Real
SCREENWRITING:
Strategies and Stories from the Trenches

Ron Suppa

THOMSON

™

COURSE TECHNOLOGY

Professional ■ Technical ■ Reference

This book was previously published in part under the title *This Business of Screenwriting: How to Protect Yourself as a Screenwriter*. That book has been revised, updated and expanded under the present title and substantial new material has been added, parts of which (particularly the sections entitled "...from the trenches") were first published by the author in modified form in *Creative Screenwriting* magazine and other publications.

Important: Thomson Course Technology PTR cannot provide software support. Please contact the appropriate software manufacturer's technical support line or Web site for assistance.

Thomson Course Technology PTR and the author have attempted throughout this book to distinguish proprietary trademarks from descriptive terms by following the capitalization style used by the manufacturer.

Educational facilities, companies, and organizations interested in multiple copies or licensing of this book should contact the publisher for quantity discount information. Training manuals, CD-ROMs, and portions of this book are also available individually or can be tailored for specific needs.

ISBN: 1-59200-957-3
Library of Congress Catalog Card Number: 2005929826
Printed in Canada

06 07 08 09 10 TC 10 9 8 7 6 5 4 3 2 1

Publisher and General Manager, Thomson Course Technology PTR:
Stacy L. Hiquet

Associate Director of Marketing:
Sarah O'Donnell

Manager of Editorial Services:
Heather Talbot

Marketing Manager:
Mark Hughes

Executive Editor:
Kevin Harreld

Senior Editor:
Mark Garvey

Marketing Coordinator:
Jordan Casey

Project Editor:
Jenny Davidson

Thomson Course Technology PTR Editorial Services Coordinator:
Elizabeth Furbish

Interior Layout Tech:
Jill Flores

Cover Designer:
Mike Tanamachi

Indexer:
Kelly Talbot

Proofreader:
Sara Gullion

THOMSON

COURSE TECHNOLOGY
Professional ■ Technical ■ Reference

Thomson Course Technology PTR, a division of Thomson Course Technology
25 Thomson Place
Boston, MA 02210
http://www.courseptr.com

to Gianna and Nicolas

My lovely living [girl and] boy,
My hope, my happiness,
My love, my life, my joy.

—Guillaume du Bartas
16th century

FOREWORD

By the real Lew Hunter

The operative word here is "real," or I would prefer to say "REAL," with exclamation points. Ron Suppa is a "from the trenches," REAL (in professional order and often concurrently) lawyer, creative executive, producer, screenwriter, professor, and author. In all of these professions, Ron has been and is a consummate FILMMAKING PROFESSIONAL, and between these very covers you will find the complete course, from soup to nuts, on everything he has learned in three decades of not only teaching it but actually DOING IT.

IT'S ALL HERE! In addition to dissecting the fundamentals of being a writer in this crazy business while simultaneously pursuing excellence in the craft, Ron gives invaluable hands-on writing tips and career strategies in simple, easily adoptable terms. And, in an approach never before taken in other how-to screenwriting books, Ron uses pitch-perfect personal and (HONEST) true stories from his own writing and producing experience to illustrate his points.

And of course he would. All of Ron's work and play hours have been dedicated to the pursuit of quality REEL entertainment. My pachyderm peeve in screenwriting education is that nearly ALL of the plethoras of books relating to screenwriting are written by people who have NEVER MADE A LIVING WRITING!! They fail themselves, then screw up legions of wannabe/gottabe screenwriters with their misinformation. (Oh, yes, some of them have been doing it for so long I suppose they have, by osmosis, gleaned some useful knowledge to pass on.) I suspect I have made enough enemies telling the world this, but them's my feelings.

Why? Well dear wannabe/gottabe screenwriter, I have been a show business professional since 1953 when I started at KFOR-TV in Lincoln, Nebraska. From there, two master's degrees, the title of creative program executive at three major networks, a working WGA member since 1969, and 100 hours of film as a producer, allowed me to believe I could run a UCLA professorial track alongside of my producer/writer career and keep a lot of people from ##&*ing up too badly in their screenwriting Holy Grail quest. In shorter words, I got chutzpah.

Ron Suppa has chutzpah, big time. And has a write/right to chutzpah. Ron has truly been a jack-of-all-trades and MASTER of all. Well, before the "truth squad" arrests me, Ron has not been a propman or most other "below the line" crafts, but "above the line," even including actor, Ron has kicked ass… to the future betterment of you, dear reader. (And to that of Sylvester Stallone, though Sly may come late to that conclusion, but I'll let Ron give you those details.)

Ron and I are so tired of people getting misinformation, we both did something about it. I wrote *Screenwriting 434* to show all wannabes and gottabe screenwriters how ninety percent of professional writers "do it". Ron does that and so much more by giving you insights into how to make a living screenwriting, with career advice on how to survive this "most misunderstood business in the world." Working with a partner, pitching, marketing, securing rights, protecting your work, agents, managers, guilds, producing it yourself, publicity… and, of course, the invaluable strategies and tips in WRITING IT! His insights into the psychological makeup of character are simply priceless and worth being the subject of an entire book on its own.

Even Ron's choice of *quotes* is inspiring, informative, and entertaining. READ THE BOOK—you'll enjoy it!

Real Screenwriting is a screenwriter's "book for all seasons." There has never been a book that has been so inclusive of the roads we screenwriters trod WRITTEN BY A PRO who has such a range of PRO experience. Including yours truly.

Lastly, and most importantly, Ron Suppa is a good and honest Homo sapian. There, I've said it without saying "I luv ya, man." (Maybe that's why he got out of the law profession.) Ron is totally dedicated to *keeping* you on the path to screenwriting success, quality, and integrity. It don't come better. He is committed to QUALITY, pulls no punches, and classes up this profession of ours a few notches, and... well, stop it, Lewis Ray; let the frog reading this book be kissed into a prince or princess by my dear friend and consummate PROFESSIONAL, world-class Ron Suppa, a man for all screenwriting seasons.

Write on, profess on, produce on, even lawyer on, Ron! After the words you are about to read, you too, dear reader, will, as they say in rock concerts... GIVE IT UP FOR RON SUPPA!!!!!!

—*Lew Hunter from near Brooklyn on the way back to his Nebraska home, October 2005.*

Contents

PART III: WHAT TO DO AFTER IT'S WRITTEN: THE SUBMISSION PROCESS 191

Author's Preface

"Becoming a writer is not a career decision, like becoming a doctor or a policeman. You don't choose it so much as get chosen, and once you accept the fact that you're not fit for anything else, you have to be prepared to walk a long, hard road for the rest of your days."

Novelist Paul Auster wasn't targeting screenwriters in particular when he wrote this, but he may as well have been. Few of us set out after high school or college to embark on a career as a writer. At some point though, it seems that just about everyone says they have a *desire* to be a writer. Question them further and you'll find most really just want to *have written*, to be instantly crowned as writers as though a genie waved a magic wand over their head.

Face it, if the desire to write is not followed by actual writing, then the desire is *not* to write. And that's okay. The world already has plenty of writers; what we really need are more readers. But if the desire is truly brimming over in you and you are worried that you came to this realization too late to succeed, don't fear. That's why I wrote this book. It's the real deal, as I've experienced it, on the art and craft, the business, and the everyday screenwriter's life. It should be all you need to kick-start your writing ambitions. As for that other profession you are working at right now, take heart: 100% of all working screenwriters were at one time not writers at all. We were tradesmen and professionals and dreamers of all ilk, just like you, doctors like Michael Crichton, lawyers like David E. Kelley, Pulitzer-prize winning novelists like Norman Mailer or Richard Russo, waitresses like Diane Thomas. The various and circuitous paths that we take to the blank page would make a good book in itself.

For me, other careers intervened, but somehow I always knew I would be a writer. The clues were there in plain sight. In college, I wrote poems and short stories and devoured William Goldman's haunting early novels written before he gained fame as a screenwriter. My heroes were Byron, Flaubert, Sarte, Henry Miller ("Don't ya' know"), Gabriel Garcia Marquez, D.H. Lawrence, Hemingway, Ayn Rand, Tom Robbins, Kurt Vonnegut, Milan Kundera (in French, no less), Ian Fleming, and even, I confess, Emily Bronte. Later, as an entertainment lawyer, I often paused in admiration of a nicely turned phrase or a perfect metaphor. I kept a journal. I savored two novels a week. Poetry was on my refrigerator. *But being a screenwriter never even occurred to me.*

As a producer, I read twenty scripts a week. I spent my happiest working hours with screenwriters. But I never gave a screenwriting career so much as a glancing thought. Then, one fine day, to borrow from poet Pablo Neruda, screenwriting arrived in search of me:

> ...and suddenly I saw
> the heavens
> unfastened
> and open,
> planets,
> palpitating plantations,
> shadow perforated,
> riddled
> with arrows, fire and flowers,
> the winding night, the universe."

Since you're reading this book, the muse may well have come for you also. According to a survey allegedly conducted one fine Saturday on Hollywood Boulevard, 150 random people were asked, "How is your screenplay coming along?" and more than four out of five gave a progress report. I applaud their ambitions and I pray for their success. But most will quickly learn, as I did, that as a career, screenwriting is one of the toughest.

To begin with, for a business that traffics in dreams, the "business" gets all the emphasis. The writer's hard work in crafting a beautiful, taut, well-structured story with memorable characters and a gut-wrenching theme is often no more than bait to lure a star. If the star passes, another writer (the flavor-of-the-month) is hired, then another, until finally no one can recall why they got involved with the script to begin with. If you truly have something to say, a unique and personal vision of the world, you may find yourself doing more soul-searching than writing. To quote William Goldman:

> "If all *you do with your life is write screenplays, it ultimately has to denigrate the soul. You may get lucky and get rich, but you sure won't get happy… if I have managed to maintain any sanity at all after nearly two decades [four now] of movie work, it is mainly because of this; I was a novelist first and I am a novelist now, but one who happens also to write screenplays."*

As for the glamour of being *in the biz*—your dream of coaching Jennifer Aniston on her lines—in the words of Tony Soprano: *faagettaboutit*. The screenwriter is to the filmmaking process as the turkey is to Thanksgiving dinner. As you present yourself on a silver platter for carving, remember that film is a collaborative art. Your job is performed *between* the idea and the actual making of the movie. If you envision meeting with the director and stars, going over your scenes line by line until they connect with your unique vision, perhaps you'd do well to catch the reruns of *Project Greenlight*.

But there *is* gold in them thar' mountains, right? All those reports of multi-million-dollar spec sales don't lie, do they? Here's a fact: Over three-quarters of the members in the Writers Guild of America are out of work at any given time. (Hey, don't blame the messenger—this book *is* titled Real Screenwriting.) On the bright side, it's true that it's good work when you can get it and the potential rewards are great indeed. Informed that copies of his scripts were selling for $100 on the black market, screenwriter Joe Eszterhas (*Flashdance, Basic Instinct*) told William Cash of the London Times: "I guess they're bought by guys who want to figure out how the hell you can be paid millions of dollars for a few weeks' work."

Compared to other forms of writing, screenwriting has always been at the top of the salary heap. Even famed writers such as William Faulkner, F. Scott Fitzgerald, Bertolt Brecht, and Gore Vidal have answered the financial—if not the artistic—call of Hollywood. In 1926, Herman Mankiewicz, co-author of *Citizen Kane* with Orson Welles, lured Chicago newsman Ben Hecht to Los Angeles with the following cable: "Will you accept $300 per week to work for Paramount Pictures? All expenses paid. The $300 is peanuts. Millions are to be grabbed out here and your only competition is idiots. Don't let this get around."

Of course it did get around. Today, busloads of screenwriting wannabes are descending on Hollywood, not only for the money, but also for the glory. Critical recognition has finally caught up with the notion that films are written, that they are conceived in the mind of a writer. Until recently, this has been a fairly well-kept secret; the spotlight focused on the director, the star, sometimes the producer, but rarely the writer. Well, the secret is out. Not only on Hollywood Boulevard, but in Boston, Chicago, Miami, and Washington, D.C., writing a screenplay has quietly become the new American Dream.

> Director Steven Spielberg, in *Words*, a documentary short by Chuck Workman, echoed this sentiment: "Most of my life has been spent in the dark watching movies. Movies have been the literature of my life. And I think in our romance with technology and our excitement at exploring all the possibilities of film and video, I think that we have partially lost something that we now have to reclaim. I think it's time to renew our romance with the word."

Over the years, I have worn many hats—entertainment lawyer, film company executive, producer, director, screenwriter, script consultant, teacher. I have read nearly 10,000 screenplays and had the good fortune to know, in some small way, over 5,000 writers. As both a buyer and seller of screen stories, I have become convinced that all jobs in the film business come down to one: finding a screenplay that can attract talent and, ultimately, an audience. My first book and numerous magazine articles were written to help the writer who had done the hard work and written well to navigate the murky eccentricities of this most misunderstood business in the world and connect to that audience.

But, until recently, I believed everyone knew that the *writing* comes first. That to be a writer is to be a student of the human condition. That a writer must first have *something to say*. That any new writer must *say* it, preferably in a full-blown screenplay. A general idea about sharks may lead to *Jaws* but without characters and story it won't make you a screenwriter. Just as having a nasty encounter with the police, a courtroom, an ex-spouse, the government, or a noisy neighbor does not mean you have a gripping movie-of-the-week drama on your hands. And just because your dog died, doesn't mean we all feel your pain. The power of your art has to bring us there.

As a teacher of writing, I assumed that there would be in any student of writing a reverence for the enormity of the task of the writer, for the power of the work wrought, for the artistry of the old masters, for the triumph of *creation* over naked commerce. But the get rich quick mentality of lotteries, lawsuits, and real estate investments seems to have spilled over to the world of screenwriting. Where once patience and hard work marked a writer's apprenticeship, now there is bitter remonstration over the inability to get an agent with one's first submission. Instead of wonder for the magic in the first stirrings of the writer within, there is anger at the vile suggestion that one actually must write anything when one has a perfectly good three-sentence idea to pitch. Anyone who can write a good letter home should be able to match the pap on TV and in theaters, right? Haven't we all said at some time, "Gee, I could have written that." Some of us added: "In fact, I'm not so sure I didn't." So why not flock to a good weekend seminar, put a new twist on what seems to be selling now, and rake in your share of the pot of gold?

I'll tell you why. Because if the writing comes from your mind, but not your heart, if it is a part of who you think you want to be, but not who you are deep inside, the art suffers. Instead of being elevated in our consciousness, your subject and your characters are diminished. And we, your audience, suffer and diminish along with them.

That said, no one curls up at night with a good screenplay. The writer's work is necessarily incomplete until it is read, purchased, produced, and released in the marketplace. And new markets created by cable television, reality television, and the rebirth of the independent film have opened wide Hollywood's once closely guarded gates. In my work with the New Members Committee of the Writers Guild of America, west, I have welcomed over fifty new members in a single month. All wrote well enough to sell to or be hired by Guild signatory production companies. But the methods by which each found his way to these companies—through the sometimes mystifying maze of agents, attorneys, producers, and studio executives—varied as widely as their personality, age, and ethnic background.

I wrote this book as a survival guide to help all writers through that maze. There is no reason for any writer, even those living far from Hollywood, to feel left out of this opportunity. For those who are approaching the blank page for the first time, I have tried to offer tips to help you fill that page with your voice and your art. For anyone who has persevered and written a screenplay or teleplay, whose good work is left to wither unseen in a desk drawer or under a pile of magazines, it is my hope this book will expand your contacts and your resolve. The various strategies offered here and stories written from my personal experiences are meant to demystify screenwriting and the film world for you, and to make it as accessible and welcoming as it should be to the talent it desperately needs to find and nurture in order to survive.

In the end, I hope the reader will come to believe as I do that writing a screenplay may not be our choice after all—but it can be our great privilege and perhaps our destiny. And marketing and selling a screenplay is not all that mystifying, holy, or pedantic a subject either. It couldn't be; agents do it all the time.

Caveat

Throughout this book, I have borrowed freely from 30 years of personal experience in the film business to convey a taste of what the real world of professional screenwriting is like and to help even the neophyte writer compete on an insider level in that world. Yet clearly, one person's experience will differ from someone else's and no two sets of circumstances or facts are ever exactly alike. *For this reason, nothing in this book is intended nor should be construed as doctrine or legal advice.* There are exceptions and qualifications to all legal principles and it is not my intention to fully explore the complex subtleties of those principles in these pages.

If I had the influence I would use it to help everyone, just one time even, say that the emperor is naked, that craziness is craziness and that bad taste is beneath their contempt. I'd get them to tell someone they've sold their souls to what they really think of them... that they are completely unprincipled, untalented... to do that one single thing that affirms some kind of justice or standards... I wish I had that influence. I'd feel like I really made a difference...

—Anonymous

"strategy"—an artful means of implementing a plan of action or agenda.

PART I

PREPARING FOR A WRITING CAREER

Chapter 1

The Screenwriter's Life

I am for the writers. All of them. The rich, the famous, the talented, the new writers and the old. The poor and the unknown writers. The writers who have won Academy Awards and have stars buried in the cement cemetery of Hollywood Boulevard. And the unrewarded writers. The unheralded, the unwanted writers too. I am for all writers: writer-directors, writer-producers, and the "and" writers (those whose names came second or third). All the damned and blessed writers wherever you are... even the dead writers.

—Richard Brooks, writer/director

Why We Write

Novelist John Barth has said "a writer knows he's a writer."

A writer is not something you strive to be—it is something you are. I have a baseball cap with the word "writer" on the brim; it defines me. I don't write all the time, nor do I always want to, but I will always write. If you, too, must write (or explode!), if you are nothing if you are not a writer, if you would do it for free, then we are brothers.

Novels, short stories, poetry, plays, screenplays, movies of the week, episodic television—each has different challenges and rewards. But whatever the medium, the desire for the writer is the same: to communicate, to inform, to move people to laughter or tears, to set them dreaming, to touch them with your personal vision of the world.

Certainly, if you have no talent you can still write. There are plenty of untalented authors—just check any airport book rack. But, while I regard

3

the untalented author with benign amusement, I regard the talented hack—the writer whose heart and soul is not consumed with the power of dreams, the violent struggles of poverty, the cancer of racism, the loneliness of old age, the cosmic point to all this *life*—as a menace to society, and I hold him in contempt of mankind. However, if you have talent, then good for you. But, remember: Talent is not always enough. If you have nothing to say, your best writing is a waste of time and the lessons in this book are academic.

For some, the profession of screenwriting may give the impression of being only about money, deals, and commerce, but selling your work should be a prerequisite to reaching an audience, not an end in itself. The world demands more from its scribes than the worship of naked commerce. Ours is a higher calling. To paraphrase Shelley in his poem *Mont Blanc*, "… it is your charge to interpret the human experience, to feel it deeply, and to make it deeply felt."

Shelley was writing about a mountain in France, a mountain to which people come to view, to ski or hike its peaks and to fish in its streams. But the poet reserved a special place for the artist. He found in the silence and solitude of that great natural wonder, "a voice… not understood by all," a passionate voice to which only the artist, the poet, the writer, "the wise and great and good" among us, could bear witness. And he held that to be our duty, our challenge, our very *raison d'être*—whether we presume to speak for that mountain, for a battered single mother in an urban ghetto, for a crippled Vietnam vet, or for a couple of quirky strangers who meet by chance and fall in love.

In an address to a PEN[1] conference in Prague, Václav Havel echoed Shelley when he said: "[Writers] are people whose profession, indeed whose very vocation, is to perceive far more profoundly than others the general context of things, to feel a general sense of responsibility for the world and to articulate publicly this inner experience." Armed with only his poetry to throw "a sharp light on the misery of the contemporary human soul," Václav Havel went from dissident writer to President of the Czech Republic. Havel knows that all writers are political writers: they cannot sit on the fence, they must take sides, make judgments as to what is moral or immoral, good or evil. Then, consciously or unconsciously, audiences or

---

[1] PEN is an international organization of professional writers (poets, playwrights, essayists, editors, and novelists form the letters of the acronym "PEN," though the organization is open to all writers and others who contribute to the literary community). Its members promote and defend freedom of expression, stand in opposition to censorship, and work to secure the health and safety as well as obtain release of writers imprisoned throughout the world on the basis of their peacefully expressed opinions and ideas.

readers will evaluate every act of every character according to their own moral or ethical scale.

These days, some people believe the world is going to hell in a hand basket. The good news is that writers don't have to take it lying down. As writers, we have the prerogative to challenge authority, inspire rebellion, sway public opinion, arouse emotion, and motivate change. Our words have the power to disturb and disrupt or perhaps just to deliver a few good belly laughs. Our reward, and that of our audience, is the enlarged sense of life, which is the ultimate gift of art.

This became clear to me on September 11. Sure, we all experienced the pain and compassion and anger and fear and variety of unthinkable threats that followed. But some of us became writers because we had the need to publicly articulate those feelings and inform them with our own unique point of view, to lend our voice to others addressing the issues that most occupy our hearts and our minds. It's an old plot principle that the greater the adversity, the greater the opportunity to build character. September 11 gave us the chance to regain the power of our art. Writers need to read and to write, as we need water and air. And audiences need someone to articulate their feelings, their hopes and dreams, their anger and their fears. They sit in a theater in the dark and put their lives on hold for two hours because they need perspective, or perhaps, for a while, just to forget.

As the Czech novelist Milan Kundera has written: "The source of fear is in the future, and a person freed of the future has nothing to fear." Movies free us of the future, if only for a couple of blessed hours. Life is uncertain, but movies are not. No one knows if or when the peace of mind we once enjoyed will return to us, but movies have a certain emotionally reassuring finality, an endpoint, a definite conclusion in which wars end, bad guys pay for their crimes, and all our nightmares are laid to rest.

The necessity of art in our lives is unquestionable. It is, Susan Sontag tells us, "a way of being fully human." Writers write. It may be the most important thing we do.

In that regard, I offer an excerpt from the remarks of screenwriter Phil Alden Robinson (*Field of Dreams*), made at the hearings against film colorization, held in Los Angeles in January, 1990, before members of the U.S. House of Representatives:

> When we begin to write a motion picture, life stops. We write for months and months, draft after draft, and then when we're finally

done… we re-write for months and months; changing, questioning, doubting, discovering, experimenting, honing, throwing things out, and putting them back. After about 10 or 12 drafts, we put a title page on it that says First Draft. We think it's pretty good. We show it to a friend who tells us it stinks. We know he's right. So we do six or eight more drafts and put a new title page on it. It still says First Draft.

After a few more of those we finally get the nerve to turn one in to the studio. They read it. Pretty soon, we get to enjoy the helpful suggestions of studio executives who may or may not have a clue what we're trying to do… so we do five or six more drafts, slap on a title page that says Second Draft and turn it in. Now the suggestions come not just from studio executives, but from their assistants, their friends, their mothers, their friends' mothers, and their children. Actually, the children give pretty good notes.

After a very long time, if we're really, really lucky, we then get notes from a director who may have a completely different vision of the movie… from actors who feel that their character wouldn't say this or do that… we find that scenes we labored over for months cannot be filmed, or are completely changed during production, or are cut out entirely during editing… and yet we endure all this. We endure it for one reason—it's not the money, and it's certainly not the glamour; it's for that slim wisp of a hope that at the end of all the pain and angst and self-doubt and pride swallowing and politicking and fighting and accommodating and tap dancing and seven-day weeks and 14-hour days and sleepless nights—that at the end of it all—after years of all that—a MOVIE is made, a movie that somehow miraculously reflects that original vision you had long, long ago sitting by yourself with the blank piece of paper.

And maybe all over America and all over the world people will sit in dark rooms and watch something that existed only in your head. And they'll be moved, or entertained, or enlightened, or touched… and a part of it will stay with them and become a piece of their memories, a piece of their life. And this movie that you imagined, and that is the product of so many people working so hard for so long, this movie that against all odds turned out pretty good, this movie that bears your name, will outlive you. You will have succeeded in leaving something behind with the power to touch people. Something that says I was here. And I tried. And this is what I did when I was here… To have even a chance of accomplishing that is the prime reason we create.

from the trenches: WHERE ARE ALL THE STORIES?

Recently, I saw one of the summer's biggest hits. I was with a friend who loves movies and afterward we made our ritual trek to Starbuck's to do our usual critique. We stared straight ahead while in line for coffee and when we sat down, we stared some more. Finally, he said, "I don't know. I guess we got our money's worth, but I'm still not sure what we saw." I was clearer on that. We had seen another special effects extravaganza and the effects were marvelous. Not breathtaking though, not like the first ten minutes of *Saving Private Ryan*. At least not to me, not anymore. After the tenth or fifteenth of these films in the last year or so, some of the artistry in the process has been lost on me.

Both of us, by the way, are filmmakers, not critics. We've been in the trenches too long to pick like vultures at the best intentions of a whole symphony of talented and committed artists. And the pressures on them were no doubt enormous—for the studio, only a blockbuster would do. The director definitely delivered the full package: relentless action, deafening sound, slick design, and some intricate and dazzling shots. Even with wall to wall CGI, he clearly had the camera team humping, using every lens, lamp, gel, net and lighting trick in the book. As for the actors, they were, well, bouncy... anyway, appropriately pretty and physical and seemed to be enjoying themselves up there. But there was no emotional impact on the audience that I could discern. No narrative momentum. No story at all.

Even now as I jot down these notes, I get a chill when I think about it. That absence of story, that total disregard for the narrative power of film, makes me feel the very turn in my bones. And I know why. Just hours ago, set to try for some needed sleep before beginning a grinding week of shooting three commercials for a Brazilian beer company, I made the mistake of checking my watch. It was a good time to reach my agent to ask if he had finally read my new spec script. Here's part of that conversation, freshly recalled:

> **Me:** *Bisexual? Why? It's an action movie—Claire is fighting to stay alive and the only other woman there is trying to kill her and she knows it—I don't think she'd be having sex with her, do you?*
>
> **Him:** *Yes, I do. That's my point—you've got two hot women in this thing and no sex.*
>
> **Me:** *There's sex. Edith has a huge sexual appetite, but it's her way of manipulating men to do her bidding.*
>
> **Him:** *Exactly. It doesn't mean anything to her anyway, so why not have her seduce Claire for the same reason—it gets her off and she gets what she wants.*

continued

And Claire becomes twice as interesting if there is a hint of bisexuality in there, don't you see?

Me: *Well, no.* What I was beginning to see was the size of his head, how meaty and pudgy it was and how it would look with a fireplace poker sticking out from it. *I mean, I'm not saying it's not an interesting character aspect, except for that it's a true story and Claire isn't gay, but don't you think it takes us in another, wholly sensationalist direction?*

Him: *Duh! (*I truly hate that.*) So what's wrong with sensational?* Anger Management *even managed to get Nicholson naked between the sheets with Adam Sandler. Sex sells. Especially two women getting it on. You've seen female mud wrestling, haven't you? You've seen* Will & Grace, *haven't you?*

I had, actually, never "seen" female mud wrestling and failed to see the connection to *Will & Grace*, but what I said, as I hung up, was: *Okay, let me play around with it and I'll get something to you.*

Just as God left us no clue to explain the mosquito, the evolutionary point of agents is destined to remain a mystery to me. But my anger wasn't directed toward my agent. Nor at the sad fact that film and truth can rarely be used in the same sentence anymore. My anger came from knowing I *would* be getting back to him (cash flow). Today, few film writers have the luxury of creating in solitude—they write what producers, development execs, and even agents tell them to write. That's the fragile integrity of screenwriters today: writing at the behest of and to the inane specifications of those I have come to call (when I am in a charitable mood) "suits."

Let's face it; if the point of writing is freedom and self-expression, screenwriting can be a bit claustrophobic. Maybe we're fortunate to be paid to write at all, but those big spec sales in the trades aren't the tip of the iceberg—they're all of it. Ours is an increasingly for-hire profession. If your dream was never more money, a faster car, and designer curtains in the old mansion on the Strip, that can be frustrating. I know my dream was to write unforgettable characters like Atticus Finch. To make audiences care about the fate of an ape, as they did in *King Kong*. I wanted to explore the values that remain in an increasingly violent, emotionally disconnected world. My themes were existential (but with spiritual overtones), my stories mostly female-driven, full of subtleties and ambiguities and a strong catharsis. *What was I thinking?*

Such noble intentions do not endear themselves to film distributors. Where were the car chases, the women in thongs, the vapid thrill ride that could later become an amusement park attraction? I was lucky to make a few sales before the sequel craze kicked in. And my spec scripts still make a good enough read to land me the occasional assignment. Except that means no longer writing to please me. That means writing to please about as many people as crew a shrimp boat. That means writing what those people would write if only they could write, which they can't. It means being commercial comes before being brilliant.

If there is little joy in that, I can't deny a certain satisfaction in getting the commission, like a prize won. In a business in which everyone knows everyone's "quote," respect requires inching mine up every so often, which means you can't turn down everything. And so I dutifully perform on cue, like a trained seal. That's not to say that I don't put as much of my concerns, emotions, principles, and time into a script for hire as I would a pet project nurtured for years. As a professional, I don't know how to work less hard.

But I don't want to write for cars or cartoon heroes. Sure, the marketplace can support a few misconceived star vehicles or commerce driven sequels now and then. But the powerful legacy of a hundred years of cinematic art—from *Citizen Kane*, *Gone With the Wind*, and *The Best Years of our Lives* to *Casablanca*, *Godfather I and II*, and *Schindler's List*—just can't be left to recycled concepts like *Dumb and Dumberer* and *2 Fast 2 Furious*. Where have all the stories gone? The stories that inform and clarify the human condition, with unforgettable characters that inspire generations to better themselves? Record-breaking grosses and CGI magic aside, the Hulk is no King Kong and Neo is no Atticus Finch. Not even close.

I fear the simple dream of writing good movies is slipping away. But I also believe the best aspirations of most writers—those paid millions to do a studio rewrite as well as those who attend evening classes and work when the world sleeps—go beyond "getting the gig." I still believe we will find a way to get something original past the phalanx of agents and studio executives looking to clone the last blockbuster. And I still believe writers who truly have something to say will yet find a forum for their point of view in small (or big) character-driven stories that someone will produce. I hope I'm not wrong.

A 12-Step Program for a Writer's Life

Most everyone these days secretly thinks himself a writer, or more precisely, he could be a writer if only… he could type, spell, or use a computer. Makes a nice daydream, but WGA award-winning writer Burt Prelutsky (*A Small Killing, Homeward Bound*), after 30 years of slogging away in the trenches, sees it a bit differently: "Only write if you absolutely have to. It is a very difficult way to make a living, so if you have any choice in the matter, get into some other racket."

On the other hand, if you say, "what else am I going to do? I've no training, no profession, like to stay indoors when it rains, and have an unnatural love of silk pajamas," maybe screenwriting will work for you. But here's a news flash: Success as a writer requires the same commitment, hard work, and other professional courtesies you would devote to a career in any other profession, be it law, medicine, or making sandals on Hollywood Boulevard.

"A Writer is a person for whom writing is more difficult than it is for other people."
—Thomas Mann

Like all arts, writing is a way of life, not an isolated effort. You may have talent; you may have one great inspirational story that burns to be told. But latent talent and one screenplay does not a career make. Writers build a body of work by maintaining a *daily routine*, not unlike that of any standard nine-to-five job.

Consider this advice posted on the Writers Guild electronic bulletin board by Phil Alden Robinson in a message to a fellow writer on the subject of "How I Write:"

As for what my day consists of, here's my writing routine. And I highly recommend it.

I don't get up too early (as I don't want to be groggy on a day when I'm writing), feed the dog, exercise (good for clearing the head before writing), shower, eat a good breakfast (very important to prepare you for writing), read the newspapers (sharpens your mind), make some phone calls and do all the assorted little things around the house that have piled up to get them out of the way so they don't give you an excuse later for not writing.

Then it's time for lunch. I go out and eat, finding that getting out of the house is a good way to clear the mind for writing. Lunch invariably leads to an errand or two, maybe a little shopping or something, sometimes even involving the purchase of necessary items without which one cannot write, such as three-hole punch paper, or a book that you need for research or background.

When you get home, there's mail to answer, and phone calls to return, all of which are very important to get out of the way so they don't impede your writing. By late afternoon, you're faced with a dilemma: start writing now, only to have to interrupt it for dinner, thus losing valuable momentum and focus... or put it off until after dinner. I highly recommend you not start at this point. Most people are not at their peak in the late afternoons, and there's nothing worse than getting a head of steam going only to cut it off prematurely. So now's a good time for catching up on magazines, some of which might actually contain a nugget that inspires or informs your work.

After dinner, you realize there's a movie you've been putting off seeing, and let's be brutally honest here: How can we be so presumptuous as to write movies if we're not seeing them? It is absolutely crucial that we learn from our peers, profit from their mistakes, experience what the audience likes and dislikes.

Okay. The movie lets out at 10, and home you go. Now, finally, there are no more distractions, all the possible procrastinations are gone, you're primed and inspired to start writing. But here's the thing. If you start writing now, you'll be up until 2 or 3 in the morning, and that's going to screw up tomorrow something fierce, so go right to bed.

The next morning, be sure not to get up too early, as you don't want to be groggy on a day when you're writing… (et cetera, et cetera, et cetera).

I do this for weeks on end until I feel so guilty and fraudulent that I drop everything, turn off the phones and do nothing but write from morning til night until I'm done.

May I suggest an alternative method? Here is a *twelve-point strategy* you might take to prepare yourself, not just to write, but for a *writer's life*:

STRATEGY

1. **Get out of your bathrobe and get dressed.**

   This advice, once given to me by author Tommy Thompson, may be the most crucial of all. Real writers view their work as a job, not a hobby. You may enjoy writing in a flannel shirt, but don't demean your work by coming to your computer before you've brushed your teeth.

2. **Take the time to develop your craft.**

   College can take four years, a law degree three more. How much time are you willing to invest in your professional career as a writer? Two hours a day? Four? A writer friend of mine makes a contract with herself and pays herself a small salary (into the cookie jar) for the time she spends writing.

   Writing, like skiing, requires "time on the slopes" to get you over the inevitable plateaus. Consider your other responsibilities, then find a block of time that matches the extent of your commitment, the same as you might do for an exercise program. Set a realistic schedule, maybe two or three hours a day, three or four days a week. And be prepared to stick with it. Be ready to stare at a blank page, to type up recipes or lists of baseball players—anything to keep you glued to your word processor until the characters that inhabit your unconscious mind begin to speak to you and demand their place in the universe.

Pliny the Elder, circa AD 23-79, had this advice for writers: *Nulla dies sine linea* (not a day without a line).

Screenwriter John Milius (*Apocalypse Now*) claims this legendary formula brought him success: he devoted one hour a day, at exactly 5 p.m., to his writing; he did this 365 days a year.

Novelist Carolyne See advises five pages a day, five days a week, forever.

The point is to find a routine and a goal that works for you—make the process fun and attainable—then stick to it. Remember, if you hope to earn, say, $120,000 for an original feature film screenplay (Writers Guild minimum for the sale of an original screenplay is around $75,000), that equals *$1,000 per page, white space and all*. Even if it took a full week to write each and every single page, wouldn't that be fair pay for an honest day's work?

3. **Find a time and a place to write.**

Woody Allen believes that "eighty percent of success is just showing up." Be prepared to be there, *somewhere*, primed and ready to work. All writers don't write all the time, but all writers do *eventually* write.

Be aware that the duties of life can drown the fire in your belly. In England, there is a saying, "the death of the artist is the pram in the hall." Try to arrange your work schedule to avoid distractions or to keep away from those who will not respect the seriousness of your time alone with the blank page. Understand that most people will not have an inkling what it is you *really* do. (They might be wondering when you're going to get a real job.) It is up to *you* to demand respect and understanding for your very real job. (Okay, jobs are supposed to *pay* something; their mothers should have taught them that it's rude to ask people how much they earn.)

Lord Byron (*The Secret Memoirs of Lord Byron*), upon the third interruption of his work by his half-sister Augusta, left this note for her on her dresser:

> I am trying to write. I doubt you understand what is involved. Use your imagination if you can. I write. I create. I conjure up visions from inside my mind and set them down on paper, in rhyme. I know all my friends think it is merely a gift, a hobby. I feel the muse upon me and I sit down and dash off a few lines

which everyone is anxious to read. Do you really suppose it is as simple as that? Do you really suppose I would enjoy the success I do by merely indulging a hobby?... It is not a heaven-sent messenger who turns my thoughts into verse. *I* have to do that. *I* have to take a nebulous idea, delightful to dream about as I lie half-awake in bed, and turn it into some sense, some *words*.

4. **Behave like a writer.**

   Do all the things on a daily basis that are part of your art. If you head off to the beach, consider it a "writer's holiday." Use it as precious ruminating time. Always carry pen and paper or a tape recorder with you, the way a photographer carries a camera. We all have moments of inspiration, but writers jot them down.

   To have that light bulb flash in your head, you must work to heighten your powers of observation. Examine your life and the people and things around you; there's a rich mother lode there to mine. If you're reclusive, force yourself to get out more! Befriend another writer; they always have time for lunch. Make and nurture business contacts. *Listen* to people. Go to a museum, take in a play, walk to work, shoot some hoops. The human condition cannot be lost on you, nor can the charms of nature, history, politics, religion, sports, the arts, the sciences, or the fantastic.

5. **See movies.**

   See the good ones and the bad ones and learn the difference. Which movies moved you to tears or laughter or set you to dreaming? Which made your heart ache from wishing you had written them? These are likely to promote the same themes you will pursue most successfully as a writer.

6. **Read the "how-to" books on writing.**

   Read them all—there are some good ones out there. While you're at it, take screenwriting classes offered in your area. Attend the seminars on the business. Think of this as career training. There may be repetition, but if you pick up one new tip that improves your work, you've made a smart investment.

7. **Read "The Trades."**

   Daily Variety, Hollywood Reporter. It won't hurt to include others, such as *Entertainment Weekly, Screen International, Premiere.* Learn the business, the players, the jargon. Know where executives are working and what agendas they are currently espousing for their companies. Allow "the biz" to seep into your daily habits, as if by osmosis. It's vital to your career to know what agencies are hot, what players are needed to get "a package" into production, and who is at which studio this month.

8. **Read screenplays.**

It doesn't matter whether they're produced or unproduced. Most local film commissions have screenplays on file, as do many university libraries (especially those with film programs). Many screenplays are published and available at the bookstore. A number of classic and current screenplays can be purchased through the Internet. Some online sites like www.script-o-rama.com, www.simplyscripts.com, and www.dailyscript.com post current TV and movie scripts that can be downloaded for free. If you have access to the Academy of Motion Picture Arts and Sciences Margaret Herrick Library or the new Writers Guild Foundation Library, you can read screenplays or teleplays simply by posting your driver's license.

Another tip is to rent the video and then watch it while you read the script (preferably the writer's version, without scene numbers and in screenplay format) and see how the words eventually translate onto the screen.

9. **Read good fiction.**

Notice how several of these steps suggest that you "READ." Writers must first be readers. The great authors and the classic works are our teachers. Milan Kundera said in *The Unbearable Lightness of Being* that a writer must go beyond himself, beyond the boundaries of his own experience, and seek out "the possibilities of life in the trap the world has become" (himself borrowing from Kafka). Books take you out of your world and open up a universe of thematic and situational possibilities; they also help you discover your own unique style and voice.

Author Stephen King, who admits to reading "seventy or eighty books a year, mostly fiction" has little patience for those who aspire to write but are not voracious readers: "If you don't have the time to read, you don't have the time or the tools to write."

---

10. **Grant yourself the freedom to fail.**

Your first steps are bound to be shaky. Accept the fact there's a learning curve. (Van Gogh sold only one painting in his lifetime.)

It takes time to find your voice; it will also take time to find your audience. Rejection is a normal part of the learning curve for a writer. The difference between the successful writer and the failed writer is that the successful writer has *failed more often.*

"A blank piece of paper is God's way of telling us how hard it is to be God."

—Sidney Sheldon

---

11. **Never stop writing.**

Do a page a day every day for the rest of your life. When you've finished one script, start another. Better still, write at least three before showing the first to anyone of consequence. Rejection won't stop you if you're halfway through your next opus. Writer's block? That's a tired excuse from one tired of life.

Playwright John MacNicholas, in his unpublished play *Dumas*, gives us this wonderful exchange between Alexandre Dumas (*The Three Musketeers*) and his son, also Alexandre (*Camille*):

Son
I have nothing to write about.

Father
I believe you're acquainted with—let's see—Love? Beauty? Death? Those subjects have sold well for several thousand years.

Son
I don't know how to start.

Father
Dip the pen into ink, cover the page with words.

Son
But form, incidents, the style—

Father
—Just start. Farmers in Normandy say if the horse is blind, you load the wagon and go to market anyway.

12. **Don't write like a great man, just write.**

This advice, given to me by a one-armed poet who can write all of us under the table, means that you shouldn't fall into the trap of believing that everything you write must be brilliant. Allow the artist in you to create before the critic in you destroys. On the other hand, *never* submit your work until it is ready. That means it should be written, polished, and rewritten again—until it is truly your best work. The movie business isn't known for giving a lot of second chances.

Forget about the fairytales of overnight, multi-million dollar script sales that you read about in the trades. Success takes luck, timing, talent, and a lot of sweat. But if the very prospect of all that effort is anathema to you, you may be headed down a wrong-way street to begin with. Because for your work to breathe, to have life on the page, you must have passion for it. Like Burt Prelutsky, you do it because you have to. And cheer up. As Somerset Maugham said, "Writing may not be a good living, but it's a good life!"

from the trenches: A ROOM OF ONE'S OWN

Not all writers are lonely recluses. Most have well-intentioned friends and family to distract them. And few begin their career in a well-appointed private office, lined with books from their personal library, laboring over a burlwood writing desk with a fine quill pen. In his salad days, Raymond Carver wrote his novels in a car parked in his own driveway to escape the daily tumult of his young children at home. Indeed, many successful writers find they still have to make do with a countertop or a desk tucked into a cubbyhole in their kitchen. I once read that Benjamin Franklin did most of his writing in the bathtub. Still, while finding a clean, well-lighted, peaceful workplace of one's own is a challenge, look at the bright side—you also get to make your own hours and go to work in flannel pajamas and slippers lined with lamb's wool from New Zealand!

In the past, writing fiction was more an avocation than a vocation. Hours were stolen like pearls in the quiet of the night, a solitary pleasure taken while the world slumbered. For most, there was little hope of making a living at it. But in the information age, with so many resources available at the touch of a few keys, writing is fast becoming the small business of choice. The same maverick entrepreneurs who would surely eschew a desk job are cheerfully tied to a table and chair for hours on end, a "do not disturb" sign on the door. And, as always, everyone is nosing around, peering over shoulders and wondering aloud what they're doing in there. But today the writer can escape all that. Armed with the latest in laptop technology, a writer can do his thing wherever he feels most inspired—amid the frenzy of an airport lounge, tucked warmly into a mountain cabin, laying on a deserted beach, or even watching the monkeys frolic at the zoo.

A writer friend of mine, single and living alone in a quiet, registered historic building, wrote a highly successful first novel on his kitchen table. But with the kudos came new commitments and distractions, including many new "old friends." He wanted a place where he knew no one, had nothing, and where there was simply little to do but write. So he took a backpack and a few favorite books to a tiny rented room without a phone or bathroom on a small island in the Philippines. It was like a womb, he told me, and he felt oddly comforted by the barren wood floor, the hard bed and the meals all served in a communal dining room. He wrote 2,000 words a day while there.

Personally, I've had solitude and I've had chaos and have found a way to work in both—when I have something to say. But when searching for that first line, trying to find the right voice, leafing through the pages of my infertile imagination for a plot twist, I too have gone to the ends of the earth—literally—to find a location to inspire the process.

Sometimes the most challenging places have their advantages. When I was in college, I wrote poetry in a lean-to in Bali where the mosquitoes were as big as dragonflies, but all my meals were included for a dollar a day. Later, I scripted a film in a flat in London that had heat only when the ice in the pipes defrosted. But oh those rewrites in the spring! For that, I sequestered a bench in Regent's Park in front of secretaries on their lunch hour sunning themselves in their knickers on the grass. I must have done sixteen drafts of that script. Places where I don't speak the language inspire me most. They re-acquaint me with the rudiments of human communication. It's also good if they have some connection, however remote, to the story I'm working on. (IRS note—my deductions for the trips to Rio, Rome, Paris, Casablanca, and Tel Aviv were legitimate write-offs—it's not my fault if the movies are still in development.)

But not everyone feels the need to roam far from home. My dear friend, Lew Hunter, wrote his award-winning scripts and best-selling book, *Screenwriting 434*, in a little shed in the back of his house that would be cramped if it held more than three garden tools. But it fit him like a glove and he felt like he was going to an office, going off to work as it were, even if only a few steps away from his comfy house.

But then, homes are sometimes good places for writers to escape from. Even if you live alone in a quiet, comfortable workspace, the phone keeps ringing, the refrigerator beckons, and all that furniture needs dusting. If you don't live alone, no one else there is likely to be sympathetic to your need for peace—all writing looks suspiciously like goofing off. Once you've written your best seller or won the

continued

spec script lottery you may get a little more respect around the house, but don't expect your roomies to tip-toe around for long. They'll expect you to bang out a script a week. And, of course, they'll see no reason why that can't be accomplished amid deafening rap music, blaring television commercials, and, since you're monopolizing the computer anyway, accommodating a little instant messaging to their "buddy list."

Maybe that's why some writers find any excuse to "get away from it all" in the name of inspiration. They'll go to Venice or even fabled Verona to write a love story. Or—as one *very* lucky action scripter did—book three glorious weeks in a Jamaican paradise. A studio was generous enough to foot the bill for a one-bedroom villa in Goldeneye Village, the clifftop getaway of author Ian Fleming, creator of James Bond. Besides trying to channel the great one's story ideas, it was azure skies in December, daily scuba lessons included, and all martinis were served shaken, not stirred.

While I also love to travel if I can, I don't expect inspiration, just a place to escape from myself, from the boundaries of my own existence. And I don't have to travel far for that. When practicing law was my day job, I wrote a novel on yellow legal pads in a red leather booth of an all-night diner on the Sunset Strip. As a screenwriter, I dragged my colored pens and 3 × 5 cards to shopping malls, parks, and so many delis they should have named a sandwich for me. A borrowed cabin in local Big Bear Mountain helped me complete an assignment on a movie-of-the-week. I even met a long-term girlfriend—feverishly banging out television shows on *her* laptop—while writing on the next bench over at the Sherman Oaks Galleria, the teen hot spot in *Fast Times at Ridgemont High*.

Of course, those places are the highlights, not the norm. Like most writers, I log countless hours at more familiar venues:

Offices. Great when it's yours, a tad dicey when it's owned by your boss—if the dime is his, your time is his. Keep a backup disk for when you get fired.

Bookstores. Who hasn't used the local B&N or Border's like our own private living room? And most offer you a cappuccino and a croissant along with their free resource library.

Libraries. Surrounded by research tools and all those books, who can get writer's block? To avoid screeching kids checking out the latest Barney tapes, try private libraries like that of the Writers Guild or Motion Picture Academy— and they have scripts!

Cafes. While most will leave you be as long as you behave yourself, even Starbucks appreciates it if you buy a coffee now and then. Take your own flask for something more inspiring.

The point is the ideal work place can be anywhere. Some writers need absolute, tomb-like quiet. Others can only concentrate with loud music blaring in the background. Some prefer a dedicated workspace, with pencils, hot coffee, and reference books within arm's reach. Still others can put in a good day's work from a soft easy chair in a busy hotel lobby. One famous author professes to do all his writing while reclining in bed or lying on a couch in front of his TV. My vagabond ex-girlfriend, now a well-published trade-book author (but poor as a church mouse) regularly writes in stately mansions or posh vacation retreats—which she house-sits while the owners are away!

Private writer retreats and writer colonies operate for those who want a total environment geared to enhancing the meditative or artistic experience. You can find them advertised in trade magazines and journals appealing to the writer. Renting a room in a private home or B&B can be a cheaper alternative. But for my money just about any venue will suffice, even mobile ones. Airplanes or long train rides are perfect for concentrated blocks of work time—nothing else to do but look out the window or read. I wrote a short story on a bus ride from London to Bristol and back—8 hours all together—and had it published in a popular anthology without a word changed.

My most unusual workplace was the pew of a church on the campus of Stanford University. It was warm, serene, close to the food court, and a nice place for a muse to visit. These days I write in a loft office with the music on and the phones off. But I may be about to get lucky. My new writing partner on a MOW (movie of the week) has leased a two-bedroom flat on the sand in Malibu as a family retreat. The waves may be a tad noisy, but it really doesn't get any better than that (oh, all right, except maybe for that villa in Jamaica).

What's L.A. Got to Do with It?

No doubt, it is not inspiration, but perspiration, that makes a writer. But can it also be location?

The question most frequently asked by writers in screenwriting seminars around the country is: Is it absolutely necessary that I move to Los Angeles to have a career as a screen or television writer?

Unlike *Jeopardy*, there is no one right answer to this question (or question to this answer, if you will). First comes the work. Then comes the validation of the work. Both can be accomplished wherever you live. If you sell a feature screenplay or win an assignment for a television series (especially then), that's the time to make travel plans. Or not—established feature screenwriters can plug their laptops into the arctic tundra if they so choose and no one will object.

Screenwriter David Koepp relocated from Wisconsin to attend the UCLA School of Theater, Film and Television, but never quite took to sprawling Los Angeles. When mega-hits *Jurassic Park*, *Spider-Man*, and *War of the Worlds* established his uber-credentials, he was able to live and work wherever he wished. (He chose New York.)

On the other hand, while an active screenwriting community extends far beyond the borders of Los Angeles, *most* screenwriters and virtually all television writers work and reside in "Hollywood," the generic area popularly referred to by the worldwide media that can, in reality, encompass all of Southern California. If you want a career in film, cable, or network television and if you want it sooner rather than later, there is no escaping the fact that Los Angeles is where the action is. The explosion in global communication notwithstanding and recognizing the fact that many talented screenwriters *do* toil outside Los Angeles with real success, my best tip would still be the same as Oscar Wilde offered long ago: "Go West, Young Man."

"Across America and beyond," according to journalist Richard Rodriquez, "men and women are gathering their bags and suitcases, closing the family house, leaving behind common memory and heading for the great city to work. They head for Los Angeles."

Certainly, Los Angeles is where the Industry lives and breathes. It's where "the business" is headquartered and the creative meetings are held, where stars and starmakers bump into one another at restaurants and film premiers. It's also where film and television writers are represented, interviewed, hired, and, importantly, it's where they work. As critics quickly point out, it may be this very insular nature of the Hollywood writing community that contributes to the current state of entertainment, which is dominated by formulaic storylines.

In reaction to this, many novels are purchased by producers in search of a diverse viewpoint. But, as if to second-guess their own good instincts, most screenplays based on those novels are written by writers working in Los Angeles. Similarly, television production is increasingly being located outside Hollywood to escape the charmless skyline and studio sets, the sameness of the ambiance and weather. But again, the writers for those shows rarely board a plane; *Vegas* may appear to have been filmed entirely on location, but a large sound stage in Los Angeles serves as a working casino and Burbank houses its writers. *Lost* may film on location in Hawaii, but its writer/producers toil at their computers in an industrial park in West Los Angeles.

Perhaps wishing to be closer to their writers who may be needed for quick rewrites, according to the August 2005 report of the Entertainment Industry Development Corp., roughly 100 of the 134 scripted and reality series in prime time are filmed in Los Angeles.

When it comes to breaking into "the business" today, all the talent, energy, and willpower in the world takes a back seat to actually being there, able to rub your sunburned shoulders with those who make that world spin. Sure, *there* can also be Toronto or Vancouver or New York or Chicago or any other place where significant filmmaking activity takes place on a regular basis and which, in turn, supports a thriving local film community. But in the main, *there* is where the players are. It's where the baby moguls set up shop, where the agents arrange "meet and greets," where the producers pick and pitch their projects, and where the pieces of the film puzzle are assembled for production.

Want an internship with a television or film company, a position that might lead to a job as a development or production executive, which in turn will create contacts and open doors for your scripts? The film factories are in Los Angeles, as well as film schools like UCLA, USC, or AFI that regularly are asked to recommend students for such positions.

Want to get noticed by a wide industry audience? Write a play and mount it in a local (West Hollywood or the Valley) production. There is no better way to perfect your voice and develop your dialogue skills. In L.A., recognizable talent will labor in your production for no money in exchange for the opportunity to stretch their television image or impress a new agent. And the producers *will* come—they're comped and frequently open to a cheap place to take a date.

Want to enter a screenplay contest that attracts agents and filmmakers? While that can work long-distance, the ones that matter will fly you to L.A. for the winner's celebration (often the draw that lures entrants into the contest). It helps to have easy access to those who may thus discover you and wish to profit from an association with you. Most agents and filmmakers are busy types who act on impulse and schedule meetings based on boredom or desperation. They may not bother to phone if you're not near enough to commiserate with over lunch or invite to their office when they're starved for fresh material and wondering what else you have cooking.

Point: agents, managers, producers—all the fair-haired Godivas that would ride bareback on your immense talent—are in Tinseltown. And you need them in your corner (better yet, living *on* your corner). It's a people business. Executives like face-to-face meetings; they like to stay close to the creators of their projects. To maintain those all-important relationships— which translate into employment and careers—writers must do more than pick up the phone or send a fax. An occasional dinner party must be attended, a round of golf or set of tennis played, a holiday or child's birth-day celebrated together. Perhaps, in a perfect world, one could live in a cabin in Montana and write for *CSI: Miami* but, on top of all the other odds working against a new writer, do you wish to increase your chances of success or *lower* them?

I realize this is a sensitive issue. Few writers want to give up lifelong friend-ships, family ties, and green spaces to pursue a risky entry into a business located in a far-off city, based only on their passion to tell a story. I couldn't agree more. I live in Los Angeles, but occasionally I too opt out for a breath of fresh air.

In 1988, my father died reaching for a glass of ice water. After that, the year evaporated—disappeared—along with his laugh, and I was ripe for a change of atmosphere. When I came across an ad in *Daily Variety* for a house trade in England ("a flat in Regent's Park and a country house in Surrey, plus two cars, for appropriate Westside accommodation"), I notified my agent, prepaid my Guild dues and hopped a taxi to LAX.

In London, I was greeted by a freezing rain. I lugged my bags up five flights of stairs and was greeted by four dank rooms overlooking the park. I didn't know a soul; the phone never rang, and there was no one to meet for lunch (besides it was too cold and wet to go out). So, noting that every wall in the flat was lined with books, I read voraciously, devouring everything from Flaubert and Sarte to Jane

Austen and the Brontës. Even the collected works of Lenin. I talked my way into a five-year pass to the Round Reading Room of the British Library where, under the spell of its huge dome, I was rendered speechless with reverence for the power of words. I occasionally occupied the same seat at which Karl Marx or Bernard Shaw had labored at creations that would endure countless lifetimes.

I worked and networked. I wrote poems, short stories, even started a serious work of historical fiction. On Sundays, I played baseball in Regent's Park with stringers from Reuters and NBC and *60 Minutes*. And yes, I eventually met with executives from most of the British film companies and the BBC. I did have lunch with producers and directors, and I parlayed whatever Hollywood cachet I imported into a temporary membership at the Groucho Club in Soho where journalists and literary and film giants from all over Europe gathered to trade tales of their writing adventures. It was arguably the best year of my life.

But I didn't write any screenplays. No television either. No one offered. Nowhere but in Hollywood is it more true: out of sight, out of mind.

There were many such times—long vacations if you will—when my agency lost contact and patience with me: If I couldn't meet face-to-face with series showrunners or schmooze over coffee in the commissary with studio executives, how could my agents be expected to generate any heat for my career? It was always difficult after I returned to Los Angeles to plug myself back into the Hollywood system and regain anything near the industry entree I had previously enjoyed. "Up close and personal" became my new mantra.

Nonetheless, despite the importance of establishing a presence in Hollywood, I still believe it is best not to change your life and uproot your family for what, at the start, is only a chance at a career as a screenwriter. But, that doesn't mean you should compromise your dreams. After all, we live in a world of faxes, e-mails, and frequent flyer miles. Write that spec feature or sample television episode and send it across the continent. If it meets with success, you can have a career and still live in Wyoming. But be aware that most writers with long distance careers are established *feature* writers who have long deadlines and isolated writing routines. And even they must maintain strong Hollywood representation and a willingness to come to town at the drop of a hat for meetings and story conferences.

Television writers, particularly those in episodic TV, will have a harder time maintaining a flexible location. While there are stories of showrunners who manage a bicoastal existence, I know of not a single writer working in series television who lives beyond local commuting distance to the show. There will be meetings you'll have to attend, notes dispensed which require immediate script revision; the whole world of series television sometimes seems to be conducted in a state of perpetual panic by a staff facing impossible deadlines on a daily basis. Simply put, it is not a long-distance gig.

Here's the *three-point strategy* I suggest:

STRATEGY

1. **Two specs before you circulate.**

   Get a couple of good screenplays or teleplays under your belt, then circulate your work in your local film community. Atlanta, Chicago, Miami, San Francisco, Vancouver, and Toronto, to name a few, have become busy production locations. And local film commissions (probably in or near your city) have lists of film activities within their jurisdictions and names of local personnel who have worked on the productions. These are all good contacts for your career.

2. **Contact local agencies first.**

   Virtually every major U.S. city has at least one good literary agency with arms stretched out to Hollywood and most will be more accessible to local talent. Contacting a local agency can also garner a new writer a valuable (and, free) first read; whether or not this leads to representation, most writers will appreciate a professional appraisal of their work.

3. **Then, go Hollywood.**

   Once you've received comments on your work, rewritten the piece to iron out the kinks, and given it another polish, *then*, make phone calls and send query letters and faxes to Los Angeles contacts. Follow up by announcing your intention to be in the L.A. area for a few days (think of it as a working vacation) to see if you can prompt agents or producers to meet with you. Many will be considerate of your effort and time but become an invited guest before you pack your bags for a long stay. And then, many screenplays later, when your talent is self-evident, perhaps you can make the mountain come to Mohammed.

For television writers, a good time to go to L.A. is during "pilot season," or when a new show is staffing up. An agent will be invaluable to you for opening doors and setting meetings. Or, on your own, you can obtain contact information for all shows through the Writers Guild.

---

from the trenches: PREPARING FOR A WRITER'S LIFE

Why not flat out admit it. Just the other day, crawling along the freeway at ten miles an hour headed to your 8 to 5 dead-end job, you said it out loud to yourself, didn't you? "Hey, you know, maybe I should give this screenwriter thing a shot."

Anyone could have seen it coming. You're famous among your co-workers for deftly working witty retorts and clever bon mots into your e-mail. Your letters home have always brought a wicked twinkle to your saintly Aunt Edna's eye. You spend more than a few idle hours at Blockbuster in search of a single decent movie you haven't seen. And, with all those bad movies, reality shows, recycled crime shows, and unfunny sitcoms, you can't possibly do much worse, right? So why not finally toss your hat into the ring?

The question is what you do now that you've decided to plunge forward—are you ready for a writer's life and, if so, what can you do to prepare for it? Because believe me this uncertain and beguiling business can test all your boundaries.

First, you might wish to make a short list of your strengths (contest awards, other writing or industry experience, business contacts) and weaknesses (living far from Los Angeles, for example). Then assess your knowledge of the business. Do you truly understand how it works? How movies are made and how a script becomes a film? Why you need all those annoying sluglines and what they mean to a production team? If you are muddy on all that, do your homework—get some DVDs with the director comments or behind-the-scenes footage or read a critic's selection of the many books on the subject. It's your chosen field after all, so become acquainted with it.

Next, put yourself and your contacts on the examining table. What, if any, unique personal attributes or experiences can you bring to the party? Have you ever worked in the industry? Whom do you know who has? Do you keep in regular contact with them? (And not just the occasional phone call—be proactive—how about making Tuesdays an "invite a mentor to lunch" day?) Is your personality one that allows you to hear and follow good advice when it is offered to you? What are your networking opportunities and how are you taking advantage of them? Have you attended any industry seminars or relevant adult education classes where a writer's craft can be honed and business contacts forged?

Then there is the grinding daily job of staying in touch with what's going on elsewhere in the business. Have you seen the current movies and read produced screenplays (many can be found online) so you can intelligently compare and

continued

contrast in a discussion of your work? The agents and producers you aspire to meet will have done so. Have you read the trade papers—*Daily Variety*, *The Hollywood Reporter*, *Screen International*—have you kept abreast of trends and current events that are now consuming the lives of your future peers? Those powerful executives and producers you plan on pitching to soon—where are they now, where have they been, what have they been buying, and where are they going tomorrow?

Starting on the career path of screenwriting is not unlike starting any small business; the challenges and rewards are pretty much the same. Oddly, the most basic requirement of all is often overlooked: Do you positively *love* film or television? You may think you can do better than what is currently playing at the local cineplex or programmed on television, but if you *hate* television, for example, don't even try to write for it. Because all those folks who write or produce for those television shows have a deep (if somewhat begrudging) respect for what they do and for the medium in general. Don't confuse writers with the characters they write—they won't find your cynicism refreshing or even just a little cute or curmudgeonly. They simply won't want to work with you.

Speaking of which, do you know any writers? Most are usually quite happy to share their wisdom and horror stories with you. Maybe they've made mistakes you can avoid or discoveries you can capitalize on. How have they enjoyed (or endured) their stint as screenwriters? How many hours do they spend writing on a typical day? How did they get hooked up with their first agent? How often do they talk to their agent or manager? What opportunities for contacts or guidance exist through the Writers Guild? How do they feed their families while waiting for something to sell? And where do they find the inspiration and motivation to keep writing when their last script failed to sell? One person's experience may not be yours, but a little commiseration by a peer beats sitting alone fighting writer's block.

As for the changes in your own lifestyle, what must you give up to be a writer? What financial sacrifices will you have to make to survive the early unemployment and inevitable financial insecurity of a writer's life? Do you like tuna sandwiches and macaroni and cheese? Roommates? Do you have a significant other earning enough for two (or three or four) and willing to share? Or have you paid off that credit card debt and banked a sufficient nest egg to see you through the rough spots? Are you a self-starter? Someone who sets a goal and a work schedule geared to meeting that goal and follows it? Remember that nobody really cares if you write or not—you must supply your own motivation. And no one else can take over and do your job should you get sick or need a vacation—the hands at the keyboard must be your own.

Which begs the question: Are you comfortable being and working alone? A writing partner is an option, but not one I recommend before finding your own way, your own voice, and your own validation as a writer. But can you be your own boss and structure a productive work schedule without a supervisor looking over your shoulder? Are you someone who habitually quits or slacks off when the going gets tough? How are you at working at home or other non-structured environment? Can you keep the pressure on to do your best, stay off the phone, and put in a fair workday even when inspiration may be lacking? Not every person has the stamina or commitment to persevere absent the carrot and stick of a regular paycheck. Don't be too hard on yourself if you're not one of them.

Finally, how will others deal with you as "a writer"? Face it: Few civilians really understand what it is that we do all day, particularly if we don't have a best-selling novel or a blockbuster movie to our credit. Some won't be able to look past your lack of a paying job while others will wish they had the guts to follow your example and do something bold themselves. Are your family or friends generally supportive of your dreams or doubters? Can your family meet its monthly budget without a steady contribution from you? Can you still hold down a job and write on the side until your career is up and running—or at least until that first sale or paid writing gig? Many new writers find that to be the way to proceed, while others prefer the "starving-writer" commitment long associated with being "an artist."

Truth be told, there is an undeniable appeal to just forging ahead and writing, come what may, paying little or no attention to details outside the margins of your pages. If that is the way that go you must, as Thomas Mann put it, by all means follow your muse and do what makes you happy. But sooner or later you'll likely find, as with any profession, a solid business plan beats putting your head in the sand or hanging out on a drugstore barstool back home in Minnesota hoping to be discovered.

CHAPTER 2

WRITING TEAMS

"We write in a room together. Scott [writing partner Scott Alexander] sits behind the computer and types. I pace back and forth or lie on the couch and toss out ideas. Killing each other isn't necessarily a negative. Battles over content are not personal—arguing can lead to good work."

—Larry Karaszewski

"Writing with a partner means you have to share the money. That really stinks."

—Robbie Fox

The Creative Partnership

Some years ago, Jack Epps, Jr., took a screenwriting class at Michigan State University that was taught by Jim Cash. Even as they came to discover their separate points of view and writing styles, they also found, as Cash put it, "a third personality that comes together whenever we work." When Epps moved to Los Angeles, Cash stayed behind in East Lansing, but the partnership thrived when they faxed ideas back and forth, worked simultaneously on scenes and drafts via computer modem, and commiserated over the exigencies of the writing business by speakerphone. Their collaboration has resulted in such hits as *Top Gun, Dick Tracy*, and others.

Having a writing partner is a great source of comfort and motivation for many writers because they can avoid facing that blank page alone. In this sense at least, screenwriting enjoys a distinct advantage over most other fields of creative writing, such as writing for novels, short stories, or plays (where one is hard-pressed to cite even a few collaborative efforts). Celebrated screenwriting collaborations—e.g., I.A.L. Diamond & Billy Wilder, Ben Hecht & Charles MacArthur, Ruth Gordon & Garson Kanin—have helped to create a long and proud history of team success in cinema writing, a tradition continued by current writing teams like former USC students Scott Alexander & Larry Karaszewski (*The People vs. Larry Flynt, Ed Wood, Man on the Moon*); brothers Joel & Ethan Cohen (*Fargo*); Willard Huyck & Gloria Katz (*American Graffiti, Indiana Jones and the Temple of Doom*), from rival schools but who met at a UCLA function; and long-time collaborators Alexander Payne & Jim Taylor (*Sideways, Election, About Schmidt*).

Note here the use of the ampersand when naming the writing partners. Per the Writers Guild, the word "and" is used only for writers who may have worked on the same script, but who are not part of the writing team.

In the best partnerships, the writers complement each other's strengths. One writer may be better with dialogue while the other works magic with structure. Put those two together and you have a powerful writing team. Some partners write separately and combine their work later. Other teams may work better if one dictates or acts out the scenes while the other translates the words into text (changing it subtly to suit his style as he goes). Another method of team writing is to entrust Act 1 to one writer, Act 2 to the other, and hammer out the final act together. Or, the writers may want to go through every beat of the process—from the rough outline to the polished final draft—as a single writing machine.

Particularly when writing comedy, it helps to have someone else in the room laughing. (Or not.) Think: Lowell Ganz & Babaloo Mandel, who collaborated on *Parenthood* and *City Slickers* or the Farrelly brothers—Peter & Bobby—who rose from screwball comedy like *Dumb & Dumber* to innovative classics like *Shallow Hal* and *Something About Mary*. A partner is also a shoulder to cry on, a cure for writer's block, a critic who cares, or sometimes just good company.

For whatever reason two people decide to combine their writing fortunes, no partnership should be entered into lightly. Becoming a writing team is akin to entering into marriage. Many *are* married, such as David & Janet Peoples (*12 Monkeys*), who work together to evolve a story, then go back and forth leading or following as the plot develops, and TV scribes Andrew Schneider & Diane Frolov (*Northern Exposure* and *Dangerous Minds*). (Others, such as Charles Shyer & Nancy Meyers [*Private Benjamin, Father of the Bride*] traded ideas across from each other on couches in their den—before they got divorced, presumably doing their recent work from couches in separate houses.) Needless to say, it is not always a good idea to become writing partners with your lover or best friend. A professional working relationship is often best at arm's length. At the least, the two of you should be compatible and like each other enough that you're reasonably assured of staying together. Divorce can be costly. A writing team displays a single creative force to the outside world. If the partners break up, it's probable that neither will have a decent individual writing sample. Both writers likely will need new, individual spec samples and may have to prove their writing talent all over again.

Ideally, partners should grow together (Cash & Epps are still collaborating, most recently on *Anacondas: The Hunt for The Blood Orchid*), learn to resolve their differences, and be able to put aside their egos for the good of the team. Mutual respect for each other's work, opinions, integrity, and creative and business judgment is essential. Trust is crucial. Both partners must be able to handle and benefit from any critical analysis by the other. Compromise cannot be anathema to you. Sooner or later you must agree (or at least agree to disagree) so the work can move forward.

Most importantly, while partners have someone to share the workload, the business side of your work belongs to the team and is subject to team decisions—from creation of the story to the writing of the script and on to the marketing and selling of it.

The Business Partnership

Before you enter into a writing partnership, here are some questions to ask yourself:

How are conflicts over the writing and marketing of the screenplay to be resolved?

If one writer comes up with the story and both write the screenplay, how is the income from a sale to be divided?

What if one partner wants to sell and the other doesn't like the terms or the buyer—must both participate in script meetings?

What if one writer moves on after the first draft and doesn't want to participate in rewrites; can the other do it alone?

What if one partner dies before the screenplay has been completed or marketed?

Will there be separate compensation for separate work? (A writing team does not get twice the money. The WGA treats two partners as one writer and applicable scale [minimum compensation] is split between them. Presumably, a team can write twice as fast, get twice the jobs, and earn twice the money in a given period. I said presumably.)

If you and your partner decide to write as a team, you will want to draw up a Writers Collaboration Agreement which outlines the duties and parameters of your relationship, including a formula for completion of the work, rewriting assignments, ownership and copyright, division of income and expenses, representation, screen credit, etc. Following are common points that this written agreement should address:

- **The Work.**
  In agreeing to collaborate, consider the writing services each will contribute to the final product, a completion date (if warranted), and final ownership of the work. Also consider if the parties' writing services are exclusive to the partnership or if either may work on other spec projects or accept separate employment. This can often affect the candor with which partners share ideas during the writing process.

- **Ownership.**
  Shall the work be copyrighted or registered in the name of both parties? If so, each should designate the other as his attorney-in-fact to complete such registration.

- **Mutuality.**
  Shall all decisions, with respect to the completion, representation, sale, or other disposition of the work, be in writing? Are all decisions mutual or may one person, in some affairs or at opportune times, act for the team?

- **Expenses & Income.**
  How shall expenses incurred in connection with the work or its disposition be shared? How shall proceeds flowing from the exploitation of the work (whether fixed, deferred, or contingent, or whether from the sale of rights or licenses in all or any of the various mediums) be divided and paid?

- **Credit.**
  How and in what order shall the writers receive credit on the work and on any motion picture based upon the work? Writing teams most often position themselves alphabetically but some grant the coveted first position to the more experienced writer or, perhaps, to the one who came up with the initial concept. Whatever formula your team decides upon, do so in advance to ward off any potential problems.

- **Interruption of Services.**
  If one party, for whatever reason, ceases work on the project at any given point, may the other party complete it? If so, must the writer complete it alone or can another partner be engaged? How, then, will the percentage of ownership and possible proceeds from the work be divided?

- **Disputes & Termination.**
  May either party terminate the agreement, and if so, how will the work or its disposition be affected? How are disputes in general, with respect to the work or its disposition, to be handled? Should arbitration be mandatory? (The Writers Guild has a mediation arbitration procedure for its members.)

- **Agency.**
  Shall the work be represented by one agent for both parties? What if each has or ultimately acquires separate representation? The commissions payable and the procedure by which duel agents may represent the work or its authors should be set forth.

- **Further Writing Services.**
  Shall (or must) the parties share any offered rewrite assignments? What if one party is unwilling or unavailable to participate in further writing services with respect to the work—shall the other be permitted to undertake such an engagement, and if so, how shall additional compensation be shared? (For example, substantial bonuses are often attached to the purchase price of the original screenplay. But if such film is based not only on the original work but also on a one-party rewrite, should the division of the writing bonus between the partners be altered?)

- **Other Services.**
  Will either party be contributing other services (i.e., attaching himself as producer, director, or some other creative capacity)? This could affect the marketability of the work and raise the question of whether some percentage share in any related compensation is appropriate for the non-attached party.

A short-form Writers Collaboration Agreement, approved for use by members of the Writers Guild of America, addresses many of these concerns and is printed by permission of the Guild at the end of this chapter. Current versions can also be obtained for a nominal fee (currently, $1.00) from the Guild. Attach an SASE and send your request to: WGA west: 7000 West Third Street, Los Angeles, CA 90048-4329; WGA East: 555 West 57th

St., New York, N.Y. 10019. However, to fully address the intricacies of the questions above and other perplexing issues which may confront the partnership, consult an entertainment attorney; this might be the first mutual decision the partnership makes.

A Word about Loan-Out Companies

Primarily for tax purposes, writers often choose to incorporate themselves. Usually, the writer is the sole officer and the entire board of directors of his closely held corporation and he owns all the company's stock (though some writers may have a spouse or other family members on the roster as well). The writer contracts to work exclusively for the corporation (in film business jargon, the corporation is a "loan-out company"), in exchange for a salary and other corporate perks such as a car, retirement plan, insurance, and so on. The loan-out company then proceeds to "lend and furnish" the writer's services to anyone interested in employing the writer.

Advantages to this arrangement include receiving payment for services rendered without taxes being deducted by the employer and the ability to spread income over two personal tax years. Disadvantages include the loss of normal employer contributions, such as state unemployment insurance (though some employers may be convinced to reimburse the loan-out company for contributions actually paid to the government). Still, the most highly prized feature of any corporation—limited liability—will usually not apply to the writer with a loan-out company. Any savvy employer will require the writer to personally contract his services to the employer (in what is known as an inducement letter), as well as execute a second agreement between the employer and the loan-out company which contracts to "cause the writer to commence his services" to the employer (known as a lending agreement).

Recently, some writing teams have incorporated themselves into a single loan-out company. The primary reason for this action is the single tax return and one accountant required at tax time and the one state minimum tax fee that must be paid.

I believe that two tax returns are better than one lawsuit. As mentioned above, it is difficult to separate two people from the bonds of a writing partnership. Now, compound that with the legalities of extracting them from the bonds of their corporation.

WRITER'S COLLABORATION AGREEMENT*

AGREEMENT made at _____, California, by and between
_____ and _____, hereinafter
sometimes referred to as the "Parties".

The parties are about to write in collaboration an (original story) (treatment)
(screenplay) _____ (other), based upon
_____, hereinafter referred to as the "Work", and are
desirous of establishing all their rights and obligations in and to said Work.

NOW, THEREFORE, in consideration of the execution of this Agreement, and the
undertakings of the parties as hereinafter set forth, it is agreed as follows:

1. The parties shall collaborate in the writing of the Work and upon completion thereof shall be the joint owners of the Work (or shall own the Work
   in the following percentages:_____).

2. Upon completion of the Work it shall be registered with the Writers Guild
   of America, west, Inc. as the joint Work of the parties. If the Work shall be
   in form such as to qualify it for copyright, it shall be registered for such
   copyright in the name of both Parties, and each Party hereby designates
   the other as his attorney-in-fact to register such Work with the United
   States Copyright Office.

3. It is contemplated that the Work will be completed by not later than
   _____, provided, however, that failure to complete the
   Work by such date shall not be construed as a breach of this Agreement
   on the part of either party.

4. It is understood that _____ (both writers) is a/are/are
   not "professional writer(s)," as that term is defined in the WGA Basic
   Agreement.
   It is further understood by the Parties that _____ (and
   _____), in addition to writing services, shall perform
   the following additional functions in regard to the Work:

5. If, prior to the completion of the Work, either Party shall voluntarily withdraw from the collaboration, then the other Party shall have the right to
   complete the Work alone or in conjunction with another collaborator or collaborators, and in such event the percentage of ownership, as hereinbefore
   provided in paragraph 1, shall be revised by mutual agreement in writing.

* The Provisions herein are not mandatory, and may be modified for the specific needs of the Parties,
  subject to minimum requirements of the Writers Guild Basic Agreement.

continued

6. If, prior to the completion of the Work, there shall be a dispute of any kind with respect to the Work, then the parties may terminate this Collaboration Agreement by an instrument in writing, which shall be filed with the Writers Guild of America, west, Inc. [new mediation arbitration procedure in Constitution]

7. Any contract for the sale or other disposition of the Work, where the Work has been completed by the Parties in accordance herewith, shall require that the Work shall be attributed to the authors in the following manner:

8. Neither party shall sell, or otherwise voluntarily dispose of the Work, or his share therein, without the written consent of the other, which consent, however shall not be unreasonably withheld. (It is agreed that _____ to contract on behalf of the Parties without written consent of the other, on the condition that s/he negotiate no less than _____ for the work.)

9. It is acknowledged and agreed that _____ (and _____) shall be the exclusive agents of the Parties for the purpose of sale or other disposition of the Work or any rights therein. Each such agent shall represent the Parties at the following studios only:

X agent   Y agent

The aforementioned agent, or agents, shall have _____ period in which to sell or otherwise dispose of the Work, and if there shall be more than one agent, the aggregate commission for the sale or other disposition of the Work shall be limited to ten percent (10%) and shall be equally divided among the agents hereinbefore designated.

If there shall be two or more agents, they shall be instructed to notify each other when they have begun negotiations for the sale or other disposition of the Work and of the terms thereof, and no agent shall conclude an agreement for the sale or other disposition of the Work unless he shall have first notified the other agents thereof. If there shall be a dispute among the agents as to the sale or other disposition of the Work by any of them, the matter shall immediately be referred to the Parties, who shall determine the matter for them.

10. Any and all expenses of any kind whatsoever which shall be incurred by either or both of the Parties in connection with the writing, registration or sale or other disposition of the Work shall be (shared jointly) (prorated in accordance with the percentages hereinbefore mentioned in paragraph 1).

11. All money or other things of value derived from the sale or other disposition of the Work shall be applied as follows:

    a. In payment of commissions, if any.

    b. In payment of any expenses or reimbursement of either Party for expenses paid in connection with the Work.

    c. To the Parties in the proportion of their ownership.

12. It is understood and agreed that for the purposes of this Agreement the Parties shall share hereunder, unless otherwise herein stated, the proceeds from the sale or any and all other disposition of the Work and the rights and licenses therein and with respect thereto, including but not limited to the following:

    a. Motion picture rights

    b. Sequel rights

    c. Remake rights

    d. Television film rights

    e. Television live rights

    f. Stage rights

    g. Radio rights

    h. Publication rights

    i. Interactive rights

    j. Merchandising rights

13. Should the Work be sold or otherwise disposed of and, as an incident thereto, the Parties be employed to revise the Work or write a screenplay based thereon, the total compensation provided for in such employment agreement shall be shared by them (jointly) (in the following proportion): If either Party shall be unavailable for the purposes of collaborating on such revision or screenplay, then the Party who is available shall be permitted to do such revision or screenplay and shall be entitled to the full amount of compensation in connection therewith, provided, however, that in such a case the purchase price shall remain fair and reasonable, and in no event shall the Party not available for the revision or screenplay receive less than _____% of the total selling price.

continued

14. If either Party hereto shall desire to use the Work, or any right therein or with respect thereto, in any venture in which such Party shall have a financial interest, whether direct or indirect, the Party desiring so to do shall notify the other Party of that fact and shall afford such other Party the opportunity to participate in the venture in the proportion of such other Party's interest in the Work. If such other party shall be unwilling to participate in such venture, the Party desiring to proceed therein shall be required to pay such other Party an amount equal to that which such other Party would have received if the Work or right, as the case may be, intended to be so used had been sold to a disinterested person at the price at which the same shall last have been offered, or if it shall not have been offered, at its fair market value which, in the absence of mutual agreement of the Parties, shall be determined by mediation and/or arbitration in accordance with the regulations of the Writers Guild of America, west, Inc. if permissible pursuant to the WGAw Constitution.

15. This Agreement shall be executed in sufficient number of copies so that one fully executed copy may be, and shall be, delivered to each Party and to the Writers Guild of America, Inc. If any disputes shall arise concerning the interpretation or application of this Agreement, or the rights or liabilities of the Parties arising hereunder, such dispute shall be submitted to the Writers Guild of America, west, Inc. for arbitration in accordance with the arbitration procedures of the Guild, and the determination of the Guild's arbitration committee as to all such matters shall be conclusive and binding upon the Parties.

DATED this _____ day of _____, 19_____.

_____

_____

from the trenches: ANATOMY OF AN ASSIGNMENT

Sometimes a partner is thrust upon you. One lazy Sunday, an old friend who had been a successful game show producer before semi-retiring to his rose gardens, rang my doorbell. A friend of his at a new, hot production company had sent him a thin book to see if he could find a viable MOW in it. My friend was curious as to my opinion. It was a young adult book, a classic, all of thirty pages long. I read it twice while he brewed himself a coffee. I loved it. It was a coming-of-age theme set in Poland against the backdrop of the final days of World War II. The story of an endearing but somewhat damaged mother and her only daughter yearning for her approval had a simple, yet profound wisdom and a ring of emotional truth to it that crosses borders and generations. Hallmark Hall of Fame could have been stamped on its cover. I posed possible scenarios for opening it up and making it accessible to today's audience and recommended he pursue it. Instead, he invited me along to pitch it with him.

Now I had previous experience writing with partners and, though the joining of two minds is never easy, the results for me had always proven worth the effort. Still, it's not something I undertake lightly. For starters, all matters of personality, egos, and compatibility aside, the *process* must be sorted out: writing habits, who will write what, when and where you'll work, separate or together, etc. Of course you split credit and pay, but more importantly, in the eyes of the business, you are now a writing team. Your work only serves to show what *the team* is capable of; thus, future work may depend upon embarking on a longer-term relationship than either of you may have initially envisioned. And for me, that day, there was another concern. My friend was *not a writer*… but then, I did so love the story.

The pitch meeting turned into a love fest. Everyone seemed to genuinely like each other and to see the same virtues and challenges in the story before us. We were spitballing ideas around the table faster than we could jot down notes. As a closer, the development execs hinted the project was so dear to them they might finance the film in-house (music to a writer's ears—it means the movie may actually get made). We ended the day swapping the numbers of our reps so that their business affairs people could draft a deal memo (the standard: outline, first and second drafts—about a six-month commitment).

Only one moment gave me pause.

The author was alive and well and a friend of the producer. So, professional courtesy if you will, self-preservation if you must, I thought I might contact her. After all, I admired the book, was grateful for the opportunity to be associated with it, and

continued

wanted her to know that. But the producers nixed that. Oh, the author was excited, they assured us, beside herself with joy that her little book had come this far, and wanted to be kept appraised of our progress. But she had nothing to add to what she had written. Why bother her? Especially when you were about to perform plastic surgery on her child.

I've written books; I know the feeling. You've already picked the medium you felt best served the material or your talent, poured every ounce of yourself into it, exhausted the possibilities for the characters and the story, and now you've moved on to other characters and other stories because you're a storyteller—it's what you do. Retreading the old ground, crafting a new plot and dramatic structure and combining characters and inventing new ones just to serve the goal of a movie, well, it's not very appealing to most authors. But what gave me pause was what the producer said next: "Besides, the other writers tried that and it didn't work out very well."

Other writers? First mention of this, as we're walking out the door? But flushed with the success of a well-received pitch, I didn't pursue it. Instead, we went home and wrote—eventually. My new partner was often ill and had to have a grilled chicken and broccoli lunch before even discussing work. It took more than the usual while for us to iron out a way to work together and still remain friends. But finally we delivered the outline…

… and they *hated* it. I checked my notes. It was what we had all agreed upon. But it turns out we didn't really *understand* what they wanted. Which was to remain faithful to the book, *while at the same time* replacing six of the seven story beats the slight work provided, including the ending, main character, setting, period, ethnicity, and religious affiliation of the family. Okay. We rewrote the outline, for free. Hell, we all loved each other, didn't we? And we were truly committed to seeing this story achieve a larger audience.

Over the next two weeks, we brainstormed a totally new approach and promptly delivered a new outline—this time to rave reviews from the production head, the development head, and the producer. I even remember the staff giving us an ovation as we marched in for our story conference. With hugs all around, we were sent off to write the crucial first draft, which we delivered right on schedule. And the whole team met again—except for the producer, who was called out of town at the last minute. Again, *they loved it*! Heaped praise upon praise until we were blushing in embarrassment. A week later we met with the producer. She spoke quietly, almost in a whisper. She too loved the script, she told us. It was just that, well… there were a few little changes.

No problem. Only this time, so that everyone would be on the same page, we drafted a letter setting forth in detail the changes discussed and how we proposed to implement them. Then we asked the production chief and the head of development to initial their approval, point by point. Only then did we go to work. Delivered the final draft. Waited. When we met again, there were some new faces in the room. *The old ones had all been fired.* The *new* head of production began with a handshake and this greeting, "Well, as you're probably aware, it just doesn't work for us."

William Goldman called them "writer killers." They play with your mind, they sap your enthusiasm, they make you crazy. Worse, they render you useless. When you ask them if they like a particular line or scene, they nod enthusiastically. After a few futile attempts like that to narrow down the problem, they beg off specifics: "I don't really know how to explain it. It's just, when you know, you know. You know?"

Yeah, I knew. I knew the agenda had changed. It wasn't any longer about the scenes, the characters, the structure, the writing at all. All that was now clearly beside the point. What was clear was the more we wrote, the less excited they became about the movie. *Because if they liked it, they'd then have to make it.* The time for excuses would be over.

Woody Allen once called a second marriage "the triumph of hope over experience." The same goes for many execs in the development process. The sky is always a deeper blue over the next horizon. The point was to be *in development*, to have a project on the drawing board, to feel active. In fact, we were all just wasting each other's time. It was then that we learned we were the third set of writers to tackle the story. They, along with two potential directors, had all been fired before we began. Two more writers, another director, and the new head of production were fired since.

Still, there were the usual benefits. The checks cleared. (They were late, but they cleared.) My new partner and I remained friends, with the understanding that we would never, ever write together again. That is, until someone again paid us to write together, which is exactly what happened when our aborted script led to a new assignment. Which, in the end, is what having a career as a writer in Hollywood is all about—keeping the creative ball in the air. That, and still being able to put "writer" down under "occupation" on all those government forms without the fraud police breathing down your neck.

PART II

STEP BY STEP THROUGH THE CREATIVE PROCESS

Chapter 3

The Screenwriter's Work Process: From Concept to Script

By now, you've decided the writer's life is for you: You have worked out your immediate living arrangements and travel plans, your desire is strong, and the rewards are self-evident. But trust me on this—as one sage wrote, "there is many a slip betwixt the cup and the lip." Or, as Woody Allen put it in his film *Crimes and Misdemeanors* (as uttered by Alan Alda's character, Lester, a hardened film producer), "This is the real world. They don't pay off on high aspirations. You've got to deliver."

The question is: "Deliver what to whom?"

The answer is: A full-length, original feature screenplay is the *sine qua non* for entry into the "promised land" of feature films; for television, at least two "spec" writing samples must precede any contact with a prospective employer. There are no shortcuts for the new writer—*no ideas, concepts, treatments, or outlines will do.*

Books or seminars which tell you otherwise are fudging the facts to make you feel better. Still, you wonder, what about those stories in the trades of writers spinning yarns and tossing off one-liners for big bucks and Hollywood superstardom? Isn't there something short of that full first draft that will get you into the club? Well, no, but what follows are valuable screenwriter tools that serve an essential purpose in both the scripting and the marketing of ideas.

The Concept (or Premise)

An idea for a film, also referred to as a "concept" or a "premise," is as ethe-real as the vacuum in outer space. It is not a tangible intellectual property; it is not protectable by copyright and it is *not sellable*, at least for the novice writer, until fleshed out with plot, characters, and dramatic structure. Nonetheless, the idea *is*, however half-baked, the basic raw material out of which movies are made.

Some early ideas are so dumb that they seem hardly worth a second thought. Yet, study the history of good ideas, urges Arthur VanGundy, Professor of Communication at the University of Oklahoma, and the most powerful appear to come from puttering around with the seem-ingly ridiculous. The real point, per VanGundy, is to allow yourself to be wildly imaginative, without censure; to brainstorm. Some ideas may prove unworkable, but others may be like caterpillars that hatch into beautiful butterflies.

On the other hand, some ideas seem ready-made for the movies the moment they are hatched. The oft bandied-about term *high-concept* is no more than studio lingo for a unique film premise with clear mass audience appeal that may be easily grasped or summarized in a sentence or two, an idea so exciting it seems to levitate off the page. Such premises are usually conveyed in a *pitch* to producers or development executives.

Some examples of high-concept films are:

- *Die Hard*—An off-duty New York cop must single-handedly battle terrorists in an L.A. high-rise and rescue innocent hostages, includ-ing his wife.
- *Splash*—A young man finally finds the woman of his dreams, only she's a fish.
- *Beverly Hills Cop*—A mission to solve his best friend's murder leads a street-wise black cop from Detroit to squeaky-clean Beverly Hills.
- *Gladiator*—When a Roman general is betrayed and his family murdered by a corrupt Prince, he comes to Rome as a gladiator to seek his revenge.
- *Seabiscuit*—A true story of a thoroughbred racing legend, who rises from an under-fed workhorse to triumph over the Triple Crown winner, War Admiral.

- *Pirates of the Caribbean*—A 17ᵗʰ century adventure on the Caribbean Sea where the roguish but charming Captain Jack Sparrow joins with a young blacksmith to rescue the Governor of England's daughter and reclaim his ship.

- *Spy Kids*—Former spies now raising a family, Gregorio and Ingrid Cortez are called back into action—but when they are kidnapped by their evil nemesis, the only two people in the world who can rescue them are their kids.

These films don't require a lot of explanation; they scream "commerciality" and boast great lead roles for actors. But even weakly conceived high-concept movies—those short on plot credibility, characters, or dialogue, but which strain to accommodate tie-ins with fast food restaurants and toymakers—still require a strong dramatic structure that builds to a high emotional impact; the kind of movie for which the term "blockbuster" was coined.

---

from the trenches: GOT A GREAT MOVIE IDEA?

There is a secret to writing scripts that sell. Ignore this advice at your own peril. Unless, that is, you're writing a no-budget, star-free film about your great-grandmother's immigration and plan to direct and finance it yourself. If so, good luck, but this is for those who want to write a commercial movie, to submit their work to agents, producers, and talent and try for a spec script sale in this increasingly dismal, pre-sold, sequel-happy, tentpole-driven market we find ourselves in. But first, a true story.

A friend of mine recently set about to write a script himself. Now, a lot of people do that and never get to page one, but my friend is nothing if not doggedly determined. It took him less than three months to come up with "a script." It was, predictably, God-awful. But he wasn't content with the suggestion he stick to computer tech consulting, and he pressed me for the reasons I didn't like it. Not surprisingly (he's an easy-going fellow), he didn't seem too terribly offended or put off by my rather scathing commentary and was encouraged that I liked the title, two or three scenes, and an unexplored setting I felt held visual value. In fact, he apparently took it all to heart because three months later he produced a much-improved second draft. This time I gave more detailed suggestions on how to refine the plot, characters, dialogue, structure, and offered a tip on a software format program.

continued

My friend then set out to "fix" the script's problems by adding more scenes rather than rewriting those that didn't work and restructuring. His third draft was too long by a third. Worse, it had resurrected all the bad habits of the first draft, while cutting out much of the simple charm of the second. I wasn't gentle in my review. But again, my friend was undaunted—he produced a fourth draft. This one I read in a sitting; it moved that well. It had solved the problems we had pinpointed and showcased his promise as a writer. I was truly excited for him. I encouraged him to start the submission process and begin work immediately on a new script (as one should always do).

But I was too quick to praise. I was so invested in his progress, so relieved to see the story finally unfold logically and with purpose, that I had failed to measure the script by the first rule of screenwriting—*Thou Shalt Not Be Boring*. If not boring exactly, it was all very tame. That's to take nothing away from a well-crafted, sweet story that had all the markings of an "A" script in a film school class. The main character was a decent guy in wolf's clothing pursuing false success with a credible arc toward redemption and real success. All the supporting characters were well developed, the plot was structurally sound and the dialogue had the ring of truth. It was quality work. A good sample script, at the least, if anyone still accepts writing samples these days.

But it never screamed "hot." It didn't spell "must-see movie." It wasn't an event movie and it wasn't cool enough or hip enough to attract the 18 to 24 target age group that flock to films like *Mean Girls* or *Something About Mary*. "No edgy humor, no particularly fresh or challenging roles, no surprises to keep us on the edge of our seat, no new contemporary themes explored." This was what a prominent film exec confided to me upon being shown the draft. I knew in my heart this would surely be the response of most any agent, producer, or development executive. "It is what it is, nothing more you can do about it. Move on, and come back when you have something that has 'hit' written all over it." So "they" would say. And they would be right.

That's when I remembered the secret. "The very first thing every screenwriter should do before writing one word of script is ask themselves if this is a movie someone would pay $50 to see—and after babysitters, parking, the tickets, popcorn, etc., that's a conservative estimate for a couple going out to a movie today." This is what industry-savvy producer and former literary agent Diane Cairns had told a screenwriting class of mine. As a superstar agent for seventeen years, Diane is no shrinking violet. She personally spearheaded into production some of the more risky scripts of our time, such as *Fatal Attraction*, *Dangerous Liaisons*, and *Thelma & Louise*. Yet, in reading many scripts submitted by new writers, Diane wonders "Have they ever seen a movie?" That story about your great-grandmother's immigration—does it resemble any film reviewed by Roger Ebert recently? Is it something a stranger would pay $50 to see?

There are four keys to marketability that Diane looks for in reading a script. The first and most important is "a big idea for a movie"—a story that begs to be told, that only cinema can do well, with a compelling hook that grabs you and doesn't let you go till the credits roll. As daring and original as a spec script may be, some ideas just don't lend themselves to a commercial, movie-going experience. The ability to recognize when an idea doesn't measure up to contemporary cinema standards can save a writer a lot of time and activity for not a lot of potential payoff.

Diane's next two requirements before undertaking representation of a script are: how well that screenplay succeeds in its genre and that the script contains at least a few moments actors will really want to play. "A horror film that is not scary, a comedy that is not funny, or a thriller without edge-of-the-seat excitement is not going to make it," she says. And of course, all movies today are somewhat actor-driven (read star-driven). "Many actors only read the lines for their character. If they don't have a few lines that they would kill to say, some trailer-worthy action they feel challenged to engage in, they'll never get to the plot."

Which leads to Diane's fourth requirement: the logic of the plot and the compelling quality of the story. Readers want a page-turner or at least a fresh twist on an old tale, a plot not full of holes, and dialogue rich with subtext and not stilted as old cheese. On the other hand, a script that needs work on those points may still be salvageable if the basic idea is large enough to allow for it—but there is no way to sell a script that misses the mark on her first three prerequisites. As screenwriting advice goes, pin that to your corkboard.

The Beat Outline and the Treatment

How does one begin a journey? By taking the first step. This bit of wisdom is the inspiration for most books or methods on screenwriting. Professionals know that the hardest hurdle of all, especially when facing a seemingly monumental task, is getting started. Witness Syd Field's early tome, *Screenplay*; its great achievement was in breaking down those large, foreboding 120 pages of screenplay into smaller bits. (Readers learned that most screenplays contain three "acts"; that it is easier to begin an act than a screenplay; easier to write a 10-page opening than 30 pages, and so on.)

Outlines or treatments are writing tools that accomplish the same thing.

A *beat outline* can be either short or long. The short version, or major beat outline, follows the "5 C's": Character, Conflict, Crisis, Climax, and Conclusion. That is, it sets the story hook that gives the main character a goal and puts him/her in conflict with an opponent, lays out the major turning points, and reveals the ending. Think of it as a clothesline on which a writer can then hang a more complete story and all those scene-stealing moments for actors. A major *scene outline* is more involved; the story is laid bare, scene-by-scene, in simple sentences or short paragraphs, usually about 50 in total.

Many writers use *scene cards*—3 × 5 or 4 × 6 index cards—as their initial outline tool. Each card represents one scene (less important scenes, such as establishing shots, lead-ins, or those simply serving to move actors from one place to another, for example, may be set aside for now). The purpose of the scene, the characters in it, and the action of the scene are printed on the card—any additional information, such as research or sample dialogue for the scene may be paper-clipped to it.

It's also a good idea to head each card with a slugline (EXT. MOUNTAIN CABIN—NIGHT) to ground the scenes and help you track their movement and timeline. This also alerts you to stagnant locations (phone conversations, cars, offices, apartments) or to a story being told all at night, for example, without day scenes in between to ease the eyes or signal that a following night scene is a *different* night and not the one we just saw.

Unlike a computer, on which the available information is limited by screen size (forcing one to scroll up or down to try for an overview), cards are easily displayed on a table or floor or pinned to a corkboard. This allows your structure to become clear and the movements and interactions of your characters—particularly the main character and opponent—to be more easily tracked. Your intended movie is then before you and scenes can be shuffled, combined, or tossed away to serve the story structure you desire.

The cards are my way of getting research and notes organized and malleable. I use color-coded cards—white for scenes that convey plot information only, light blue for scenes that add character development, pink for plot-turning points, and red for climactic moments that carry the story or the actor's performance—the passion moments, key action scenes, comedy payoffs, big special effects, that sort of thing.

A *treatment* is the dramatic narrative of a film story, usually between 5 and 20 pages in length (although writers have been known to develop treatments that are half the length of their screenplays). It unfolds as would the film itself (if not exactly scene-by-scene), told in active voice, present tense, and can even contain snippets of dialogue, making it read much like a short story. It is not a synopsis; it does not try and summarize the movie—it *is* the movie, told in story rather than script form.

Most writers will be better off outlining than writing a treatment. The outline is more easily manipulated for changes and forces the writer to think more in images than words. The treatment is more familiar ground for most new writers (and executives prefer it because it makes for an easier read), but tends to mask a weak story or weak character development with metaphors, adverbs, smooth segues, and other literary conceits. The narrative form can also get sloppy, with the inclusion of phrases like "he realized," "he wondered," "he decided," or even "he thought." Remember that in a screenplay it is only what the character says, does, sees, or hears that can be translated to the screen.

Still, as we will see, both are essential development tools for any screenwriter. Outlines and treatments both focus on the scene-by-scene construction of the story; they refine the narrative structure and chart character growth. Line-by-line, or in a brief narrative, they are easy to follow, easy to change and rearrange. The writer is free to create and discard scenes (a crucial step in the creative process) before committing them to the apparent permanency of a screenplay. Some writers combine the two forms—writing longer paragraphs for the outlined scenes, even including brief dialogue exchanges. This makes for a detailed outline that is easier for a third party—like a development exec—to digest.

By way of example, here is a three-act feature film beat outline (using treatment elements like bits of dialogue) of key plot-developing scenes from Ernest Lehman's classic *North By Northwest*, directed by Alfred Hitchcock and starring Cary Grant as Roger Thornhill.

> *Act I (Setting Up the Dramatic Situation—wherein, to quote Gore Vidal, we put the protagonist "up a tree").*
>
> Midtown Manhattan, the tempo of Madison Avenue, streets swarming with smartly dressed people. V.O. "Would it not be strange, in a city of seven million people, if one man were never mistaken for another…"
>
> ROGER THORNHILL, tall, lean, faultlessly dressed, and far too original to be wearing the gray flannel uniform of his kind, meets

business associates for lunch. When he rises to send a telegram to his mother, LICHT and VALERIAN mistake him for "George Kaplan." They hustle him into a waiting car at gunpoint, refusing to tell him where he's being taken.

Thornhill is taken to the Townsend estate where PHILLIP VANDAMM, posing as Mr. Townsend, also assumes he's Kaplan. Vandamm accuses him of lying and grills him on how much he knows of "our arrangements." Upon Thornhill's denials, LEONARD, Valerian, and Licht force a fifth of bourbon into him.

Valerian and Licht put the drunk Thornhill behind the wheel of a moving car on a winding mountain road. Thornhill manages to steer the car until he is followed by a police cruiser and arrested.

Thornhill, his mother, lawyer, and two cops, return to the Townsend mansion to verify his story. A woman assumed to be Mrs. Townsend contends that Thornhill attended a party the night before and drove away drunk. She says her husband is addressing the UN today. As the party leaves, they are watched by Valerian posing as a gardener.

Thornhill and his mother manage to gain access to the real George Kaplan's room at the Plaza Hotel, where they find a newspaper picture of Vandamm.

Thornhill, posing as Kaplan, goes to the UN looking for "Townsend." The Townsend he finds is not the man from the mansion. Valerian watches from b.g. As Thornhill shows the real Townsend the newspaper photo, Townsend gasps and falls into Thornhill with a knife in his back. Thornhill grabs for him and is photographed holding the knife above the dead man.

Act II (Progressive Complications—wherein we "throw stones at him.")

A group of CIA men view the same photo on the front page of the newspaper. They regret Thornhill is mistaken for Kaplan but, "there's nothing we can do for him without endangering Number One."

Thornhill boards a train for Chicago, eluding police with the help of EVE KENDALL, who hides him in her sleeping compartment. But she also sends a note via the porter to Vandamm: "What do I do with him in the morning?"

In Chicago, Eve arranges for Thornhill to meet Kaplan, but instead Thornhill is attacked by a crop duster in a cornfield. He returns to find Eve with Vandamm. He follows them to an art auction where

Vandamm picks up a statue filled with microfilm. Thornhill confronts him, but when Leonard and Valerian prevent his escape, he causes a scene and is arrested.

In the police car, he confesses that he is a wanted murderer, but instead of taking him to jail, the police deliver him to the airport, where he is met by the PROFESSOR, the head of the CIA.

Thornhill learns that Vandamm is an international smuggler of secrets, that Eve is actually a CIA agent, and that his relationship with her has endangered her life.

To convince Vandamm that "Kaplan" is no longer a threat, the Professor stages Thornhill's "death" at Mt. Rushmore by having Eve shoot him with blanks.

Thornhill and Eve meet afterwards and confess their love for each other—but Eve must leave the country with Vandamm that night, never to return. They kiss goodbye as the Professor leads him away.

Act III (Conclusion—wherein we "get him back down")

Thornhill escapes the Professor's protective custody and goes to Vandamm's house to try and keep Eve from leaving. He discovers that Leonard and Valerian know she's a spy and intend to kill her.

Thornhill manages to get Eve and the statue away, but they are pursued on foot through the woods until they emerge on the top of Mt. Rushmore. Trying to climb down the treacherous slope, they are attacked by Valerian and Leonard until a CIA sharpshooter kills Leonard. Thornhill must still rescue Eve from the precipice where she has fallen, pulling her up until—

Eve lands beside him in the upper berth of a moving train.

In truth, few writers really like outlines or treatments—they're boring and they usually do not have enough witty repartee to keep the writer amused. But the fact is that *almost all successful screenwriters will admit to spending more time on the outline or treatment stage of their writing process than on the actual screenplay.*

Established writers may find a treatment/outline to be a potent *selling tool* as well, useful in accompanying a verbal pitch, for example. Many step deals often get started by a required treatment or outline stage so that the producer can work with the writer to iron out story problems before they become fixed in the cement of the screenplay. However, the treatment/

outline is an entirely different animal from a screenplay—in format, content, and tone—and neither the outline nor the treatment alone has a chance of launching your writing career. Producers simply are unable, or unwilling, to decipher screenwriting talent or the big-screen worthiness of your story on the basis of a treatment or outline alone.

Industry-savvy director Monte Hellman, who plows through two scripts a day in search of viable screen material, throws away treatments he receives. He comments, "Whatever a treatment tells me about a story is too often muddled and lost in the costly and time-consuming process of getting it into a coherent screenplay. Why should I risk that when there is a plethora of full screenplays to consider?"

Make no mistake, in an industry overwhelmed with books, screenplays, and other written materials, producers may ask a new writer for a treatment or a *synopsis* (a condensed version of a story, told objectively, not dramatically as in a treatment). But, usually, it will be requested *in addition* to a full screenplay. (Should you submit one, brevity is best; at the least, it will force them to read your script to get the complete story.) No doubt, this makes the producer's work easier, but is it to your advantage? After all, in relatively few pages, you must convey the uniqueness of your characters and the full scope of your story in a different format. If you fail, the reader will pass on the treatment and avoid reading your fully realized dramatic screenplay. If the reader likes the treatment, he will then read the screenplay anyway (thus, you get two chances to be rejected!). This might not be the ticket you were hoping for to your screenwriting career.

Don't be seduced into thinking your treatment can make money—the Art Buchwald way. Buchwald sold a treatment to Paramount Pictures but later had to sue the studio to prove that his treatment was the inspiration for the Eddie Murphy film *Coming to America*. According to former Paramount Creative Executive David Kirkpatrick, the studio optioned only one treatment in the ten years he was there—Buchwald's. And that was only because of Buchwald's formidable reputation as a writer and the attachment of a producer with whom Paramount had interest in doing future business.

The "Spec" Screenplay

In showbiz lingo, a "spec" script is a screenplay written with the hope (the speculation) that someone will buy it. Born of the writer's passion and created without any guarantee that it will be sold, a spec script, written by seasoned pros and novices alike, is undertaken with the hope that some-one—someday—will appreciate its merits and step forward with a bonafide purchase offer. *A spec screenplay is also the preferred method for a new writer to break into the film-writing business.*

As an unsold writer, only *you* know that you have original, exciting ideas and the talent to transform them into riveting stories for the screen. The spec script serves as the writer's calling card. It is designed to get your talent noticed and get you meetings, even if your first few screenplays don't actually sell.

Though spec sales in the millions still grab headlines in the trades, the true boom period for such sales peaked around a decade ago, when it seemed the studios were snapping up anything! Back then, producers looking for a quick road to blockbuster riches were scheduling meetings in 20-minute increments, just long enough to hear the one-line high-concepts that would surely be the catalyst for the next summer's worldwide box-office smash. But as those same high-rollers learned the hard way, high-concept premises do not always produce good or successful films. As a result, the studios were left with well-marketed, highly publicized, and totally unpro-ducable screenplays, for which they paid sinful sums. One such script, "The Cheese Stands Alone," riding a P.R. wave of legendary proportions, sold in a bidding war. Years later, it is yet unproduced. Changing gears, bidding wars were almost overnight confined to novels or genre work from dependable A-List screenwriters.

But, just as quickly, there seems to have been another turnaround: The dol-drums seem to have been shaken out of the spec marketplace. Spec scripts are pouring out of word processors and flowing directly into development. Agents are setting up scripts for big "coming out" parties, getting overnight reads, and orchestrating furious bidding wars. Expensive spec sales are back in the headlines. If one can believe the stories in the trades, the spec screen-play no longer "sleeps with the fishes"—it's the newest Hollywood star.

(My note of skepticism is derived from meeting writers who reportedly sold specs for high six to low seven figures—and are living in a studio apartment. It is to everyone's advantage—agent, writer, and even buyer—to proclaim megabucks sales in the trades. Later, when the deal falls out or the actual conditions to receive the bonuses that add up to the reported price are not met, it is to no one's advantage to report that fact.)

What are buyers looking for in a spec script today? First, refer back to the four points listed in "Got a Great Movie Idea?". Some buyers will tell you they want nothing more than "a good story." Some are in search of a particular genre or a vehicle for a particular talent, be it star or director. Others are more specific—they want "passion" in the writing or "dialogue that levitates off the page." Whatever they say, all buyers are after the same thing: a surefire hit or, at the least, a hot new writing talent. But, be forewarned—one thing is certain: no one screenplay will please every buyer.

At a conference on spec selling at the Writers Guild of America, west, William Morris agent Alan Gasmer espoused at length on the virtues of movie concepts which could be reduced to one powerful, easily grasped, easily repeatable, sentence. It's all about marketing, he explained, and studios getting audiences into the theater. He added, studios do this with a visual effects extravaganza that features a main character attractive to a male star. The fact that 18 of the top 20 highest grossing films of all time are visual effects-laden films aimed at males (i.e., *Spiderman I & II*, the *Lord of the Rings* trilogy, the original *Star Wars* trilogy and three prequels, *Raiders of the Lost Ark* and its sequels) is not lost on these executives. Gasmer was forthcoming with his opinion that no *current* female star other than possibly Julia Roberts is considered strong enough to "open" a movie. As for family-oriented material, Gasmer pointed out the obvious: currently, there are no strong 14-year-old stars. Studio lingo for a "family movie" is *Men in Black* (which made more money for Sony Pictures than any film in that studio's history) or *Batman* or *Independence Day* or *Spiderman* or some other PG-13 film. A story that is compelling in image and character and that provides a catharsis of emotions (but which does not meet the above criteria) may be limited to the independent market—an arduous journey in which the writer must essentially package and find financing for his own work.

Many agents prefer to hear their clients' stories first. For example, it is not unusual for a writer to want to cash in on a box-office trend with a new twist on a hot genre. A plugged-in agent will gently remind the writer that he may be jumping on a ship that has already sailed. (Why waste time developing an idea that is outdated or oversold?) But, you may be wondering, the agent as creative censor? Consider this: Agents earn their commission by knowing the current state of the entertainment industry. No matter how competitive the agencies and studio executives may appear to be, in reality, they breakfast together, party together, sleep together, and trade positions like baseball cards. With e-mail, it takes only the click of a mouse for every development executive in town to know the details of every other one's reading list.

There is a famous story floating around about an executive at a major studio who was livid that he had lost out on a high-concept comedy (eventually made by DreamWorks SKG) because he was in the restroom when the agent phoned for final bids.

To be a successful representation of your talent, it is generally agreed that a spec screenplay should be bold and risky, about a highly personal subject, and featuring characters you know intimately. (Look closely and you'll find writers—all artists really—confronting the ghosts of their past over and over in their art. The existential dread that runs through Ingmar Bergman's films may have roots in his strict upbringing by a Lutheran minister father who would lock him up in the closet for punishment. It is rumored that George Lucas' troubled relationship with *his* father, combined with his boyhood refuge at Saturday matinee serials, gave birth to the *Star Wars* films. Notice how the main character is named "Luke" and that Vader recalls the German word "Vater," which means "father.") The technical aspects of screenwriting—solid dramatic structure and clean screen format—can be learned. What sells is your unique point of view—your fears, your fantasies, your passions. And for the pure joy of writing about your dreams (or your nightmares), all you risk is your time.

For the novice screenwriter, shortcuts should not be taken. High-concept one-liners, treatments, and verbal pitches are selling tools for the writer who is already a known quantity, whose track record commands recognition and respect in the marketplace. (Even then, such writers are usually limited to pitching ideas in the genre in which they've already staked out a reputation.)

For the unknown writer, a full-length, original feature screenplay is still the key with which to unlock a screenwriting career. The spec screenplay doubles as the writer's resume, especially in an industry in which most work is "on assignment" (and assignments are handed out only to writers with a track record or viable script samples). With your spec screenplay, you will have a product for sale and a potent sales "brochure" for the main product in your warehouse—YOU!

The spec script also maintains your creative integrity. As you'll discover when you are hired to write a script (based on your idea or someone else's), you will be writing under the supervision of an employer and your creative instincts will be "guided" by well-intended, but often infuriating, "story notes." Your screenplay will then become what is known as a "work for hire."

Under the 1976 Copyright Act, all written work done under contract or "on assignment" essentially belongs to the employer. In fact, not only is the employer considered the owner of the work ("the owner of all the rights comprised in the copyright": 17 U.S.C. ¶ 201 [1976]), but the law actually goes so far as to consider the studio or other employer the author of the work written for hire. Is it therefore any wonder that the studios feel free to change, revise, rewrite, and alter the material written for them on assignment?

This is why spec writing isn't for new writers only. Even seasoned veterans will forego a guaranteed "work-for-hire" paycheck (along with the "helpful suggestions" of producers and studio executives) in exchange for the freedom to quietly develop their next screenplay in the privacy of their own thoughts.

Spec writing also allows writers to create stories in different genres from that in which they are pigeonholed. And, on the sale of original material, spec writers who are members of the Writers Guild will retain a small portion of rights, known as "separated rights" (e.g. novelization and publication rights) and are accorded, per Writers Guild rules, first crack at the rewriting of their work. Freedom is the byword here.

Spec writing too often translates (in the new writer's mind) as "free" writing; the thought of writing for free can be the death of good work, passion, and self-worth. Instead, consider it as one way of having dominion over yourself and your work. No one has to give you permission to write (unlike acting or directing, for example). What you write has future value and you own it completely. As an added kicker, whenever a spec script sells, it has potential for spawning a bidding war, which almost always commands the highest purchase price.

There is a downside to spec writing. Of course, the most obvious is that there is no paycheck attached to your work. And, truth be told, most first, probably second, and even third spec scripts by a new writer may not sell. There are thousands of unsold spec scripts lining the shelves of story departments in every studio in town. Only a fraction (under 5%) of the scripts sold—those put into development and which have time and money and often teams of good writers working on them—ever get made.

On the other hand, good work usually finds a champion. A screenplay needs only one buyer. If you are driven to write, fear of failure should not enter into the equation.

In poker, there's a saying: scared cards can't win. The film business rewards its players, not those who quit at the first sign of rejection. Screenwriter Michael Tolkin (*The Player*), while a guest speaker at a UCLA Extension seminar, put it succinctly: "If you write something that no one has ever read before and it's good, stick with it, you'll get it made."

From July 2004 to July 2005, there were 65,000 registrations (mostly scripts) at the Writers Guild of America, west. Considering that as of July 2005 there were only 7,467 active members in the WGA, west (50 % more are associate, caucus, retired, or "emeritus" members), most of the scripts were by newcomers. The truth is, many try but few succeed at making a consistent living as a screenwriter. Success is a combination of luck, patience, talent, and timing. But, why dwell on the odds? Some of the world's most successful people achieved success because they were too naïve or too oblivious to know or care about the odds against them. Paul Allen, one of the founders of Microsoft has said, "If I knew how impossible what I was trying to do was, I would've never started."

The "Spec" Teleplay

The writer occupies a special place in television. The creators and head writers in series television often control the show and a staff writer can rise to producer status over the course of a single season. There is also the immediate gratification of seeing your work performed and broadcast in a matter of weeks as opposed to the years that may pass between the writing and the production of a feature film. Yet television writers earn those credits with long hours and a relentless work pace and often must sacrifice their creative autonomy to a group writing effort that may involve twenty writers in a room all contributing to your developed idea. All in all, it's a different ball game from features.

Submitting your work for television involves a slightly different approach also than for features. Television networks and TV series showrunners (the head honchos) rarely buy completed scripts—they hire writers. A typical series (sit-com or hour drama) will have a group of writers on staff primarily responsible for plotting out the season's story and character arcs and for writing most of the shows. As needed (both for fresh ideas and because of staff burnout), most shows also hire one or two freelance writers per season—primarily on the strength of a pitch meeting in which the writer offers up a number of story ideas—to supply individual episodes. These freelance writers may later be asked to join the staff or be invited back to pitch more story ideas and interview for a staff position. (May is staffing season, when writers vie for full-time jobs for the fall season.)

So, how does the novice writer get that all-important pitch meeting? First comes the work—writers must have track records or writing samples appropriate for the market in which they hope to sell. If your spec samples convince them of your writing talent, you will be invited to pitch. If they like your ideas or just like you, you'll get a final meeting with the show-runner. At that crucial point, the job is yours—to lose. They already like your work—the clincher involves the boss liking you.

For longer projects, like a movie of the week (MOW), new writers have a harder time breaking in. The networks rarely buy a MOW from a spec script, tending instead to develop issue-oriented concepts or ideas from recent events in the news. They usually do this in partnership with production companies that have a track record of their own and with writers selected from lists of "network-approved" writers, ranked according to their history of ratings success, organized by genre (comedy, action, romance, etc.), and listed by the writer's contract price and availability. How does a new writer get on that approved writer list? Only via your existing track record or powerful writing sample.

The staff writers for a television series receive extra pay and credit for episodes they write, as well as career boosts if their episodes win awards. (When I confronted a writer/producer of a top-ranked series about the uncanny resemblance of several recent episodes to storylines I had pitched him months earlier, he said, in a rare moment of candor, "Why should we give you the Mercedes?") Still, heavy workloads force many writer/producers to parcel out at least one or two freelance writing jobs per season. Your sample scripts should showcase your ability to write either hour drama or sitcom; it also should illustrate your knack for getting to the heart of any dramatic or comedic truth and demonstrate your grasp of the individual voices for the show's continuing characters.

So let's start with a basic *five-point strategy* for writing that sample series script or two that will get you noticed and get you pitch meetings.

STRATEGY

1. **If you're going to write for TV, you must watch TV!**

    Shunning the medium won't get you far in a world comprised of people who eat, breathe, and sleep television. Television writers love their shows! It's foolish to attempt writing a spec episode of a TV series if you have rarely seen the show. Come staffing season, most freelance writers tape at least a few episodes of *every* series for which they may be considered. They study these shows until they have a solid grasp of the individual "tics" of the series regulars and plots the series has explored. If possible, they also obtain the series "bible" which often includes future plotlines and character arcs. I strongly recommend taping and studying at least a dozen episodes of any show for which you wish to write a spec script. If one of the show's principal characters eats cereal, you should be able to name the brand and whether or not he talks when he chews.

2. **Don't waste your time writing a *pilot* (the initial episode for a new series).**

   Pilots by writers without a track record of well-received, previously produced work are never seriously entertained. Producers want specs of existing shows to showcase your abilities to write within the confines of a given show and given set of characters. That means *your spec should be of a show now on the air and one that also has a foreseeable future.* Even as a sample sent to other shows, a script from a canceled show dates your work—and you. (Haven't you kept current with what is happening on television?) Sorry, but no one will want to read your *Friends* or *Frasier* spec now. Chalk it up to experience.

3. **While it is sound policy to submit a sample script to a show of the same format (sitcom to a sitcom; drama to a drama), *it is not necessary to submit a sample script of a particular show to that same show* (i.e., a sample of *Alias* to the producers of *Alias*).**

   A rare few producers (the staff of *Frasier* was known for this) prefer samples only of their show, but current wisdom is that the best home for your spec is just about anywhere else. This is because the showrunners are way ahead of you; storylines have been tacked to their corkboard for months. It is hard to surprise a staff that spends its every waking hour writing or hearing pitches about their own show. While your spec is absolutely necessary to get you that pitch opportunity—which could lead to employment—it will rarely, if ever, be purchased outright. Series producers read to find talent, not story ideas. A sample of *The King of Queens* can serve that purpose if sent to *Will & Grace* or any other half-hour sitcom. The same is true for hour dramas (an episode of *CSI: Crime Scene Investigation* could easily be submitted to *ER* and vice-versa), though you wouldn't want to submit a sample *Joey* (a half-hour sitcom) to the producers of *Lost* (an hour drama).

4. **Don't showcase new characters or make drastic changes to the unfolding storyline of existing characters.**

   Keep the current stars at the center of your spec plot and respect the boundaries of their running plotlines. The television audience enjoys a certain familiarity with the existing characters and premise of the show—so should you. New characters are fine as long as the story doesn't revolve around them. For example, a spec would not have been the place to introduce Bette Midler to Kramer on *Seinfeld*. The decision to attract a major guest star is one that the producers like to keep for themselves. For the same reason, don't develop major new story or character arcs for the existing stars. The producers are way ahead of you. They'll decide if Jerry gets married or not. They want writers to contribute to their show, not take it over.

5. **For MOWs or miniseries, know the general parameters of what the networks are buying.**

   MOWs, for example, have recently favored true stories (docudramas) or issue-oriented themes centering on a woman's challenge or dilemma. Even with the recent trend toward "epic" programming (movies based on best-selling books or classic novels) and tabloid topics, women-in-peril dramas continue to be MOW staples. If you have such a concept in the works and/or have obtained the rights to a true story (see Chapter 6), and even with a reputable agent in tow, do not go directly to the networks. The preferred method is to seek a producer or a studio with a network track record of projects similar to yours that can then champion your project.

The WGA, west magazine, *Written By*, no longer publishes the names and phone numbers of television series contact people, but this invaluable information is available on the Guild's web site, www.wga.org. The trade magazines, such as *Variety*, also chart the career path of key TV executives and what the networks are currently buying or developing. Most accept submissions from agents only, but don't let that discourage you; a little dogged ingenuity can open doors. Try obtaining a copy of the show's bible (general guidelines, requirements, and format) or a script from a produced episode. Also, as advised above, tape at least four or five episodes of the show and study them, to gain a grasp of the characters, setting, theme, and structure.

A good writing sample, an enthusiastic approach, and bull-headed (but charming) persistence can bring you assignments and also a staff position. There is great turnover. The currently employed writers invest long hours trying to be original week after week, season after season. Successful shows need new blood. The sheer pressure of writing yet another exciting or funny show for those well-known and much-loved characters can deplete energy and imagination. That's why there is always room for the ambitious, hard-working writer to break in, to do the grunt work, and to move up the ranks to producer and, eventually, the lofty position of "showrunner" (head writer/executive producer).

Caveat for Guild members:

Any writer may labor for himself, but spec writing in the employ of or at the direction of another is strictly prohibited and applicable Guild minimums must be met. Prohibited spec writing includes any services for which payment is contingent upon the acceptance or approval of the material ("Write it; if I like it, I'll pay for it"). Also, pursuant to the "second meeting" rule, television producers or network executives may not request a second meeting without entering into a "story commitment"—if the first meeting concerned the writer's original idea. Nor may they meet with the writer a third time without entering into a binding obligation.

Adaptations

Wouldn't most of us love to be paid to write a screenplay for which we would not have to invent the story, the setting, the characters, the plot, and even, in many cases, the dialogue? Well, more than half of the screenplays written for films produced in Hollywood are based on material previously produced or published. Most are based on best-selling novels or previous film classics. The studios pay a great deal for the rights to tinker with these underlying properties, and pay celebrated writers a lot more to adapt them into films.

It's smart business for the studios, used to putting out millions for the services of a star or celebrated director. Weekend grosses have proven that a pre-sold product trumps all other marketing strategies. There is simply no way that betting the farm on beloved novels such as *Harry Potter* or *Lord of the Rings* or on comic book super heroes like *Batman* or *Spiderman*—all capable of tentpole (holding up the studio) business—is anything more than a conservative and prudent investment decision. And that's what the film factories want—protection against downside risk. This also means, of course, that with such a huge initial investment at stake, it is rare to trust an adaptation to a writer without a track record.

Nonetheless, every so often, a lost classic or a forgotten book is dusted off and brought down from a shelf and adapted for the screen by a devoted fan. It's very tempting for the writer. Why try and make up what some other author already vetted past an editor and publishing bureaucracy? In truth, there is some great stuff lying around out there. Reach back into Victorian England for the works of Jane Austin to yield *Emma* and its modern version *Clueless*, for example, or Emma Thompson's more reverent adaptation of *Sense & Sensibility*. As a bonus—Austin's work being in the public domain—not a penny had to be spent to acquire the rights. More recently, screenwriter John August reached into his childhood memories for the latest incarnation of *Charlie and the Chocolate Factory*. From an interview by Mark Olsen in *Written By*, Summer, 2005, August said:

> "I've done a lot of adaptations, explains August, and usually I have to take the characters and basic storyline of the book and find a new way of doing everything. Charlie was one of those rare cases where I could literally go through the book with a highlighter and figure it out. *I can save this sentence and part of this sentence and I can use a lot of this dialogue just as Roald Dahl wrote it.*"

Sounds easy, right? But while the terror of the blank page *is* somewhat mollified in the adaptation process (characters, settings, and plot being mostly predetermined), imagination and artistry are no less a requirement. Screenwriters must be brutal in culling or redesigning those aspects of the work that will not play for the particular medium of film. For example, some plays offer as few as two characters and serve their plot needs within one set, while film begs to open up the story to use the full scope of the medium.

This is a lesson lost not only on the inexperienced. David Koepp, one of the most respected and highly paid scripters in Hollywood, wrote and directed an adaptation of a Stephen King novella, *Secret Window, Secret Garden*. The movie, starring Johnny Depp as a man who naps and makes phone calls while the world spins, worked well enough for King on the page, where he could explore the sanctity of the heart and mind laid bare. But whoever decided the silent ruminations of such a loner could carry a feature film— where sound and fury reign—were as self-deluded as the producers of *My Dinner With Andre*.

So it is that, for many adaptations, scenes may need to be modified, more diverse locations written in, and action substituted for long speeches.

Conversely, the sprawling novel may require characters to be combined, entire subplots lost, and new material written to fit in its place. The novel, *The Godfather*, by Mario Puzo, was too rich for even one epic film; it found its first formidable sequel in whole chapters discarded from the first film.

The mantra of the adapter is cut, cut, cut. And the screenwriter may be vilified for it. Novelists, critics, and loyal readers may understand that their beloved work must undergo a substantial transformation on the way to film, but they are often no less vituperative toward the result.

Novelist John Le Carré (*The Constant Gardener*) has been quoted as saying that turning a book into a film is "like having a cow turned into a bouillon cube."

Some will not argue the process (as co-screenwriter of the adaptation of his own novel, *The Prince of Tides*, Pat Conroy had little about which to complain), while others like Richard Russo, author of *Nobody's Fool*, may find that his sprawling novel was no better served by a faithful adaptation and the presence of Paul Newman; writer/director Robert Benton adhered slavishly to the text, but, to my mind, the subtle charm of the characters and setting were strangled in the two-hour format of film. Perhaps that's why Russo later decided to do his own adaptation for his Pulitzer Prize-winning novel, *Empire Falls*.

Should you set out to adapt a novel, play, true story, or other material for the screen, you will first need to secure the rights. This subject is dealt with in detail in Chapter 7. Of course, you don't need anyone's permission to write your screen version of any published or produced work—but you can't sell it without the rights to the original material (this is known as delivering a "clear chain of title"). Unless, that is, you sell it to someone who already owns those rights. Such legalities notwithstanding, you can always use your work as a writing sample to showcase your screenplay talent.

Or here's a thought: How about taking that lost, rejected, or never-submitted *script* of yours out of your drawer and adapting *it* (backwards, so to speak) into a novel? Screenwriter Allan Folsom did it. After years of trying without luck to sell his original script *The Day after Tomorrow*, he didn't shelve it—he turned it into a novel. The novel became a smash best-seller—and then was greedily snapped up (by the very execs that ignored it the first time around) to be adapted into a motion picture. A circuitous route, sure, but an option for screenwriters who have carved out compelling characters and a riveting plot only to butt up against the growing aversion to anything that doesn't come with a pre-sold audience.

Other Media: Is a Screenplay Your Best Option?

There are many ways to have your point of view reach an audience. Your particular writing talent may be in exploring the inner discourses of the mind, the murky world of dreams and thoughts. You may shy away from "action" writing, aspiring instead to the direct connection that language itself can make between your heart and mind and that of an audience. You may like the freedom of moving back and forth in time or even of moving between different points of view. Or maybe you just do not wish to be artificially constricted in the format or length of your work. As an avid reader it may be books that turned you on to writing to begin with, so why not, then, consider putting your efforts into a novel?

Hollywood has always had a love affair with the publishing world. Not only do books come pre-approved by editors and publishers with as tough a set of writing and marketing criteria as any film studio, but they also come with a pre-sold audience of loyal readers. As a bonus, novels usually offer strong, well-structured stories and vivid, three-dimensional characters. And your reward as a novelist? If the rights to your book are sold to a studio or producer, you'll likely receive a celebrity stature rarely achieved as a screenwriter, as well as a lucrative deal for the screen rights. Best-selling authors may even be paid for unfinished works. And many novelists are paid to write the screen adaptations of their screenplays. (Not that everyone jumps for joy at the prospect: One novelist recently described the process as being like "a cannibal eating his own foot.")

If dialogue is your strong point and you have little need for either the vast mindscape of the novel or the expansive physical arenas possible in film, perhaps you will find greater satisfaction and more immediate gratification in writing for the stage.

Once you have established your voice in one medium, you can transfer that voice to the screen. Neil Simon and David Mamet are playwrights who have forged successful screenwriting careers. Indeed, Mamet is one of the few screenwriters (William Goldman is another) who stipulates that the words he writes shall be altered by him alone. While common for playwrights, this is unprecedented creative power for a screenwriter.

Find the medium that best suits your writing talents and the needs of your story. That may be the single most important creative decision you make as a writer.

Chapter 4

The Art of the Pitch

Pitching is the art of selling ideas (and often fully developed screenplays) in Hollywood. Some writers, including many established writers with produced credits, seem to have quit spec writing all together. Instead, they expend their creative energy in meetings with producers and film company execs spinning elaborate stories of movies they would like to write, and would be willing to write, if only someone would pay them first to do so. According to WGA records, far more spec script sales than pitches result in money changing hands in the feature film world, but the allure continues.

On the positive side, pitching can save a writer a lot of time developing ideas in which no one may be interested. Plus, the writer doesn't toil for months on end without being paid. And it *can* be lucrative—the trade papers keep the myth of easy fortunes alive through nearly daily reports of pitches resulting in a wildly extravagant sum paid to the "author." On the other hand, through the luck of the draw, you may not get the pitch meeting with the person who *would* be excited by your story ideas. Also, you may be a lousy verbal story-teller and a super-fantastic writer. Or the idea you have may be half-baked now, but so what? Most *great* ideas come through the process of writing—in the heat of research and development—so who knows what your concept could morph into with a little effort. A lot depends on how committed you are to your own story ideas, but my personal belief is that if it's worth putting your reputation on the line in a pitch, it's also worth writing.

That said, pitching is a large part of the screenwriter experience and, as you'll see, it's crucial if you wish to write for television. Which may lead new writers to wonder why they must agonize at their desk over character arcs and structure when, apparently, most producers view their time as too valuable to actually read, preferring to have writers present their story ideas in a pleasant chat over cafe lattes in an air-conditioned suite.

Something light and easy to remember, like a commercial jingle, so that it easily can be repeated at the Monday morning round table to a bleary-eyed production and marketing staff. Something that offers a vision, a promise of what a blockbuster it could be if only one added a star or two and a hot director and a barrel full of money and… oh, of course, later maybe, a script? But can a brief, entertaining pitch of a barely fleshed-out, but catchy little high-concept really launch your screenwriting career? Such is the mystery and allure of the infamous "pitch meeting."

Preparing the Pitch

What could be a more civilized way to do business? The writer meets the executive, shakes hands, and presents his story and himself in a brief, entertaining performance. You can even enlist the executive's help—most want to believe they have something valuable to contribute and are only too happy to interrupt your pitch with their own. You need only appear enthusiastic about *their idea for your idea* and you may find yourself granted a development deal. It happens. But while I don't wish to dash your hopes of winning lucrative development deals without actually having to write a screenplay, sorry, there is a reason why I call the easy money to be had from selling a pitch a myth. It's an avenue generally reserved for *recognized talent only*. That means writers with a track record of produced work or a solid reputation as a writer "who delivers."

Still, a talented few new writers may get in the door—if they have a hot writing sample (preferably, a feature film) and a strong contact behind them (like an agent, manager, or lawyer) to set up the meeting. If you don't have such a contact, try selling your wares door to door. It may be a last resort, but if it's your only resort, use it. Start by making a list of your contacts, weak as they may be, and exploit them (in the good sense). Then, peruse a current issue of the *Hollywood Creative Directory* (available at bookstores or try them online at www.hcdonline.com or phone toll free at 800-815-0503) for production company information. You'll want to target a development executive—not someone too high up the food chain—though getting through to one still may not be easy. Try and find a connection to the person or, through engaging in a little online research, find as much as you can about the companies or films they have been involved with. Be persistent, but not overbearing, and they may wish a writing sample first. But keep in mind that no matter what they say ("We only accept pitches through agents we know."), everyone is looking for new talent. Development execs who read your sample script and find a fresh writing style or a deft handling of a particular genre are usually only too eager to meet you. Perhaps you will be right for a pet project they're hot to develop or you'll have a bombshell answer to the question: "So, what else have you got?"

Feature Film Rule:

no credits + no script sample =
no agent + no pitch + no sale + no job

In television, as discussed in Chapter 3, the pitch meeting is the lifeblood of the business. This is not necessarily good news for a new writer, however. Producers and production company executives know that to option or buy a completed teleplay can be an expensive and futile waste of time and money, especially for telefilms (MOWs) where there are very few buyers and limited venues. It is simply good business sense, now ingrained into practice, to develop the concept in-house with established writers practiced in the techniques of writing to strict act breaks (for commercials) and tailoring their work to stars pre-packaged into the show for the demonstrable viewer loyalty they may carry.

Still, for series television at least, fresh blood is always in short supply. Even new writers may be awarded freelance slots and eventual staff positions if they are able to display a fertile imagination, a wealth of ideas, and an infectious enthusiasm in their pitch meeting. But new writers armed only with story ideas probably won't be invited to pitch at all.

The classic school of thought is that a new writer must have two spec episodes of a currently running television series to demonstrate writing talent and a grasp of the essence of the show for which the episodes are written. (As previously noted, it has never been necessary to present episodes of the very show to which you are pitching.)

Today, however, many series producers are telling freelancers to submit feature scripts, plays, short stories, even magazine articles as writing samples. These execs are looking for more than good scripts—they want imagination, a fresh voice. Deeply drawn characters, fresh dialogue, and a well-crafted structure are most important to them. After that, it is up to the writer not to blow the final interview with the showrunner and to make everyone in the room feel that they have met a true colleague. In the crush of May staffing season, where hundreds of writers compete for one or two available slots on a series staff, both the writing sample *and the writer himself* must make a lasting and irresistible impression if they are to even register as more than a blip on the exec's radar.

Writers invited to pitch a movie of the week or a pilot for a new series, or those brought in to develop a miniseries (sometimes parceled out in parts to various writers), usually are seasoned television veterans with long track records. Or, they are writers who may be attached to producers or star acting talent with whom the network or cable company would like to be involved or with whom they already have programming commitments. On occasion, a new writer may find himself in this position; make the most of this rare opportunity. While it is unlikely that any kind of arrangement will be approved for your long-term involvement with the very show you have conceived, don't despair; one idea does not a career make. Negotiate the best credit you can, make every attempt to include future writing assignments into your deal, and trust that the success of the show will alert everyone in the business to your talent and potential and future work will follow.

Plus, you'll meet people who do the hiring. This is the hidden side benefit to pitching that is lost to the writer laboring alone at home. Of course, many people choose writing as a career because they *want* to labor alone at home and socializing is simply not their forte. But if you are someone possessed of a shy, reserved personality who never comes off well in groups, think again about film or certainly television writing. Maybe novels are the way to go for you. Pitching is a participatory art. The writer brought in to pitch must coherently organize a storyline and bring it to life before an often-distracted executive who has just possibly heard four hundred pitches this month alone. If you hesitate, repeat yourself, can't adjust to interruptions or feedback without losing your composure or your momentum, you may need to find yourself a writing partner, someone who can play off your best moments with enthusiasm, clarity, and convincing salesmanship.

If you do have a writing partner, be in agreement; complement each other's rifts and moves; don't argue or contradict each other. (The buyer of your pitch wants to feel secure; he wants to feel that he's a part of a well-oiled team, a member of the gang that backs each other up, not the one whose members stab each other in the back.)

from the trenches: THE POLITICS OF THE PITCH

The event was billed as the "Hollywood Pitch Festival." Like a poetry reading at a beat cafe, each participant had only a brief moment on stage to deliver a strong emotion to a crowded room of sometimes-distracted listeners. Seven minutes was the allotted time to make their impression on the "buyers" (development execs? interns?). At the last minute, the pitches were scheduled five minutes apart, including getting one party in while another attempted to decorously make his or her way out. This forced most participants to scramble to reconfigure the "pitch" they had no doubt labored dutifully to perfect in front of a mirror and assorted friends and family for weeks preceding the event. It was a carnival atmosphere, one guy even dressed in costume. Another brought a suitcase full of props. And most left happy as clams for the sheer liberating joy of having been given a shot at all.

Pitching has become the new get-rich-quick lotto for many that aspire to be screenwriters. In the New Hollywood, getting an agent or producer to read a script by an unknown can prove as daunting a task as dating a supermodel. To those who shelled out $350 apiece for the privilege to attend the festival, this may have been as close as they were ever going to get to someone paying attention to them, much less giving them a grab at the golden ring.

Some of the participants are no doubt damned competent writers, with concepts, outlines, and treatments as dazzling as many which wind their way through the development process. A lot of them have even written full screenplays. They just can't get anyone to read them. And too many haven't yet grasped the single most important concept in the film business—it is a real business, run by professionals who expect to deal with other professionals, especially where the expenditure of large amounts of money is at stake.

I'm sorry, life can be cruel, but here's the real skinny: Pitching is *not* a realistic selling opportunity for those without a track record or a hot writing sample or who are not otherwise connected to a star producer, director, or actor with whom a buyer wishes to be in business. A screenplay (or two spec TV scripts) is the cover charge to the dance. Even then, without a solid reference from someone trusted in the business, reading new talent is rare. The undiscovered writer is simply not going to be asked to pitch to anyone, anywhere, unless they pay for the privilege. Pitch seminars have cropped up and prospered because *in the ordinary course of business* that door is closed to would-be writers.

continued

Studios don't commit hundreds of thousands of development dollars on people they don't know who claim to have had an interesting dream one night. Despite all the hoopla and grand announcements in the trade papers that would lead one to believe otherwise, there's a catch. Yes, deals are done and riches won on the strength of a pitch, but the underlying facts are a bit more sobering. Read on a bit past the headlines for hints like "the project *reteams* [the writer] with [the production company]" or a spokesman quoted as saying "it's great to be back in business with… " or other clues that tell you this was no carpetbagger off the street selling ideas to strangers.

There *is* no shortcut to becoming a writer that bypasses the act of writing. Writers write, everyone knows that. Even the Harvard Business School types that run Hollywood are pretty damned sure that writers seeking bushels of money ought to have written *something*, a script sample at least, first. Many also won't accept submissions until an agent or other trusted business associate clears the playing field and makes a solid recommendation. This may be bad news to those who want to reap the profits of a writing career without investing any sweat equity, but at least it means there is a God. The good news is that later perhaps, if you work hard, you may yet get to make the pitch that encapsulates six months of mind-twisting labor in fifteen or twenty minutes of casual banter over a complimentary Pepsi.

And when you do get that chance, there are some secrets and strategies you ought to bring into that room with you because you don't get a second chance to make a good first impression. Most important, relax, because you're in the driver's seat. They may be burnt out, overworked, or understaffed, but if you've been called, they've read your work and *they already like you*. Their agenda at the pitch meeting is to discover talent, to hear what it is you've got to sell, to harvest your imagination and hard work, and to log on to your internal search engine for fresh ideas, plots, and characters. All you have to do is smile and pitch. But the art of *successful* pitching is about way more than your pitch. Every pitch meeting is a carefully orchestrated negotiation. And as with every business transaction, there is a politics to pitching that you ignore at your own peril.

Here is a *ten-point strategy* for pitching I picked up over the course of many such encounters on both sides of the table.

STRATEGY

1. **Know the basic etiquette.**

   Most execs will have penciled you in for 30 minutes. In that time they expect a handshake, some easy banter to ease the tension, your pitch, and a pleasant goodbye. If they offer you coffee or a soft drink, take it. It extends your stay and honors their gracious hospitality. Pay attention and you'll know when it's time to leave.

2. **Know your audience.**

Do your homework. Know the track record and any personal details you can find by searching the trade paper archives. Look for something you have in common. Find a way to give them what they want. By understanding their needs, you can deliver solutions. Remember that the meeting is ultimately not about you or your script, it's about them. It's about how buying from you or being in business with you can help further their career. Show them the way to a mutually beneficial relationship.

3. **Be prepared to sell.**

That's your agenda. You presumably have either a full script or a well-developed story in mind. Now sell it with confidence and enthusiasm. Visual aids are okay, but don't be a prop comic. Start simple. Hook them in immediately with a strong, clear, single-line premise. Fully believe in (love) your characters, the sheer entertainment value of what it is you want to sell. No one makes a development deal on a project about which the writer is lukewarm. Be prepared to dramatize key scenes and involve your listener in the memorable, plot-twisting moments that a good trailer (another sales tool) often provides. And here's a little trick: Speak lower and slower than normal—lower pitch conveys authority and forces them to lean in and give the good parts time to sink in.

4. **Pitch story.**

Not plot (too detailed), not character (not at first), not you (not ever). What's the genre? Then give them the broad strokes: the goal, the dire consequences of failure, the similarities your story has to X (insert any block-buster), and your unique twist. You can't underestimate their attention span. Save the complexities of the plot and the details of the character arc for the script. In any case, never tell them everything you know. Like in any good love affair, you'll want to hold a little back to keep them wanting more.

5. **Listen well.**

Questions show they're involved and interested. Never forget that you know they're only guessing. Don't be afraid to stray from your agenda. Be open to suggestions. Ask them questions. Take notes. And don't take offense (their imagination and capacity for original thought is scuttled by more influences than bad films). Besides, notes given in pitch meetings are rarely well thought out and should never be taken as etched in stone.

continued

6. **Preach to the converted.**

   Sitting down to pitch to one person is a different dynamic than addressing a room full of execs with pencils poised. (They may play to the crowd, offering ideas to show they have something to contribute.) Isolate the most interested person there and ask him a question related to your story, such as "If the genie gave you the magic lamp and you had only one wish, what would it be?" Involve him and the others will follow.

7. **Have an alternate ready.**

   Be committed to your pitch, but always have a viable alternative (just one, never more) prepared. If they cough and say, sorry, we've heard this before or we have something similar in development, you still want your fifteen minutes. (You also don't want to be a one-trick pony, but having too many ideas tends to make your passion less convincing.) Also prepare for the buyer's propensity to switch to a project of his or her own. Listen carefully, ask questions, make suggestions, and take notes. It could mean they like you, if not your story, and want to hire you for a script or rewrite assignment.

8. **Don't pull literary rank on them.**

   Nobody likes a smarty-pants. Don't talk theme, tone, inciting incidents, or character arcs. They know the jargon. And no literary allusions. They won't get them. It'll only make them defensive, get their backs up, make them resent you, want to put you in your place, recover their self-esteem by lowering yours, and on and on.

9. **Don't be intimidated by how impossibly young they all are.**

   They have brains, even street smarts, but you figure they lack the wisdom that comes with time and experience and grants a certain perspective that youth can only pretend to enjoy. Oh, get over it. Everyone brings their own insecurities to the table. Your job is to show respect (if not awe) for what they have achieved, make them value you, and make everyone in the room feel comfortable.

10. **Think long term.**

    People in the film business tend to do business with their friends. Your pitch meeting is an opportunity to forge future alliances, future collaborations. In the final analysis, your real, long-range success in the business will depend on your ability to deal with and make allies of whomever you encounter along the way—secretaries, assistants, development execs, producers, and heads of studios alike. Some you'll befriend, some you'll involve, some you'll teach, some you'll entertain, but ideally you want to leave them all excited to have met you and committed to doing business with you in the future.

Making the Pitch

Here is Marc Norman's winning pitch for *Shakespeare in Love* (although none of it showed up in the eventual film):

"You're 23. You live in a small town in the country. You had to marry a girl you knocked up when you were 17. You have three kids. You work for your father in a pretty boring business. You're miserable. When a traveling theater company comes to town putting on shows, you go with your parents and wife. You're sitting in the audience watching the actors on the stage, and you think to yourself 'I should be doing that.' The next day, when the theater company leaves town, you go with them. The year is 1584, the town is Stratford on Avon—and you're William Shakespeare."

At its best, pitching can be an electrifying experience; more often, it's frustrating, humiliating, and downright bizarre. (Some very respected writers find themselves twisting balloons and wearing arrows through their heads to get their points across.) In other words, this is not an ordinary job interview. Fellow writers relate horror stories like the one about the award-wining producer famous for seeking "sensitive" material who walked out without a word in the middle of a pitch by a renowned novelist. The producer ambled back in five minutes later with a Diet Coke in one hand, a cell phone glued to her ear, murmuring, *sans* apology, "Can we begin again, I may have missed something here."

Or how about the star who called for a pitch meeting in his mountain cabin *in another state*, causing four people to fly, change planes, plan overnight stays, etc. Then he kept everyone waiting while he finished a round of golf, finally taking the entire pitch with his girlfriend on his lap. And, my personal favorite, a writing team desperate enough to execute three uncompensated rewrites at the behest of and based on the notes of a wildly enthusiastic development executive. At the appointed hour to "sell" the script to the studio head in a meticulously rehearsed pitch complete with puppets, storyboards, props, and a soundtrack, said d-girl turned to the team at the very emotional height of their pitch and said, "I think you guys are great, you know that, but—and correct me if I'm wrong here, Ricardo—I think we may already have something like this in the hopper. What else have you guys got?"

My own protocol for such meetings is to always arrive on time, stay relaxed, and have both short (to open with) and long versions (when they're thirsty for more) totally rehearsed. Be ready to dazzle, entertain, listen, adapt any story to new suggestions, and always have an answer to the question, "So, what else have you got?" Also, be polite to everyone you meet with (and their entire staff) and show genuine gratitude for their time.

It also helps to realize that the person(s) you are pitching to is both the buyer and the seller of concepts. Once you have convinced that person, he in turn must convince someone else of your story's merits—by pitching it, of course. So what the executive wants is something fresh, new, and exciting, yet as familiar and comfortable as an old shoe. "It's just like X, only in this show… " Television programmers shy away from taking risks. They know that audiences have only a few lines in *TV Guide* and a few minutes of on-air promos to grasp the show's concept and decide whether to watch.

I was once told by a Vice President at a major network that my concept was such a natural for television, she was shocked that it wasn't already on TV—but she couldn't buy it because television wasn't doing it already!

Some development executives and story editors hear as many as 2,000 pitches a year. So think of your pitch as a TV commercial—you've got a few precious minutes to sell your wares. Therefore, keep it short and simple. But, that doesn't mean you have to be too brief or too businesslike, either. A few sincere pleasantries exchanged before you launch into your pitch are expected. Remember: to turn your pitch meeting into a job and a career, try to be someone they'll want to hire because they like your enthusiasm, attitude, grasp of the show, or even because you'll be fun to hang out with!

Should you get a pitch meeting, here is my *ten-point strategy* for pitch meetings:

STRATEGY

1. **Go in prepared.**

   Practice until you know your pitch cold. Know the show, its running characters, their relationships, and the setting they're in. And, of course, know all there is to know about your story.

2. **Go in loaded.**

   Use props if you need to, but always give them a good show. For a television series pitch, five or six storylines are expected. Feature or MOW pitching is usually limited to one, more highly developed, concept.

3. **Start simple.**

   Have a strong, clear, single-line premise and give a brief overview of story and characters. The decision to buy or pass is usually made within the first two minutes. Use these to focus on memorable scenes, the big, plot-twisting moments.

4. **Be prepared to perform.**

   Deliver your pitch with passion, clarity, and confidence. Be enthusiastic and animated, but don't overdo it. The point is to keep them awake, not to frighten them.

5. **Keep it short.**

   Five to ten minutes for a TV series show, shorter if you see their eyes begin to glaze over, and never more than 15 minutes, even if you're on a roll; 15 minutes or longer for a feature or MOW is usually expected. In every case, never tell everything you know about your story; keep the imagination engaged. And never make up on the spot what you don't know about your story—they'll catch you.

6. **Play to your audience.**

   Adapt to the tone of the group. When possible, take the lead, but keep it light and cheerful.

7. **Listen.**

   Don't take offense at questions. Invite them into the pitching process. Be flexible and open to suggestions. Take notes and don't be afraid to ask for help. Often it's easier to sell them *their* idea for your idea than it is your own.

8. **Know when to stop.**

   If you pay attention, you'll see the signals. It's an art to know when to walk away before you're asked to leave.

9. **Leave as little behind as possible.**

   A page or two, at the most, to refresh their memories and give them something to pitch. Remember that most pitches take on new identities, as new ideas are grafted onto the original idea, so don't have your concept so etched in stone that it differs from the one the executive thought he bought.

10. **Smile and say, "Thank you."**

    If they like you, they'll want to find a way to work with you.

And then, leave. Avoid the long goodbye. If they've already accepted working with you, why hang around and give them time to question their judgment?

from the trenches: HOW *NOT* TO TAKE A MEETING

Some are called "meet and greets," some "doing lunch," some are actually called "pitches." But don't fool yourself: Every meeting in the film business is a pitch meeting. Either you're pitching someone or someone is pitching you. You may be having a meal together or networking at a seminar or off in the corner at a party, but it's the very prospect of doing business with one another that fuels the encounter. Your fine spec script may have paid your way into the dance, but careers are made by how good you are at "working the room."

And as important in such encounters as the commodity you are pitching—your film, your screenplay, your series concept, yourself—may be how well you observed the unspoken rules of conduct. Did you offend or make a friend? Did you leave them wanting more? Did you give "good meeting?"

Years ago, when the most powerful woman in our film business today, studio chief Sherry Lansing, was a development executive at MGM, my then-agent, Bill Haber at powerhouse agency CAA, thought it would be a great idea if Sherry and I met. I was a young producer with offices and a deal at Universal Pictures, a movie with the hottest movie star in the world in pre-production, and a bittersweet love story by an equally hot writer under my arm. Sherry, a former model, already had a track record as a savvy executive with great story sense. We were both, in film parlance, young, ambitious up-and-comers. Oh, and we were both single and available, not that arranging our meeting had anything to do with that.

Sherry had read the love story and assured me that everyone at MGM loved it. Written by Alan Trustman, writer of *Bullet* and *Thomas Crown Affair*—two films that cemented Steve McQueen's stardom—the script had already attracted a director and a dream cast. The ostensible point of our first meeting was to discuss writers for the inevitable rewrite of this script that everyone was so crazy about before MGM actually signed a deal to purchase it. I came armed with a list of available A-list writers, and by all accounts the meeting went well. I was to submit the script to those writers agreed upon and inform their agents of MGM's interest in seeing the movie produced. Sherry and I set our next progress meeting at the Polo Lounge of the Beverly Hills Hotel, a breakfast meeting, 8:30 in the morning.

This is where things took an interesting turn. I am, you see, a night owl. Mornings are not my forte. The morning of my meeting with Sherry I set an alarm, but I was still running late. I arrived at the hotel at about 8:45, entering the lobby just as an agent I knew stood off the main staircase with actor Peter Finch, that year's Academy Award nominee for his standout performance as newscaster Howard

Beale in Paddy Chayefsky's film classic *Network*. The agent saw me, waved me over, and introduced us.

Now I swear that what I am about to tell you is the God's Honest Truth. Just as I had finished pumping his hand, Peter Finch dropped dead in front of me. Collapsed onto the floor in a heap. The rest of the next half an hour was a blur to me then, much more so now, but this much is sure: The agent and I undid his shirt and tried to help him breathe. Paramedics quickly arrived and took up that task. The last image I had of Peter was of his body laying on the cold floor, stripped to his underwear, as a female passer-by, perhaps a hotel guest, pointed and exclaimed loudly, "Oh, look, it's Peter Finch. I wonder what movie they're making?"

Somehow I remembered my appointment and staggered into the Polo Lounge where Sherry sat, sipping what must have been her fourth cup of coffee, seemingly unperturbed by my rude timing and also seemingly unaware of what had just transpired a few feet away. After I told her, she was most gracious and agreed that this was no time to discuss business, especially as she was now late herself for her next appointment. So we reset the meeting for the following week, this time at the El Padrino room of the Beverly Wilshire Hotel.

Sherry again suggested breakfast. Blame a faulty alarm or a poor calendar system, but, predictably it now seems, I was either hopelessly late or forgot the date all together. The fact is I had stood Ms. Lansing up—a stunning woman sitting alone in a power restaurant for the whole film world to observe—for the second time in a row, and this time I had no excuses. When I realized my unforgivable *faux pas*, I phoned and apologized profusely. Always the class act, Sherry took my call, but I could swear icicles were forming on the power lines between us. I quickly arranged for The Wine Merchant to send over one of their finest Bordeaux, which may have been acknowledged, I can't recall, but we never rescheduled. The whole thing put a damper on what was once a hot project. Never after was the script discussed in the same sentence as MGM and, for whatever reason, it remains to this day the finest script I've ever read that was never ultimately produced.

For our purposes, the above, in a nutshell, can now serve as an abject lesson in how *not* to conduct yourself at a meeting. The larger point is that all meetings in the film business are personal. Whether or not you have the hot bidding-war script of the month or just wild blond locks and legs that go to the moon, a judgment is being made on whether or not you are someone they want to be in business with. Either they *like* you or you better have a whole basket full of talent for sale. Toward that end, let me make a few suggestions.

continued

Pre-pitch. Have a real agenda going in. What do you want? If it's a story pitch, practice telling the story. Give yourself fifteen minutes to paint the big picture. Forget the scene-by-scene details and go for the juicy character moments that will attract a star and what makes the plot marketable. Have a back-up plan in case they say, "No thanks, we've something like that in development, what else have you got?" Then get a good alarm clock. Two. Also carry two good pens, aspirin for those sudden migraines, breath mints, a toothbrush and floss if it's a lunch meeting, and a power bar for those hunger pangs if it's not. Dress casual. New writers don't wear Armani. No suits or ties. Generally, sneakers, jeans, T-shirt, and decent jacket is the accepted writer look, though for women, it's obviously more flexible.

Pitch. Relax. The people you are meeting are not likely to be studio heads. They have as much to gain from getting along as you do. If they suggest lunch, that's a good sign they are in some way going to be pitching you. Dinner and you're a shoe-in. (And remember—they always pay so don't go digging around in your purse.) But most meetings will take place in an office. Turn off your cell phone and go to the bathroom *before* you walk into the outer office. Always take the coffee or water or soft drink when it is offered—it buys you precious time and helps cut the natural first date tension in the room. A little chit-chat to loosen everyone up always helps too. (Something about the traffic on the way in is not the best indication of an interesting talent with a unique way of viewing the world.) Then tell the story you rehearsed as though it's the very first time these words have ever rolled (oh, so effortlessly) off your lips. Give them your full attention when they ask questions or make suggestions. Try to ignore it if they don't give you the same courtesy.

Post-pitch. Give them a warm but firm handshake. Leave as little behind as possible. Try and arrange a follow-up meeting or phone call. Let them know you appreciated their time. And leave before they have to show you the door.

Chapter 5

Designing the Marketable Screenplay

"I have been told… that I seem to love all my characters. What I do in writing any character is to try and enter into the mind, heart, and skin of a human being who is not myself. Whether this happens to be a man or a woman, old or young, with skin black or white, the primary challenge lies in making the jump itself. It is the act of the writer's imagination that I set most high."

—**Eudora Welty, from the preface to her Collected Stories (Harcourt Brace Jovanovich, 1980)**

Part One: The Hollywood Film

"Now Playing at a Theater Near You"

Screenwriters are, first and foremost, storytellers. We tell our stories with pictures, dialogue, and sound. While a novel can deal with the interior life—thoughts, feelings, emotions, memories—dramatic writing is limited to describing what we see and what we hear. Those are the parameters within which we must create.

Of the thousands of decisions a writer makes, our first and perhaps most important is what story to tell. We can choose from among the mythic themes of destiny, immortality, man vs. woman, good vs. evil, or write a fairy-tale of princes and princesses or stick to the staples of modern drama, which explore the more personal and complex subtleties of human behavior and relationships. Some will aspire to write a commercial story, epics even, with universal themes and characters whom actors will kill to play. Others will want to craft "smaller" films to satisfy a very personal sense of art—"slice of life" stories perhaps, with few characters and locations and no special effects. Whatever your choice, finding a worthy screen story is usually the result of trial and error, looking into your own heart and discovering what it is you truly want to say.

Some say that writing is a gift, not a skill to be learned. But talent can be nurtured and craft can most definitely be taught. Yes, it can be difficult at times to deliver to the page exactly what you want to express, but that usually improves with practice. Some will get it eventually and some won't. Not all start out with the same degree of talent. But most everyone starts by learning the time-tested techniques and craft that have been the hallmarks of good writing over the years. And for better or worse, a virtual cottage industry has risen to help you do that.

New writers may feel especially flummoxed by the avalanche of writing primers or the almost religious fervor of writing seminars and their "rules" for success. Put your ear to the ground and you may hear "The Seven Steps," "The 12 Stages," "The 22 Building Blocks," "The 30 Stations." (Ask about films like *Memento* or *Vanilla Sky* or *Requiem for a Dream* and watch the gurus develop a hernia trying to fit them into their staid theory.) But a well-told story is not the result of a mathematical equation. Aristotle introduced the basics centuries ago: A story must have a beginning, middle, and an end. Others after him have added "not necessarily in that order." Success, I have come to believe, is all in the art of the telling.

So is there really that much to know before you can write (and sell) a screenplay? Well, yes and no.

All art has form. It's a waste of time to argue whether or not there are or should be schools or rules for writers (for any form of art, for that matter). The passion to write may be the only prerequisite. But films require an audience. And there *are* storytelling standards that film audiences have become conditioned to respond to and that anyone in the mainstream film business will expect your script to meet: *strong characters involved in a crucial central conflict that is solidly structured in dramatic form to deliver a satisfying emotional experience to an audience.*

Moreover, in a world that accepts Hollywood movies as among America's most influential and desirable cultural exports, films today must be able to play as well in Bangkok as in Burbank. They must convey story points and basic human emotions through powerful images and not simply through words. It stands to reason, then, that the *universal appeal of your work has a great deal to do with its marketability.*

Finally, never forget that your primary goal as a working writer is to appeal to readers or development executives whose task it is to find viable screen stories. These executives must then convey the merits of your story to senior executives who wield the power to "green light" a movie (send it from development to production). These senior executives, in turn, may see their careers being made or broken by the audience (the final arbiter of the true worth of your story). And, the audience has expectations of its own.

Noam Chomsky, the distinguished MIT linguistics professor, has theorized that all of us are born with "cognitive structures" that underpin our grasp of human communication. I would go further and propose that we are all born with a cognitive structure for story. My own children learned to use the VCR/DVD and TiVo and to channel surf at warp speed before they were in preschool. They studied films like they were preparing a doctoral thesis; they watched some classics hundreds of times until they could anticipate exchanges of dialogue like fans at a midnight screening of *Mommie Dearest*. This is one factor in support of formula films and TV shows: *Audiences arrive subconsciously preconditioned in their expectations of what a story is and what it must fulfill to satisfy them.*

Because of this, making a study of the art and the medium—its boundaries and its possibilities—is well worthwhile before setting out to write within its constraints. There *are* time-tested writing tools to help writers find their voice and express it to as large an audience as possible. Still, too many barriers are erected to discourage new writers—usually by non-writers, those I have come to call the artless and crafty.

---

from the trenches: LIES OF THE ARTLESS AND THE CRAFTY: PART ONE

In my office there hangs an etching. It depicts a dozen penguins in a cheerleader-like pyramid. Five penguins at the bottom brace up four penguins perched precariously on their heads, and those four strain under the weight of the two above them, who in turn support the top penguin. None of them, save one, looks remotely happy. Guess which one? Well, it's not the one on the top, for the future holds but one direction for him—the long way down. It's one of the two just below him, one who climbed up on the backs of the rest, his smiling eyes fixed firmly on the top perch. The etching is entitled "The Corporation."

continued

To me, that's the heart of the matter. The film business is like one large corporation, an exclusive club really, and its members don't want to let you—the competition—in the door. Your potential success threatens their entrenched position. So they conjure up a lot of urban myths—assorted horror stories and mystical passwords, barriers to climb over and hoops to jump through—to discourage all but the very resolute and tough-minded. They'll say your story lacks "structure," that your main character lacks a clear "arc." That your "inciting incident" comes too late or too soon and that your "plot points" aren't popping up at the right page.

Even for those who have done their homework, written thoughtfully and well, the naysayers bar the way. They'll create circuitous career paths that lead nowhere, tell lies designed to mislead and discourage you. They'll say they have all the writers they need already, that you need an agent to get to them, and that good agents are too busy to read or be bothered with new writers. They'll tell you "nice try, but don't give up your day job."

Words of wisdom from those who don't write, who don't have a clue what it means to put your heart and soul on the line for everyone to pick apart. Don't you believe it. If you're driven to tell stories, then go with your passion, go with your pleasure, go with what you love or what you fear, go right to where the pain is and get it out of you and onto the page. If you love movies or television, then write those stories in script form. If you've never seen a script before in your life, there are simple, cheap, computer programs to help you lay out the sluglines and write within the page breaks and indent the dialogue and do all the rest of that nonsense that has nothing to do with writing for you. The important thing—the one thing you must never forget—is if you write because you must, you'll find a way to get it read. Maybe even produced. Nobody ever said it would be easy, but it's not impossible.

Here are just a few of the lies that writers are told by the non-writer gatekeepers every day in this business:

- **Lie number 1:** *Before you can be a screenwriter, you have to master the basic rules of structure, character development, dialogue, and screen format.*

  Before you can be a screenwriter you have to be a writer who loves movies. That's all. Yet this lie pours from the lips of Hollywood know-it-alls like it was the word of God. And it works. Because new screenwriters so badly want there to be defining, teachable rules to guide their work. And a few time-honored truths of storytelling do give one a solid grounding upon which to build. Sure, you'll want a plot, a narrative drive, and characters that move us. Also dialogue that actors can speak without sounding like wooden puppets. But you can put all that down in verse on a roll of toilet paper as far as I'm concerned. Because the ultimate truth of all creative art is this: *There are no rules.* As Thomas Mann wrote about one of his characters, "he went the way that go he must." All writers must sooner or later develop the confidence and freedom to go off on whatever wayward path their creative voice leads them.

Still, it's fair to say that most movies are based on screenplays that adhere to certain time-honored storytelling traditions. And there is a form and format to achieving a professional-looking script that most writers must follow if they are to get their work past the gatekeepers. The need for a certain degree of hard work and talent should also not be discounted. Many potential screenwriters are hopelessly in love with their 160-page first draft or don't want to hear the fact that even a rewrite by David Mamet won't resuscitate their weak premise and woefully underdrawn characters. But that said, a lot of viable babies are being tossed out with the bath. Any season of film offers but a few truly great movies—movies that surprise and delight—and these most often spring from scripts that follow the beat of a different drummer. Those are the scripts I can't wait to read.

- **Lie number 2:** *Your good screenplay should remind us of other great movies.*

As with most lies, there is a grain of truth to this one. Readers of screenplays—those that provide the coverage for the agents, producers, and development execs—are an insurgent first strike force trained to trash anything that doesn't tell a recognizable cinematic story. And they are not completely misguided in their demands. It's advertising dogma that it's better to position a new product comfortably within the parameters of an already accepted product. That's why the studios love genre films—the audience has a pre-sold idea of what it is they're about to see.

Unfortunately, that's also why a documentary, *Bowling for Columbine*, won the Writers Guild of America's top prize as the best *original screenplay* of 2002. The film business is stewing in its own witch's brew of sequels, remakes, and adaptations, and too many spec scripts have, as their only source of inspiration, other movies and TV shows. Maybe a seasoned vet can churn out these old standbys, but when evaluating a new writer, it's the offbeat styles and stories, the dark and strange, the surprising, the quirky and the weird that capture an agent or producer's eye. Only something new and different will set you apart. Give us that, and there are those who will

continued

find your work among the ruins, cherish it, and champion it. Don't, and your retreaded movie ideas and formulaic scripts are destined to lie there useless as an old tire.

So, okay, maybe there is one rule: Take a good look at life—not movies—and have something new to say about it before wasting anyone's time with your script. Your challenge is to escape the ordinary, accepted, and done and define your own voice.

- **Lie number 3:** *Before you can write movies, you must have an encyclopedic knowledge of movies, you must study, critique, interpret, and attempt to emulate the very best of them.*

  Why? You're not auditioning to be Roger Ebert's sidekick, are you? Save your thumbs; you'll need them if you're going to be a writer. Of course you have movies that you love—we all do. You wouldn't write movies if they weren't an influence on your life and, in some way, a creative inspiration. But you don't have to become a film scholar to write movies. Referencing other movies to write your movie is a sure way to write derivative and formulaic films. On the other hand, screenplays can offer technique as well as inspiration. Once you could only find the writer's draft at the Writers Guild or Academy libraries in Los Angeles, but today, no matter where you live, any number of Internet sites offer them. If possible, watch the movie as you read the script. Figuring out why the two differ may be the best screenwriting instruction you can get.

The writer's real challenge is to create dangerous, magical, intimate moments for actors, stories rich in human behavior that deliver the most entertaining, disturbing, haunting, or most satisfying emotional experience of which he/she is capable. That in mind, here are the ingredients that make up a recipe for a marketable screenplay—but never forget: *all rules, once mastered and understood, can be creatively broken.* And I encourage you to do so whenever possible.

A Viable Premise

Films are all about *story*. And all screen stories are about what happens (action) and who it happens to (character). A solidly crafted and clear *premise*, like a thumbnail sketch of the plot, sets forth your main character, his goal, and suggests the obstacles he must overcome to reach it. This single sentence or short paragraph can help you stay focused on the story and keep you from veering off into different directions.

The Verdict offers an example: "An alcoholic lawyer has one last chance to gain his self-respect: by winning justice for his comatose client." This sentence supplies the main character, his story problem (both personal and professional), and his chance for redemption.

But what is a story? In the simplest version, you get your protagonist up a tree, throw stones at him, and get him back down. But I'm partial to William Faulkner's definition: "a likable character, facing seemingly insurmountable odds, toward a worthy goal." It would seem true that the central conflict of most films revolves around an early event that requires a main character to act and puts him in conflict with others, but what many movies are *really* about is the internal struggle of the main character which surfaces as a result of such an event. In better stories, striving toward the external goal takes on greater and greater *personal* significance, requiring the main character to grow and change as a person in order to achieve it.

So how do you choose your story? Write about what intrigues you, what excites you, what you believe no one else has said quite the way you would. And then aim for the heavens. Don't be misled by the number of Hollywood films that seem to be derivative hack jobs. (It's hard to single one out of such a growing plethora of drivel, but, on the other hand, have you seen *Stealth*?) Many such movies are made because they *can* be made—the formula has worked before, talent has been paid, and the distribution pipeline must be filled. But new writers will need to demonstrate a penchant for imaginative storytelling. Find a fresh story, a unique voice. Take risks. Write what you are most curious about. But understand that your story will be expected to follow a classic *narrative structure*. The five basic questions of good journalism can help with that.

- *Who* is your movie about? (As we'll see, most movies have one main character that drives the plot.)
- *What* is your movie about? (The subject of your film—both the dramatic situation and the central question that the film asks.)
- *Why* is achieving the goal so important to the main character? (The character's motivations are the single most important element in determining his actions.)
- *Where* and *When* does the film take place? (Setting and context—location, period, culture—can help focus the story and supply metaphor and detail that enriches the plot and characters.)

Certain essential *strategies* also should be considered in picking any film story. Four were stated in Chapter 3:

STRATEGY

1. It should be a big idea for a movie.
2. It must succeed in its genre.
3. It must contain at least a few moments that actors will really want to play.
4. It should have a logical plot and compelling quality to the story.

Here are eight more:

5. It should be and stay fresh and interesting enough to engage our full attention.
6. It should lend itself to constant dramatic or comedic conflict.
7. It should be dripping in violence, sex, and passion.

    (Okay, emotional violence counts, but I don't want to soft sell this point—dramatic conflict is often played out in the extremes of human behavior, from the ancient storytellers who gave us *Hamlet* and *Medea* to the modern ones who gave us *The Godfather* and *The Lord of the Rings*. Do not shy away from the very tools of drama that have succeeded in gripping audiences for centuries. (Though some subjects, such as violence toward women, racism, or child abuse, may offend audience sensibilities.)

8. It should avoid clichés, stereotypes, and obvious film and television retreads.
9. It should take risks.
10. It should evidence real imagination, not just research (though research is important).
11. It should showcase one multi-dimensional main character that is required to grow and develop as a result of having gone through the trials and tribulations of the plot.
12. It should make the audience dream about the myriad possibilities of life.

Flaubert has said that the highest goal of art is not to raise laughter or tears, but to make your audience dream.

This last consideration is what moves me towards the stories I choose to tell. Audiences watch movies to gain understanding, escape reality, or experience a work of art. My stories are thematically driven—they aim to teach, to make a difference. I prefer real-life dramas that have simmered in me a while, that have made me angry, that have taught me much, and that have made me care deeply. I wish I had written *Hotel Rwanda* or *Traffic* or *Maria Full of Grace*. But as those films demonstrated so well, I also understand that people go to the movies to be entertained, not to be preached to. We learn our deepest and most lasting lessons obliquely, while we are laughing or taking a thrill ride or witnessing an intimate moment not meant for prying eyes. As many before me have done, I counsel you: *write story* and let theme flow naturally from it.

Premise vs. Theme

The premise differs from theme in that it concentrates on the *story dynamics* rather than on the sentiment the author wishes to convey. As an example, the theme of *The Music Box*, the drama written by Joe Ezsterhas that starred Jessica Lange, might be described as, "the conflicts a woman faces when someone she loves and trusts has his most basic morality questioned." This theme—general as it is, it could apply to any number of stories—cannot guide the author in crafting a plot. On the other hand, the premise might be stated as: "In 1990, a criminal attorney must defend her father who is accused of Nazi war crimes." Now we know the underpinnings of the plot that drives and influences the actions and decisions of the main character. The theme—the moral dilemma (does she choose love/loyalty over truth/justice?)—follows from that.

Themes from the Heart

Milan Kundera says, "Whenever a novel abandons its themes and settles for just telling the story, it goes flat." A theme can be as simple as the triumph of good vs. evil (as in *Star Wars*); it can be as obvious as the film's title (*Sense & Sensibility*, which offers a theme of reason vs. passion); or, it can be as complex as finding heroism in the face of failure (as in *Saving Private Ryan* or *Apollo 13*). Some hold the main theme of *all* drama to be personal identity, asking the question: "Who are we really?" Whatever the theme, your work must have a personal point of view, whether it be derived from your heartfelt passion or your keen perception. *As a writer, you must eschew the safe middle ground; you must take sides.*

It almost doesn't matter if the side you take is not the most popular. In *Das Boot*, the main character is a German submarine commander during World War II. The author's strong POV presented this character as simply another human soul caught up in the horror of war. As a result, even American and English audiences found themselves rooting for the Germans to escape detection from the Allies and win!

Films deal with truths that flow indirectly—through our emotions, not our reasoning, our heart, not our mind. This allows the truth to take a deeper, more sustainable root in our subconscious. To do this, writers involve the audience directly in the *experience* of the characters. Theme is not what the story tells, but rather what it *reveals*. Ancient Zen philosophy tells us that one cannot always hit a target by aiming at it. You may not be certain what theme will emerge from your story, but, as a writer, you are both a student and teacher of human behavior. Don't limit your work to your knowledge or experience; write about what piques your curiosity and what drives you to learn and experience—a powerful theme will follow.

The Illusion of Reality

A common indication of a work by a new writer is the sense of it all being a little too true-to-life. Conversations sound like they would in the street; people make entrances and exits by saying hello and goodbye; actions are too real. Take the writer to task for something that doesn't ring true and they'll cry defensively: "But that's what really happened!" The truth is that audiences don't care what happened—they don't want to see real life. For reality, they need only look around them. They don't pay $10 for that. The writer doesn't transcribe life—he dramatizes it, arranges it to delight, excite, or surprise the audience.

The painter Matisse once presented one of his stylized portraits to a lady who exclaimed, "but a woman isn't like that." Matisse replied simply, "It isn't a woman, madam, it's a picture." Likewise, the audience knows it isn't life, it's a story. They make a deal with the filmmakers to suspend disbelief in exchange for the chance to escape reality for two hours.

As writer/producer Ed Zwick said when asked in an interview in *Playboy* magazine if people tuned in to see real-life problems on his TV show, *thirtysomething*:

> It is not reality… We are distilling reality the way one reduces sauces. It becomes more potent. We are giving the illusion of reality while using

the traditional elements of film: rising action, complication, climax, and denouement… You're left with a sense of truth and reality, but it's calculated in dramatic terms.

While a good film must convince us that what we are seeing is real and immediate enough to involve us, it is *believability*—not reality—that the audience craves. This means that characters must have the skill and internal and external motivations to render their actions credible in the circumstances in which they have been placed. Not real life, but *reel* life.

A Recognizable Genre

Producers may say they want new and different, but the first question asked in most pitch meetings is: "What's the genre?" In Hollywood at least, where the marketing tail wags the dog, genre translates to time-tested audience appeal and identifiable characters that attract stars. And yes, that also means movies we've seen (or think we've seen) before—that's the appealing common language of genre. But it does not mean that you should create a piece of formulaic writing. "Genre" simply implies a story that offers a clear theme (good vs. evil; truth; honor; heroism; passion) and a strong central character within a recognizable story format. How you tell the story remains your creative choice.

Some conventional genres and a few examples (without attempting a laundry list) you might find sectioned off in your local video store are:

- **Action-Adventure** (*Die Hard, Raiders of the Lost Ark, Lethal Weapon, The Seven Samurai*);
- **Biography** (*Ray, Amadeus, The Coal Miner's Daughter, Patton, Shine*);
- **Comedy** (*Arthur, Wedding Crashers, There's Something about Mary, The Waterboy, Meet the Parents, A Beautiful Life*);
- **Black Comedy** (*Dr. Strangelove, Network, The War of the Roses, Prizzi's Honor*);
- **Drama**—this category is often subdivided into:

    Family (*Terms of Endearment, Ordinary People*),

    Period (*The Remains of the Day, Dangerous Liaisons*),

    Legal (*The Verdict, A Civil Action*),

    Epic Historical (*Gone With The Wind, The English Patient, Lawrence of Arabia*),

Coming of Age (*Stand By Me, Diner, Breaking Away*),

War (*Platoon, Saving Private Ryan, Das Boot*),

Prison (*The Great Escape, The Shawshank Redemption, Midnight Express*),

Psychological (*Memento, Awakenings*)

- **Film Noir** (*Sunset Boulevard, Body Heat, Basic Instinct, LA Confidential*)
- **Gangster** (*The Godfather, Scarface, Bugsy, Goodfellas*)
- **Horror** (*Alien, Scream, Saw, The Devil's Rejects, Psycho*);
- **Detective/Mystery** (*Chinatown, Basic Instinct, The Maltese Falcon, The Big Sleep*);
- **Love Story** (*The End of the Affair, The African Queen, Officer and a Gentleman*)
- **Romantic Comedy** (*Sleepless in Seattle, You've Got Mail, Touch of Class, When Harry Met Sally…*)
- **Sci-Fi** (*Alien, Star Wars, The Truman Show, War of the Worlds*);
- **Thriller** (*Silence of the Lambs, Psycho, Se7en, Jagged Edge*);
- **Western** (*Red River, The Searchers, High Noon, The Unforgiven*);
- **Fantasy** (*The Lord of the Rings, Harry Potter, Spiderman, It's a Wonderful Life*);
- **Musical** (*The Wizard of Oz, Cabaret, The Sound of Music, West Side Story*).

Many films are *mixed-genres*, in which the main plot often is carried by the controlling genre, while the subplot carries the thematic genre (e.g. *Witness*, an action-love story, or *Titanic*, an adventure-love story). Some films toss genres in like they were making a chef's salad (such as the action/horror/sci-fi/love story *The Terminator*, or how about an action/adventure-sci-fi-love story-epic historical combo like *Raiders of the Lost Ark*). Of course, some genres (try a musical action/adventure or a satire/romance) are about as compatible as lemon juice and heavy cream. And never forget the Academy's favorite genre, what I like to call: The Moral Superiority of the Handicapped (*My Left Foot, I Am Sam, Forrest Gump*).

Each genre sparks an audience expectation, ingrained over thousands of hours of storytelling, of what they are about to see. That's because each genre makes its own unique thematic argument—the horror film challenges our notion of what is human and what is inhuman, for instance—and has its own set of conventions. A love story, as an example, emphasizes the passion; its characters are very human, vulnerable; the external opponent is always the lover; the internal opposition—immaturity, fear of commitment, etc.—is always strong; and the growth of the main character is in learning how to love selflessly. The love story espouses the "one right person for each of us" theory. The audience wants to see them get together, believes they must get together (but they keep missing each other, and all those misunderstandings!), becomes certain they can't get together (how can they ever get past that!), until, "ah, they got together—I should have seen that coming all along."

But just because a genre script may be less risky for the marketplace doesn't mean that it shouldn't *take* risks and explore new boundaries. Once you identify the common traits of a particular genre, you can experiment with *reversing our expectations*. Allow the conventions of a genre to set up your story and then give a twist in plot or character to surprise an audience that expects the usual thing. Examples of this include:

The Shining (a horror film in which the monster is the man of the house);

Unforgiven (where the western "hero" shoots a young man in the back as he attempts to crawl to safety);

Platoon (a war drama in which the individuals in the unit betray and murder each other);

Sleepless in Seattle (a love story in which the two lovers are never physically together until the final shot).

The TV series *Columbo*, based on a notion by the mystery writer Ellery Queen, is a great example of turning a genre upside down to the writer's advantage. A detective story usually centers on the detective's own major need (or the plot is viewed as an abstract exercise). Not *Columbo*. He has no personal angst to be worked out on screen. He's never at home (he has an unseen wife), in a police station, jail, or courtroom. In the normal police procedural, the audience discovers clues and learns the killer along with the main character. In *Columbo*, we are, instead, taken into the writer's confidence, witnessing the crime (always sanitized and barely seen), and given every fact that could possibly be used in solving it. The murderer is always a pillar of society—rich, powerful, educated, and untouchable—until the bumbling man in the rumbled raincoat wears him down. Unlike a typical cop show, *Columbo* avoids all the harshness of real police work—there are no prostitutes, drugs, thugs, or other cops. There is no family of regulars, no love interests, no car chases or fights, no violence at all. He doesn't use or even carry a gun. Yet in the realm of "TV detective," Columbo seems to have set the standard.

A Visual Setting and Context

The setting for your story is also a character. Our environment shapes us all; likewise, film characters must live in and make full use of their world. Deserts, oceans, mountains, and rivers act as crucibles by which characters may learn about themselves in the crossing (*The African Queen, Apocalypse Now,* or *The Mission*). Islands can be used to explore new societies, basic human needs, or political metaphors (*Lord of the Flies, The Man Who Would Be King*). A particular time period can heighten social irony (*Planet of the Apes, The Enemy of the People*). Homes (*Poltergeist, The War of the Roses*), families (*The Brady Bunch Movie, The Munsters*), small towns, isolated locales (*The Shining, Friday the 13th*), and violent weather conditions (*Alive, Twister*) all offer settings rich in metaphor to make your story come alive with hidden meaning.

Use the medium. Take advantage of the wide range of available locations and tap into the possibilities of special and digital effects and sound. If you write a film like *Top Gun*, craft scenes that let the audience hear and feel the power of the jets. Avoid static settings like offices, restaurants, cars, apartments, and phone booths. Instead, make the background a lively character in your film; have it brimming with all the relevant details that make your characters insiders in their world. If you are doing a police procedural for a TV series, know the culture of cops on the beat, what a cop does when he first approaches a crime scene, what happens with the dead body, what does the street, the apartment, the alley, look and smell like?

Research

There are entire web sites devoted to movie goofs, flubs, flaws, and mistakes. Finding them has become a game for film buffs. Few spoil the movie-going experience. So I try not to get too bent out of shape about little things like the Battle of Sterling Bridge in *Braveheart* having no bridge in it, or a recent cable channel airing in which it not only states that Anne Boleyn was executed by guillotine (which wasn't even invented for nearly another 300 years), but that the subject device is "on display at the Tower of London."

Research not only gets the details right, but can lead to the discovery of information that can expand your premise and enrich your characters. (For example, Anne's husband, Henry VIII granted her final request: the honor of being beheaded standing up, with a single blow by a special swordsman imported from France. The sword, however, is not on display anywhere.)

If you've set a caper comedy in Casablanca, at least leaf through travel books for interesting locations and local customs. Then contact the Moroccan consulate for information on customs, police procedures, Interpol jurisdiction, firearm use, or other details that might inform your plot. Help is usually just a phone call or key click away. Libraries allow free access to their online archives by posting your library card number. Most government and private agencies have public relations officers to answer questions and impart useful information—police, fire departments, hospitals, crisis centers, the FBI, DEA, CIA, the military, foreign embassies, etc.

You'll find that a little research goes a long way toward helping the audience suspend its disbelief and confer credibility upon your characters. If your main character is a small town waitress longing for love in a seedy diner, for example, you'll want her to be comfortable and believable in her actions, lingo, and daily routine. When Al Pacino tells her she's beautiful, we have to believe in her shy appreciation of the compliment—and forget she's Michelle Pfeiffer, one of the world's most beautiful women.

Too many writers neglect this critical step in designing plot, character, and context. But I'll let a TV legend make my point. In a scathing three-page single-spaced memo to his head writer, Erle Stanley Gardner, the creator of the original Perry Mason TV series, had this to say (in part) about the written episode, *The Case of the 12th Wildcat*:

> *"Why in hell is it that Hollywood script writers are ignorant of the basic facts of life and won't take the time to verify physical facts which are well known to almost every adult and quite a few children in the audience? Here we have a story founded on a gimmick with everything including geography twisted around to suit the gimmick.*
>
> *The Daylight Limited makes the run from San Francisco to LA in around 10 hours. The Lark, loafing along at night, makes the run in 12 hours. Here we have a high-priced football team on a train that somehow manages to consume nearly 20 hours in the run—and apparently has to consume that time in order to give the gimmick a chance to work. Let's take a timetable of the Southern Pacific and get this time element straightened out...*
>
> *If the police sealed off the cars, they wouldn't leave a trunk between the cars without searching it... the idea of the police acting in this way is simply absurd. I think the script was started with the idea of the trunk trick and then the writer got stuck with it.*

I doubt that any chemical will consume the bones in a body in the length of time the fire raged in that car. I would have supposed that some checking had been done on this chemical, but after what happened with the train schedule, I doubt it. And Mason, or any lawyer, would have demanded a corpus delicti. While this is not the body of the victim but the body of the crime, there are times when the term is synonymous and this is one. In order to consume a body, it takes a lot of time. Bones are very, very difficult to reduce to ashes and the smell of a burned body is overpowering. A fire fierce enough to destroy a human body isn't going to burn undetected in a stateroom for 50 minutes. A five-minute call to the fire department would have given these writers a lot of valuable information they should have had—and probably would have destroyed their whole plot idea.

A body being entirely consumed in the stateroom of a train with no odor of burning flesh, no sign of a fire until after the body is consumed, presents a problem that doesn't have an easy solution as far as I am concerned."

A Dynamic Opening

The preparation and research over, now it's time to write the script. Our notes and outline at the ready, we approach the first blank page. What do we write on it? Whatever will make our eventual readers turn that page.

Busy story departments plow through the hundreds of submissions they receive per week the way we might clean out our garage—anything that can be tossed, must be tossed. If you are a successful, known quantity (on a par with David Mamet, William Goldman, or Alvin Sargent, for example) most readers will grant you some latitude and read your entire screenplay to see how it develops. But the new writer has maybe five to ten pages, tops, to grab the reader with fresh, interesting characters that actors will want to play, clever dialogue, budding conflict, and a premise that screams "blockbuster."

In Hollywood, first pages are like first dates—impress, or it stops right there. And readers are like prom queens: everyone wants a shot at them, so they can afford to be picky. So many scripts, so many stories, and oh so little time. Is it any wonder that most wade through their weekend reading assignment by closing the cover on a writer's dream as soon as the first false note rings, as soon as a typo crosses their eye, as quickly as a cliché inches its way up a character arc? No fifteen-page courtesy read anymore. A few paragraphs are all it takes to spot a turkey. The incessant beat of the reader's clock is pass,

pass, pass. Passing makes their employer's job easier. It's why they were hired in the first place—to lighten the load. There is only one sure way to keep their interest: blow them away in those first brilliant pages.

Maybe sooner. Think of some of the great first *lines* in novels that are forged in our literary consciousness. "Call me Ismael." (Melville) "It was the best of times, it was the worst of times… " (Dickens) I particularly like Patrick Suskind's opening line in *Perfume* (soon to be a major motion picture): "In eighteenth-century France there lived a man who was one of the most gifted and abominable personages in an era that knew no lack of gifted and abominable personages." Lines like these seduce the reader into loving the work.

And that is your goal—to have them fall so deeply in love with your style, your tone, your premise, your context, your characters, your command of language, that they are predisposed to love the next 119 pages despite all the flaws that may develop. Great openings have a way of grabbing the reader and forcing admiration for and allegiance to *the writer*. Some scripters, like Shane Black (*Lethal Weapon, Kiss, Kiss, Bang, Bang*), design their first pages to take on multiple tasks, and always rely on high-impact, evocative language that impart the author's attitude and point of view and set the tonal integrity of the story. Experienced scribes know pages one to five may be the only time many readers are reading for pleasure, willing to bond with the writer's stylistic charm. As a fellow writer once put it to me, style is the wrapping that makes your reader want to open the box. A truly great opening then should do more than introduce context, characters, or plot information—*it must turn the reader into a fan*. Some take great risks to do that, even if it may mean alienating the reader. Take the opening paragraph of the Diane Thomas script, *Romancing the Stone*:

> INT. MOUNTAIN CABIN—DAY
>
> A size 16-eee boot kicks through the door, ripping the old board from the wall. GROGAN's grisly body stands framed in the doorway, a dirty foul-smelling beast. The shotgun in his grip is cocked. A strong-hearted beauty, ANGELINA, in buckskin poncho, eyes him guardedly from behind a table and surreptitiously slides a boot dagger out of its sheath. In the rafters, a spider faints.

Now upon first glance, quickly scanning the paragraph, this writing may so infuriate a reader with its use of cliché upon cliché, stereotype upon stereotype, and all those dreaded adverbs (the –ly words), that the script may easily stop dead in her mind right there. But wait. There is that final sentence. "In the rafters, a spider faints." That's kind of funny, isn't it? Not filmable, but stylish, sure. Can there be more here than meets the eye? As we now know, yes. Diane was giving us not *her* writing, but the claptrap of a romance writer (her main character) pounding out her latest commercial potboiler, the melodramatic result destined for a sepia-toned soap opera. That last sentence was put there to let us in on the joke. And in that vein, Diane hit the writing nail squarely on the head.

Recall the powerful opening image of *The Godfather*? Against pure black, the weathered face of an Italian-American slowly reveals itself, filling the screen as the first great line of dialogue breaks the silence: "I believe in America." In measured, broken English, struggling to maintain his dignity, the man seeks a desperate favor to avenge his daughter's disgrace—from the only source of justice he can count on, a man whose very way of life threatens everything he respects in the America he loves. This is an opening that engages the audience dramatically and emotionally and hooks the reader into becoming a page-turner.

As a sometime story analyst, three things in particular tend to turn me off in the opening of a script I'm reading: large blocks of scene description, the immediate introduction of way too many characters (after three I have a hard time keeping them straight), and early scenes or (worse) flashbacks designed to set the (oft-misunderstood concept of) "backstory." The opening page is no place for the writer to clear the fog from the murky story to follow. It is no place to get the motor running. The train is already moving down the track.

A "true beginning" as it is known in the trade, doesn't even start at the beginning—it cuts right into meat—the very *raison d'etre* of the scene—and starts there. Just as you would want your characters to make an auspicious entrance, so must you, the writer. Make things happen "too soon" or have your character say things now that will reverberate down to the climactic moments of Act III. A line or two of dialogue that sets the character's voice, hints at a past (is he/she damaged?) or future (is he/she too happy thus vulnerable to sudden change?), and drips in potential irony or conflict never hurts.

Keep a lot of white space. A minimum of description or short bursts of dialogue—Lagos Egri calls it "the art of terseness" (relying solely on subject and verb)—usually sets the right tone. And never forget style—in the early pages of a script the writer can choose *not* to disappear in the work, to let his voice be clearly established. A judicious use of capitals to punctuate action or the novelist's tools of personification, metaphor, foreshortened time, or mood manipulation, can form a seductive mental bond directly from writer to reader. Here, for example, are the first few paragraphs of M. Night Shyamalan's *The Sixth Sense*:

INT. BASEMENT—EVENING

A NAKED LIGHTBULB SPARKS TO LIFE. It dangles from the ceiling of a basement.

LIGHT, QUICK FOOTSTEPS AS ANNA CROWE moves down the stairs.

Anna is that rare combination of beauty and innocence. She stands in the chilly basement in an elegant summer dress that outlines her slender body. Her gentle eyes move across the empty room and come to rest on a rack of wine bottles covering one entire wall.

She walks to the bottles. Her fingertips slide over the labels. She stops when she finds just the right one. A tiny smile as she slides it out.

Anna turns to leave. Stops. She stares at the shadowy basement. It's an unsettling place. She stands very still and watches her breath form a TINY CLOUD IN THE COLD AIR. She's visibly uncomfortable.

She moves for the staircase in a hurry. Each step faster than the next. She climbs out of the basement in another burst of LIGHT, QUICK FOOTSTEPS.

WE HEAR HER HIT THE LIGHT SWITCH.

THE LIGHTBULB DIES. DRIPPING BLACK DEVOURS THE ROOM.

Just as the screenplay may be one long metaphor for your theme, the opening (which establishes that theme in context) may be thought of as a metaphor for your screenplay. A good opening should set the tone and context, introduce your main character in a fresh, interesting way, and hint at a possible hole in his life that needs to be filled. And it should begin the conflict by engaging the story hook.

The Story Hook

The *true beginning* of any story, also commonly known as the *inciting incident* or *primary event*, the story hook is an event that radically upsets the ordinary course of life for the main character and compels him to act. It's the event that gives the character his goal (at least the initial goal). It should occur as early as possible in the story—as soon as we know just enough about the main character to bond with him. And it *must* occur: It is the one essential element every story must possess. A story without a story hook never quite gets off the ground.

In *North by Northwest*, it is the moment when Roger Thornhill is mistaken for George Kaplan and hustled away from his pleasant lunch at gunpoint. In *Thelma & Louise*, it occurs when Susan Sarandon (Louise) shoots the would-be rapist and tells Thelma that what's done is done and it can't be undone—in effect, life will never be the same from this moment on and we'll have to deal with the consequences. In *Field of Dreams*, it's the moment that Ray Kinsella first hears the voice in the cornfield. Choose any movie you like. It should be easy to identify the event, the person, the moment that alters the world of the main character and that truly kicks off the story.

In finding a viable story hook for the movie you wish to write, ask yourself why you chose this character and this subject in the first place. Perhaps your character is so trapped in a destructive relationship with his past that he fails to recognize the deep truth of his potential. No doubt, you love your character and know that he can be a happier person if he can only lift off that yoke the size of the Titanic he's carrying around on his shoulders. Because God sees through to our deepest and best qualities, our true nature, he loves us despite our faults and weaknesses and errors in judgment. In the same way, your character is your creation, your child, and you want the best for him. So ask how God would intervene if one of His children were under a misapprehension as to their true nature—a misapprehension which was weighing him down and preventing him from enjoying all the potential of his being. Wouldn't the best structure for a story be one that places him in a situation—a predicament—that gives him a challenge most congenial to the discovery of his true inner nature? Aristotle called this primary event *energeia*, meaning "the actualization of the potential which exists in character and situation." Once this incident occurs, your character's agenda will be set, the wheels of the plot will begin rolling, and the pages should practically turn themselves.

Characters We Care About

Movies are about us—you, me, our neighbors, our families, our tragedies, our heroics and our shame too. Actors play or lend their voice to characters, and those characters lend their voice to us. It should come as no surprise then that characters are what audiences remember from a film: Rhett Butler in *Gone with the Wind*, Atticus Finch in *To Kill a Mockingbird*, Travis Bickle in *Taxi Driver*, Don Corleone in *The Godfather*, Rocky Balboa in *Rocky*. And if you examine your response to most great films, you will find that you have a strong concern for those characters as people. You may not always like them—that's a personal choice—but you are forced into a human empathy with them, to bond with their common everyday struggles in "the trap that the world has become" (to quote Milan Kundera, himself borrowing from Kafka). We look to movies to explain the human condition and we look to actors to mine the depths of the truth in human behavior. This is true whether your film is populated by humans, aliens, animals, fish, insects, or cartoon characters.

Milan Kundera in his novel, *The Unbearable Lightness of Being*, wrote, "Characters are not born like people, of woman; they are born of a situation, a sentence, a metaphor containing in a nutshell a basic human possibility that the author thinks no one else has discovered or said something essential about."

And that's the larger point. A character is not a real human being—it is a work of art. The writer, in order to deliver a specific emotional response to an audience, manufactures the principal character, his goals, needs, obstacles, pressures, responses, and motivations. The plot is how the writer "sells" this character to an audience—as the character passes through a series of physical, emotional, and psychological hoops, we begin to identify with him, root for (or against) him, care for him, and invest emotionally in the outcome of his struggle.

My four rules for the principal character (the protagonist) of any film are:

1.   He must be charismatic and *interesting* to watch;

2.   He must be possessed of a very definite *attitude*;

3.   He must be *credible* in the circumstances in which he is placed;

4.   He must be highly *motivated* in his actions.

There is an old Native-American saying, "the stronger the wind, the stronger the trees." A person is capable of doing just about anything if the adversity that he faces and the conditions that motivate him are strong enough. Knowing this, the writer creates life-altering situations to test the protagonist's (often mistaken) beliefs about himself. In this sense, the real goal of every story is to reveal the true nature of the protagonist and to witness how he learns and grows as a result of the pressures put on him in the story.

Action is not what *happens* to your character; action is what your character *does* about what is happening to him.

Actors find the truth in their characters by creating a world of inner motivations for the decisions demanded by the script. Similarly, a writer must imagine himself in his character's shoes, from birth onward, and intuitively grasp his character's motivations—his fears and desires, successes and failures, disappointments and dreams, values and ideals. Only then can the writer depict human, identifiable, and memorable characters acting and reacting with emotional accuracy.

Write parts actors want to play. Characters should be multidimensional, motivated, and vulnerable. They should be engaged in risky human behavior and be faced with life-altering challenges.

In designing a cast of characters for a feature film, the writer will usually create a main character, possibly possessed of a backstory, with a clear goal that puts him into contact and conflict with an identifiable opponent and a key supporting cast of kinsmen, allies, enemies, and others there to serve the needs of the story. The following sections will examine these elements in order.

One Main Character

As there is one author's voice, there is usually one character to carry that voice. That character possesses sufficient strength of will to undergo the trials and tribulations of the plot, sufficient interest to arouse the empathy of the audience, clear and convincing motivation, and is actively committed in body, mind, and soul to their objective. That character is almost always the hero or anti-hero—the story's protagonist, the central character whose actions drive the plot. The clear rooting interest.

But hold on. In *Die Hard*, Hans, the villain, the antagonist, orchestrates the action—McClane only reacts. But the story evolves from McClane's point of view and, as the hero, the audience is invested in his fate as he carries the torch of societal values. So maybe we could say the main character is the one with a backstory that motivates key actions in the film, or the one who changes and grows as a result of going through the struggle in the film—McClane is both of those. But while those are all good clues, none are definitive—as Quentin Tarantino proved in *Pulp Fiction*. John Travolta appears to be the main character; his actions structure the beginning, middle, and end of the film (he dies somewhere in there, but his character is resurrected). Samuel L. Jackson has the character-changing epiphany. And Bruce Willis seems to carry the author's point of view as to how we should act toward others. But I'll go with Travolta as the film's central character, because in the final analysis, the plot and most other characters revolve around or at least intersect with him. The writer must love all his characters, but here I think Quentin surely loved John's character most.

Nietzsche remarked that upon choosing a wife, "ask yourself if you are willing to have a conversation with this woman for the next forty years." The main character must also fascinate and hold your interest—if not for forty years, at least for the next year or two of your life.

Those anomalies notwithstanding, *one clearly defined main character* (often the "hero") is a staple of American movie making. He can be good or bad, win or lose (or change his goal at the end), but he offers a clear point of view, as well as focusing and lending purpose to the plot. Even in ensemble films—structured around a series of thematically linked subplots in which the whole is truly greater than the sum of the parts—there is usually one character around which all the action seems to coalesce. Think of Kevin Kline's character in Lawrence Kasden's *Grand Canyon* or *The Big Chill*, or, John Travolta's "wandering angel" (the gentle, confident, strong, movie-loving, above-it-all guy that no evil sticks to) gangster in *Get Shorty*, who calmly and gracefully centers and binds the film's swirl of four plot lines of money, betrayal, greed, and film allusions.

In classic two-character stories, such as love stories (*Romeo & Juliet* or *When Harry Met Sally...*) and buddy stories (*Butch Cassidy & The Sundance Kid* or *Thelma & Louise*), you will find that one character's actions primarily move the plot and it's usually (but not always) that character who has the most to learn in terms of acting toward others and who exhibits the greatest amount of growth. Look carefully and you'll usually find that character is also introduced first, has the most scenes, and has his name come first in the title.

In *Romeo & Juliet*, Romeo goes to the ball, seeks Juliet on her balcony, slays her cousin Tybalt, and is banished for it; when he finds her "dead," he is the one who takes his life first. In *When Harry Met Sally...*, Harry makes love to Sally but is uncomfortable with the aftermath and must reconcile the ideals of love and friendship. Sally stays essentially as she was from the very start of the film.

In *Butch Cassidy*, Butch is the gang leader who decides that robbing banks is getting too risky and ultimately opts to move to Bolivia, taking the Sundance Kid along. In *Thelma & Louise*, many thought Thelma (played by Geena Davis) to be the main character since she changes the most. But look closer: Louise (Susan Sarandon) opens the film telling a couple in a diner that "smoking will kill your sex life" and then smokes herself (signaling she is damaged somehow). She then encourages Thelma to make the trip, shoots the would-be rapist, and makes the decision to run due to her past woes in Texas and subsequent fear of being unable to receive justice in a man's world (the backstory—a device we examine further below). It is also Louise who finally achieves "freedom" for both of them by driving their car off the edge of the cliff. Clearly then, Louise, possessed of both the backstory and actions which drive the plot, is the main character.

But then there is the Michael Mann crime drama, *Heat*, pitting two colossal movie stars against each other: Al Pacino and Robert DeNiro. I have to believe Mann intended two main characters here and balanced their screen time accordingly. Pacino plays the cop, "the good guy." But while society's morality is on his side, his personal morality leaves much to be desired. He treats his girlfriend and his poor snitches badly and we're not at all sure we'd like him as a friend. DeNiro, on the other hand, "the bad guy," is a master thief and worse. But he treats his girlfriend with kindness and respect and acts with life and death, stand-by-you loyalty toward his band of thieves in whom he inspires equal devotion. In a way, we respect his morality more than Pacino's. (If this were a gangster movie, we'd root for DeNiro's, the gang that gets along, as opposed to Pacino's, the gang that double-crosses and stabs each other in the back.) This creates a conundrum at the inevitable battle to the death between the two rivals. DeNiro can't escape—if he does, the little morality bell that rings in the back of our heads will toll: "he must eventually pay for his crimes." Yet we don't want him to die either. And for him, a life behind bars is a fate worse than death. So when Pacino's bullet finds DeNiro, Mann has Pacino act out what the whole audience must have felt—he takes DeNiro's hand in his and, in his own way, he mourns him.

If for this reason alone—the audience's desire to not have their emotions split—most movies center on a single protagonist, someone with at least one clearly admirable trait and at least one small weakness (nobody's perfect). *Making the main character as fully human, unique and interesting as possible is the single most important job in screenwriting.* This requires a ruthless psychological investigation. Who is he/she and what truly motivates him/her? What are his values, his personal beliefs? What will he die for? What are the lies he tells himself every day in order to survive? Only when we understand all of that can we truly know what his response will be in a crisis situation. Life is difficult, after all, and the choices we make under pressure often define us more than what others believe we stand for.

The Indian Goddess of Mercy says, "If we can see all, we can forgive all." Let us in on the secrets of your characters' lives. Let us see what they would show no one. What finally drove Ernest Hemingway, for example—obsessed with courage in all his writings, a man who raged against suicide—to decide to take his own life? This is the secret that a movie on his life must explore.

There are few great films that do not in some way turn on the moral decisions of the main character. What are your character's ethics? If put on the witness stand to testify against a friend—in a situation where telling the truth would be to act as a witness against the friend—does he lie? What is first in his hierarchy of values: truth or loyalty (as in the aforementioned *The Music Box* example)? What are the outside limits of his morality? If he rubbed the magic lamp and the genie gave him one wish: he could either end world terrorism or become a world famous, rich and successful screenwriter married to Michelle Pfeiffer—and the world would never know his choice—which would he choose? These are questions an author must first ask himself. Inevitably, it is the author that must take sides on the moral question posed for the main character. It is the author's emotions, judgments, and point of view that will inform the character's actions.

Try to picture your main character toward the end of his life, sitting by a roaring fire telling stories to his grandchildren. What would be the events of his life that he would recall? When he met his wife perhaps, or the moment he decided to embark upon his career, or perhaps he would choose that one defining moment of great adversity that challenged all he ever thought himself to be and which was ultimately responsible for his becoming the man he is today. If he were writing a book on his life, wouldn't that be the moment he would write about? Wouldn't that be the moment his audience would be most interested in?

Sartre has written that characters reveal themselves only in the extremes of love, hate, anger, fear, joy, hope, despair.

Of course, feelings expressed under pressure are not always a true indication of their meaning. It is a screenwriting maxim that Action is Character (what a character does defines him)—but in reality, motivation and context determine the interpretation of that action. David Milch, creator of seven television series, including *NYPD Blue* and *Deadwood*, posed this question at a recent writing seminar. "Peter denied Christ three times. Judas kissed him on the cheek. Can we tell by their actions who really loves God more?"

Some writers give their characters *masks* to hide their true feelings. One technique is to have a character initially behave antisocially to mask his pain or to deflect the rejection he fears will result from trying to fit in with society. *Lethal Weapon* features a cop who hides his grief over the loss of his wife by acting as a borderline psychopath. In the 2003 Jean-Claude Van Damme prison drama, *In Hell*, this voiceover comes at the climax of the film: "Most of us know that the mask we hide behind is garbage. Sooner or later it shatters. That's when you find out the man you really are."

Spiderman and Batman hide their true identity and their hearts behind literal masks. The cartoon ogre, Shrek, masks his fears and vulnerability in his attitude: "I don't like people anyway, so stay away!" When what he really means is "I fear they will find me so loathsome, so hideous, that they will ridicule and reject me and I can't take that pain any longer." Of course, the dramatic irony is that Shrek's great love, Fiona, hides behind a mask as well—a beautiful face and body created by a spell.

With that I offer a *ten-point strategy* for discovering your main character:

STRATEGY

1. **My anti-character bio tip.**

   Some writers do a detailed biographical study of their main character. I do not. You never need to know more about your main character than you are prepared to reveal in the story. What's the value in knowing his best friend in second grade unless that information is used in the pages of your script? Yet many such irrelevant details, once conceived, worm their way into the story and blur the focus.

2. **No long lives.**

Shakespeare said that he wrote about human experience, with the dull parts cut out. Don't force your main character—through too broad a premise—to deal with too much. A long life is the stuff of novels. Screenwriters must economize, choose what is really important. Movies are about life-altering, defining moments. What are the key choices of your main character's life, the choices that truly moved him one way or the other (though such moments may be imperceptible when they occur)?

3. **Be autobiographical.**

Find the quality in your main character that is most like your own and use it to shape your character's decisions and actions. As Chekhov said, "Everything I learned about human nature, I learned from me."

4. **Give your character a reality.**

That means give him a name and stick with it, give him an environment, a cat or dog, a girlfriend or wife, a best friend, a boss, a full life.

5. **Challenge him.**

Constantly. Never let anything come to him easily. No good should come to him except through conflict. It is your job to keep him actively engaged.

6. **No surprises.**

Make your main character's responses to those challenges be consistent with who he is or who he believes himself to be. At the least, that means never give him any last-minute powers, like he suddenly knows karate or can fly a plane.

7. **Commitment and communication.**

He must be totally driven—body, mind, and soul—to meet those challenges and he must convey that commitment through his actions.

8. **There are no small coincidences.**

The only coincidences that should occur past the first few pages are those which make life *worse* for your main character, never better.

9. **No retreat, no surrender.**

He faces challenges he can't walk away from, with all the physical and moral courage he can muster. He must not dwell on the odds.

He does not see himself as weak or powerless—he believes that if he acts, he can win.

10. **The anti-deus ex machina rule.**

   Never, under any circumstances, take the climax of the film away from the main character. Only he can solve the story problem. No third party can come in and do it for him. The problem can't go away on its own.

   There is this moment toward the end of *Heat*: The thief (Robert DeNiro) steps out of a hotel room having just claimed righteous vengeance on a renegade former gang member—when a hotel security guard places a gun to his head. If, for a second, the audience thought he was caught, the writer delivered the feeling he intended. But we should know better. There is no way the audience can be put through two and a half hours of a dramatic standoff between Pacino and DeNiro and have some cast extra catch the thief!

Backstory

Movies are about secrets. The audience is a voyeur, peeking in on the hidden underbelly of human behavior. To make a main character (like a good date) interesting, he should be flawed, quirky, dark, charming, full of contradictions—with an air of mystery about him. That mystery is often tied to the character's backstory—drama's pop-psychology answer to the dark and deep motivations that inform the character's sometimes downright bizarre behavior.

While all characters bring aspects of their past to the film, only the main character is given a true backstory. Used properly, it can be a tool for the writer to shape and motivate the main character's actions and decisions in the film. As discussed earlier, it's why Susan Sarandon's character in *Thelma & Louise* decides to run rather than trust her fate to the legal system or take the most direct route through Texas to escape, and why Paul Newman's lawyer in *The Verdict* has allowed a past wrong to destroy his faith in justice, leading him down a path of personal and professional self-destruction. In these films, the backstory not only provides exposition about such past events, but also the motivation that informs and drives the dramatic conflicts and issues confronting the character now—conflicts and issues that are crucial to the unfolding of the central actions of the movie.

Also, as those films show, backstory serves another crucial function: *It allows the story to start at a later point in time.* Instead of burdening the audience with too much information (*exposition*) too soon, the audience is gradually let in on character-defining past events as the story develops. But whatever past you conjure up to enrich your own concept of your characters, if it does not directly affect plot and character *in the screenplay* then it is not backstory. If we are not to learn the character's backstory in the movie, it may as well not exist.

Clearly Rick's mysterious past is one of the reasons *Casablanca* endures as one of the most popular films of all time, but I have in my library (courtesy of Prof. Rennard Strickland of the University of Wisconsin) a "memorandum of screen development" dated 12/11/41 from an executive at Warner Brothers to the effect that Rick was a "famous criminal lawyer," having practiced in New York and Paris! The memo reads in part as follows:

> "*Rick Blaine…. is a taciturn man of mystery to his patrons…. Only Rinaldo, French Prefect of Police, knows of his background as a famous criminal lawyer [and of] his abandonment of career and flight into oblivion.*"

Now it is true that Howard Koch, one of the screenwriters who transformed the script for the unproduced play *Everybody Comes to Rick's* into the Oscar-winning scenario for *Casablanca*, was a Columbia Law School graduate and a member of the New York Bar. And it is possible, I suppose, that there are hints in the film of Rick's legal prowess, subtle clues such as negotiating the sale of his café to Blue Parrot owner Sydney Greenstreet (representing his own interests as badly as most lawyers do when representing themselves). But I seriously doubt that Rick is the image that most people conjure up when they think of silver screen lawyers. I doubt that it informed Humphrey Bogart's performance in any way, and I doubt it adds one bit to the popular success of the film, the plot, or our appreciation for Rick's character. And as such, it doesn't qualify for what we are defining as "backstory" at all.

You can find backstory lurking in the "I coulda' been a contender" line that Marlin Brando delivers in *On the Waterfront*, or in Clint Eastwood's past failure to protect the President as a Secret Service officer in *In the Line of Fire*, or in the demons that haunted the self-pitying Nick Nolte since childhood in *Prince of Tides*.

Finally, backstory serves one more crucial purpose: It is often the engine that drives the theme, causally related directly to the main character's psychological need in the film and to the key thematic question of all drama, "*Who am I?*"

In designing a main character, a writer asks *three key questions*:

1. Who does he think he is?
2. Who does he appear to be to others?
3. Who is he really?

A character's self-image—who he believes himself to be—is shaped by his experience. If a man (call him "Jim") faces enough courage-failing moments in his life, he may think himself a coward. Jim's friends, knowing who he has become, may think him meek. But the author, his creator, knows that underneath that frightened shell is a man capable of true courage—*if only* Jim were given the right opportunity to face his fears and a strong enough motivation to overcome those fears.

The writer's task then is to examine not only present reality but the mystery of existence, the complete panorama of human *possibilities*—all that man can become, all that he is capable of becoming—and give him both the opportunity and the motivation to change.

What happened to Jim so long ago? What is the secret to the damaged person we see emerging in the story? How does the specter of his past affect his life now? Jim's past can be used to explain and shape who he is and appears to be at the start of the movie. Because *we do what we do in order to be consistent with whom and what we think we are.* Having failed to live up to his own standards, Jim believes himself a coward and acts accordingly. This poor self-image is his existential problem. Making a character come alive means getting to the bottom of this existential problem and finding whatever has shaped who he is now or what he has become as a result of the problem. In Freudian psychology, a person stuck with such a self-image can become crippled emotionally and rendered unable to participate fully in the possibilities of his life. Jim must go back and face the "ghost that haunts him from the past" if he is to overcome the dramatic conflict and issues that confront him in the story, gain freedom in the present, and move on to a higher plain in his life.

Of course, not every main character is possessed of a secret past. James Bond or the Clint Eastwood characters of *The Man with No Name* or *Dirty Harry* are too busy dusting off the filth of the world to dwell on or dramatically require a backstory. In *The Graduate*, Benjamin is a bored, purposeless college graduate seduced by an equally bored, purposeless housewife—then he meets her daughter. It's all straight-line love/obsession from there on out—no secrets needed (though Mrs. Robinson has one—why she married in the first place).

A Clear Goal

Unlike the novel, a screenplay is too tightly structured to allow for creative detours from the plot. So it has become axiomatic to say that before writing the first page, you must know the last. To set up an action you need to know its consequences, its dramatic or comedic payoff. You must also know what you want the movie to accomplish from an audience point of view before you can set the main character to accomplishing it. Ask, what is the defining moment of your character in the film? Then place your character in a circumstance that leads up to and away from that defining moment. You'll want things to get as awful as possible for that person so that the audience is practically off their seats with the need for the character to act. *The true heart of any film is the moment that your main character makes the choice to take action.* The culmination of all that he has learned and experienced as a result of going through the plot—this is the moment that delivers emotional satisfaction to an audience.

Screenplays are goal-oriented. The goal must be specific, clearly identifiable, as crucial to your character as life and death, and not subject to compromise. And yet, it is not the goal itself but the character's journey toward the goal that matters most. In fact, in some stories the goal is a *MacGuffin*— a term coined by Alfred Hitchcock—an object of desire for the conflicting characters (such as the statue of the falcon from *The Maltese Falcon* or the silver suitcase that Robert DeNiro and everyone else chases in *Ronin*), a red herring that triggers the plot but has no other inherent story value. But even in the striving toward such an illusory goal, true depth of character can be gained. For in our struggles, in defeat more than victory, we grow. As Ernest Hemingway said, "The world may break us, but afterward many are stronger at the broken places." This is the very essence of the film hero and his cinematic struggles. James Allen, the 19th century English author, put it this way, in his pithy but enduring classic, *As a Man Thinketh*:

> "*A man should conceive of a legitimate purpose in his heart, and set out to accomplish it... He should make this purpose his supreme duty, and should devote himself to its attainment... Even if he fails again and again to accomplish his purpose (as he necessarily must until weakness is overcome), the strength of character gained will be the measure of his true success, and this will form a new starting point for future power and triumph.*"

And in a movie, characters can attain such success only through conflict.

Conflict

"He who would achieve much, must sacrifice much."

—James Allen, As a Man Thinketh

True character growth in a screen story requires *dramatic* (transitional) conflict—*a great and sustained effort against the forces of true adversity toward a worthy goal*—that can challenge all the protagonist's resources. (A football game has conflict, but absent a story beyond the score, not dramatic conflict.) In fact, nothing of any value can be achieved except through conflict. This conflict can be external or internal. Most film stories utilize both.

The plot is shaped by the *external conflict*—the event that sets up the main character's desire, opposition, and goal. This places the main character at odds with a human opponent (other adversity often attaches as well, but a flesh and blood opponent focuses the conflict). The more well developed the opponent—with his/her own history, motivations, needs, and character arc—the more powerful the external conflict and the more credible the main character's growth as a result of that conflict.

The *internal* conflict is formed by pressure from the character's inner need—sometimes revealed in a backstory—which forms the deep motivation for his actions and decisions.

Presenter Charlie Rose recently made this comment in a televised interview: "Motivation is perhaps the single most important thing in turning potential ability into realized ability."

It is the first law of physics that a body in motion will stay in motion until acted upon by an outside force. Everyday experiences are usually not powerful enough to derail us from our present life course, certainly not strong enough to cause us to consider seriously the deeper meaning of our existence. The same is true of our main character, which is why a character's transitional conflict begins with a life-altering moment, the story hook or inciting incident—though that moment can seem quite benign when it occurs.

In David Mamet's *The Verdict*, it is the moment that Frank Galvin, an alcoholic ambulance chaser packing up the remains of his seedy office, gets one last chance for redemption: a case. Not a huge event for most lawyers—but for Galvin, it's his *only* case, and it directly causes a series of progressive complications that raise the stakes to do or die proportions.

Galvin is a flawed, frightened man bucking the system against impossible odds, but he has greater personal motivation than winning money. If he fails to win justice for his comatose client, he may also fail to regain *his* sense of justice and self-respect (his internal conflict) and, for him, this is an emotional life and death issue.

This internal conflict is the true heart of drama—the main character's struggle within himself to resolve a difficult moral dilemma, or to come to terms with his past, his drinking or drug use, his sense of failure or other psychic misgivings, or to confront his psychological flaws: his fears, weaknesses, insecurity, immaturity, low self-esteem, even self-hatred. While the character's initial *goal* may be money or fame or even self-preservation, this is never a real matter for concern with an audience. Let's just say it— *they know it's only a movie.* But in spending two hours with a character's internal struggle, the audience identifies, empathizes, and often learns more about the possibilities for their own lives. It is experiencing the struggle against such internal conflicts *with* the main character that gives rise to the *catharsis* Aristotle called the point of all drama.

The *dramatic need* of Galvin's then—to regain his faith in justice and in himself—is the *inner conflict* at the heart of *The Verdict*. His past experiences have left him feeling abandoned by the system and by the concept of justice itself. Both Galvin and his opposing attorney, Edward Concannon, are savvy Boston lawyers. But for a twist of fate years earlier that took him down a different path, Galvin—like Concannon—could be senior partner at a large, successful law firm. But what derailed Galvin then, shaped the person he became now. Both are lawyers paid to win, but for Concannon, winning is everything, while for Galvin, justice and truth have become more important. The dramatic conflict in the story comes from these conflicting values. And so Galvin's backstory—the primary tool the writer uses to build deep conflict and character growth —is what motivates his obsessive drive to attain justice for his client and himself.

The final conflict of a movie is the climax. Using tension and conflict to hold and tease the audience to the end, *the climax of the movie must always be the battle between the main character and the opponent.* In *The Verdict* this occurs in the classic courtroom confrontation between Galvin and Concannon—a battle representing all that they believe in and all that separates them. In undergoing this struggle, Galvin learns to let go of the past and the audience can have the catharsis of believing a person can overcome his inner demons and walk away to a richer, fuller life.

Of course, other sources of conflict can also generate dramatic tension in a story. The forces of government or the confines of culture or society (Kafka's primary themes) can create significant challenges for the characters, as can the forces of nature (fire, flood, wind, rain, snow, earthquakes, avalanches, and tornadoes). But it has been said that while "a man can have an enemy or he can be his own worst enemy," a man's real enemy can never be society, a country, "the woods, fireflies, gardens, sunsets, waterfalls, and mountains." These are obstacles, not enemies, and never sources of true conflict. For that we need an identifiable opponent.

An Identifiable Opponent

Faulkner tells us that the most powerful stories emerge from "a heart in conflict with itself." In terms of a character's ultimate, inner need, this is accurate. But the visual immediacy of film requires a living opponent to personify the struggles taking place within the character's psychic makeup.

In *Shane*, Jack Palance is the personification of evil as he lures an innocent farmer into a gunfight and then mows him down mercilessly. As the savior of the town, champion of decency and family values, Shane, wounded, must ascend the hill and go in and kill him.

But all opponents are not so easily drawn. In most love stories, for example, it is the very sympathetic lover—usually the female—who provides the thematic opposition to the immature male who must learn how to love. In fact, the opponent is often the mirror image of the main character—a "there but for the grace of God go I" person—who personifies who our hero would have become had life not taught him a different lesson. In *The Verdict*, James Mason portrays a lawyer who believes he is paid to win. Not a wrong sentiment exactly, and had life not handed Paul Newman a raw deal, it's possible he would have shared the same smug point of view as Mason. But instead Paul Newman seeks justice, not just victory, for his client—and that is presented to the audience as making all the difference.

A good writer loves his opponent as he does his protagonist and endows that opponent with all the human qualities which will make him believable to an audience; even a villain must be given a heart. Arguably, the most purely evil dramatic character in Shakespeare is Iago from *Othello*. Yet, the actor chosen to play Iago is often a handsome, charming man. Theater lore tells us that even Shakespeare knew that this evil character had to be made human or the audience would never be able to take him seriously, and thus cast some of the most beloved actors of his day in the role.

But not every movie has a single strong opponent. *Apollo 13* had only bad luck to overcome in a story about heroism in the face of failure. Forrest's girlfriend in *Forrest Gump* kept him on his toes through life, but his character's "disability" held our attention. The lack of anything more than serial opposition gave *Mr. Holland's Opus* an almost fated ending. Ensemble films like *Husbands and Wives* and *Grand Canyon* never seem to confront their opponents directly, though there is much opposition, just as *JFK* and biographies like *Ray* and *Nixon* are like detective stories, with opposition shrouded and overpowered by the mystery or the enigma of the man himself.

But like most principles that guide good storytelling, the exceptions only support the rule.

Supporting Characters

When designing a cast, your main character gets the spotlight—keep him/her interesting and complex, motivated and active. Supporting characters are purely functional. They live so the main character has someone to talk to, someone to oppose, someone to love. They may be advancing the plot, supplying key background information, or contributing to the ambiance of the main character's life—but their prime reason to be in the story is *to serve the needs, desires, motivations, challenges, and plans of the main character.*

Giving minor characters too much to say or do can slow down and disrupt the action of the plot and detract from the focus on the main character. That doesn't mean they shouldn't be interesting. They should be given their individual personalities, skills, quirks, and attitude, *all the better to complement and draw out the various facets of the main character's (or opponent's) personality.* But never make them complex or too interesting or the audience will expect them to return to the story at a later stage. And don't strain yourself to develop them all. They don't get a backstory. They don't get to take over the movie at some point. They must have a clear reason to be in the story, and they don't get to be there at all if another character is adequately serving the same function. You may not even give them a name. If the audience has no occasion in the story to learn a minor character's name, you may wish to assign them numbers (Cop #1) or name them by the job they do in the story (Coat Check Girl). (Actors of course would prefer a name, but they would also prefer eight additional scenes.)

And you should never have too many of them. In fact, for most features—except those that contain multiple story lines, thematically linked—eight principal characters is about all that can be given any personality or dimension or given sufficient story beats to develop beyond the superficial. Beyond the principal opponent, these are the principal supporting characters like allies, love interests, partners, key opponents, family members, etc. Most serve more than one function—one or more of five categories (my "5 Cs"):

1. **A confidant.** Someone in whom to communicate their thoughts, feelings, and plans.

2. **A catalyst.** To help kick the main character into action.

3. **A conscience.** To make them face the inconsistencies and lies in their life.

4. **For comic relief.** Even torturers know that at some point you have to give the victim a sip of water to revive them if you're going to continue the torture.

5. **For contrast.** The arguments in a script, direct or indirect, need balance.

A Balanced Structure

All art attempts to bring order to chaos, so it's perhaps only natural to impose structure and rules upon the subject. Most such rules in screenwriting are derived from dissecting produced screenplays (or films) that are deemed successful. Maybe someone looks at a hundred and a dozen fit some sort of paradigm, so a rule is born. Kind of like scientists who point out the seven warning signs of a coming tsunami 24 hours after one hits. So if you're skeptical about the validity of plot points or second act curtains or rules in general, I empathize. But I still believe it's important to have a healthy respect for the traditions of good storytelling. And the cornerstone of those traditions is story structure.

We've all told stories or heard stories told and we know good storytellers from poor storytellers. The poor ones give away the punch line too early or don't set up the surprise ending properly or get you confused about who and what the story is supposed to be about, or worse, how you're supposed to feel about it. By story's end, your eyes have glazed over, you don't care, you don't remember it two hours later, and if you did, you'd never re-tell it to a friend. That's because a good story is about more than plot, characters, or dialogue—it also has to be a *story well told*.

Gustave Flaubert said: "It is not the pearls that make the necklace, but the thread." Wonderful scenes and quirky characters are wasted if the incidents aren't structured along a clear, defining line that lends them purpose and dramatic power. Stories are structured much like life: every day you die a little, come closer or farther away from your goals, even if only in time. So it is with story: every scene advances the plot, moves the character closer or farther away from his goal. In a well-told story, there is cause and effect in everything, but even more so than in life. Because in life, certain causes *may* produce certain effects, but in a story we believe they *should* produce those effects—the storyteller having started a causal chain, must deliver us satisfaction. To achieve this, writers design a story as an architect designs a house. First they ask a series of questions to establish the pillars that will support the structure:

1. How and where should I begin the story and why just there?

2. How best should I organize the scenes so that they have the greatest emotional impact on the audience?

3. How can I maintain dramatic tension and involve the audience in the fate of the main character?

4. What is the true end to my story and how can I build to it so that it is both surprising and inevitable?

"Begin at the beginning," the king said gravely, "and go until you come to the end and then stop." That's how Lewis Carroll in *Alice's Adventures in Wonderland* succinctly defined the writer's challenge: finding the true beginning—or point of attack—of the story and of every scene. *And* ending it before tacking on that one scene too many that may blunt the emotional impact.

Beginnings and endings, and how to get from one to the other—basic story questions. One facile answer is that all screen stories should start too late and end too soon. Get into the story as quickly as possible to hook the viewers and end it while they're still on the edge of their seat. Structuring the film around setups and payoffs—the main plot payoff being the climax—can help you do that.

Structure is the ordering of story incidents to create the greatest emotional impact on the audience. From the very first page, storytellers set up moments that will pay off later in the story. They may introduce a line of dialogue that will hint at a backstory or foreshadow a future event. Or plant an object in Act I that can be resurrected for use in a completely different way in Act III. A small action, barely noticeable at the time, may foreshadow the moral dilemma the main character will ultimately face. Or they may erect various building blocks in the first few pages (time locks, motifs, taglines are but a few examined below) to twist around later to cause or make more meaningful the actions climaxing the film.

When they are included (not all stories have them) *subplots* are also structured with their own beginning, middle, and end. Sometimes they set up a competing desire in the main character (he gets A, he loses B, he gets B, he loses A). Or they may enrich the main plot and enlarge the characters. While in *As Good As It Gets*, Jack Nicholson's attraction to Helen Hunt remains the A-plot focus, his B-story relationship with his gay neighbor adds a humorous triangle to the love story and plays up Nicholson's personal quirks to mine further conflict from his bizarre lifestyle. But more often the subplot addresses "what the movie is *really* about" by carrying the theme and/or taking the conflict into the character's personal relationships. The love story in *Witness*, for example, completely overshadows the main action plot and becomes the controlling genre in the movie.

Most films have only one or two subplots, but some have three or four or more that build to a thematic climax, as in director Robert Altman's films, *Gosford Park*, *Nashville*, and *Short Cuts*, John Sayles' *Lone Star*, or Lawrence Kasden's *The Big Chill* or *Grand Canyon*. The goal of such films is a cohesive story that gathers smaller interrelated stories together for greater impact in the film's final act.

Structure, then, is the dominating principle in a screenplay; the bungee cord that prevents scenes from straying too far; what keeps springing everything back to point. There is no great mystery to it; if you play an instrument, if you can dance, you know structure. It's an instinctual grasp of rhythm and timing; it hits highs and lows; it never stands still, but it all stands together. And it must work its magic within a set time frame. From the ancient bards who went from town to town selling their stories like so many pots and pans, to the modern multiplex theaters that pack in audiences at two-hour intervals, storytellers have tailored their yarns to audience boredom levels. That's why some action producers call for a "whammy" (explosion, car chase, gun battle, or the like) every ten minutes or so in the plot.

But if the viewer does not need a car chase every ten minutes or even a happy ending, he does need to be captivated, surprised, and entertained. He puts himself in your hands and he expects to be taken on a skillfully designed thrill ride. And, he appreciates a satisfying ending—a reward of sorts—for having gone along on the journey.

TYPICAL 3-ACT STORY STRUCTURE FOR A FEATURE FILM

BEGINNING:

Set tone, context, and introduce the main character.

Introduce and involve other key characters but keep the focus on the main character.

Engage the story hook (a desire that is urgent, important, and difficult to achieve).

Introduce the opponent and set a dramatic time-lock for the problem's resolution.

Imply theme and raise the stakes to propel the story into the second act.

MIDDLE:

Problem intensifies as solution begins to evade the main character.

Temporary triumphs for main character, but opponent wins key confronts.

Subplots and/or relationships complicate and make main character's problems complex.

Character learns from failed options. Build clues and insights, but hold back key information from main character.

Make natural progression to the black moment when all victory seems impossible.

Main character changes/acts (perhaps confronting backstory) to reverse downward spiral.

ENDING:

A new stimulus kicks in to help main character in the final battle with opponent.

Final solution, based in clues built in, comes at lowest point in battle.

Climax is between main character and opponent.

Ending is a victory to audience satisfaction, unless main character changes goals.

One final dramatic twist is usually anticipated.

Tie up subplots, personal relationships, and moral point of the story (theme).

Main character ends at a different place from where he began.

A Strong Protagonist Spine

John F. Kennedy said "a man does what he must, in spite of obstacles, pressures and the opinions of mankind, and that is the basis of all human morality." In film (the ultimate morality play), events happen—sometimes disturbing, often morally ambiguous—which force a character to tap into his deepest reserves to overcome them. He may stumble, he may fall, but as he does he learns. And as he learns, his true character develops and he realizes he is more than what he has allowed himself to become. This physical and spiritual quest, these actions in pursuit of a goal, form the protagonist spine upon which the body of the movie rests.

Animated films clearly dramatize this journey toward self-discovery. In *Aladdin*, the song, "A Diamond in the Rough," tells the audience, via music, what the movie is all about—a true Prince placed by fate in the rags of a pauper. In *The Lion King*, the wise old monkey asks Simba, "Who are you?" Simba responds, "I thought I knew. Now I'm not so sure." The voice of his father later reminds him: "You are more than what you have become. Remember who you are." As with many films, Simba's revelation of his true destiny (and responsibilities as king) is the second major plot-turning point and powers the film into its final act.

Most screen stories are told from the main character's point of view. His actions not only drive the plot, but also bond the audience with the moral point of view the author wishes to impose. To accomplish this, the main character is typically introduced in one of three ways:

- **damaged** (as in *Leaving Las Vegas*, *Thelma & Louise*, or *The Verdict*),
- **happy** (but vulnerable—as in *North by Northwest*, *A Civil Action*, or *Jerry Maguire*), or
- **drifting through life without apparent purpose or happiness** (as in *Rocky*, *On the Waterfront*, or *Casablanca*).

The inciting incident will then upset his ordinary course of life, force him to react, and challenge who he is at the start of the film. The film then dissects and challenges the possibilities that exist for the character and allow him to adjust his actions, grow, and elevate his life accordingly. Most studio films apply the storytelling conventions of a 3-act structure to the main character's journey in the film:

- In Act I, the main character (usually morally strong, but weak and vulnerable in other ways) is introduced in his world. Whatever balance or order he has achieved in that world is upset when the inciting incident occurs. This gives him his goal or *conscious desire* and puts him into conflict with an opponent (stronger than the main character in many ways, but morally weak). This leads to the complications of Act II.

- Act II, which often illuminates the character's need or *unconscious desire*, is tied to the backstory. This results in a raising of the stakes—

the emotional or physical ante—and a greater and more obsessive desire, all seeming completely out of reach when the character suffers an apparent fatal defeat (sometimes called *The Black Moment*).

- Act III often kicks off with a personal "taking-stock" that challenges the ghosts that haunt the character from his backstory—the emotional core of the film—and gives him new confidence and focus to forge ahead against all odds. He then engages the opponent in a battle that decides all, often leaving him in a better, psychologically secure, place at the end of the film than he occupied when he began it.

All drama, in the final analysis, is about this quest of the main character to discover who he is and what he is made of when the chips are down. His desires, actions, and decisions are the driving force and focus of the plot. These actions and desires form the "spine" of the movie and propel it to its conclusion. Aristotle expressed in *Poetics* that the ordering of the incidents is the first duty of the writer—but those incidents (scenes) are not haphazard, but rather, connected by the motivated actions or unconscious desires of the main character.

I once got a sneak peek at the storyboards for an animated feature film. Scenes were typed on 3 × 5 cards and pinned to a corkboard. At the top of the board was a graph dedicated to the main character. As the story unfolded, the graph charted the character's progress toward his goal, scene by scene. (A character can only rise if he has fallen, but even as he spirals down there is hope, a chance to recover.) Thus, the *character arc* was formed, which peaks at the film's end (when the protagonist typically develops into a stronger person, with a greater understanding of himself and thus at a higher place in life). This progression of character actions is the spine that determines the logic and the strength of the underlying story—the very clothesline upon which the story is hung.

Tellingly, the lower half of the graph was dedicated to the viewer, who should be on an emotional roller coaster, too. Was he scared, happy, excited, sad? If he was on the edge of his seat too long, he was given a moment to sit back and relax, only to have his emotions rekindled in the next segment of the film. (Hence, the expression, "comic relief.") But the greater point is that the emotions of the audience were *directly tied* to the progress, the journey, the ups and downs, the arc, the growth chart of the main character.

Advanced Structure Tools

As we've seen, a well-told story is balanced and the ending possesses a certain inevitability. There is reason and logic behind events and we appreciate being given the clues necessary to divine the end, even if we were too caught up in the action to catch their significance when they first appeared. But give us less and we will feel cheated and manipulated. There is good reason for this. The writer has all the power in this relationship of ours.

Years ago, I was in the audience at the Writer's Guild for a screening of *No Way Out*. Kevin Costner starred as a CIA liaison officer in this taut thriller about a murder and cover-up that reached into the highest levels of government. It was a great film right up until the very end, when the writer delivered a final plot twist: Costner is revealed to be an undercover Russian spy. The collective groan from the writers in the audience over this "surprise ending" was a reaction to it being both totally gratuitous and completely out of left field—no clues were set up anywhere in the film to validate it. Of course, we know that a writer can make anything happen in a story, but for a twist to work requires *dramatic set up*. Absent that, it is like the writer is playing poker with us and, just before he lays down his cards, he announces that—guess what—sixes and eights are wild!

Audiences love to be surprised, as long as the writer prepares them for the surprise. Witness the twist endings of M. Night Shyamalan's *The Sixth Sense* or of Christopher McQuarrie's *The Usual Suspects*. Go back and view the movie over again and there will be the satisfaction that everything was plausible, logical, and right before our eyes, if only we had thought to look. The set up must be there for the payoff to be truly rewarding. Conversely, this is but another reason not to attempt the opening of your movie if you do not know the ending. How can you set up something you don't yet know will occur?

Tying endings and beginnings together is one of the structural challenges of screenwriting. Fortunately, a variety of structural devices exist to help balance the opening and ending and lend logic and inevitability to the climax. Used properly, these devices can be invaluable storytelling tools, but beware: used inexpertly to mask problems or weaknesses in the story, they tend to only call further attention to them. Some of the more common devices are:

- **The Storyteller (or narrator).** There are first-person narrators, third-person narrators, omnipotent narrators—even graphic presentations to open or close films, like the story crawl that leads off each *Star Wars* film, setting the sci-fi tone and feeding us exposition all in one large gulp. *Network* and *Casablanca* use opening newsreel type voiceovers to help authenticate the sorry state of the main character's world. In the gangster film, *Goodfellas*, the main character's voiceover lends sympathy to a basically unsympathetic thug. The first-person narration in the television series, *The Wonder Years*, contrasted the innocence of the boy we saw on screen with the mature irony of the adult remembering his youth. In *Taxi Driver*, it's our window into the twisted mind of Travis Bickle. In *Casino*, Director Martin Scorsese has so many characters talking over action without warning that he seemed to be parodying the device. One thing is certain: after a few years of being relegated to the bench by most screenwriters, narration is making a strong comeback. Once considered a lazy writer's means of telling the story without having to actually make up scenes to do so, we're experiencing a renaissance of characters talking over or even right into the camera (thank you, Woody Allen and Ferris Bueller).

At its best, this is a literary tool borrowed from first-person novels—where it directly reveals the character's inner thoughts and feelings. If the storyteller is the main character—let's say a detective as portrayed in the television series *Magnum P.I.*—we have the advantage of getting a broader picture of the strategies that are motivating his actions. Series creator Don Bellesario had a more creative use for the device though—as a tool for skipping over the boring parts of detective work (like interviewing suspects) by having Magnum dispense with them in a voiceover while the action stayed with the more audience-pleasing repartee between Magnum and his stuffy English friend, Higgins.

A storyteller can also help span long periods of time and various locations as in *The Great Gatsby*. In *Days of Heaven* the third-person narrator brought a wonderful tone and style to the film through the use of a Brooklyn twang to tell this Midwest period saga. Or narration can give an overview of the larger forces affecting the main character, as in *Platoon* or *The Shawshank Redemption*. It can be used as a plot device by making the act of telling the story have an effect on the outcome of the story—especially when the story goes on beyond the storyteller—as in *Road Warrior*. It can add depth of character, frame a story in time, pull together and unify disparate pieces of a long, episodic life, as in *Million Dollar Baby*. It can lend a literary feel to a beloved novel by repeating literal lines from the book—as in *A River Runs Through It* or *The Prince of Tides*. In short, it's a multi-purpose tool.

But for all these valuable cinematic uses, it's not a very cinematic tool. The reason: It fails to generate conflict and it disengages the audience from directly experiencing the action of the film. Instead, they are told what is happening on screen or the result of action already taken out of their sight (like the difference between witnessing a carjacking or reading about it in a newspaper). The best advice is to avoid using it to move the story forward by what is being related in the voiceover (Don Bellasario's use being a creative exception), and never use it in a mystery where suspense is crucial.

■ **Flashbacks.** These are scenes of events occurring prior to or previously in the story and inserted into the chronological timeline of the film. Used well, a flashback can help to start the story later and communicate information better than verbal exposition. The flashback in the middle of *Casablanca*, for example, allows the story to begin in Rick's café instead of Paris and conveys the essence of Rick's past relationship to Ilsa without Rick awkwardly (and out of character for him) telling it to some third party in the story.

In films such as *The Usual Suspects* or *The Man Who Shot Liberty Valance*, the central story *is* the flashback and the present scenes supply a crucial framing story, lending a reason and gravity to the telling of the story in the first place. For memory fragments or the dramatization of the main character's past trauma (his backstory), a flashback can be invaluable in showing rather than telling these crucial points of exposition. But often flashbacks (dream sequences too) are used by lazy writers to fill in gaps in the plot or supply easy motivation for an action otherwise without one. If flashbacks are not fully integrated into the structural framework of the film and used to further context and tension, it can stall the forward momentum of the story. My belief is that if your story truly *needs* the flashback to move forward, you should not use it. Find a way to tell the story in the present first; only then may you use a flashback to enrich the telling.

■ **Flashforwards.** These are scenes of future events inserted into the chronological timeline of the film. One excellent use of this device was in Atom Etoyan's *The Sweet Hereafter*, in which an attorney tries to gather clients for a lawsuit from among the small town survivors of a terrible bus crash in which many of the town's children perished. As the lawyer is a very guarded and private man, scenes in an airplane, chronologically occurring after the main events of the story, are brought forward to gain insight into his character. But this device is not often used as it can destroy the illusion that the main character has choices, and can reveal and render the dramatic outcome predetermined.

- **Foreshadowing.** The cause and effect relationship between scenes, sequences, even small visual moments and lines of dialogue, is what creates the sense of a well-told story and a complete movie experience: everything counts, everything is connected, nothing is wasted, it all adds up in the end. Something is said, an object is introduced, a look is exchanged, and later in the plot, when we almost forgot, it all comes back to haunt us. This device is closely allied with planting something in an early scene that will be used or pay off, perhaps in an entirely unexpected but completely logical way, in a later scene. At its best we will hardly take notice of the plant when it is first set before us—be too obvious and you are guilty of telegraphing it, making the writer seem less than adroit.

When Thelma packs her husband's gun in her purse in the beginning of *Thelma & Louise*—holding it at arm's length by two fingers, it is so alien to her—we can almost hear Chekhov warning us that a loaded gun onstage at the start of a play must be used before the play is over. Of course it must. When Q gives James Bond an exploding pen, is there any doubt that we must see it used? Reason tells us there is no way McMurphy can lift a bolted-down water fountain as he tries to rally his fellow patients in *One Flew Over the Cuckoo's Nest*. The scene is over—the fountain served its purpose. Man has his limits. We forget about it—until the very final frames of the movie, when the Chief, tall and strong and clearly in homage to the now lobotomized McMurphy, wrenches it loose from the floor and tosses it through the barred windows to make his escape to freedom.

- **Timelocks.** These are deadlines placed within the plot by which time something must be accomplished to avoid dire consequences. The audience can almost hear the clock ticking as options are tried and fail and the deadline approaches. The classic use of this device was in *High Noon*, at which time—as quick cuts to the town clock remind us—the gunfight is to occur on the streets of the town. In *War Games*, a computer is programmed to launch nuclear missiles in X minutes—which tick down dramatically—unless someone can find a way to stop it. In any mystery or crime drama, a time limit for solving the crime allows the dramatic tension to build. "If I don't catch the killer by Friday, my client on death row dies."

- **Motifs and Taglines.** These are balancing devices involving an image or sound (motifs) or a line of dialogue (tagline) that appear early in a story, is often repeated at least three times, and gains significance over the course of the story. The motif of water signals the calm and fury of nature lending metaphor to the scenes of a failed marriage in *Shoot the Moon*. Grain provides the metaphor for community in *Witness* and is used to seal the villain's fate in the end. In Frederick Raphael's *Two For The Road*, we take a road trip with a married couple (through flashbacks) from the joy of when they first met to their present marital problems. When they are falling in love, they observe two lovers jump in a fountain naked and one says, "Who would do something like that?" The other answers "Married people." Years later, bickering after a car accident, they see two people at lunch saying nothing to each other. The same question is posed, but, sadly, the answer is also the same, "Married People." In *Driving Miss Daisy*, a black gentlemen takes his orders from the white lady he is employed to chauffeur with "Yes, Ma'am," the words of an employee to a boss. Later the same words are those spoken friend to friend, and when delivered at the end the movie to a dying old woman, they are clearly spoken with love, punching up the emotional catharsis for the audience.

- **Montages.** A rapid succession of shots, a montage can be useful *if not overused*. Serves a good function as a series of establishing shots to give an overall sense of time and place. Or to show the passage of time, as in *Notting Hill*, for example, with Hugh Grant crossing busy Portabello Road as the seasons of a year change in his path. Or to condense the arc of a relationship into a few choice visuals (perhaps connected by a musical number) that fluidly show what a half-dozen fully scripted scenes might stumble over. As music videos became popular, so did montages as the backdrop for a song that could cross-promote the movie. But, like dream sequences (the use of which I associate more with tired stories than tired characters), they too often signal a laziness or inability on the part of the writer to fully dramatize the action. Or a shortcut to exposition the writer knows in his heart is so damned boring and repetitious he resists scripting it.

Scenes and Sequences

From a little acorn, a great oak grows. That's the secret of writing a movie. You start like any good gardener by marking off your territory: what is the film you want to write and who is it about? You research the landscape of your story, you map out the seeds of a plot, and then you begin to plant. Little beats follow little beats into full scenes, scenes that in turn cause other scenes to happen. Those scenes join together and form sequences and ten or twelve of those later you find that your little bits and pieces—those little seeds you planted long ago—have grown into an organic and majestic first draft screenplay.

As movies have structure—beginnings, middles, and ends—so do scenes and sequences. Each scene is composed of a series of beats, each beat representing a single action or emotion or exchange of dialogue. These form mini-movies in a way, telling mini-stories, delivering information, involving and developing characters, and creating and evoking emotion—much like a commercial on television, even one that runs only 15 seconds.

Usually, only about 50 or so scenes (as distinguished from shots—many shots or angles can make up a scene) can comprise an entire movie (not counting establishing shots or small transitional scenes that may, for example, facilitate entrances and exits).

Each scene is announced and introduced by a *slugline*, indicating whether the scene is inside or outside (INT. or EXT.), the location, and when it takes place (DAY or NIGHT). The body of a scene contains scene description and/or dialogue, the purpose of which is to develop the character and reveal essential information *to move the story forward*. The writer must determine the true beginning of the scene—the *point of attack*—and the earliest, most economical and dramatic way to end the scene and lead into the next. But the single most important thing to remember is that *something happens in every scene*.

Ten important questions to ask when writing or outlining scenes for your movie are:

1. What is the purpose of this scene—what do I want to show or accomplish?

2. Is this the most visual and dramatic way of expressing this information?

3. Does this scene advance the story—i.e. do I need this scene?

4. Is there a natural cause and effect from the scene before and after?

5. What does this scene set up or pay off?

6. What is the subtext of this scene?

7. Is this a scene an actor will want to play?

8. What can be cut from this scene?

9. Does this scene go as far as it could go dramatically?

10. Is this still the movie I first set out to write?

A *sequence* is a group of such scenes that have a common story-telling purpose, usually linked around a single action or undertaking, becoming another movie within the movie. Examples are the long wedding sequences that open *The Godfather* and *The Deerhunter*. Both set a clear tone, introduce many characters (principal and supporting), set up and foreshadow events to come, inter-cut between activities in various places in and around the event, establish key relationships, and set the wheels of the plot in motion. One or two such sequences can form a first act, maybe four or five can form a second act, and it is not uncommon for a movie's final act, especially in an action/adventure film, to be comprised totally of a single sequence as well.

The value of linking scenes into sequences is that it highlights the causal relationship between them and gives a cohesive and easy-to-follow structure to the story. It also prevents a film from rambling along episodically, each scene seeming to bob on its own, like an island in a vast sea. In *Mr. Holland's Opus*, for example, the story follows the life a high school music teacher through many years, with a family we see born and grow and a series of students on whom he has a life-changing impact. This type of story is always in danger of losing dramatic momentum—e.g. students graduate after 4 years and any emotional investment we placed in them or their relationship to the main character is lost as a new group enters school. But in this case the writer interwove a series of sequences—linking the family drama with the teaching drama with a third drama involving the school staff—and the result was a series of mini-movies that each impacted and built upon the other and seamlessly added up to one emotionally satisfying experience.

Action sequences are one of the biggest challenges a writer faces. Must you choreograph every blow in a fight scene, every twist and turn in a car chase? Before an action sequence makes it into the hands of stunt coordinators, *it's the writer's job* to fill the story with original, exciting, suspenseful action, unexpected obstacles, obstructions, reversals, and barriers. Something like a horse chasing a motorcycle through the crowded streets of a city into a swanky hotel. But talking about action belies its raw physicality and evocative language, so here's the sequence from *True Lies*, screenplay by Claude Zidi and Simon Michaël and Didier Kaminka, starring Arnold Schwarzenegger. We join the action at page 43.

INT./EXT. GIB'S CAR—NIGHT
Gib is weaving furiously through traffic. He slides into a turn.

GIB
Copy that.

HARRY
And make it fast. My horse is getting tired.

ON GIB, mouthing "Your horse?"

EXT. STREET—NEXT TO PARK—NIGHT

Malik explodes through the bushes and out onto the street. Cars skid around him, out of control. He turns south. Weaving through TRAFFIC. Harry leaps the hedgerow behind Malik and gallops among the spun-out cars. He goes right over the hood of one blocking his path. The driver ducks as the horse's hoof cracks the windshield.

EXT. STREET/ HYATT REGENCY HOTEL—NIGHT

Up ahead traffic is stopped jammed tight at a light. Malik goes into the oncoming traffic lanes, which are empty. Gib's car slides around the corner in a blare of horns and comes barreling down the street toward him. Gib cranks the wheel and slides the car broadside, blocking both lanes. Malik locks up the brakes and the bike slides to a stop. Then the terrorist pops the clutch and wheels the bike around—jumping the curb and going straight into the lobby of the HYATT REGENCY HOTEL.

BELLMEN and GUESTS scatter as the bike roars right at them. The sliding doors are opening for a bellman coming out with bags and Malik blasts past him into the lobby.

Harry ducks, galloping through the doors after him.

INT. HOTEL—NIGHT

Acres of marble and red carpet. Liveried PORTERS. GUESTS dressed for evening, the men in suits, diamonds on the women. And sudden pandemonium as Malik roars through the lobby, with Harry charging along behind him. Malik guns it across the lounge, knocking over tables. He gets air at the top of the steps going up to the RESTAURANT.

Harry swerves to avoid a panicking guest and finds himself careening toward the JAZZ QUARTET at a full gallop. He gathers the animal and leaps (in glorious SLOW MOTION) over the bassist, who is diving for the carpet. Harry and horse land deftly and then he urges his mount right up the steps after Malik.

INT. HOTEL RESTAURANT—NIGHT

Malik roars between the tables, looking around wildly for a way out. Harry charges in, ducking to avoid the chandelier. Waiters, trays, dinners, tables… everything seems to be flying at once as people dive out of the way.

INT. HOTEL—MAIN HALL—NIGHT

Malik skids out into the main hall by another door and sees—THE ELEVATORS. The door is just closing on one of them. He guns it and slides through the doors.

Harry rides out of the restaurant in time to catch a glimpse of Malik as the doors close.

INT. SCENIC ELEVATOR—NIGHT

Harry canters the horse into the next elevator, which has just been boarded by an OLDER COUPLE. He has to practically lie down on the horse to fit through the door. The animal barely fits, nose to tail, in what turns out to be—

A GLASS ELEVATOR with a view of the whole atrium of the hotel as it rises, right to the top of the building. Harry looks through the glass at the elevator car next to him, fifteen feet away. Malik is inside, punching a button. He glances up and sees Harry. Their eyes meet for a moment, just before Malik's car ascends rapidly. Malik's malevolent glare is etched on Harry's retinas.

The older couple is jammed against the side-wall by Harry's panting, snorting horse. It clomps around the tight elevator. The woman is trying to crawl between her husband and the wall.

                    HARRY
        Can you just press the top floor, please.

The man nods mutely and complies. Their elevator takes off, rising after Malik's.

INT. HOTEL LOBBY—NIGHT

Gib runs in with Faisil and Keough. They follow the path of destruction, growing more and more amazed. Gib yells to one of the porters.

                    GIB
            The guy on the horse?!

The porter points at the elevators.

INT./ EXT. SCENIC ELEVATORS—NIGHT

Harry has slid off the horse to get next to the control panel. He can look up at an angle and see Malik in the car above him. His thumb hovers over the emergency stop button. If Malik gets out at any floor, Harry will stop. Malik can look down and see this—he knows Harry's got him. He just keeps going, floor after floor, using the time to think.

The older woman is just staring, trying not to breathe. The horse flicks her in the face with his tail.

INT./EXT. ROOFTOP—NIGHT

A spectacular view of the city. TRACKING WITH Malik as he comes out of the elevator, rides to the far edge of the roof and slides to a stop. He looks down twenty stories.

The second elevator arrives. The doors part and Harry comes out, his Glock poised and ready. He sees Malik revving his bike. The terrorist brodies the bike into a fast one-eighty and speeds back toward the edge of the roof. Amazingly he increases speed, ROARING RIGHT OFF THE EDGE, ARCING THE BIKE SUICIDALLY OUT INTO SPACE!

Harry rides to the edge in time to see Malik on his bike CLEAR A 60 FOOT JUMP and SPLASH INTO THE ROOFTOP POOL of a LOWER BUILD-ING next to the hotel!

Harry is out of control now, seeing the guy get away. He wheels his mount and charges across the roof to get some running space. Then he turns again, back toward the edge Malik jumped from. He kicks the horse's flanks and yells HAAHH!! The horse's hoofs thunder on the roof as they go full tilt toward the edge.

But a horse is not a motorcycle. It is slightly smarter. It slams its front hoofs down together, stopping suddenly. Harry goes right over its head. He flies forward, almost right off the roof. He slams to the edge with his legs dan-gling over, holding onto a piece of pipe with one hand. His Glock tumbles down into the darkness.

Harry sees Malik far below, climb out of the pool, running to the roof door of the other building. Getting away. Harry clambers up onto his own roof, breathing hard. He walks over to the horse.

> HARRY
> What the hell were you thinking? We had
> the guy and you let him get away.

He looks into the horse's innocent brown eyes. Pats its neck fondly.

> HARRY
> What kind of cop are you?

"Reel" Dialogue (Movie-speak)

Forgive the cliché, but a picture is worth a thousand words. Unlike novels or stage plays, movies don't have to rely on words to tell the story. In fact, the first movies were silent. If today's action blockbusters are any indication, we may be heading back that way. And for good reason—communication in film is primarily a non-intellectual, emotional process. The ideas expressed in film are best expressed through dramatization, not by stating them out loud. It's an intuitive process—one that appeals directly to the heart.

But ask an actor what he reads first in a script and he'll tell you the dialogue. Ask a producer or agent or studio exec and you'll get the same answer—they read the first few pages and after that their eyes tend to skip down the page to the dialogue exchanges. That's because the first job of a marketable screenplay is to attract talent (in the world of movies, when we say "talent" we mean actors) and the clearest window into the heart, mind, and emotions of the characters the talent is asked to play is screen dialogue.

Screen dialogue is fundamentally different from words spoken in stage plays, or certainly in everyday life. Stage actors have little besides words to tell the story and to give nuance and depth to their characters, so long speeches are sometimes necessary. In film, everything from a wayward glance to a series of quick cuts in a montage can fill those needs. And though movie-speak may sound like the way people speak in life, that's only a creative construct—put five minutes of movie dialogue up against what real people say in a five-minute conversation around a dinner table and you would see the difference.

Characters in a film converse to communicate plot and character—not to pass the time. They cut to the heart of conversation and never waste words. (Six sentences on screen can seem a lengthy speech.) Heroes, in particular, like to act, not talk. When characters do speak, they have a tight agenda: movie-speak is not repetitious, doesn't go on and on, doesn't interrupt (often), doesn't beat around the bush (another cliché), is not full of awkward pauses, non-sequiturs, mindless chit-chat, or even polite formalities like saying goodbye at the end of a phone call. Because movie-speak isn't real dialogue at all—it only mimics real dialogue. The goal is dialogue that *feels* real. Movie-speak is direct, terse, purposeful, informal, and often delivers just the perfect turn of a phrase we might say if we could consider our words, write and rewrite them, and polish them to a shine.

Words in film serve the same story function as the scene in which they are spoken:

- to advance the plot
- supply information
- reveal character, and
- foster dramatic conflict.

Since you have the medium of film at your disposal, use it. Express your story in cinematic terms. Convert a talky scene into one with more action; don't have a speech tell the story, dramatize it. When your film plays in other countries, you don't want it to be a reading assignment. The whole world loves brevity. It saves time and is easier on the eyes. (Yes, eyes. Audiences read lips when they watch a movie. Ever see a film where the soundtrack is a millisecond out of sync with the actors speaking? You didn't realize you were lip-reading, did you?)

As an exercise, cut out all dialogue and see what you have left. Do the visuals tell the story? Is it at least an interesting visual experience? If not, take the characters out of cars and apartments and off phones or analyst couches and have them talk while jogging across Central Park or shooting hoops in a YMCA. Or juxtapose necessary exposition with bizarre locations or circumstances, such as a cop questioning a doctor about an affair with a victim as the doctor autopsies that very corpse in a pathology lab.

With special effects and CGI driving many plots, more is asked of less dialogue than ever before. The few precious scenes in which characters actually speak with each other in between the quick cuts and rapid pace of action sequences is often all we have to discover their character and complexity. Yet writers cannot give in to the temptation to use those moments to expound on the theme or wax poetic. Film is a visual medium. Long exchanges of dialogue or lengthy speeches can bring the visuals to a grinding halt. And actors will resist saying anything at all ("Here, take my sword.") if they can simply perform the action or give a reaction (a nod of the head instead of having to say "yes").

Of course, there are wonderful examples of long speeches lighting up a movie: Robert Shaw in *Jaws* revealing his scars along with the personal source of his hatred for sharks; Jack Nicholson exploding on the witness stand in *A Few Good Men* and telling Tom Cruise that "you can't handle the truth"; a rain-soaked Peter Finch, in *Network*, informing the world that he's "mad as hell and not going to take it any more"; Mel Gibson in *Braveheart* rallying his troops for a battle that looks certain to be a suicide mission; Al Pacino giving his final statement to the jury in "*... And Justice for All*", pointing to his own client and saying "the son of a bitch is guilty!" But these classic movie moments are memorable *precisely* because such speeches are *rare* and, even more rarely, done well. If you feel you must do a long speech, try and make it a turning point in your movie and pace it out through interweaving reaction shots or cuts to parallel action.

One important caveat: While dialogue is used to indirectly *expose* a character's feelings, needs, flaws, and motivations, never have the character *state* any of those things directly because *we won't believe him*. Real character revelation is almost squeezed out reluctantly through *conflict*. In *Thelma & Louise* we learn about Louise's terrible experiences in Texas through the eyes of the detective on her tail. Thelma figures it out on her own somewhere toward the end, but Louise never mentions a word about it. In *The Verdict*, Galvin's friend and ally tells his girlfriend how things went down long ago and how Galvin got royally screwed, but Galvin's not in the bar at the time. To be there or mention it himself would not only be self-serving, but would make him into a whiner.

And though Paul Newman can get away with doing it in the speech-friendly context of a final argument to a jury in *The Verdict*, avoid having your characters be mouthpieces for your theme, or have them tell us what we're seeing, or worse, what we've already seen!

Here is a *twelve-point strategy* for creating good screen dialogue:

STRATEGY

1. **Characters don't talk to each other, they argue.**

   No pleasant chitchat, please, and don't have your characters preach to us. Dialogue maintains the tension and dramatic conflict between the characters. Especially if forced to reveal expository information, having characters scream it at each other may be your best choice.

2. **Give each of your characters his/her own voice.**

   They should speak as one would with their education, background, occupation, personality, experience, country accent, or regional dialect. They have their own characteristic rhythms, their own sense of humor or lack thereof, and they react to situations in their own unique way. Mel Gibson's psycho cop in *Lethal Weapon* will respond to a crisis, a woman, a felon, or order a sandwich much differently than his more grounded partner, Danny Glover.

3. **Limit parenthetical character directions.**

   They are an admission of failure by the writer to have written the line or the scene powerfully or accurately enough. It's better to risk the director or actors coming to the wrong conclusion than to give into the fear that makes you want to control the words. Tolerate uncertainty. Let the actors discover the work for themselves. Our accidents are God's purpose.

"No one in the world tries to cry except bad actors," veteran performer Martin Landau points out. "Good actors try not to cry. No one tries to laugh except bad actors; people try not to laugh. No one tries to be drunk; drunks try to be sober. How a character hides his feelings tells us who he is."

4. **When you've cut your dialogue to the bone, cut another 25%.**

"The art of dialogue is in its terseness," advises Lajos Egri in *The Art of Dramatic Writing*. *Economy* is so crucial to good dialogue that I'm making the point again. Steven Zaillian, who wrote the screenplay for *Schindler's List*, said his first draft includes everything the characters have to say on the subject. Then he cuts and cuts, until if he cut one more word, the dialogue would make no sense whatsoever.

5. **Avoid talking heads.**

Give actors physical *business* to do. Keep their hands busy. And tie the business into their character. No one smokes a cigarette or takes a drink in a movie without purpose. In *The Graduate*, Mrs. Robinson uses a cigarette in bed to punctuate key dialogue, allow for tense pauses while exhaling, and as a weapon to threaten Benjamin when he announces he'll take out Elaine.

6. **Don't bring out the home movies.**

In *From Russia with Love*, James Bond's ally lights a cigar and tells a tied-up enemy "I've had a long and interesting life. Would you like me to tell you about it?" He was being sarcastic, of course. Genre can also determine dialogue—heroes in action films want to walk the talk, not vice-versa. And when they speak they want everyone to lean close and pay attention. Know someone who talks a lot? Others tend to tune him out. As opposed to the person who never says much at all: when he speaks, everyone else shuts up and listens.

7. **Limit profanity, racism, and misogyny.**

If that's the way your character is wired, fine. But just a little in the script goes a long way—no sense in alienating your readers—and will be enough to tip the actor or director willing to take it to another level.

Writer/director Kevin Rodney Sullivan (*Barbershop 2, How Stella Got Her Groove Back*) puts it this way: "I think when you get people in a dark room for two hours, that is a privilege... Now, if you're going to celebrate violence, marginalize women, make racial statements, unanswered, you are abusing that privilege."

8. **Let your characters be understood.**

Accents, dialects, inflections, and slang can be indicated with a word here or there to give *the flavor* of the speech. A Frenchman may toss in a "Oui, Monsieur" instead of "Yes, sir", or his accent or language may be noted once in the character's description or in a parenthetical when he first speaks. But don't try and mimic a Scotsman or a Louisiana bayou accent in every line—it'll drive a reader crazy. It's better to note characteristics of speech, such as foreigners rarely using contractions: "You can not go there," instead of "You can't go there."

Filmmakers find their own solution to language concerns. In *The Hunt for Red October*, Sean Connery portrays a Russian submarine commander. He and his crew briefly speak their native tongue to convey the reality of the situation, but obviously that can't continue. In a shot, we fade from him speaking Russian and when he comes back in focus, he and the crew are speaking English. We all got the point.

---

9. **Avoid clichés and prompts.**

"Drop the gun. Do it. Now!" Or the hero grabbing the fence and screaming, "Nooooooo!" as his partner/lover/friend suffers some horrible fate. Or an extra making an innocent comment only to have the main character say, "What did you just say?" before revealing his brilliant plan. And don't let characters repeat lines just to fill space in the script: "I told him to go home." "You told him to go home?" Or ask questions just to prompt an answer: "So, what did you do then?"

10. **Avoid introductions.**

Cut right into a scene. Actors don't like to say "yes" or "no" or "hello" or "goodbye" or introduce themselves. Let names spill out naturally—and only use them at all for principal characters. Don't use "well" or "so" or "actually" or other such openings either.

11. **Limit names and questions.**

It's awkward and unnatural for characters to call others by name in a dialogue exchange: "Well, Tom, I don't know, do you?" "No, Clara, I never found out." People don't use names every time they address someone. And main characters don't play the straight man for jokes and they don't stand around in scenes asking leading questions like "Really?" and "Is that what he said?" or "What happened then?" so supporting players can draw the clever conclusions.

12. **Hold a cast reading.**

Cast your friends, though actors are better if you can get them. Nothing improves dialogue like hearing someone new to the script try and get his mouth around the words. Sit back and listen, don't comment, don't try to direct, don't fill everyone in on the hidden meaning behind your clever motif. And don't distract them by taking notes. (Blue pencil reminders of where they fidgeted, their eyes glazed over, or they got up to stretch are fine—but try to avoid nodding maniacally and feverishly starting your brilliant rewrite.) In fact, don't do or say anything except serve refreshments and say thank you when they're done. You've just been to school.

Subtext

I've been holding something back from you—the one dialogue tip so crucial it needs its own subsection: *What you say in dialogue is never as important as what you don't say.* The subtext gives life to the text. Screen dialogue must be emotionally charged, informal, purposeful, economical, and—here's the part I left out—*brimming with subtext.*

And the key to understanding subtext is this: *Subtext is directly determined by context.* In HBO's *Curb Your Enthusiasm,* for example, series creator/star Larry David writes a detailed story outline—perhaps 7 or 8 pages long for each episode, but doesn't include a single line of dialogue. The context— the comedic situation that he places the characters in—provides not only the framework for the intersecting stories, but also a comedy setup so strong that the dialogue can be *improvised* by the actors. Nothing need be particularly witty or clever; actors can give honest reactions to the situation they're in, and it works!

An acting coach gave me the following non-specific (no story) actor's dialogue. As you read, picture a couple that just returned from an idyllic honeymoon.

HE
Good morning.

SHE
Good morning.

HE
How do you feel?

SHE
Great.

HE
I'm sure.

SHE
What do you want for breakfast?

HE
Whatever.

SHE
I'll fix you some scrambled eggs.

HE
Fine.

SHE
You going to work this morning?

HE
Have to.

SHE
Oh.

HE
Do you want me to stay at home?

SHE
It's up to you.

HE
Can't.

SHE
Like I said, it's up to you.

I'm sure you can picture our couple very much in love and not wishing to part on this morning after their honeymoon. But read it again. Only this time change the situation: The couple has been married for five years and just had their first, much-wanted child. This morning is one week after they lost that child to sudden infant death syndrome. Go ahead, read it again.

Still hold true for you? To borrow from Bill Clinton, can you feel their pain? Their depression? It works, right? Okay, one last time. Now it's the morning after the wife has found out that her husband has been having an affair with his secretary. He knows that she knows and she knows that he knows that she knows. Okay, read it again.

I'm betting you made it work there too. Maybe you even put in a little inflection when she said, "You going to *work* this morning?" But what made this dialogue work for us was not the words themselves—open to interpretation and dramatically weak as they are—but the *context*—the dramatic situation in which we placed the characters, and the emotions, and underlying feelings that truly motivate their statements and responses.

What characters say is the product of who they are in the story and the situation they find themselves in. If the context is dramatically strong enough, you can script practically any words. Two adult women sitting across from each other at lunch is not a very dramatic scene premise. But even ad-libbed dialogue will suffice when one (a lower-class white woman married to a white man) has just discovered the other is the sophisticated daughter she never knew she had—and that she's black! (*Secrets and Lies*)

As long as the audience is let in on the underlying subtext, they can interpret the true meaning—and hidden psychological need—behind what the characters say and do. This helps make the audience less a passive voyeur and more an active participant in the drama before them. They learn, like good detectives, who the characters really are as they decipher their words and actions in the story based on the clues they are given.

What does a character mean when he says, "I love you?" That depends on who they are in the story and what their intentions in the moment may be. Are they trying to be honest, manipulative, polite, deceiving, placating, or kind? Maybe they mean, like Jack Nicholson's character in *Terms of Endearment*, "Sure I love you, baby," which might not be exactly what Shirley MacLaine hoped to hear. Was he trying to deflect her interest with humor or was he being deliberately cruel or perhaps masking his own fears of commitment and getting too close? Who he is in the story up to that point will be our clue. Because we understand that people tend to avoid addressing emotional issues directly, we will substitute what we believe is the real emotion behind the words they say.

In good writing, it is the unspoken emotions that convey the deeper meaning. Ever attend a funeral when the deceased's relative is weeping and gnashing her teeth? We feel horrible for her but we detach ourselves because *she is doing the crying for us.* But if she delivers the eulogy with measured words and quiet courage and, suddenly, her voice cracks just a little—look out, open the floodgates, there won't be a dry eye in the room.

In *The River*, when Mae and Tom Garvey (Sissy Spacek and Mel Gibson) argue in bed over the dwindling fortunes of their farm, we know their argument is really over the worsening state of their marriage and we feel the deeper levels of emotions they cannot say to each other. But, if either character was to come out and say, "Hey, we have a problem in our marriage. Let's talk about it," it would undercut the life-like, participatory quality of the drama and, hence, the power of the scene.

This "on-the-nose" dialogue, as it is known—a character saying exactly what it is he wants without subtext or context helping define the words—is to be avoided at all times.

A Cathartic Ending

It's near the end of *Alien*. Ripley is in the shuttle-craft. She watches the final destiny of the mother ship as it scatters to the stars, presumably taking the remains of her crew and the alien with it. She strips to her underwear to prepare for the long sleep on her voyage back to Earth. Then, from behind her, the creature rises, chewing on a large piece of flesh. It has been in the shuttle-craft all along. Looking for a place to hide, Ripley dives for the open door of a small locker containing a pressure suit. Hurls herself inside. Pulls on the helmet, latches it into place. Turns on the oxygen valve. The creature rises. Faces the locker.

As written by Dan O'Bannon, this is a perfect battle scenario—compromise is impossible, the main character and the antagonist must fight and only one can win. The audience can, for that critical moment, doubt the ending that we thought was ordained—there is simply no way Ripley can possibly survive! (She does.)

But such endings are difficult. We must know them in advance in order to set them up and yet some stubbornly evolve even as we script them due to the subtle way characters and circumstances alter over the course of the story. Nowhere in Buck Henry's final draft screenplay of *The Graduate* is there any hint that he intended for Benjamin and Elaine to be anything but deliriously happy sitting at the back of that bus at the film's end. Director Mike Nichols tells us he directed Dustin Hoffman and Katherine Ross to "get on the bus and laugh." But what we got instead is an enigmatic ending that was as unexpected as it was classically perfect for the tone and final moments of the film.

To "feel right," endings must do more than logically follow everything that has gone before and wrap up every plot and subplot that has preceded them. They should also maintain the integrity of the character and story arcs and climax with a "final button" scene that conveys the feeling the writer wants the audience to leave the theater with. Michael Corleone, sitting all alone, the last brother, at the end of *The Godfather II*. A long line of cars snaking its way through the pitch black night to a phantom baseball diamond in an Iowa cornfield in *Field of Dreams*. Or those final moments in a fog shrouded airport in *Casablanca*, when Humphrey Bogart looks into Ingrid Bergman's eyes one last time as he sends her off on a plane with her husband, just because it's the right thing to do. And even that kind of scene only works if the audience has identified with and built up a deep reservoir of emotional attachment to these unforgettable characters, so deep that the audience shares in the characters' emotions as their own.

From the story hook on, the ending may be inevitable, but how we get there is not. Most main characters are given a lot of obstacles and life baggage to overcome. Most will hold fast in the face of great adversity and battle down blind paths where sometimes an awful price awaits even the victorious. But it is only as the struggle becomes personal to them, as it burrows into the very core of their humanity, that it becomes personal with us too. That's the moment we truly suspend our disbelief—it's no longer a movie and these aren't fictional characters anymore. They represent us—our hopes, dreams, and fears are tied together with theirs. For the final outcome to have the power to affect us deeply, we only ask that it be the honest result of all that has gone on before.

Most moviegoers want happy endings. It's the can-do American way—a light at the end of every tunnel, every enemy defeated, no past too dark to overcome, and every hooker gets a second chance. Who didn't root for

Richard Gere to rescue his poor Maiden at the end of *Pretty Woman*? After falling in love with Julia Roberts, the audience may not have responded well to the darker but more realistic ending of the original screenplay that spawned the movie *3,000*.

But make no mistake: Audiences want the characters to *earn* those happy endings, not have them tacked on to garner higher test audience scores. And they'll still turn out for a solid drama with a dark side, like the gut-wrenching tragedy of a double suicide in *House of Sand and Fog*, or a young cop uncovering the severed head of his sweet wife in *Se7en*, or the thematically-linked disasters that pile one on the other to plague the principal characters in the multilayered *Crash*.

Yet, with all the myriad tasks the ending must fulfill, every film journey has only three possible conclusions: win, lose, or draw. Audiences want a cathartic release for the investment of their time and emotions, so a draw is pretty much unacceptable. If the writer has done his job well, any other ending, even a "surprise" ending, is as inevitable (though only in hindsight) as it is satisfying.

Much was made of the shock ending of *Thelma & Louise*, taking their own lives by plunging their car over the Grand Canyon. But given the chain of events leading up to it, was any other ending viable? Could the women have surrendered? For the most part, the audience wanted an emotional payoff, not an end scroll telling us that, for example, Thelma got two years of a suspended sentence and Louise returned to waitressing after serving four years for manslaughter. Could they have escaped? Escape would hardly have been credible given a plot that has the two hurdling toward a grand precipice at the end of a desert plain with police forces from three states in hot pursuit. Should they have been gunned down? The tone of the movie and the audience's empathy with the characters would have been violated (besides, it was already done in *Bonnie & Clyde*). At its core, Thelma and Louise were characters trapped in a world in which the determinants of law and society were so strong that redemption could only be achieved by rejecting those determinants as false and by having them take charge of their own destinies. The ending validated this for the audience and so was accepted. Or, this could be looked at as winning by losing, as in *Rocky* (he loses the fight but gets the girl) or *North Dallas Forty* (he gives up football but gets a life) or … *And Justice For All* (he loses the case but gains some measure of self-respect). As contrasted with losing by winning, as in *The Godfather Part II*, where Michael has defeated all his enemies, but at the cost of losing his family.

Even in films in which the ending is not in doubt, the tone of the film must be respected. For example, in *The Lion King*, the audience easily could predict that the lion cub, Simba, would grow to adulthood and defeat his evil Uncle Scar in a final battle and thus regain his kingdom. But how? In one scenario, Simba, a healthy, brave young lion, could kill Scar, an old, weak lion (and his uncle, no less). The audience might cheer for the moment, but something would sit uneasily with them: It wouldn't be a fair fight. Instead, Simba judiciously bans Scar from the kingdom. But the writers knew that while this punishment was "humane," the audience would feel deprived of a real catharsis (after all, Scar planned and carried out the murder of Simba's father). So, a final battle ensued in which Scar double-crossed his own gang (the merry but deadly hyenas), rewarded Simba's kindness by tossing hot ashes in his eye, and caused his own demise by unintentionally catapulting himself into his band of revengeful hyenas. This scenario appeased the audience's desire for vengeance while preserving Disney's requisite family values—and, more importantly, met and satisfied audience expectations.

Audience Expectations

As evidenced by the example in *The Lion King*, the audience builds many subconscious expectations over the course of a film. Screenwriting legend Paddy Cheyefsky addressed this, while first acknowledging the four basic plot questions:

- Who is your main character?
- What does he want?
- What's keeping him from getting it?
- How does he get it?

To which he added one more:

- What does the audience want for him?

Whatever fate a writer envisions for his characters, Cheyefsky knew the writer must also walk in the shoes of the audience, which has its own expectations for characters they care about.

Imagine a film in which Clint Eastwood is stalked by an escaped murderer he put in jail years before. Imagine also that he is a widower with a five-year-old daughter. Finally, imagine that the writer, reaching that tough second act curtain, decides to have the stalker kill Clint's daughter. He's thinking this will propel the action into the third act and whip the audience into a frenzy rooting for Clint's revenge. The writer has just committed the cardinal sin of misreading audience expectations. Screen villains usually lose; we know that. But, after coming to care for the little girl, she is now irreplaceable to the audience and they would emotionally "check out" of the film at the point of her death. Clint's character, unable to save his own daughter, would be rendered powerless—a flaw that could not be redeemed by any kind of revenge killing.

Or take the film *Black Rain*, in which the writer failed to anticipate or properly manipulate the affection the audience would feel for the likable Andy Garcia, partner to Michael Douglas' street-wise cop. When the two travel to Tokyo to pursue a Japanese gangster, Garcia endears himself to his Japanese handler (and to the audience by proxy) by singing Karaoke together in the film's lightest moment. Seconds later, he is beheaded in the parking lot by some nameless, faceless villains while Michael Douglas looks on helplessly, screaming, "*NOOOOOO!*" The author doubtless felt this would both raise the stakes and the rooting interest for Douglas. *WROOOOONG!* With Garcia dead, the film evaporated into a revenge/chase movie in which there was never any doubt about the outcome—an outcome that left the audience cold and feeling emotionally cheated by Garcia's pointless slaughter.

But one writer got it right. In *Witness*, the frankly overused "corruption in the police department" main plot sets up the thematically crucial love story that is at the heart of the film. In the "fish out of water" scenario, a hardened Philadelphia police detective being hunted down by elements in his own force must go underground in a pacifistic Amish community to protect a small boy who was witness to a murder and can finger the cop who did it. The detective is cared for and sheltered by the boy's beautiful mother and thus the audience expectation of a thrilling love affair is set in motion. Except the author knew he had a problem.

How can the film end? The audience knows the bad guys and the detective will battle and the good guy will win. There's no real mystery there. We can also be fairly certain the lovers, Harrison Ford and Kelly McGillis, aren't going to die, and most certainly not the little boy (for the reasons we just set forth above). But what rooting interest exists in the love story? Would we really want this sweet Amish widow to leave behind her family, her bucolic farm life, and her community and uproot her son to go and live with a violent detective in the mean streets of Philadelphia? Or, would we truly believe or root for this tough street cop suddenly remaking himself into a gentleman farmer joining his woman in an Amish lifestyle? And how would we feel if the two parted at the end, leaving the poor widow with a small son, who had given herself so selflessly to this man, abandoned on her farm? None of these are very satisfying outcomes for an audience and having Ford catch the bad cops is not likely to provide consolation.

But the writer anticipated that. Early on, a gentle, kind, strong, and committed Amish man, played by the handsome and charismatic ex-dancer Alexander Godunov, is introduced as a rival for McGillis' affections. Yet neither Ford nor Godunov take actions or hold animosity against each other. Instead, they bond as buddies, sitting for lunch side by side after raising a barn together. And in the movie's end, when Ford leaves alone, as he must, to return to his life—as he drives down the path away from McGillis' farm in the final shot of the movie—there is trusty Godunov with his hoe on his shoulder, trudging up the very same path. And we know in our hearts that McGillis will be fine and the boy will have a good father.

And because the writer knew the ending, he kept the love affair of Ford and McGillis at arm's length. They never share a bed or more than a kiss. If they did, even in the enthrall of love, the audience would not accept Ford's leaving, feeling he "loved her and left her." And that little moral bell that rings in the back of our head would be telling us McGillis could not then go with Gudunov either—or she would be a loose and tainted woman, jumping from man to man, bed to bed, in our eyes.

A Clear Narrative

Screenplays are not written to be great literature. No one curls up at night with a good screenplay. But they are meant to be read—if properly circulated, most first drafts can expect an audience of maybe 50 to 100 readers. They should be kept simple (no complex sentences or show-off vocabulary), clear, and economical. Yet staccato dialogue and bare scene descriptions make for a boring read. Some style is encouraged. It is, after all, the writer's task to put the movie into the reader's head—to do more than lay down characters in a setting, but rather to describe the sensation, the *flavor* of the scenes as they unfold. Take this example from William Goldman's *Marathon Man*:

> THE SHOPS on First Avenue and here is the first indication of one of the central images that will recur: cities in crisis. Stores are empty. Lots of them. And a lot of others have "sale" signs across their fronts. Others have steel gates pulled across their doorways—you can make out the salespeople behind the gates, but they don't look happy. From the storefronts, you can tell this was once a German neighborhood, and maybe there's a swastika amateurishly drawn across a deserted window…

Goldman not only describes what we see, but gives us (and, incidentally, the production designer) powerful clues as to *how* we should view the scene. This is a clear indication of a competent writer who has done his homework. This is where talent plays a part. The writer's expressive skills—command of language, voice, style, tone, point of view, and pacing—will reflect (favorably or unfavorably) on the quality and enjoyability of the reading experience and may make all the difference in how the script is accepted in the marketplace.

Notice also that Goldman underscores one phrase. This is done more often in directing the *inflection* of a character's dialogue than in scene description, but either way is an acceptable tool—along with exclamation marks, capitalizing for dramatic emphasis, and onomatopoeia (Buzz, Bow wow)—as long as it is used judiciously. Ellipses (…) to indicate a pause (as in a phone conversation heard only from one end) or for a sentence that goes unfinished, or dashes (--) to mark interrupted speech are also fine. (But there is still a lingering old school aversion to the use of italics in scripts.)

Particularly for scene description, you'll find useful this *ten-point basic writing strategy:*

STRATEGY

1. **Write in present tense, active voice.**

   The time is always now, even in flashbacks. It's "John opens the door." Not: "The door is opened." "They run." Not: "They are running."

2. **Spell correctly and use proper grammar.**

   Commas have a purpose. If English is not your first language, have a friend help you edit and polish your work. And don't rely exclusively on your software's spell check—check it yourself. Spell check won't catch "there" for "their" or "your" for "you're" or "effect" when you mean "affect" or "its" when you mean "it's."

3. **Avoid metaphors.**

   ("The curtain of night fell") or similes ("a heart as big as all outdoors"), though okay in small doses in describing your principal characters ("She is like her refrigerator, well-stocked and perfectly organized with nothing out of place." *Ordinary People*).

4. **Keep it easy to read.**

   Clean, liberally paragraphed, lots of white space on the page.

5. **Use a dictionary and a thesaurus.**

   Mark Twain compared the difference between the right word and almost the right word to "the difference between being pregnant and almost pregnant." Name things as specifically as possible. A tomahawk is not an ax. Objects are a window into character. Does she drive a car or a Mercedes? Live in a house or a beachfront trailer? Be specific with verbs too. "He hits him." Okay, but does he jab, poke, slap, whack, clout, punch, or punish him?

6. **Don't overwrite.**

   Don't write mood ("doom" spelled backwards), don't overdescribe (especially in the opening when you think we need so much more than we do), and cut down on the adverbs. "The adverb is not your friend," Stephen King writes in his book, *On Writing*. Slowly, quickly, happily, angrily, expectantly, timidly—what do they add, especially in directions for the actor? Tell the actor what to do, not how to do it. This goes for adjectives as well. Less is more.

7. **Keep description clean and lean.**

   Here, by way of example, is a sentence written many ways, only one of which is correct:

   There is a car pulling into the driveway.
   A car starts to pull into the driveway.
   Angle on: a car as it pulls into the driveway.
   Camera follows a car as it pulls into the driveway.
   We see a car pull into the driveway.
   A car pulls into the driveway.

   The final sentence is sufficient; all the rest contain superfluous words.

8. **Don't write camera directions, design wardrobe, or dress the stage.**

   Okay, if you have a doctor who wears bunny ears to work, you better tell us that. But otherwise, don't embarrass yourself. A director will decide when the star gets his close-up and a whole bunch of talented experts can choose the best shots and camera angles, dress a debutante for a ball, or pick out appropriate posters for a college jock's dorm room.

9. **Don't say "we see," "we hear," "begins," or "starts."**

   Of course "we" (what if only one person is watching the movie?) see or hear what you've written—it's a movie! Remove the words and there is no change in the meaning. And characters don't begin to speak, they speak. They don't start to answer the door, they answer the door.

10. **Don't describe what we can't see or hear.**

"John Smith (a former green beret who won two purple hearts flying helicopters in Iraq, was divorced twice and is now an absentee father and out of work carpenter) is putting a pail of nails into his truck." Okay I've picked a particularly egregious example—but it's from an actual spec script.

This last caveat is a huge stop sign for me. There is simply no excuse for attempting to convey story or character information in the stage directions. Okay, an occasional author aside or "summing up" comment to punctuate the end of an important or particularly long sequence *can* be acceptable style. We are *writers*, after all, and must be allowed a little poetic license, especially when it serves the tone of the story and lends authority to the writer's voice. But style is never an excuse for bad writing.

Here is a paragraph from a student script offered purely in the interest of higher education, one so poorly written as to make me feel unkind including it here. Only the names have been changed to protect the innocent characters. See if you can spot the errors.

INT. MEETING HALL—LATER

About 30 or so community members sit on homemade bleachers. Most of the audience is male and in their thirties and forties. However, there are a few single and married people present, and a small variety of ages and looks. Still, the crowd is predominantly old hippie/new age/working class/libertarian/slightly disenfranchised/not-quite-able-to-fit-in types. Joan sits near the front with her friend, PAULA/CONSUELA (originally called Paula by her family and now called Consuela by community members). Next to them is the young girl that Eric called out to last evening as she was getting on a school bus just before the scene in which we saw Eric tell the old woman that he was talking to her "heart, mind, and soul." Piano music drifts in from an adjoining room, where Annette plays an extended improvisational piece. A bottle of wine, her glass, and a smoking cigarette sit atop the piano.

A Professional Screen Style and Format

Screenplays, like people, are judged first on appearance. The reader makes a snap decision: Does this look like something I want to spend my whole evening getting to know? If it weighs as much as the Orange County phone directory, sports a spiral binding, has coffee stains on its blue iridescent cover, and a flip inside reveals the dialogue running down the left side of the page, the screenplay is not going to be read.

Feature screenplays and scripts for television have a distinctive format, which has evolved little in the last fifty years at least. Some established writers have tinkered with that form, have tried to create a style maybe a little more hip, a little more fun to read, a little more twenty-first century. But readers and production personnel—the audience for whom the script is intended—are notoriously slow to accept change. Going against the generally accepted form is risky and should be undertaken only if you are already successful in the prevailing form. Sure, styles change over time—for example, some older classic screenplays are replete with camera directions, considered poor form today—but hasn't your first script challenges aplenty to face already without trying to break new ground?

The film business is not a school. It doesn't grade on a curve or give an "A" for effort. Your spec script must compete on an equal basis with those of professional Hollywood screenwriters. No one will say, "Well this isn't as good as Mamet's, but the screenwriter is new and it's not too bad, so let's put our $100 million into this one." No one (including the audience) cares if the script was cheap to buy or how long it took to make the movie—only how good it is. And the readers of your spec expect a professional look or will assume it's not the product of a professional quality writer.

By far, the best way for new writers to get a firm grasp of proper format (and its occasional idiosyncrasies) is to read screenplays, preferably produced and preferably the writer's draft. The final shooting script (which may contain colored pages to mark various drafts) or continuity script (which may omit scenes written but not shot) or published scripts (which may number and print scenes in a book-friendly format) are poor substitutes. As stated in Chapter 1, a number of online sites post current TV and movie scripts that can be downloaded for free. (**Caveat:** you often get what you pay for. Anyone can put anything on the web—the scripts may bear only a passing resemblance to the writer's draft, and their formats are often completely wrong.) Best source: both the Academy of

Motion Picture Arts and Sciences Library or the new Writers Guild Foundation Library offer thousands of genuine screenplays, MOW's, hour dramas, and sitcoms for anyone who visits.

This book will set guidelines for a feature film script only. That format is substantially the same as for a spec MOW or an hour drama (such as *Alias* or *CSI: Miami*), *except* that a MOW has seven distinct acts and the hour drama four, plus a possible teaser and/or tag (epilogue) for each. Each half-hour sitcom (taped, three-camera format) has its own unique style, but the major differences are: two acts (and a possible teaser and tag) clearly set forth in the script, a length of about 45 to 55 pages, and *double-spaced* scene direction and dialogue (the most obvious difference).

All this has become so much easier for the new writer with the availability of formatting programs such as *Movie Magic* and *Final Draft*, which do all the hard lifting for you in all formats. Programs can also be created on your PC or Macintosh with very little effort. Or a few minutes surfing the web should yield you a number of screenplay and sitcom style sheets and templates to download for free.

Here are 14 other important guidelines for screenplay appearance:

1. Covers are discouraged. If you feel you must, use plain, thin, card stock covers that are easy to roll back—an agent or producer will put theirs on when the time is appropriate.

2. Use a good stock of white, 8 1/2 × 11-inch, three-hole punch paper and bind with brass brads of good quality (ACCO #5 or #6 heavy-duty fasteners is preferred) in the first and third holes. Print on one side only. (Yes, production companies often do double-sided pages to save paper—but that's not okay for your spec, sorry.)

3. Your cover page is your title page. It should include title, written by [name], and contact information. No date, no "first draft," no copyright or WGA registration notice. As the Writers Guild of America likes conformity in the title page, here is the complete approved format (per Article 37 of the Minimum Basic Agreement):

Project Title

by

Name of First Writer(s)

(Based on, if any)

Revisions By

(in order of work performed)

Current Revisions By

(Current writer, date)

Name

Address

Email

Phone of Contact

4. Use Courier 12-Point type, though Times New Roman, Bookman, or anything similar will do. Don't use italics, bold, or different size fonts—it marks you as an amateur.

5. Don't give character lists, casting suggestions, detailed set descriptions, or a synopsis.

6. No dedications, quotations, or artwork, please.

7. Your first script page is not numbered, all others beginning with page 2 are numbered in the upper right-hand corner.

8. Keep the length within 100 and 130 pages. Each script page generally translates to a minute of screen time. Readers don't want three-hour vanity epics from new writers.

9. Margins should be 1 $1/2$ inches on the left (to accommodate the holes and brads) and 1 inch on the top, bottom, and right side.

10. Don't number your scenes. Scripts are given scene numbers when they are budgeted for production. If your software program does this automatically, disable that function.

11. Don't use (CONTINUED) at the bottom right margin of one page and the top of the next to indicate a scene continuing on to a new page. Again, if your software program does this automatically, disable that function. EXCEPTION: If *dialogue* must be continued to the next page, end on a complete sentence, add (MORE) at the bottom center and put (CONT'D) after the character cue that continues the dialogue on the next page.

12. Don't break scenes up into shots. Use master scenes only, which describe the entire action in that setting.

13. *Proofread* your work for grammatical, punctuation, or spelling errors (do not trust Spell Check). Don't break sentences from one page to the next and be on the lookout for **widows**—character cues or scene headings left by themselves at the bottom of a page. Bring them up to the top of the next page.

14. The more reader-friendly the writing style, the better:

    Paragraph freely.

    Use short sentences.

    Present tense and active voice.

    Spell out two digit numbers, personal titles, and indications of time.

    Do not hyphenate long words, breaking them from one line to the next.

    Never break a sentence from one page to the next.

What follows is the first page of the screenplay for the feature film, *The Pirates of the Caribbean: The Curse of the Black Pearl* (screenplay by Ted Elliott & Terry Rossio, Screen Story by Ted Elliot & Terry Rossio and Stuart Beattie and Jay Wolpert, Based on Walt Disney's Pirates of the Caribbean). Notes at the end will explain the numbered notations on the script.

FADE IN: ①

EXT. CARIBBEAN SEA—DAY ②
③   ⑤
④A gray, impenetrable wall of fog. A massive SHIP emerges from the mist, the masthead looming: the *H.M.S. Dauntless.*
                                                     ⑥
EXT. DAUNTLESS—FORECASTLE—DAY

FOCUS on a⑦little girl, ELIZABETH SWAN, standing at the bow rail, gazing at the sea, singing, slow tempo.
                        ⑧
                  YOUNG ELIZABETH ⑨
          … Yo, ho, yo, ho, a pirate's life for me…
          … drink up me hearties, yo, ho… ⑩

She is startled when a hand clutches her shoulder. The hand belongs to JOSHAMEE GIBBS, born old, skin a dark leather.

                        GIBBS
                     (sotto) ⑪
          Quiet, missy! Cursed pirates sail these waters.
          you don't want to bring them down on us now,
          do you?

Elizabeth stares wide-eyed at him.

                    NORRINGTON
          Mr. Gibbs.

NORRINGTON, a dashing young man, Royal Navy to the core, glares at Gibbs. Beside him is GOVERNOR WEATHBY SWANN, a man of obvious high station—and Elizabeth's father.

                 NORRINGTON (CONT'D) ⑫
          That will do.

                        GIBBS
          She was singing about pirates. Bad luck to be
          singing about pirates, with us mired in this
          unnatural fog—mark my words.

                    NORRINGTON
          Consider them marked. On your way.

GIBBS
'Aye, Lieutenant.
        (as he moves off)
Bad luck to have a woman on board, too.
Even a mini'ture one.

He returns to his deck-swabbing duties, surreptitiously takes a quick swig from a flask.

---

1. Most scripts begin with **FADE IN:** capitalized and flush with the left-hand margin. Other openings are possible, such as DEEP SPACE or BLACK SCREEN or whatever works for your story. Most scripts end with **FADE OUT** capitalized, right-margin justified and ending with a period.

2. This entire line is the **scene heading** or **slug line** and provides the three basic bits of location information for the scene that follows (whenever any of the information in the slug line changes, a new scene begins):

   EXT. (exterior) or **INT.** (interior) to indicate whether the scene is shot outdoors or indoors (scenes in moving vehicles—cars, trains—count as interior);

   place (the location for the action in the scene) which can get as specific as you wish (FOOTBALL FIELD, FIFTY YARD LINE) within reason; and

   time, for which **DAY** or **NIGHT** is sufficient, though DAWN or DUSK is sometimes used. Specific times (11:14 PM), season, or year can be included in parentheses after the location, but if it is meant to convey story information, it will have to be communicated in the body of the scene.

3. Double-space between the scene heading and the text that follows.

4. The text is sometimes called the **description**, sometimes **stage direction**. All description of the action of the characters in a scene is called the **business**. It is always single-spaced, though you double-space *between* paragraphs. And liberal paragraphing is encouraged. Big blocks of description tend to be skimmed by a reader. Isolating separate actions or images in short sentence fragments, capitalized, on a single line, is a technique that is catching on for highlighting key information.

5. Capitalize all **music, sound, and special effects** and the **first appearance of any character** (even bit parts and background characters) to make them easy to find and follow. In the writer's discretion, **key objects**, such as SHIP here, may also be capitalized. After the first appearance, all character names should be lower case.

6. Every scene is an implied cut needing no **transition**, as is the case here. Some writers however still use transitions: **CUT TO:** after every scene or to emphasis action cuts, **DISSOLVE TO:** to show the passage of time or to enter (or between) scenes in montages or dream sequences and **FADE TO:** to indicate a longer passage of time, to punctuate the mood, or just to slow the pace of the film. When used, these transitions should be double-spaced from the preceding text or dialogue, double-spaced *after* the transition to the next slug line, and positioned flush right.

7. If **camera directions** are used, they should be capitalized as well. As previously noted, camera directions are discouraged unless necessary to make a story point.

8. Double-space before the character name.

9. The name of the speaking character, or **character cue**, is capitalized and begins about 4 inches from the left side of the page. Never center the name as it should line up with other character cues to form an even line down the center of the page.

10. Single-space to the **dialogue** immediately below the character cue. Dialogue is left justified and indented approximately 3 inches from the left side of the page and 2 inches from the right. All dialogue text is single-spaced and no unused space is left in a section of dialogue.

11. **Actor direction** is a parenthetical suggestion placed about 3 1/2 inches from the left side of the page directly under the character cue. It most often attempts to direct tone of voice (angrily), manner of speaking (sotto), or dialogue that goes against the expectations of the situation (irony or sarcasm). But it also finds favor as a means of expressing small bits of action (as he moves off) so as to avoid having to interrupt the dialogue with business that stretches across the page.

12. When a character's dialogue has been interrupted within a scene by description (*not* by another actor's dialogue) the abbreviation in parenthesis for continued (**CONT'D**) is often placed after the character name when he next speaks. Many writers are now avoiding this as cumbersome except where it is deemed necessary for clarity.

Finally, writers have devised myriad solutions to the problem of expressing visuals accurately while maintaining a clean and reader-friendly page. Here are a few:

- use INTERCUT for a phone conversation so that you don't have to go back and forth between phone locations and can run the dialogue as a single scene;
- use a single slug line direction such as:
  EXT./INT. BLACK'S CAR—CITY STREETS—MOVING SHOT—DAY to cover a car moving through various locations seen from both inside the car and out;
- use (**beat**) as a pause in dialogue to indicate a change of subject or a new thought (a beat is really a small psychological moment for an actor, but it has gained acceptance in this form through use);
- use INT. HOUSE/VARIOUS for when you want your characters to freely move about a variety of rooms and don't want to crowd the text with sluglines. For example, you could write "he walks into…" double-space down to KITCHEN and double-space down to the new action from there;
- The use of CREDITS BEGIN or TITLES OVER before text if you desire to control the roll of the credits (END CREDITS or END TITLES can close them out for you).

Read scripts for more formatting ideas or create your own solutions. Just be clear and be imaginative!

Rewriting

Finishing a screenplay is like giving birth: after the initial burst of accomplishment—the elation that it's done, over, you took it full term—comes the realization, especially if you've done this sort of thing before, that the really hard work is just about to start. Sure you'll be tempted to sing from the rooftops, to send autographed copies to everyone on your contact list, but if I could give you just this one… teeny… word of advice: don't.

All writers know writing is rewriting, the final ingredient to the marketable screenplay. Screenwriter Robert Rodat wrote 11 drafts of *Saving Private Ryan* before presenting it to Paramount for the first round of their "notes." Renowned authors Joan Didion and John Gregory Dunne did 29 rewrites of the Michelle Pfeiffer-Robert Redford vehicle *Up Close and Personal*. M. Night

Shyamalan wrote 10 full drafts (starting from scratch each time, by hand on yellow legal pads) of *The Sixth Sense* before bringing it forth as a first draft to his agent. Even novelist Vladimir Nabokov (*Lolita*) states, "I have rewritten—often several times—every word I have ever published. My pencils outlast my erasers."

For most professionals in the film business, the biggest turn-off when being submitted a script is to hear the words "I know it could use a rewrite, but see what you think of it." Sure, sometimes the magic takes time to find its way into the story. Rarely will a truly tight structure and fleshed-out characters that have achieved their maximum dramatic potential emerge on the first go-around. But that's all the more reason why writers must develop the discipline to stick with their material long enough to smooth out the rough edges and to make it as good as it can possibly be.

No matter that you edited every line three times while you were writing that first draft. No matter that you've held a cast reading, cut some more, and polished all your dialogue. There were shortcuts you took when you were so close to the end, weren't there? Scenes that could have been cut or added, plot holes ignored, dialogue that remains indulgent? This script that took so long to conceive, outline, and write is still, trust me, an unfinished first draft. Send this draft to your precious contacts now and you will be doing yourself and your screenplay the greatest disservice. Once they pass, there are no second chances.

Instead, put your first draft away for a week or two. Don't look at it once. Go to the theater. Take a vacation. Read a book. Get a girlfriend. Do all the things you put off to write your script. Then bring all your new experiences with you and see how you feel about your script now that you have a fresh perspective. Put yourself in the position of a reader. All she cares about is whether or not it is a *great* script. Not a good script. Not a potentially great script if only it had one more rewrite. It must be a GREAT script as is, or it's a pass. In fact, if it *is* a great script and they love it and buy it—it will still in all likelihood undergo a number of rewrites, mostly by writers other than you. That's just Hollywood's way. The script money is the cheapest money the studio can spend. A director and star will have changes they'd like to see made before they commit, and after. They'll have writers who they've worked with before and must now hire again. As the birth mother, your greatest ally down the home stretch may be the WGA's tough arbitration rules, crediting the original writer unless hell freezes over.

But for now, before you sell it, *you* are the rewriter. The script can benefit from your complete knowledge of its sources and themes. Begin with the structure. Like a good gardener, weed out the beats that don't work, make sure all setups are paid off and payoffs are properly set up. Don't be afraid to go back to the beginning if you discover the climax simply doesn't hold water. Make sure the ending matches audience expectations—or have a solid reason why not. Eliminate plot holes, explore the visual or metaphorical value of an alternate context, and hear every line spoken out loud. Dialogue can always be trimmed, pacing and scene transitions refined, actions more clearly defined. Be coldly efficient in eliminating excess camera, stage, or actor directions. Make it a clean and easy read.

And never forget the words of Ernest Hemingway: "The test of a good story is in how much good stuff you can leave out."

Here is a *ten-point rewriting strategy:*

STRATEGY

1. **If the character conflict seems weak...**

   Track the main character and opponent. See where they interact, react, and otherwise appear. Check that their storyline is the focus of the plot and that each is acting in character and in constant conflict with the other. Are the stakes clear for each of them? Are the stakes increasing? High enough? Are each in active pursuit of their goal? Are their motivations clear and convincing? Are they interesting and credible adversaries? Does each have credible skills and limitations? Why do we care who wins or loses?

2. **If the main character seems boring...**

   Are the motivations driving his actions strong enough? Does he have any compelling personal problems (a backstory) in addition to the story problem caused by the inciting incident? (Think about a strong subplot.) Is there sufficient subtext in what he says and does to keep him mysterious and interesting and keep us actively involved with him? Can we give the main character some interesting trait or skill (or family) that a supporting character now possesses?

3. **If the story seems to go flat at times...**

   Too much narrative will slow a script down. Cut out what can be implied. Pull out the dialogue to see if scenes are showing rather than telling. Strong dialogue can mask a dramatically weak scene. The dynamics of a scene should be clear enough that actors can improvise dialogue as well as you can write it. Are these scenes we've seen before? Find a more interesting location for the scene.

4. **If the plot seems hard to buy…**

   Are the characters acting consistent with who they are or believe themselves to be? Are the special effects in keeping with the tone of the story (there's a difference between a fantasy and a horror film)? Is there credible cause and effect in the scene progression? Do flash-backs, dream sequences, montages, and/or narration succeed as good storytelling tools—or are they crutches bolstering a weak story? (Hint: if you need such a device to tell the story, look for a hole in your story structure.)

5. **If the dialogue is sounding all the same…**

   Does each character have his/her own voice? Is the dialogue stiff (often, the earliest dialogue has yet to find the voice of your charac-ters)? Are the characters stuck spouting exposition or character history? (Try working the exposition into action. Character is best shown through behavior.) Are they being asked to mouth the theme? Do they have anything interesting to say?

6. **If the scenes or characters seem repetitious…**

   Can you eliminate scenes or combine characters? Do supporting char-acters have their own personality and voice? Are the scenes too long? (The more economy a scene has, the less déjà vu seems to set in.)

7. **If the script seems talky…**

   How many words can you cut from every scene, from every dialogue exchange? (Hint: cut as many as you can, until one more and the scene would make no sense.) How many words can you convert into actions?

8. **If you haven't resisted the temptation to direct on the page…**

   Make sure camera directions are necessary and scene descriptions aren't indulging in wardrobe design and set decoration. And check parenthetical directions for actors—necessary? If so, your scene is not written clearly enough.

9. **If the script is too long…**

   Do you need all the subplots? Have you repeated information? Does more than one character serve the same purpose? Did you remove camera angles, musical cues, or other elements which distract from the dramatic unfolding of the story? *Most* feature scripts average about 110 pages (translating to approximately one minute of screen time per page). Yours can be longer or shorter, as long as its quality can justify the length.

10. **If the script is too short…**

Your story or characters may be underdeveloped. Can a subplot help? Or maybe you've done too much rewriting—tossing the baby out with the bath. Make sure you haven't sacrificed character complexity, personal consequences, or scenes that have sheer entertainment value for the sake of a fast moving plot.

When you've finished that, get new feedback from one or two trusted friends. (*Friends*, not wanna-be writers who may be jealous or angling to be your partner.) Listen to them. That doesn't mean you have to agree with them. Keep the strength of your convictions, and remember William Goldman's famous line: "No one knows anything!" (On the other hand, if ten people tell you your boat's sprung a leak, it may be time to start swimming.) But if they love it, if they wouldn't change a word—polish it one more time. Until you can objectively say, "this script is no longer getting any better, just different." Then stop.

---

from the trenches: WHY IS YOUR SCRIPT SPECIAL?

The FedEx man was at my door again. His name is Frank. He has three kids and his wife's name is Connie. We chat like old friends as I sign for yet another screenplay. I remember asking for this one—the query letter got my attention—so I get right to it. It looks clean enough. Three brads hold together 114 pages in proper script format. No glaring typos, notes scribbled in the margins, or illustrations artfully intermingled within the pages. Sadly, it becomes apparent that it doesn't measure up to its pitch. Minutes later, it's tossed in the bin. Someone's hopes and dreams into the recycler.

And this was one of the good ones. The flood of screenplays that never come close to measuring up to pro standards swells with each passing year. Their authors seem never to have read a script or writing primer and either don't own a good script format program or know how to use one. They don't spell check or proof. I often question whether English is their first language. They submit screenplays as thick as phone books or thin as a list of intelligent actors. Some arrive bound in steel rings, as though to protect them from theft or with pages stapled together like a term paper. They're dirty, covered in coffee and tea stains (I hope) and have "First Draft, 1986" proudly etched on the cover page.

continued

Many writers seem to work harder on the gimmick designed to get their script read than on the script itself. One submission was posted ten pages at a time to heighten "the suspense." Some come with drawings to accompany the text or surveys to be completed by the reader. Some have dedications or poetic quotes the author undoubtedly feels adds a literary quality to the work. An e-query offered an elaborate puzzle to solve in order to "win" the right to read the script. I once received a script with a tiny hand-painted hat glued to the cover, a sombrero about four inches around. The story being about Daniel Boone, I suppose they couldn't figure out how to construct a coonskin cap.

All this is before I turn the first page. Inside, scenes are replete with directions for the camera, wardrobe personnel, and set designer, while giving the actors little to do besides twiddle their thumbs while reciting rambling, expository dialogue. Parenthetical comments are interspersed in the stage directions to give us background information. ("He was once a colonel in the Green Berets, decorated with the Silver Star for valor in the Vietnam War"—Don't describe what you want us to *know*—script what we will *see or hear*!) But the ones I loathe most are those accompanied by cover letters that rival the script in length. Some give a "synopsis" that dwells on each excruciating detail while trying to remain "coy" to preserve the surprises in store for us. Or contain chatty notes that apologize for the perceived flaws in advance ("it just needs a good rewrite"), while also lecturing the reader on the profound "hidden" implications of the premise.

The overall impression is that the script was written by an amateur and rushed to market. Pop it out and send it off. No rewrites. No polish. No rethinking or retooling the first blush of creativity. Faced with heavy competition, new writers act as if the roses go to the first horse out of the gate. Gimmicks, promises, and purple prose cover letters only make a script stand out for all the wrong reasons. Good or bad, the writing speaks for itself. No use making excuses for it. There is no excuse for sloppy writing by someone who professes to be a writer. And bad form and desperate measures only make your script special in the wrong way, an instant candidate for oblivion.

Most word processing software has spell check, but you have to turn it on! Then there are the cover letters from writers complaining about the business not giving them a break, when *the letters themselves* are a mess of misspelled words, grammatical errors, and bad punctuation, capital letters seemingly inserted at random and handwritten corrections in the margins. Readers are easily persuaded *not* to read. And every written communication by a writer—even a post-it note or an e-mail—is a *de facto* writing sample and judged as such.

What does an agent or producer look for in a script? A page turner. Something that makes her fidget, feel an emotion, or find a heart she didn't know existed. A truly perceptive take on human behavior or a concept so sexy, risky, shocking, or unorthodox that it screams "fast read, quick sale, easy money." Today, the focus is on what's hot, new, and undiscovered, and that translates to youth: someone just shy of eighteen, trying to break a modeling contract from Ralph Lauren, and using a return ticket to Milan as a bookmark. Check out *Thirteen*, which the print ads proudly proclaim to be the age of its co-author (and which, ironically, you have to be over seventeen to view). But if puberty is a distant memory and you haven't been to the gym since high school, it's all about the strength of a well-written story. If readers and their bosses took out an ad, it would read:

"**Wanted**: writers with exceptional storytelling skills, demonstrated by two fabulous specs loaded with great ideas, clever lines, and memorable moments for actors."

Even if you do connect with an agent or mentor who knows what the money guys like and has massive enthusiasm for your writing, they need a story to pitch. Only story sells tickets. It's not stars. Check the embarrassing grosses on Affleck and Lopez's (too-early) valentine to each other, *Gigli*, or Harrison Ford's bomb *Hollywood Homicide*. And it's not sequel power, as attested to by *Charlie's Angels: Full Throttle*—despite a massive publicity push and the smothering coverage of Demi Moore's hook-up with that '70s kid, Ashton Kutcher. Even a hugely anticipated sequel like *The Matrix Reloaded* floundered when no one could figure out what was going down, to whom, or the point of it all.

Visual clarity, narrative momentum, and emotional impact define a well told story. Top those with an imaginative, timely premise and you have the makings of a bidding war spec sale. A tightly woven plot and a polished final draft are a must. On the other hand, no one is waiting with baited breath for yet another slice-your-wrist dramedy about impossibly beautiful, slightly wacky, spoiled, out of work teens desperate (over a few beers) to trade hooking up for love. We've seen that one. Something mildly original and mature would be like a breath of fresh air. Is some glimpse of the truth in human affairs too much to ask?

In the normal course of things, your best is rarely achieved on the first draft. Writing requires a brutal self-honesty. Where can it be improved? Have you addressed the plot holes, pared the dialogue and scene description to the bone? Removed the unneeded technical directions? Made every beat as visual as possible? Proofed each and every page by hand? How many words can still be cut?

continued

And if the most you've written before turning your passion to screenwriting is a postcard to your Auntie Mame from Florida, get a good critique from two honest friends before maxing out your industry contacts. The worst notes of your life are the greatest gift a writer can receive. The first draft is the writer's time to learn. Don't shy away from a non-laudatory critique—or take up the popular defense that someone else told you the exact opposite, as if that gives your version justification. Judgments can differ, even directly contradict each other, but they do not cancel each other out. Hear what your readers have to offer, use what sounds right and forget the rest.

Or the script may not be fixable. Live with it. Put it aside—it's not a final judgment on your talent—and move on. One script can start a career, but it doesn't have to be your first. And it should certainly never appear that way to the recipient of your efforts.

Some Final Thoughts on Writing the Hollywood Film

As the *average* studio feature film budget nears $100 million (production and advertising) and the target audience is geared to younger and younger moviegoers, it is difficult to discuss seriously the psychological motivation of character and the need for subtext in dialogue to accomplish a myriad of subtle storytelling tasks. I'm just not sure if anyone cares anymore. Then again, the adult audience, at least, seems to care; the drop in summer 2005 box office admissions indicates that they are staying away in droves.

Today a film is not measured in superlatives for the writing, directing, or acting; it is measured in box office grosses. It's no longer uniquely quirky characters or a brilliantly woven plot that excites a studio executive—it's the number of explosions, bathroom jokes, and movie stars it can accommodate. The marketing brass bet their megabucks on those movies and when they score big at the box office, they say, "see we were right." No, I don't see. Just because you coax a number of bored teenagers out of the sun or out of the house on a Friday night with relentless advertising and commercial tie-ins, doesn't mean they like what they are seeing. It may just mean they never had much of a choice.

But every year, in November, as new snow caps the Rocky Mountains and visions of Academy Awards dance in the heads of studio execs, films that do speak to the human experience are rolled out like a Trojan horse into the marketplace. Suddenly comes a *Sling Blade*, an *American Beauty*, a *Million Dollar Baby*, a *Sideways*, or a *Crash*. Most are made or released by the "art house" divisions of the same studios that gave us *Stealth* or *The Island*. But at least they point to awareness that reaching for the potential of the medium to illuminate and enrich our lives is still a worthy goal. That multicultural human characters we can identify with can attract as wide an audience as cartoon superheroes. That the saturation level for serial violence, over-the-top special effects, cardboard characters, dumb dialogue, and wall-to-wall mayhem has to come soon. If I were betting the studio's megabucks, I'd start by betting the farm on something that has a heart.

So trusting that nothing I have written above will encourage you to write formula pictures with stock characters and no noble thematic ambitions, here are some general thoughts:

Keep your best storytelling instincts tuned to *creative deviations* from the accepted wisdom. As Quentin Tarantino demonstrated when he twisted the structure in *Pulp Fiction*, there can be variations on even "the beginning, middle, and end" rule. Use the general guidelines offered in courses and books to develop your instincts as a storyteller, not to replace them.

The whims of the audience change. Since it takes most films years to come out of development and into your theater, don't try to anticipate studio wish lists or current trends. (Beware also what I call the "law of opposites": a star who has just completed a high-tech hit may look for a quiet family drama next or a director just returned from six months in Columbia might opt next for an urban drama to be closer to his family.) Instead, start your own trend. Take risks with your work. Appeal to our wildest fantasies. Surprise us. Get personal. Or, as one now famous writer who struggled for years without a sale put it: "Get away from what you think movies are supposed to be and deal with your own nightmares."

But don't preach. Don't make your work a place for clichés or stereotypes. And, don't shy away from the sex, violence, and passion that is inherent in life and the heart of dramatic conflict in film. All the great and terrible truths of the world are too big to fit into our hearts; a writer must carve them into images that move us. It is possible to be both commercial and tell a worthwhile story, even one infused with poetry!

And, whether you are a novice writer or a successful one, don't fall into the trap of writing for the money. Of course, to reach true financial heights as a screenwriter, you must write movies that people want to see and that means: good stories, which are entertaining and emotionally involving, and which are well told.

Finally, never forget: Let your audience dream, if just for a while. (Viewers may want to see *War of the Worlds*, but they want to be Tom Cruise.) And, that's reason enough to post on your corkboard the following advice from screenwriter Larry Ferguson (*The Hunt for Red October*): "The way you get screenplays on the screen is you write parts actors want to play." That's the ultimate test of a truly marketable screenplay.

Chapter 6

Designing the Marketable Screenplay

Part Two: The Independent Film

"Dollars and Sense"

"Kiss me, will ya, kid." Those words were whispered to me nearly 30 years ago, over the expanse of a mahogany desk, by a cigar-chomping pro in an expensive but ill-fitting suit. I had just pitched him a tale of international intrigue that was also a love triangle and a story of grifters and gypsies who found themselves in a complex web of deceit and murder and... that's when this guy leaned forward, his eyes glazed over, and said it. He wasn't coming on to me; he was giving me advice. Good, sound advice. "Keep it simple, stupid." The KISS method of storytelling.

Welcome to the world of low-budget, independent filmmaking, including those staples of what used to be known as the B-movies: teen-oriented genre films. *Beach Party* with Annette and Frankie. *The Blob* with Steve McQueen. *I Was a Teenage Frankenstein*. Movies of horror, sex, violence, comedy, and oddities that independent giants like producers Sam Arkoff, Roger Corman, and Lord Lew Grade pumped out for decades to feed the appetite of Saturday matinees, drive-ins, and an international market starved for American product. These were the films once known as exploitation fare, though more than a few of them were brilliant, with quirky points of view, depressingly real storylines, or odd characters that shocked the established film industry.

And some became cult classics, such as *The Little Shop of Horrors* (which Roger Corman shot in only two days in 1960), George Romero's *Night of the*

Living Dead (1968), Dennis Hopper's *Easy Rider* (1969), Gerald Damiano's pornographic *Deep Throat* (1972), John Waters' *Pink Flamingos* (1973), Martin Scorsese's *Mean Streets* (1973), John Cassavetes' *A Woman Under the Influence* (1974), *The Rocky Horror Picture Show* (1975—the horror movie spoof still packs in a midnight audience), John Carpenter's *Halloween* (1978), and David Lynch's *Eraserhead* (1978).

By the time five friends from the University of Central Florida cleverly used the Internet to hype their pseudo-documentary horror film, *The Blair Witch Project* (1999)—made on a $60,000 budget, it scared up a worldwide box office of $248 million—they were firmly in the indie tradition of turning the very limitations forced upon them through a lack of money to their creative advantage. Forty years earlier, French New Wave filmmakers such as Jean-Luc Godard (*Breathless*), Francois Truffaut (*The 400 Blows*), and Alain Resnais (*Hiroshima, Mon Amour*) also had to make do without fancy equipment, exotic locations, and expensive talent in front of and behind the camera. They concentrated instead on superb and insightful *storytelling* and a bold cinematic style forged of necessity that pioneered the use of stock footage, improvised dialogue, documentary-style camera work, and jump cut editing. And their best films all shared one critical quality: *a great story well told.*

This pioneering spirit persists in shaping cinema today. "If you want to be independent, you have to be flexible," points out writer/director Wong Kar-Wai (*2046*), "and sometimes those restrictions become the source of your inspiration."

In that spirit came Spike Lee's *She's Gotta Have It* (1986), shot in 16mm in 12 days and completed for under $115,000, Errol Morris' *The Thin Blue Line* (1988), John Sheridan's *My Left Foot* (1989), Carl Franklin's *One False Move* (1991), Neil Jordan's *The Crying Game* (1992), Jane Campion's *The Piano* (1993), Kevin Smith's *Clerks* (1994), Mike Figgis' *Leaving Las Vegas* (1995), Anthony Minghella's *The English Patient* ("Best Picture" 1996), John Sardi and Scott Hicks' *Shine* (1996), Billy Bob Thornton's *Sling Blade* (1996), Mike Leigh's *Secrets and Lies* (1996), Alan Ball's Oscar-winning *American Beauty* (1999), and Sophia Coppola's *Lost in Translation* (2003). And the foregoing is by no means a definitive list—more like picking cherries while dancing through a great and bountiful field.

The point is that the term "independent production" is no longer synonymous with "small" or "unimportant," "exploitation" or "art house fare." In fact, nothing could be further from the truth. The key word is "independent"—used here it means a movie financed and produced outside the studio system. And the vast majority of such movies today, even ones with mini-budgets in the thousands of dollars, strive to be as compelling, significant, influential, and entertaining to a mass audience as any film showing at your local cineplex. In fact, it is the rare film festival screening where one can find the very exploitation fare that formerly was the staple of independent production—the direct to cable or video movies. Independent production is no longer branded by a lack of quality. Instead, what is desirable and achievable is a measure of artistic freedom and creative autonomy that may be hard, if not impossible, to attain within the strictures of studio oversight, richly compensated talent (with their paid entourages), and budgets that equal the GNP of a small country.

For those reasons, writing a low-budget film (the Writers Guild Independent Film Program will sign Low Budget Agreements for theatrical films budgeted under $1.2 million) is not only for the novice or unproduced writer. Many established scribes, discouraged creatively, led the Guild to forge an exception to the "Schedule of Minimums" so they might labor on their works of love for little or nothing if they so choose. And if producing your screenplay won't break the bank, you'll likely find less resistance to the notion of your directing it too—should you have any slight leanings in that direction. (For more on this, see Chapter 10, "Building a Writing Career: Strategies for Marketing Yourself.")

And that doesn't mean your script must be limited to low-budget fare either—many films tagged as "indie fare" today are in fact financed and produced by large quasi-independent studios operating within the studio system, set up to encourage the production of more risky material. Currently there is Searchlight Pictures (Twentieth Century Fox), Focus Features (Universal), Sony Classics (Sony), Fine Line Features (New Line), Paramount Classics (Paramount), Warner Independent Pictures (Warner Bros.), and Miramax (Disney), though the legendary Weinstein brothers have recently broken away and formed their own company. Many more independent films are bankrolled by dot.com billionaires and wealthy entrepreneurs willing to spend production dollars that rival that of the studios. The result is that "independent" no longer translates into ultra low-budget or experimental filmmaking—just strong narratives and a clear directorial vision, produced and financed with a thumb of the nose at the establishment.

According to the Motion Picture Association of America, in 2004, the average cost of production for a motion picture of a member company was $63.6 million. That's an 85.5 percent increase from 1994 and a 341.3 percent increase over 20 years ago, in just the negative cost alone. On top of that, distributors spent an estimated average of $34.35 million on advertising campaigns and prints. That equals nearly $98 million per film. On the bright side, that represents a 5 percent decrease from 2003's record high of over $102 million per film, mostly attributable to a 12 percent decline in domestic marketing costs.

Out of 483 films released in the U.S. in 2004, only 200 were from the "majors." The number of films increased from 453 ten years ago, with total box office gross jumping to approximately $9.54 billion, increasing from $5.34 billion in 1994. But these films were spread over roughly the same audience. In fact, admissions declined 6.3 percent to 1.54 billion from its peak year of 1.64 billion in 2002. Those wide and expensive marketing campaigns have not had the effect of making more people want to go to the movies.

And somebody has to write these films. Literary agents say that all this sheer activity means more and greater opportunities for writers. After all, script material can't come from the same handful of studio darlings. Those darlings are busy writing films for studios, studios *not* in business to make low-budget films, but in business to make money. If it takes money to make money, so be it. That's their philosophy. And at the high cost of making their kind of films, the studios are not anxious to take risks on "new" material or on untried talent that the audience hasn't previously validated and accepted. So they will continue to hire the costliest talent and adjust their development or production schedules to accommodate their availability. But that leaves the independent field wide open. For most screenwriters, both union—not the few who make the big bucks we read about in the trades, but the rest, the 60 percent of nearly 8,000 active WGA members who never report a dime of income in any given year (of the 40 percent who do, the median income is still less than $50,000)—and the countless thousands of nonunion screenwriters who churn out those low-budget films, there are worse things than a steady income and a chance to have a forum for their work.

Years after enjoying the "privilege" of working with studio execs, big budgets, and superstars, I was lucky enough to be hired to produce a film with a simple script, no stars, a first-time director, and a budget of around $1 million (every Friday, I held my breath until the paychecks cleared). And a funny thing happened: I found myself less stressed than I had been in ages and having one hell of a good time! The writer was beside me on the set, working on dialogue with the actors and director. We made the script better and found practical, fast, and cheap solutions to problems. Filmmaking had finally become the fun and collaborative gig I had dreamed of.

The downside is that the battle for screens in the marketplace is highly competitive. The vast majority of independent films will be unable to find distribution. And that short film you labored over through four years of film school is even less likely to ever see a public viewing. Beyond the lack of box office stars or spectacular special effects to draw in the public, let's be honest: many low-budget entries do lack quality. Many contain the same plotless sex or violence that is often found in major studio films (but without those big stars and special effects). Still, on the bright side, they too can find an audience. These are the films that feed the cable stations and line the shelves of the sprawling video stores in your neighborhood (though there is a decreasing demand for straight-to-video films that have not had at least a limited theatrical release). But even more importantly perhaps, these films can sometimes help introduce your talents to agents, producers, film executives, the critical press, and even your target audience should they be accepted for screening at the growing network of *film festivals* both in the United States and abroad.

The penultimate event for American independent cinema, the Sundance Film Festival, held in Park City, Utah, often turns into a feeding frenzy by distributors scrambling to acquire the rights to the unconventional and often very personal work of independent writers and directors. More than anything, it was the mainstream critical and box office success of Sundance entries like Steven Soderbergh's *sex, lies and videotape* (1989) and Quentin Tarantino's *Reservoir Dogs* (1992) that forced upon the studios the fact that a modest budget does not always translate into modest achievement. If the studio chiefs still had any doubts, Robert Rodriguez's *El Mariachi* (1993), made on a budget of $13,000 and playing cheek to cheek with $50 million dollar offerings at the suburban mall, and Tarantino's *Pulp Fiction* (1994), which cost $8.5 million to produce and grossed $200+ million theatrically alone, most likely put them to rest. (Interestingly, both *sex, lies and videotape* and *Reservoir Dogs* were spawned at the world's most celebrated workshop for independent film and filmmakers, the Sundance Institute—created by actor-director Robert Redford and which predates his famous film festival.)

As you might expect, the competition for a spot in the festival is fierce. In 2005, 250 films were selected for screening at Sundance out of 5,617 entries (2,171 features and 3,446 short films). The festival's success has also spawned a nearby competitive offshoot, the Slamdance Film Festival, which tries to accommodate the rapidly accumulating avalanche of worthy films that don't, for whatever reason, make it into the Sundance competition. In the past years, Sundance has received such massive industry attention that there is now serious talk of moving it to a new venue, such as Salt Lake City, to handle the growing crowds and increasing need for screens.

Executives have been quick to groom the hottest film festival prospects for stardom. Some independent writer-directors, who have roots in low-budget genre films, like Sam Raimi (*Darkman*) and John Sayles (*Brother From Another Planet*), shuttle back and forth between making personal, independent films and studio-made mainstream films. Others, such as seasoned veteran Jim Jarmusch (*Stranger Than Paradise* and the recent *Broken Flowers*), call themselves "film outlaws" and shun Hollywood altogether in favor of the control they wish to maintain over their vision. But this is the way it always has been in the independent world—and the motion picture art form is the better for it.

So if you aspire to the rebellious side, or just want the simple validation of writing a movie and seeing it produced with your images and words reasonably intact—or if what you really want to do is direct—writing for the independent marketplace may be for you.

To help you along, following is a *13-point low-budget strategy* that may convince an independent producer that you have what it takes to write a quality, cost-conscious film:

STRATEGY

1. **Character-driven stories.**

   Dialogue is cheaper than planes, boats, and trains. But don't create too many speaking parts; even low-budget actors have to be fed, housed, trucked, clothed, and rehearsed.

2. **Limited locations.**

   Don't move your story around too much (e.g., drop the airport scene if you can have your characters do it while they're packing their bags).

There's a reason why so much art-house fare is set in an isolated cabin in the forest or a haunted house or a deserted amusement park.

3. **No complex stunts.**

These require time to block and stage and time costs money. There's little time available for rehearsals and there's even less for filming multiple takes or angles (a master shot and a close-up may be all the coverage a director will get).

4. **Day scenes preferable to night.**

Lighting is difficult and time-consuming and dark movies don't go over as well with the mass market.

5. **Interior preferable to exterior.**

The director will shoot outside if the light is right, but for an interior scene, the lighting and sound can be controlled.

6. **No special effects.**

Consider your genre: a space film without money looks tacky (remember *Plan 9 From Outer Space?*); the same is true of those blow-everyone-away in the middle of a crowded street scenes. Action believability is not easily achieved on the cheap. In fact, it's not a bad idea to banish guns altogether—even the blanks and squibs require weapons experts onset as well as expensive insurance. Don't forget: Special effects are not just computer-generated images (CGI)—don't even think about fires and explosions—rain, snow, wind, or even heavy traffic have to be faked and achieved and so are deemed special effects. (Different seasons in the same script can create havoc; in fact, use the blue pencil on any kind of weather you write, besides sunny summer days.)

7. **No children or pets.**

Your budget will skyrocket if you have scenes with children—their hours are strictly regulated and there's also the cost of a teacher who must be on the set. (Plus, there can be pesky parents hanging around.) The same goes for animals—the horror stories you've heard about getting animals to act on cue are most likely true (see the famous cat-sipping milk scene in *Day for Night*). And animal trainers can be prima donnas, too.

8. **No period pieces.**

You might incorporate stock footage to give the film scope, but period pieces are a problem unless you have an "in" at a costume house or access to a "wild west" town in the desert which has banished every vestige of the late 20th century.

9. **Stick to terra firma.**

   That means stay off the water and out of the air. If you don't, you'll regret the insurance rider you'll need. Boats, water stunts, airplanes, helicopters, and blimps are verboten to all but the most technically experienced and well-heeled productions.

10. **No complex crowd shots.**

    Don't have the main characters chatting away while jogging in between traffic and crowds. Extras may work cheaply, but they need proper clothing, makeup, and direction (and don't forget the extra fee for Craft Services—that can add another $200 a day in doughnuts!). And police are expensive; save the traffic control for the line to get into your movie.

11. **No fancy camera directions.**

    Let your plot tell the story. Crane shots, dissolves, pans and sweeps, dolly tracks, and Steadicams are not cost-effective. Getting "fancy" should mean no more than rubbing a little gel on the lens.

12. **No specific music cues, products, or protected work.**

    The license fees can break the budget, if proper licenses are even negotiated. In fact, some wonderful films are still languishing in studio vaults, deprived of a video/DVD release, because the music rights were never properly licensed for all media. In addition, brand name products and recognizable art or trademarks must be licensed and even a doctored photo of a celebrity may violate valuable publicity rights. (Actor Dustin Hoffman sued a national magazine for using a photo of the character he portrayed in *Tootsie*—artfully displayed in a current designer's dress. A jury awarded him $3 million in damages.)

13. **Be realistic.**

    I read one low-budget film in which the opening scene had the main character dragging his wounded leg up the crest of a hill where he found himself directly in the path of "a stampede of a thousand white buffalo!" Unless you want white to be the new color of your producer's hair, understand your budget limitations and be realistic.

That cigar-chomping pro? That was Sam Arkoff. Undaunted by his gruff dismissal of my first idea, I pitched him another one that same day—an idea I thought would be simple and inexpensive enough for AIP. It was the story of a small-time clubfighter who gets a fluke shot at the heavyweight title. He wants only to be standing at the end of the fight and not be "just another bum from the neighborhood." It was titled The Italian Stallion back then, and was later variously known as Hell's Kitchen and Pepper Alley, among other titles. You probably know it best as *Rocky*. Sam passed on that, too.

Shortly afterward, I made my first studio deal and was happily ensconced in offices at Universal Studios, nestled snugly between Sly Stallone and Steven Spielberg. I promptly forgot all about low budgets and concentrated on making studio pictures. I thought I'd never see Sam again.

Then, years later, on one sun-drenched morning at the Cannes Film Festival, I was sitting on the terrace of my hotel, watching the blue water cascade over white rocks and enjoying my breakfast, when my nostrils became aware of the wafting smell of pungent cigar smoke. I looked over my shoulder and there was Arkoff, who, without missing a beat, mumbled in my direction, "What about that script, kid, huh? Guess I should've bit on that one."

Right again, Sam.

from the trenches: WRITING THE SHOWCASE SHORT

It's how Spielberg, Coppola, Lucas, and Scorsese got their start. As a producer, I found the first three filmmakers I ever worked with through short film showcases. Always on the lookout for new talent, I still try my best to make it to film festivals, film school screenings, and private showings of independent films. USC, UCLA, NYU, Columbia, and AFI, in particular, all do a great job of exposing student work to the film community. A host of other film schools make an annual trek to Hollywood, blanketing the town with postcards and full-color brochures and renting theaters to champion their school's talent.

But things changed not too long ago. With the growth of the Internet and DSL, a few clicks of a mouse were all any producer or talent scout needed to bring thousands of showcase shorts streaming right into his or her living room. Even a technophobe like me was soon surfing over 100 sites that offered up a seemingly endless crop of narrative, documentary, or experimental shorts, many produced with a department store video camera and edited on a home computer. (Beware: the docs and experimental films are not likely to garner interest from the main stream movie world.) It sure beat sifting through a pile of scripts and toting home

continued

a dozen or so to read over a fine spring-like southern California weekend. Grab a tub of popcorn, sit back, and surf! It's so easy who could resist? But that, of course, soon became the problem.

Overnight, it seems, anyone with a camcorder was making movies. Every pimple-faced 13-year-old was a budding filmmaker. No script, no problem. No actors, so much the better. What was once a novel and facile way of introducing acting, writing, and directing talent to the industry quickly gave way to a glut of amateurish, poorly conceived, and horribly produced schlock. The players in Hollywood quickly tired of the next slice-of-life, Gen-X or Gen-Y youth-angst offering. Spending an evening viewing out-of-focus, unedited, plotless wonders became a chore akin to watching paint dry. If it's possible, it even began to make reading scripts fun again! Predictably, many sites suffered a swift demise with the bursting of the dot.com bubble, and I would have bet the flurry of shorts available over the net would have diminished at least by half as a direct consequence.

Not so. Instead, it's doubled. And I still watch them, though with limited patience and a very discretionary and very expeditious "delete" instinct. Why do I bother? Because the flood of new *screenplays* making the rounds each year has not doubled, it's *quadrupled* and covering them—as any agent, producer, or film exec will tell you—can be an expensive and time-consuming nightmare. If "everyone" is writing a screenplay, you can bet most of them are pretty bad. And though there are no doubt an equal number of occasional gems in the script and the short film format, *watching* (as opposed to reading) a movie does seem a more economical (and enjoyable) use of time and resources.

There is another reason also. For anyone who has been in the trenches and actually made a movie, a knee-jerk respect exists for any maverick digging into his own pocket, gathering the resources, and cranking out one of his own. The short film marks the filmmaker as a person who has tackled the physical, financial, and creative challenge of putting words into moving images that tell a story. Nothing quite compares with making a movie to prove you have what it takes to make it in this highly competitive business. And the agent or producer can see the work of a whole range of talents at the same time.

In 2004, Australians Leigh Whannel and James Wan patched together a short script as the basis for a four-minute DVD they shot in their basement to use as a pitch for their screenplay, Saw. A round about route, sure, but their script was ultimately produced on a shoestring budget of $1.2 million. Whannel went on to star in the film and Wann directed and the movie grossed $102.9 million worldwide—$55 million in North America alone.

Which, in turn, is the one big caveat for the screenwriter: *no one reads short film scripts.* Shorts are popular with producers and agents precisely because they can just pop them in the VCR/DVD player. It is the film, not the writing, which impresses. Short film scripts are viewed as production tools. The storytelling talent the short showcases is generally accepted to be that of the "filmmaker," an ego title often usurped by the director (as if any one person can take credit for a film). And, fair or not, short films serve primarily as calling cards for feature or television film *directing* careers. (On occasion, one acts as a springboard for the writer to develop a feature film based on the short—as when James Dearden was asked to expand his 40-minute short, *Diversion*—resulting in the 1997 block-buster, *Fatal Attraction*, directed by Adrian Lyne.)

Sure, the more discerning agents and producers will also use the short film to ferret out the writer, knowing that's the truly rare creative commodity in Hollywood. But for the most part, the scribe is way down the list when kudos for the best short is handed out. Because agents and producers sell features, not shorts. That's the business they are in. They're interested in people who make movies happen. That's why when your short hits the circuit, you are strongly advised to have a *feature* concept or screenplay (something you would like to do next) ready to pitch to whomever should come a'calling.

And if you're going to write a short, and you can raise the funds to film it without attaching a third-party director, why not direct it also? As did the four poster boys for a film school education whose famous last names began this column. They wrote, as well as directed their early shorts, and their writing talents have had a great deal to do with their ultimate success. But it was the features they were burning to make that got them development deals and offices on the studio lot. And it was the universal tendency (sprouting from the French "auteur" theory) to regard the director as the primary creator of the film that made them household names.

If a painfully shy George Lucas can do it, you can do it too. If you can't afford 16 mm, just grab a Super-8, hi-8, digital, or VHS camera and practice saying "action" and "cut" with panache. Stick to a sync sound narrative short and don't get too experimental unless you're only doing it to entertain your friends. It'll help form your creative vision, you'll get full credit for any eventual success and, trust me, you'll be happy you did. (Is there anyone, really given the chance, who doesn't want to direct?) If nothing else, you'll learn more about screenwriting—and the real world challenges of translating words into images—than from most film school curriculum.

continued

In that spirit, I would like to offer a *10-point short film strategy* gleaned from my own limited experience writing short films and my much more extensive experience watching them.

STRATEGY

1. **A short film is not a short feature film.**

   (Maybe the most important, if obvious, of all.) It is the length most appropriate for the theme, subject matter, or character(s) explored. You can't just cut down that old spec script to size. *Originality* is prized above all else.

2. **Short films can and should take risks.**

   The budget is less, the purpose more defined, the appeal does not have to be universal. Unlikable, even abhorrent, main characters are possible. Non-politically correct themes may be explored. Structure can be manipulated. Use the freedom inherent in this non-commercial medium.

3. **Short films are highly focused.**

   The premise should easily fit into a sentence. One main character, one main conflict, sometimes revolving around only one incident. Taking on too much is a sure recipe for disaster.

4. **The mark of a well-scripted short film is fresh characterization, inventive visuals, proper pacing, and a quick, satisfying ending that hits your audience in the gut.**

   Even if you are not the director, even if the film is a *visual tour de force,* your contribution can still shine if the film is possessed of a *clear narrative thrust* that marks the writer as a skilled storyteller.

5. **The context should be a rich one, the setting metaphorical, the climax satisfying or disturbing but never without emotional impact.**

   By having the external world reflect the internal struggle of the characters, the audience gets a bigger emotional bang in less screen time.

6. **Conflict, choices, commitments, and action define character, in the short as well as the feature film.**

   The staple of old-fashioned storytelling—a strongly drawn main character facing a difficult moral quandary, ultimately resolved through motivated action (or a unique twist on same)—is still that which lures producers to festivals to "discover" screenwriters.

7. **Because of the shorter length, use screen time judiciously.**

    Each scene should carry tone, plot, *and* character. Visual setups, payoffs, and leaps in action are preferable to dialogue-heavy exposition or plot development. Wherever possible, remove dialogue and replace with action or visual exposition. If you do have a dialogue based short script, set the verbal style from the start and offset it by adding clever, creative, inventive visual elements to the backdrop of the scene. The director will love you for it.

8. **If you are writing, for example, a fifteen-minute film, ask yourself: What are the ten to fifteen shots that will tell the entire story for you?**

    Strong juxtaposition of powerful images will not only save screen time and allow you to tell a much richer story in a shorter time, it will result in a much tighter pace and structure and allow the film to tell its story with as few images as possible.

9. **Use sound, music, and image to full advantage.**

    These are often mistakenly labeled as production tools, but particularly in a short the writer must utilize them as a primary means of storytelling, not just as icing on the cake.

10. **Short scripts need a 100% solid, workable structure.**

    There is no room for slack, meandering, or bare expository scenes in your story. Take out everything you don't absolutely need. Grab the audience immediately, hold them the entire way, and resolve the story as economically as possible. Write it long and condense it to a quick inventive setup, carefully planned cuts to move the story along, and the cleverest, most surprising resolution you can devise. Leave the audience feeling that they've been on a short roller coaster ride which ended much too quickly.

CHAPTER 7

SECURING THE RIGHTS (AND OTHER CONSIDERATIONS) FOR ADAPTATIONS AND TRUE STORIES

As noted in Chapter 3, more than half of the screenplays nominated for Writers Guild of America Awards or Academy Awards are for works *based upon material previously produced or published.* And television has an infatuation with dramas based on real people and true stories culled from the headlines. But would-be adapters take note: The credo of successful adapters is, "I know how to tell a story, so don't confuse me with the facts."

In that regard, adaptations are not so different from original screenplays. Screenwriters must *make up, adapt, and re-order* the most compelling incidents to serve the screen drama. A novel, a play, a true story, or one based on events in the news—all may be worthy *premises*, but the screenwriter must create from them a unique motion picture event. The screenplay will still require complex main characters, a supporting cast, tightly structured scenes, visual settings, terse movie-speak dialogue—the same ingredients that go into creating an original script. The only difference is the adapter starts with someone else's core ideas.

For bestselling books or historical events and characters—even for stories based on current affairs or events in the local news—audiences may well bring their own preconceived notions about who did what to whom and how they are to be portrayed in a film. But the screenwriter is not a journalist nor is he held to journalistic standards. He is creating a work of art unique to film. Historical fact or public record shouldn't be lightly tossed aside—unless to do so makes for a better film. If your screenplay centers on the White House during the time of the Cuban Missile Crisis, for example, you may want to respect the event—the crisis is well-documented. The players are also somewhat set by history and public awareness—the Kennedys and their staff. But you get to choose the point of view character and what was said and done is subject to dramatic license; if your intention is to do revisionist history, you can even alter the participants, events, and outcome. Maybe we'd all speak Russian at the end of your film.

Similarly, for those beloved novels, it's *usually* a good idea to maintain a healthy respect for the themes and values set forth in the underlying work, but that's the writer's call—what's best for the story and what must be changed. If you are adapting a previous film or a television series, then sure, let the fair-haired characters inspire your writing, allow the plot and themes to serve as *source material*. But your task is not to replicate art, but rather to *create* art, an entirely new film that will stand on its own dramatic or comedic merits.

That said, for the writer who desires to tap into such a rich wellspring of ready-to-wear character and story, certain rudimentary guidelines can save valuable time and costly legal fees.

Adaptations of Previously Produced or Published Work

Good story material may be found as near as your own bookshelves or the dusty back room of a neighborhood used bookstore. Of course, to adapt a novel, play, or other written or produced material for the screen, you must first secure the underlying rights, usually referred to as *the motion picture, television, and allied rights* in and to the material to be adapted. These rights are severable from the bundle of rights encompassed by the copyright and are normally retained by the author when publication or live theater rights are sold. Acquiring these rights may require you to put on your producer's hat. Don't be intimidated; as some executives say, a producer is only "someone who knows a writer." Here's how it's done.

For *books*, a simple phone call or letter to *the subsidiary rights or ancillary rights* division of the publisher, or a letter to the author addressed in care of the publisher, should establish if the film rights are available. If they are, determine who owns or controls the copyright and has the power to grant such rights to third parties such as yourself. If the book or play you seek is not a recent publication (e.g., a book 40 or 50 years old might catch your fancy), you may find that the publisher is out of business or is under new management and the information you desire may not be available or readily forthcoming. In this case, you will have to go directly to the author.

Your local library should stock author directories that may be helpful, including the *Writers Directory*, which lists writers from around the world who have at least one work published in English, and *Contemporary Authors*, which at 165 volumes and listing over 100,000 authors may be the most complete source of author information available; for information about either book, contact Thomson-Gale Research, toll-free at 800-877-4253. You can also communicate with The National Writers Union (212-254-0279) or The Authors Guild (212-563-5904); either will access their membership files to help you locate an author.

For *bestsellers*, past or present, it is best to invest in a copyright check by an attorney versed in copyright law. Two firms that are well known for their expertise in title searches on literary properties are Thompson & Thompson and Brylofsky & Cleary, both based in Washington, D.C. and accessible through their own web sites. The U.S. Copyright Office charges only $20 an hour to search its indexes for information on copyright ownership and/or assignments, or you can do a search yourself through an established checking service like the Library of Congress (202-707-3000) or other companies offering the service (for a small fee) on the Internet. If film rights do appear to be available, you will want to know if such rights have been previously transferred and to whom (namely, producers—have they already shopped the work in Hollywood with no success?). Keep in mind that since copyright owners are not required to register their work or their ownership, even the best research may prove inconclusive.

Obtaining rights to a bestseller can be expensive (tens of thousands of dollars), so you will likely want an agent or lawyer to help you craft a deal that is fair to all concerned. For a lesser-known work, the author or his representative may be inclined to grant a writer a favorable arrangement since your interest may help sell the film rights to a dormant novel. With both parties going on good faith, the option fee can be as little as one dollar (or, it can even be free), and a one-page deal memo (setting forth in plain English who gets what, for how long, and on what terms) is often the only documentation needed to get the ball rolling.

The Writers Guild has carved out a *"no option" exception* to their minimum payment schedule for a work targeted for television, where a few phone calls may serve to cover the universe of potential buyers. In such cases, option money need not be paid to the writer for the period during which the potential purchaser of the rights actively seeks financing for the project. This practice is referred to as an *if-come* deal. In such a deal, a purchase price, while agreed upon beforehand, is only paid upon setting the project up at a network or other television venue.

To adapt a *stage play*, contact the author or his agent and proceed as above.

To embark on a *sequel or remake* of a previously produced motion picture, begin your rights inquiry with the distributor (usually one of the major motion picture studios). In most cases, your quest will end there as well. (Studios are not keen on unsolicited attempts to exploit their libraries.) But don't be dissuaded if you truly believe in the project. Your enthusiasm or your spec script written on a wing and a prayer may spark a renewed interest in a previously forgotten or ignored gem. While the studio is under no legal obligation to connect you to the project they own, the executives may decide to work with you if you provide a *truly novel and substantial twist* in story or approach—in which case, an *implied contract* may be deemed to have been entered into, which could protect you against the studio exploiting your ideas without compensation. (Although ideas are not protected by copyright, the California Supreme Court, in the case of *Desney v Wilder* nearly a half-century ago, held that an implied contract—a legal fiction—could arise when the circumstances surrounding a script submission or even a concept pitch create an *implication* that if the work is used there will be payment for it; consult your lawyer if you suspect it may apply in your case.)

The implied contract claim came under question recently when certain federal district courts in Los Angeles held that if a claim was based on the submission of material eligible for copyright—such as a screenplay—a claim for breach of implied contract was preempted (barred) by the federal Copyright Act. But then, in late 2004, the Ninth Circuit, the federal appeals court with jurisdiction over California, ruled in *Grosso v. Miramax* that a writer who submitted a screenplay to a studio (or, presumably, to any person or entity who traffics in such ideas in the regular course of business), could sue the studio for producing a movie containing ideas similar to those in the screenplay, even if the movie was not deemed similar enough to support a copyright infringement claim.

Finally, if the rights you seek are not available, you can still contact the current owner and offer to share your vision and enthusiasm for the material; you just might land a contract to perform writing services on the project.

Advice worth repeating: You can *write* a screen adaptation of any published or produced work without acquiring the rights. But, you can't *sell* your screenplay based on that work without them (unless you sell it to someone who already owns or plans to acquire those rights). Any other buyer will require a clear and complete chain of title from the "based upon" material through to the final draft screenplay. Still, you can always use your adaptation as a writing sample to showcase your talent at adapting plot, characters, and dialogue to the screen. But, such a work may offer little hint of your talent for creating story and character from scratch.

The Limits of Copyright: Public Domain

Copyright is not granted in perpetuity. When it expires, the work falls into the public domain. This means it is up for grabs by anyone—for free. (The writers who brought the novels of Jane Austen to the screen were paid—not Austen's heirs.)

You don't have to go back to Jane Austen's time to find public domain material. *For work created before January 1, 1978,* the copyright survives for 28 years after the registration date or the date the work was first offered in the marketplace. The copyright is renewable for a term of 47 years (effective with the Copyright Act of 1976), for a total protectable term of 75 years. However, due to neglect or oversight, many copyrights are not renewed.

For works registered with the copyright office or first offered in the marketplace after 1978, the copyright term is for the life of the author plus 75 years. For joint authorship of a work (the creation of which is deemed not to be separable), the 75 years runs from the demise of the last surviving partner. In the case of a work "for hire," the protected term is 95 years from publication. When these terms expire, the work falls into the public domain and is free for the taking without permission or payment.

Adapting True Stories

In writing classes across America, students are urged to delve into their personal experience to find material about which they can write with knowledge and passion. Do you hate your boss? Write a thinly veiled character in his likeness and let the world know what you think of him. Did your girlfriend leave you for another woman? And poor you left with only those juicy secrets shared into the night… it beats seven years of therapy, doesn't it? But what if they recognize themselves in your work and decide to sue you? Doesn't the First Amendment protect freedom of speech and aren't you, as an artist, allowed a little artistic license with the facts? What about libel? You're only writing the truth and isn't the truth considered an absolute defense to a libel action? Or, what if you believe you have found the perfect subject for an MOW from yesterday's headline news: the cheerleader mom who plots to blot out her daughter's competition or the beauty contestant found strangled in the basement of her parent's home.

What rights must you obtain to depict those people in a movie and why?

Fine Print Caveat: what follows, for reasons of brevity and ease of comprehension, is an overview of the subject. It does not attempt to cover all the intricacies, exceptions, and technical minutia of the applicable legalities and their exceptions. For a legal opinion on your specific circumstances, you should consult with an entertainment attorney.

The Law of Libel

The law of libel protects against false written statements, communicated to another, which damage the reputation of the defamed person or entity, or subjects him/it to hatred, contempt, or ridicule. (The law of slander applies to the spoken word.) The deceased are excepted; you cannot libel the dead because defamation is a personal right that does not descend to the estate. Defamation of the deceased could, however, lead to liability to members of his family, partners in his business, or others directly damaged by your libelous statements.

There is also an exception for so-called "*public figures.*" In order that the press may freely publish opinions and criticism about individuals in the public eye (politicians, celebrities, or other subjects of media attention), the published statement must *not only* be false to be actionable, but the writer or publisher of the statement must have either known it to be false or have held a negligent and reckless disregard for whether or not it was false.

Even if everything you've written about an individual can be proven to be true, you may still have legal problems. The rights of privacy and publicity may carve out exceptions to your ability to protect yourself with even the veil of truth.

The Right of Privacy

While libel seeks to protect a person's reputation, the right of privacy seeks to protect an individual's damaged feelings.

Even if they are true, if facts are revealed which are "highly offensive" to a person of "ordinary sensibilities" and are of a nature to which the public has "no legitimate concern," they are not protected by the "truth" defense to a libel action.

> It may be true that your girlfriend engages in kinky sexual activity, but the law does not condone your revealing the sordid details to the world. Of course, if your true love is sadly departed, that's another matter; like libel, an individual's right of privacy ends with death.

And, there is yet another weapon given to the aggrieved and sensitive victim of the poison pen: *the law of false light*—a close cousin to libel law, false light has all the characteristics of the law respecting invasion of privacy. A false light lawsuit must prove not only that materially false facts objectionable to a reasonable person have been published (a term of art extending to any medium), but also that the way those facts have been presented has placed the complaining individual in a false light in the public eye, hurting his feelings or interfering with his ability to exist peacefully in the community. A public figure must also satisfy the "knowingly false or reckless disregard for the truth" criteria outlined above to successfully sue under this admittedly murky legal theory.

The Right of Publicity

Recognized in about half of the country, including the entertainment capitals of California, New York, and Florida, the right of publicity protects against the unauthorized use of a person's name, face, voice, or image for commercial benefit. You may not, for example, appropriate the likeness of Kevin Costner to help sell your video spoof on golf without his prior approval or consent. Moreover, this is a right that can survive the individual—it is capable of being passed down to heirs and estates. (You can't put that likeness of W.C. Fields on a cereal box without paying a royalty to the attorney paid to administer the Fields estate's right of publicity.)

As you may guess from the above examples, these are not often screenplay problems, as the First Amendment protects the use of names and likenesses in that arena. But if your work is destined for multimedia exposure, such as on billboards or games used for "purposes of trade or advertising," you may have legalities to consider.

Obtaining Releases or Acquiring the Rights to Life Stories

Here's the good news: *No one sues on a screenplay;* they wait until the movie comes out. In the ecstasy of creation, the writer has a free hand. But then again, there is that pesky warranty and indemnity writers are asked to sign should they actually *sell* their script. So before a production lawyer puts you on the hot seat (or breaks your deal over it) you might wish to consider this advice: Unless the real-life person you intend to portray is a public figure or deceased and you don't have a prevaricating or malicious bone in your body, the rights of privacy and of publicity and laws against defamation make it advisable to obtain, in writing, the rights to his life story and a release of liability for your portrayal of that life.

If you can't manage to obtain a free release (for a limited period and with payment of a stated sum due should you sell the project), you may have to buy it. This usually involves an option and a purchase price attached to an exclusive term (say, one year). During that term, you have the right to seek the development and production of a film based on that true story. If you fail to exercise the option, all rights revert back to the individual from whom they were obtained.

What you are buying is his complete cooperation, and that of his family and heirs, in depicting the events of his life, including your access to private conversations and writings (such as letters and diaries). And no matter how he pleads for it, *never give him script approval.*

Any such agreement should also include the following:

1. A representation that the person understands he is giving the right and permission to depict the events of his life in a movie or television film and that the purchaser of those rights (or his assignee) has the right to embellish, fictionalize, dramatize, and adapt the facts of that life story in any manner in which he chooses, at his sole discretion.

2. A representation and warranty that he agrees never to bring suit in any court of law in any venue based on defamation and invasion of rights of privacy or publicity.

3. That the rights granted are fully assignable to any other person or entity.

A bit of paperwork, sure—but better than the potential legal liability from a film based on the life of an uncompensated, living, breathing, sensitive, and angry individual. Besides, a studio or network may demand nothing less. It is common practice for producers of biographies, fact-based fiction, true stories pulled from the headlines, etc., to require the writer to *annotate* as to source each line of dialogue, each twist and turn of the plot, every detail of setting or characterization that is not totally invented.

Annotation requires the writer to substantiate the source of every non-fictionalized word, whether by taped interviews or courtroom transcripts or from double and triple substantiation by witnesses and testimony to actual events or conversations. In some cases, the writer may create a scene necessary for plot or character development and annotate it by showing that, from what he can prove was said or done, the character in this circumstance *could have, would have, or should have* displayed the character traits exhibited.

The validity of the above caution notwithstanding, in April 2005, the Florida Supreme Court ruled against the surviving family of the fishermen portrayed in the movie, *The Perfect Storm*, in their suit for *commercial misappropriation* or invasion of privacy. The film's producer, Warner Bros., had never compensated any of the ill-fated fishermen depicted nor did they obtain permission to portray them in the film. Nonetheless, the state court held that the Florida statute on misappropriation applied only to situations in which a person's name or likeness was used for commercial trade or advertising purposes. The court found that although the purpose of the movie was to make money, it was not the kind of commercial exploitation covered by the statute and to hold otherwise would infringe free speech.

Conclusion

As the above may serve to illustrate, there can be no clear rules in an area of the law that seeks to assign monetary damages for bruised egos and tarnished reputations. Perhaps free speech and literal truth give license to say that Miss Milky Way has put on so many pounds that her title refers to a candy bar rather than an asteroid belt. But remember—anyone can bring a lawsuit and people that are hurt badly enough by someone generally do. In the end, being right or ruled non-liable may be little consolation to you for the lost time and legal fees incurred defending yourself.

Where real people are concerned, your best protection is in your art. *Fictionalize.* Use your relatives, friends, and enemies as springboards, not as substitutes, for your imagination. Change men to women, jocks to nerds, doctors to lawyers. If someone has to stretch to identify himself, he'll have a hard time getting a lawyer, much less a court, to find merit in his case. And you'll likely sleep a lot better.

PART III

What to Do after It's Written: The Submission Process

Chapter 8

Protecting Your Work

"Trust in Allah, but Tie Up Your Camel"

Whatever the peculiar vagaries of the business, one fact is certain—producers won't be able to purchase or produce your work if they don't have access to it. In other words, as a writer, you cannot be unduly afraid of theft but also hope to circulate your work to buyers. No matter what its merits may be, your unread script will remain unsold in the dark recesses of your desk drawer unless you expose it to the light.

That said, there are legitimate concerns about protecting your material from uncompensated appropriation (i.e., having it stolen, ripped-off, snatched in broad daylight—this may sound like an overexaggeration, but it's an emotional issue). To hear the horror stories circulating in restaurants and studios around town, this sort of thing happens all the time. Major producers and directors often exact confidentiality agreements from their employees and will assign code numbers to script submissions, etc. But represented writers rarely give story theft a second thought—the reputations and business practices of their agents, managers, and lawyers provide the protection of a Kevlar vest.

Certainly, each year, several movies appear which seem to have lifted their plots from the same source material. (You may remember all the "body exchange" films that came out around the time of *Big*? I can think of six offhand.) But does that mean plagiarism took place? *Conscious stealing* happens less often than we may believe. To most mainstream film executives or producers, stealing an idea is not worth the trouble. Movies cost too much to produce—it makes little sense to cheat on the relatively small amount it would take to secure the appropriate rights. (That's what development budgets are for.) Also, in the long run, it's in the best interest of the studio executives to establish relationships with people who have bright ideas.

Unconscious stealing is a whole other story. Thirty years as an entertainment lawyer, producer, and film company executive has taught me this: You absorb a lot of ideas during the course of hundreds of pitch meetings and thousands of script submissions.

In a story conference, with plotlines and dialogue tossed back and forth or as writers, producers, directors, and executives try to beat a deadline or solve a script problem, who really can say where any particular thought originates?

One judge in the Midwest is said to have found, as a matter of triable fact, that there are only 29 basic plot ideas in the world, with the most enduring of those realized in the repeatable genre movies that form the staple of Hollywood's diet. Critic Northrop Frye seems to agree: "Poetry can only be made out of other poems; novels out of other novels."

In fact, the very concept of "originality," suggests Los Angeles copyright attorney S.M. Moore, may be more a matter of incorporating old ideas into new form than the solitary creation of an idea that is assumed by copyright. After all, if writers mine the human condition for stories, isn't it likely those stories have already been told and retold, born anew each time through a unique voice, a fresh perspective? And when a TV series is based upon a film that is based upon a novel, the lines of "originality" blur even further. (Perhaps this explains why the single most litigated issue under the Copyright Act is whether a given work is an infringing derivative work "based upon" another copyrighted work. For while copyright protection does not extend to "underlying ideas" but only to the expression of such ideas, neither does infringement require a word-for-word theft of the original work. Courts have found infringement whenever the new work is "substantially similar" to the copyrighted work.)

Of course, it is perfectly acceptable for a writer to incorporate *public domain* material (for which copyright protection has expired or was never attached) into his own literary work. Charles C. Mann, writing in the *Atlantic Monthly* on the question of copyright and the theft of ideas, made this point:

Shakespeare derived some of the language in *Julius Caesar* from an English translation of a French translation of *Plutarch*; he followed a printed history so closely for Henry V that scholars believe he had the book open on his desk as he wrote. In this century Eugene O'Neill gleaned *Mourning Becomes Electra* from Aeschylus.

Personally, I subscribe to psychologist Carl Jung's theory of "the collective unconscious." Sometimes ideas are out there, like dreams floating in space, and any number of people laboring over a story might pull them out of the air and adopt them as their own. The novelist P.D. James echoed this, saying "a good idea, whether related to plot or theme, is like a benign infection borne on the air, waiting to be caught and used by others if one doesn't get [it] written quickly."

Still, make no mistake, you have rights with respect to your work product. Even if you have put a new twist on an old plot or you have only presented it orally in a pitch meeting, it is protectable, either by federal copyright or by various state laws which claim that an implied contract exists between you and the potential buyer if your material is submitted, orally or in writing, with the expectation of payment for its use and is, in fact, subsequently used.

As stated in Chapter 7, in late 2004, the Ninth Circuit, the federal appeals court with jurisdiction over California, ruled in *Grosso v. Miramax* that a writer who submitted a screenplay to a studio, could sue the studio for producing a movie containing ideas similar to those in the screenplay, even if the movie was not deemed similar enough to support a copyright infringement claim.

All writers are advised to afford themselves the best protection possible against theft of their work. A written agreement is best. If that's not practical at the time (pitch meetings leave writers particularly vulnerable to theft, conscious or unconscious), try to get an oral agreement that your work is being submitted for sale and won't be used without payment. Keep in mind that blind, unsolicited submission of your work is a risky, no-win proposition.

Here is a *four-point strategy* to protect your work:

STRATEGY

1. **Submit wisely.**

   Submission through established channels, like agents, entertainment lawyers, or literary managers, offers your most basic protection. Regular business relationships are less likely to be put in jeopardy by a rogue attempt to circumnavigate the author's interests.

2. **Maintain a paper trail.**

Keep records of all correspondence between you and any potential buyer who has been given access to your work. (If you have an agent, they will do this as a matter of course.) Never submit your material without a cover letter. Save your rejection letters. Take notes of meetings or telephone conversations, being careful to chart date, time, person spoken to, and subject matter (these can serve double duty when claiming business expenses on your tax return).

3. **Copyright your written work.**

This is your simplest and best protection. Article 1, Section 8, of the U.S. Constitution gives Congress the power to secure "for limited times" to authors "the exclusive Right to their respective Writings."

What is copyrightable?

Under current law, every "original work of authorship" expressed in a tangible medium is copyrighted at the moment of creation. Mere ideas, concepts, names, titles, facts, etc., are not copyrightable, per se, though other forms of protection may apply. Titles, for example, when registered with the Motion Picture Association of America, are protected from use by other members of the MPAA, though only for a set period of time. Also, a title can become so well publicized that it acquires a "secondary meaning"—public identification with the title is so strong that to allow it to be cloned would likely cause confusion in the public's mind. (One could not, for example, release a movie about underwater predators and call it Jaws.) True events are not copyrightable but any original expression of those events, as in a news or magazine article, is protectable.

Who owns the copyright?

The creator of the work is the owner of the copyright, unless that work is created "for hire," in which case the employer (the producer or studio) is considered the author of the work, for copyright purposes. A work "for hire" is any treatment, screenplay, or other work (including films) created by an employee for an employer or pursuant to a written contract that expressly provides that it is a "work made for hire." In such case, the creator has no ownership rights to the work created.

The bundle of rights encompassed by the copyright are property rights, protectable from unauthorized use, trespass, or encroach-ment—the same as a piece of land. Similarly, they can be sold, bartered, assigned (all rights), transferred (one or more rights), passed on in a will, or even broken up and auctioned off in parts (but only in writing). For example, a writer may sell the adaptive rights to his work, i.e., the right to make a film or television show based on it, while maintaining the right to publish the work or have it performed on the live stage.

How do I register the copyright?

Register your copyright by filling out Copyright Application Form PA, a copy of which and instructions for completing can be downloaded from the U.S. Copyright Office's web site at http://www.copyright.gov/forms/. (I've also included a copy at the end of the chapter.) The current copyright fee is $30 and a copy of your material must be included in the same envelope as the completed form. Your material is copyrighted as of the date of receipt, but allow about three months for confirmation. An original can be obtained by writing to: Copyright Office, Library of Congress, Washington, D.C. 20599. Recorded information is available 24 hours a day by phoning (800) 688-9889 (toll-free), or call (202) 707-3000 on weekdays to speak to someone in the Copyright Office. You may also call the forms and registration hotline at (202) 707-9100.

Under international copyright law enacted March 1, 1989, pursuant to the Berne Convention, registration of your copyright is optional, but it is strongly recommended. It puts the world on notice of your claim to creation, it establishes proof of authorship as of a certain date, and it is a prerequisite to the extended benefits of any infringement suit you later may be forced to file. On a similar note, it is also *no longer necessary* to preserve your copyright (or risk having it fall into public domain) through the use of a copyright notice (placing the word "copyright," it's abbreviation, or "©" on the cover page, followed by your name and the year of copyright). In fact, for screenplays, a copyright notice is rarely seen.

How long is the work protected?

The Copyright Act of 1976, effective January 1, 1978, and just recently revised by the U.S. Congress, extends copyright protection to individuals for life, plus 70 years (now the same term as for British works); and to a company, in the case of a "work made for hire," for a term of 95 years from the date of publication. For works written prior to 1978, a protected term of 75 years from publication applies. ("Publication," as defined, includes films of the work, although works under the current act need not be published to be granted protection.)

While it is not possible here to cover all the specifics involved with copyright protection, you can contact an attorney who specializes in that area of the law (ask for references from your local bar association). Also, the Writers Guild of America, west, Inc., recently published a thorough pamphlet called *Plagiarism & Copyright Infringement*. It can be obtained for a nominal fee by writing the Guild at: 7000 West Third Street, Los Angeles, CA 90048-4329.

---

4. **Register your work with the Writers Guild.**

Both the Writers Guild, west (address above; phone: 323-951-4000) and the Writers Guild, East (555 West 57th St., New York, NY 10019; 212-767-7800) operate a registration program that is widely used by all writers, both Guild and non-Guild. This service is also available over the Internet by contacting the Registry at http://wga.org.

Guild registration is recognized throughout the industry as an effective means of corroborating a claim of authorship because it establishes a specific date by which you authored the registered work. It does this by sealing received material (no bindings, covers, or brads) in an envelope, recording the date and time, and giving you a numbered receipt. The Guild subsequently can be called upon to produce the material in its signed, dated, and sealed envelope when necessary.

Guild registration accepts a wide range of material, including scripts, treatments, synopses, and outlines for radio, television, or film and even for stage plays, novels, short stories, poems, and lyrics. However, Guild registration is valid for only a five-year period (renewable), after which it is authorized to destroy the material without notice.

For recorded information on how to register your work, call the Writers Guild, west hotline at (323) 782-4500, or see the Guild's informational pamphlet included at the end of this chapter. Keep in mind that Guild registration is not a substitute for copyright.

A recent alternative to both Guild and copyright registration is The National Creative Registry. It is priced similarly to the Guild registration but provides a longer registry and certain unique services. You may write to them for information at: 1106 Second Street, Encinitas, CA 92024 or phone them at (619) 942-2660.

Q. Is it okay to just register my script with the WGA to protect it or should I go through the effort to copyright it?

Sherry, Los Angeles, California

A. There is no effort. Put down your pen and your work is copyrighted. *Registration*, on the other hand, is about proof of when you wrote it and your rights to sue for infringement. WGA registration is cheaper ($10 for members or $20 for non-members versus $30 to copyright), more people friendly (if you go to trial, someone will testify as to your date of submission), and perfect for the busy writer (you can register over the Internet). But that's where the comparison ends. Guild registration is for 5 years (renewable) whereas copyright registration is (for natural persons) life plus 70 years. To sue, you must copyright it first anyway and, if you get to court, only works copyrighted *prior to* infringement (if found) are entitled to attorneys' fees and statutory damages and even, under certain circumstances, to prima facie proof of ownership. So it's a no-brainer. Copyright it—and if you can afford the few extra bucks, register it too. You'll likely sleep better at night.

Finally, there persists in writers' folklore a practice called a "poor man's copyright," in which the writer sends his material by registered mail to himself or to a few close friends. If push comes to shove, he can produce his script in a sealed, postmarked envelope, thus establishing the date of authorship. This costs almost the same as a copyright or Guild registration and you must be responsible for keeping your envelope safe and preserving its seal, etc. It is not a recommended practice.

Copyright Office fees are subject to change. For current fees, check the Copyright Office website at *www.copyright.gov*, write the Copyright Office, or call (202) 707-3000.

Form PA
For a Work of Performing Arts
UNITED STATES COPYRIGHT OFFICE

REGISTRATION NUMBER

_____

PA   PAU
EFFECTIVE DATE OF REGISTRATION

_____
Month   Day   Year

DO NOT WRITE ABOVE THIS LINE. IF YOU NEED MORE SPACE, USE A SEPARATE CONTINUATION SHEET.

1

TITLE OF THIS WORK ▼

PREVIOUS OR ALTERNATIVE TITLES ▼

NATURE OF THIS WORK ▼ See instructions

2 a

NAME OF AUTHOR ▼

DATES OF BIRTH AND DEATH
Year Born ▼   Year Died ▼

Was this contribution to the work a "work made for hire"?
☐ Yes
☐ No

AUTHOR'S NATIONALITY OR DOMICILE
Name of Country
OR { Citizen of _____
{ Domiciled in _____

WAS THIS AUTHOR'S CONTRIBUTION TO THE WORK
Anonymous?   ☐ Yes ☐ No
Pseudonymous?   ☐ Yes ☐ No
If the answer to either of these questions is "Yes," see detailed instructions.

NATURE OF AUTHORSHIP Briefly describe nature of material created by this author in which copyright is claimed. ▼

NOTE

Under the law, the "author" of a "work made for hire" is generally the employer, not the employee (see instructions). For any part of this work that was "made for hire" check "Yes" in the space provided, give the employer (or other person for whom the work was prepared) as "Author" of that part, and leave the space for dates of birth and death blank.

b

NAME OF AUTHOR ▼

DATES OF BIRTH AND DEATH
Year Born ▼   Year Died ▼

Was this contribution to the work a "work made for hire"?
☐ Yes
☐ No

AUTHOR'S NATIONALITY OR DOMICILE
Name of Country
OR { Citizen of _____
{ Domiciled in _____

WAS THIS AUTHOR'S CONTRIBUTION TO THE WORK
Anonymous?   ☐ Yes ☐ No
Pseudonymous?   ☐ Yes ☐ No
If the answer to either of these questions is "Yes," see detailed instructions.

NATURE OF AUTHORSHIP Briefly describe nature of material created by this author in which copyright is claimed. ▼

c

NAME OF AUTHOR ▼

DATES OF BIRTH AND DEATH
Year Born ▼   Year Died ▼

Was this contribution to the work a "work made for hire"?
☐ Yes
☐ No

AUTHOR'S NATIONALITY OR DOMICILE
Name of Country
OR { Citizen of _____
{ Domiciled in _____

WAS THIS AUTHOR'S CONTRIBUTION TO THE WORK
Anonymous?   ☐ Yes ☐ No
Pseudonymous?   ☐ Yes ☐ No
If the answer to either of these questions is "Yes," see detailed instructions.

NATURE OF AUTHORSHIP Briefly describe nature of material created by this author in which copyright is claimed. ▼

3 a

YEAR IN WHICH CREATION OF THIS WORK WAS COMPLETED This information must be given in all cases.
_____ Year

b DATE AND NATION OF FIRST PUBLICATION OF THIS PARTICULAR WORK
Complete this information ONLY if this work has been published.
Month _____ Day _____ Year _____
Nation _____

4

See instructions before completing this space.

COPYRIGHT CLAIMANT(S) Name and address must be given even if the claimant is the same as the author given in space 2. ▼

TRANSFER If the claimant(s) named here in space 4 is (are) different from the author(s) named in space 2, give a brief statement of how the claimant(s) obtained ownership of the copyright. ▼

APPLICATION RECEIVED

ONE DEPOSIT RECEIVED

TWO DEPOSITS RECEIVED

FUNDS RECEIVED

DO NOT WRITE HERE
OFFICE USE ONLY

MORE ON BACK ▶ • Complete all applicable spaces (numbers 5-9) on the reverse side of this page.
• See detailed instructions.   • Sign the form at line 8.

DO NOT WRITE HERE
Page 1 of _____ pages

EXAMINED BY	FORM PA
CHECKED BY	
CORRESPONDENCE ☐ Yes	FOR COPYRIGHT OFFICE USE ONLY

DO NOT WRITE ABOVE THIS LINE. IF YOU NEED MORE SPACE, USE A SEPARATE CONTINUATION SHEET.

PREVIOUS REGISTRATION Has registration for this work, or for an earlier version of this work, already been made in the Copyright Office?
☐ **Yes** ☐ **No** If your answer is "Yes," why is another registration being sought? (Check appropriate box.) ▼ If your answer is No, do **not** check box A, B, or C.

a. ☐ This is the first published edition of a work previously registered in unpublished form.

b. ☐ This is the first application submitted by this author as copyright claimant.

c. ☐ This is a changed version of the work, as shown by space 6 on this application.

If your answer is "Yes," give: **Previous Registration Number** ▼   **Year of Registration** ▼

5

DERIVATIVE WORK OR COMPILATION Complete both space 6a and 6b for a derivative work; complete only 6b for a compilation.
Preexisting Material Identify any preexisting work or works that this work is based on or incorporates. ▼

a

6

See instructions before completing this space.

Material Added to This Work Give a brief, general statement of the material that has been added to this work and in which copyright is claimed. ▼

b

DEPOSIT ACCOUNT If the registration fee is to be charged to a Deposit Account established in the Copyright Office, give name and number of Account.
Name ▼   **Account Number** ▼

a

7

CORRESPONDENCE Give name and address to which correspondence about this application should be sent. Name / Address / Apt / City / State / ZIP ▼

b

Area code and daytime telephone number   (   )   Fax number   (   )

Email

CERTIFICATION* I, the undersigned, hereby certify that I am the

Check only one ▶
☐ author
☐ other copyright claimant
☐ owner of exclusive right(s)
☐ authorized agent of _____
Name of author or other copyright claimant, or owner of exclusive right(s) ▲

of the work identified in this application and that the statements made by me in this application are correct to the best of my knowledge.

8

Typed or printed name and date ▼ If this application gives a date of publication in space 3, do not sign and submit it before that date.

Date _____

Handwritten signature (X) ▼

X _____

Certificate will be mailed in window envelope to this address:

Name ▼

Number/Street/Apt ▼

City/State/ZIP ▼

YOU MUST:
• Complete all necessary spaces
• Sign your application in space 8

SEND ALL 3 ELEMENTS IN THE SAME PACKAGE:
1. Application form
2. Nonrefundable filing fee in check or money order payable to *Register of Copyrights*
3. Deposit material

MAIL TO:
Library of Congress
Copyright Office
101 Independence Avenue, S.E.
Washington, D.C. 20559-6000

Fees are subject to change. For current fees, check the Copyright Office website at www.copyright.gov, write the Copyright Office, or call (202) 707-3000.

9

Rev: June 2002—20,000   Web Rev: June 2002   ♻ Printed on recycled paper   U.S. Government Printing Office: 2000-461-113/20,021

WGA
INTELLECTUAL PROPERTY
REGISTRY

The WGA's Intellectual Property Registry receives over 30,000 pieces of literary material annually and is available to members and non-members. Writers are invited to submit their material to be archived by the Writers Guild to protect their work. For more information on this service, contact the Registry at (323) 782-4540.

PURPOSE AND COVERAGE
The WGA Intellectual Property Registry is available to assist all writers in establishing completion dates for particular pieces of their literary property written for the fields of radio, theatrical and television motion pictures, video cassettes/discs and interactive media.

Registration provides a dated record of the writer's claim to authorship of a particular literary material. If necessary a Registry employee may produce the material as evidence if legal or official guild action is initiated.

The Registry does not make comparisons of registration deposits, nor does it give legal opinions, advice or confer any statutory protections.

Registration with the Guild does not protect titles.

PROCEDURE FOR DEPOSIT
Materials may be submitted for registration in person or by mail. The Registry must receive:

1) One (1) unbound, loose-leaf copy of material on standard, 8 1/2" x 11" paper.
2) Cover sheet with title of material and all writers' full legal names.
3) Social security number (or equivalent), return address and telephone number of one writer (the registrant).
4) Registration fee:
   WGAw and WGAE members $10.00
   Non-members $20.00

Payment accepted in cash, check, money order or Visa/MC (expiration date required).

When the material is received, it is sealed in an envelope and the date and time are recorded. A numbered receipt is returned serving as the official documentation of registration and should be kept in a safe place.

Notice of registration shall consist of the following wording: REGISTERED WGAw No.___ and be applied upon the title page.

MEMBER STAMP
At the time of registration, WGAw members may request that a maximum of two (2) copies of the material being registered be stamped with the legend "MEMBER WGAw." The stamp indicates only that one or more of the writers listed as an author on the title page was a WGAw member at the time the material was registered with the title page bearing the stamp. There is no additional fee for use of the stamp.

REGISTRABLE MATERIAL
We only accept written materials.
Registrable material includes scripts, treatments, synopses, outlines and written ideas specifically intended for radio, television and theatrical motion pictures, video cassettes/discs, and interactive media.

The WGA Intellectual Property Registry also accepts stageplays, novels and other books, short stories, poems, commercials, lyrics and drawings.

DURATION AND EXPIRATION
Registration is valid for a term of five (5) years and may be renewed for an additional five (5) years at the current registration rate. Renewals will be accepted up to three months prior to the expiration of the original registration. A grace period will be extended allowing renewals as late as three months following the expiration of the original registration.

At the time of registration, or renewal, you authorize the Registry to destroy the material without further notice to you on the expiration of the first term of registration or any renewal period.

REQUESTS FOR REGISTRATION INFORMATION

It is imperative that we DO NOT confirm any registration information over the phone.

Only the writers listed on the registration receipt may request confirmation of the registration, the registration number, date of deposit, or any other information.

The Registry will honor such written requests from writers regarding the registration of their own work(s) only if accompanied by photo identification. All verification or confirmation requests from a writer should contain as much specific information as possible, such as registration number, title of material, effective date, and social security number of writer, and may be submitted by facsimile, mail or in person. The fax number for the Registry is (323) 782-4803.

REQUESTS FOR COPIES OF DEPOSITED MATERIAL

Because the deposited material cannot be returned to the writer without defeating the purpose of registration, registered material may not be withdrawn. It is therefore important to always retain a separate copy of the material being registered.

If a writer finds it necessary to obtain a copy of deposited material, duplicates may be purchased for the price of registration upon written request by one or more of the listed authors, identified by photo identification. In the event an author is deceased, proof of death and consent of the representative of the heirs and/or estate must be presented in order to obtain a copy of the material.

Requests for duplication of deposited material must be submitted by 5:00 PM Thursday of any week. Duplicates will be available Tuesday of the following week.

In no event, except under these provisions, shall any deposited material, copies of deposited material, or information regarding deposited material be provided unless an official guild action, court order, or other legal process has been served.

FREQUENTLY ASKED QUESTIONS

Does Guild registration take the place of copyright registration?
No. Any questions regarding copyright should be directed to the U.S. Copyright Office in Washington D.C. at 1-800-688-9889 or to an attorney specializing in that area of law. Copyright application forms are available to walk-in customers only.

Does registration with the Writers Guild protect titles?
No.

Does registration help a writer become a member?
No. Questions concerning the rules for admission to membership in the guild should be referred to the WGAw Membership department at (323) 782-4532.

Does registration help in determining writing credits?
Generally, no. If there is a dispute as to authorship or sequencing of material by date, then registration may be relevant.

Questions concerning the WGA credit determination procedures should be directed to the Credits department at (323) 782-4528.

REGISTRATION HOURS
Monday through Friday, 9:30 AM to 5:30 PM

LOCATION AND MAILING ADDRESS
WGAw Registration
7000 West Third Street
Los Angeles, CA 90048

TELEPHONE NUMBERS
(323) 782-4540   Information
(323) 782-4803   Fax

WEBSITE
www.wga.org

CHAPTER 9

REPRESENTATION: AGENTS, LAWYERS, MANAGERS, AND GUILDS

You've finished the final polish of your script, satisfied there is nothing more that you can do to improve it. There are only two things left to do, begin work on a new one and get your first script in the hands of someone who will actually pay you money for it.

How do you find that person and how do you get him to read your work? Accept this simple caveat and save yourself wasted postage and time waiting for a phone call or letter that will never come: *Most production companies have a firm policy against accepting any material unless it is submitted through an established agency or some other contact with whom they already enjoy a business relationship.*

If you don't have direct contacts in the movie and television industry, you must get in touch with someone who does. Traditionally, the answer was clear: Hire an agent—someone who can not only get exposure for your script, but also for *you*, which leads to writing assignments, the bread and butter of the screenwriter. But the position of the agent as the primary sales force for the writer is changing. With many new markets to cover and a heavy concentration on packaging clients as a means of circumventing the straight 10 percent screenwriter commission, agencies are left with little time for grooming new writers or nurturing an existing client's career. To gain some insight into why no one seems too happy with the resulting state of affairs, settle back and meet my agent—a hard working, much maligned, underappreciated, at times annoyingly needy ten-percenter, whom I am fortunate enough to call my friend.

from the trenches: MY AGENT MAKES A POINT

(and she does have one!)

We were scheduled for a lunch meeting, but it was over 100 degrees in The Valley. My agent suggested sushi take-out from a Trader Joe's near my house. Not exactly The Palm or The Ivy at the Beach, but okay, I thought, whatever. It wasn't until this otherwise delicate waif snagged a six-pack of some exotic ale that I suspected something was brewing other than beer. We headed to Paradise Cove where it cost $20 to park but the sand is clean and empty enough during the week for a little quiet time. As we sat back against the cliff, she popped her first brewski and let out a deep sigh.

"I know you've been with me a long time," she said, "but I just don't think I can take the pressure anymore." Uh oh, here it comes, I thought, I knew I shouldn't have called her at home at 2 a.m. just to see if she was back from New York yet. "I think you know so and so, don't you?" She didn't actually say so and so, but I did know the name as do you if you go to the movies and pay even token attention to the writing credits. "Well, he left me this morning, and not for another agency. That's the third big gun I've had stolen from me this summer." She was referring to the growing trend of high priced talent—yes, writers included—abandoning their agents for sole representation by managers and/or lawyers.

"I've spent 20 years taking on new writers who have had little or no exposure to this business and developing their talent and reputation until they become real players in this town. And then I've had to stand by helplessly and watch as they move on to bigger agencies or, like now, just move on. There's no loyalty anymore; they're all just a bunch of whores." I didn't mention the uncanny similarity of her last sentence to some excellent dialogue written by David Mamet in *The Verdict*, but after 20 years of representing writers, I'm sure her entire life is full of subconscious movie references. Besides, she had struck a chord with me. Despite all my allusions to sharks and dog dooey whenever I reference agents, the best of them have integrity and street smarts and bust their butt in the service of their clients. As I devoured our spicy tuna roll, she poured out her heart, illuminating the hard realities of a job that writers would do well to understand, if not empathize with.

First of all, there is the growing workload. Besides weekly agency pow-wows to learn who is doing (or would like to be doing) what with whom, agents must make regular rounds of studios and production companies to keep up their contacts and remain on top of what is being sought and bought in the marketplace. Then comes the agent's client list. Some writer-clients are in constant demand, thus generating phone calls, meetings, contract negotiations, and all else that goes into stoking the flame of a busy and successful writing career. Others on the list may need closer career guidance (suggesting spec script topics, the giving of rewrite notes, etc.) and even handholding when the client may feel that his interests have been neglected. When a writer's livelihood is at stake, the expectations for the labors of his agent always run to the high side, particularly in the lean times.

Moreover, as clients leave for whatever reason or go through long periods of non-productivity or just no longer respond to the agent's nudging to produce more or better material, there is the pressure to find and sign new talent. It is commissions, after all, that keep the doors open. (And we're not talking small change here; my agent informed me that she was desperate. She needed to earn over $3 million for her clients in the next six months just to cover her draw, her car lease, the salaries of her assistants, the rent on and overhead of maintaining her newly leased, celebrity-designed, and opulently furnished offices.) So there are lunches and the clandestine after hours rendezvous to court the A-list writer who may wish a change of venue. And the phone never stops ringing. With the explosion of interest in screenwriting, thousands of aspiring writers as well as seasoned novelists, journalists, poets, and college lit teachers are banging at the barn door. They took the seminars, read the how-to books, and have written that all-important spec script.

There are over 100 new scripts *a day* being registered at the Writers Guild. And, God willing, their authors hope, more than anything else, to find an agent willing to take on new writers. So these out-of-work, unproduced, aspiring writers armed with nothing more than a naked script, send query letters, hit up any contact they may have, however remote, and try every trick imaginable to get an invitation to place that script in front of a ten-percenter. And rightly so—at this point that's the writer's job. For their part, agents *are* looking for professional work and talent to represent. So against all odds of finding something truly worthy, with all the work already on their plate, and notwithstanding an openly stated agency policy to never accept unsolicited material, *I know of no agent who cannot be somehow coaxed into accepting a submission from a new writer.*

True, most agents will want a submission to come with a recommendation from a respected associate in the business or be preceded by an intriguing and well-crafted query letter. True also that scripts will be tossed at the first sign ("feeling her cheeks grow hot") that they are not dealing with an author conversant with the basic demands and mechanics of the profession. But, such criteria having been

continued

met, even new writers will find that getting their scripts in front of an agent eager to sell them may well be a daunting challenge, if not the impossible task they feared. The problem for the agent is *finding the time to read them all*!

Yes, all those spec scripts must be *read*. To do even one script justice takes a good hour of an agent's time. Even with assistants and readers to share the load, there is evening and weekend reading material to fill any outside *life* the agent may have hoped to enjoy. Yet if most writers don't hear back from an agent within a week or two of submission, they panic and send their material elsewhere. Should the agent then finally find the time, do the work, discover that rare grain of sand that can be squeezed into a pearl through careful nurturing and clever representation (none of which he has time for), it may be too late. The script, passed around town, is now "covered" and as dead as Marilyn Monroe. The agent will have wasted money, his valuable time, and perhaps his reputation in the bargain. For this reason, I recommend that if a writer does get an invitation to submit to an agent, he do the polite thing and give the agent a reasonable and exclusive (or an openly disclosed nearly exclusive) period of time in which to consider the work. Four weeks seems fair.

Even if your work is found to be riveting, entertaining, and unique, there are many practical points to consider before calling you in to sign a contract. Is your work marketable now or would it benefit from a rewrite or polish? Is it a difficult subject, not likely to garner bids, but so indicative of writing talent that it is worth the agency's time and effort to promote *the writer* as a commodity? Is it star-castable? Does it beg for a particular director's vision? Where and how should the material be presented? Does it call for a high budget, suggesting a studio production, or should it be carefully and selectively shopped to talent or producers who may be new, hot, and cutting-edge? Is it such a high-concept film that the agency should raise the heat on it and stir the competition into a possible bidding frenzy? Or is its appeal limited to a few, risk-oriented production companies known to take on more artistic, remote, or controversial material? Should the agent first try to associate actors or a director to the project? (*Packaging*, as this practice is known, can be done from within the agency or by reaching out to top talent wherever they may be found.) Taking the long view, it is in both the agent's and writer's best interest to choose the path most likely to lead to the actual *production of a film* and not just a high-priced script sale. Too many bidding war screenplays languish neglected and unproduced on studio shelves.

Should a sale be imminent, there is the delicate question of pricing it so as not to turn off prospective buyers and still maximize the return to the writer. Major deal points must be negotiated, including profit participation and the writer's possible continued involvement with the project. An aggressive agency may yet use their connections to associate other talent after the fact to further enhance the project's chances of being produced. And, of course, the deal must be closed with a well-drafted deal letter that nails down all the important details for a lawyer's follow-up contract.

Returning to my agent's original lamentation, there is also the continual job of keeping the writer contented, well fed, and creatively busy after the sale. Hopefully this will prevent him from bolting for greener pastures at the first sign of a career downturn or, worse, the great sudden success that spawns greed and betrayal and naked self-interest the likes of which we never thought ourselves capable.

As the sun faded on our "lunch," the six-pack (I had two cans) had done its work and my agent felt somewhat mollified by the prospect of the prodigal client returning to the fold, tail between his legs. She wasn't about to throw away 20 years either. And, when you come right down to it, she had made some good points. Agents work hard and, in the end, 10 percent of nothing is nothing. Why begrudge them if they're a little hard to reach sometimes, temperamental in their own right, and do occasionally get to tag along on our wild ride.

Agents: The Writer's Sales Force

Perhaps the single most important concept to grasp in the film business is this—*it's a business of relationships.* Simply put, agents know more movie producers and studio executives than you do. They spend their days cultivating relationships with buyers. And the buyers love agents because agents save them time and money. Agents may not have infallible taste, but they are counted upon to distinguish a professionally formatted and potentially viable screenplay from one that, quite frankly, is just not up to marketable standards. This saves potential buyers piles of money on "coverage" (having your work read, summarized, and critiqued). Later, the agent can also act as a buffer zone between producers and clients—a service that becomes more and more indispensable to both as a cherished work winds its way down the rocky path of development.

Agents also confer instant credibility to the new writer: if you have one, *you belong.* (It's a club, after all, and your agent is a member.) In addition, regardless of the individual egos that comprise it, *film is a collaborative art and the business of screenwriting is ultimately about the writer developing into someone with whom others in the business will want to work.* When bonds form, writing assignments—the lifeline to health and pension benefits for the freelance writer—can follow and careers can become established.

Agents are also the first line of defense in protecting studios and producers from "nuisance" lawsuits. Find a successful film and you'll find someone who claims, sometimes justifiably, that he sent or phoned in the idea first. *Air Force One*, the nation's top summer box office draw for 1997, was immediately hit with a lawsuit claiming that the original idea was hijacked by the producers from a former helicopter mechanic and his sister. Without commenting on the merits of the case, the film's executive producer stated that, "Unfortunately, in our business, this has become an undesirable sign of success."

Most spec scripts by unknown writers do not sell and agents know this. After years of working their way up the agency ladder, from the mailroom to the assistant's desk to the small windowless office they occupy now, they are not anxious to toss their career on the fires of your writing fantasy. To get their attention, you have to bring something to the party. And face it, you have nothing else to offer them but the words you put on paper.

Producer Brian Grazer (*A Beautiful Mind*, *Cinderella Man*), tells about a meeting he had early in his career with MCA/Universal Studios founder Jules Styne. "He asked me if I had money. I said no. He asked me what I owned that might interest him. I had to admit there was nothing. So he handed me a piece of paper and told me to write something on it. I did and he said, 'There. Now you have that.'"

Your original spec script is your professional calling card, a means of getting you in the door to take the meetings that can lead to assignments. And one spec script—unless it's a sure-fire, high-high-concept, bidding war, slam-dunk sale (good luck with that!)—is often not enough. You have to make your prolific talent and career commitment unquestionable. Most screenplays are written for hire, but it is also true that most writing assignments are doled out to writers with a track record of delivering movies. Agents already have such writers to sell. They accept *new* writers based on *long-term potential.*

Any new writing talent trying to make an impression on an agent today has an uphill battle. There are simply too many new writers and too many new scripts being written for what is essentially a flat buyer's market. Agents need *both* a script that they can sell now and an obvious talent that is worth the investment of their time in building a writer's career. Even then, the agent's challenge will be getting that talent exposed in the marketplace. But for that to happen, the agent needs a way around the buyer's (or showrunner's) reluctance to consider new talent. If he can just tantalize the buyer into reading the script—even if it is not what the buyer wants at the moment—the hope is that the buyer will become engaged by the writing and ask to meet the writer (to see "what else" he's got or to determine if he may be right for an open staff position or another project slated for development).

Particularly in television, where the pitch is the lifeblood of series, cable movies, and MOWs, the entree of an agent may be critical in setting up those all important face-to-face meetings with producers and television executives.

Think of screenwriting as a business with two assets—your inventory of scripts and yourself. An agent is your sales force for both. Writers and their agents should respect and value each other's contribution—that would be the winning attitude. On the other hand, maybe you've tried everything and just can't land an agent. I say, don't despair.

from the trenches: LIES OF THE ARTLESS AND CRAFTY: PART TWO

■ **Lie number 4:** *To sell your work, you need an agent.*

Well, no, you don't. But if you want rejection that makes you feel really, finally, in the game, start the proverbial hunt for an agent. You may find you can get your script read by Spielberg and Hanks before most agents will give it the time of day. To be fair, they have their reasons. They're busy, they already have clients with track records that can't get arrested, and they've seen too many—far too many—spec scripts by new writers that suck. That's if they read those spec scripts at all, or very carefully, or were ever the right audience for what was written. You'll never know. Yet I've heard many good writers say, "So and so at such and such agency liked it, but they want me to make these few changes." Listen to me: you never, *ever*, change your script to suit the momentary whims of anyone but yourself. And that's what the agent is giving you—his or her momentary whims. Don't take them to heart so quickly. They're not writers. They're not your teachers and you're not begging for a grade. They're telling you whatever first comes to mind to get you out of their in-basket. Give them the same script next week—they may not even remember it or may offer up a whole new reason for rejecting it.

continued

I'm not saying that having a good agent in your corner won't help. I hope this chapter will help you recognize their potential value to your career. It can be a big shot of adrenaline for your spirits and can get you meetings and jobs you might otherwise miss. Send the query letters. Go for it, by all means. But having an agent read your script and champion it to the hot A-list buyers is not the *only* way to sell it. There are entertainment lawyers, literary managers, good friends with contacts and, of course, you. You have the primary responsibility to market your script any way you can, to whomever you can. But don't wait for anyone else's validation. Don't depend on strangers to give you a career. I am as truly tired of hearing a writer ask, "so what should I do with it now" as I am hearing "so what should my character do next?" You're the writer, you figure it out—that's your job! Sooner or later, you'll connect with someone who loves what you've written. That's not a promise, but it'll have to do for now.

How to Get an Agent

A tall, dignified man with dark, piercing eyes approaches a well-known Hollywood agent at a trendy restaurant and drops a thick sheaf of paper on the table between them. "I am Satan and this is the story of my life." The agent barely looks up as he tips the last of a double espresso down his throat. The tall man waits patiently in silence. "So why are you bothering me with this, Mr. Satan?" the agent finally asks. The tall man takes a seat beside him. "Because I am Satan and my story will make you rich and powerful beyond your wildest dreams." The agent picks up the first few sheets of paper and thumbs through them. "Pretty racy stuff, all right. What are you looking to get for it? A million? Two million?" Satan tosses up his hands, "I only want my story told." The agent looks around and then leans closer, "C'mon, just between us, what's your angle, what do you really want?" Satan leans in even closer, "Only your soul, that's all I ask." At this the agent smiles. After a moment, he says, "So what's the catch?"

Agents may be the butt of many a Hollywood joke, but finding a good one is no laughing matter. Sometimes it seems as if you need an agent to get an agent. When I asked my own former agent to speak to students in my screenwriting class, this was his reply:

> "I'd be happy to speak at your class, but on one condition: tell
> them not to phone me, not to come over to my office, not to send
> me scripts. Let them do the work, find a prominent person in the
> film business, a successful producer, director, or writer or a super-
> successful actor, have them read it first and personally recommend

it to me and then, and only then, will I read it. There is no shortage of writers or work to represent. It's a highly competitive business and only those who stand out in the eyes of a professional whose opinion I respect are—percentage-wise—worth the investment of time needed to read new writers or evaluate their work."

Not all agents are so blunt (I got lucky), but most conduct business in the same way: through referrals. You, on the other hand, have contacted every person you ever went to school with and simply cannot connect yourself to anyone in a position to personally recommend you and your work. Do not despair; you can get an agent. You'll just have to work at it.

The first thing to be done is to check the current list of Writers Guild signatory agents (those that agree to abide by the Guild's writer-friendly rules). (Updated lists may be found on the WGA web site: http://www.wga.org.) *The Guild will not recommend individual agents nor assist writers in any way in gaining access to agents.* Besides the annual *Writer's Market*, another popular industry source book is *The Hollywood Representation Directory* (which lists agents, managers, and entertainment attorneys), c/o Hollywood Creative Directory, 5055 Wilshire Blvd., Los Angeles, CA 90036; telephone: (323)525-2334 or (800)815-0503; fax (323)525-2393; or contact them online at www.hcdonline.com.

Any of the above sources may list agents outside of Hollywood, but most of these resources are geared to agents in the greater Los Angeles area. The big advantage to Los Angeles or New York representation is *access.* You want an agent who doesn't have to make long-distance calls to keep up his contacts.

In Los Angeles, you'll find a high concentration of agents in "Agent's Alley," that small cluster of streets near Sunset Boulevard and Doheny Drive, or along Wilshire, Beverly, or Santa Monica Boulevards.

If you live far from Los Angeles or the New York metropolitan area, consult your city directory listing for local literary agencies. Contact them, then follow through—determine whether they are Writers Guild signatory agencies and inquire about their client list. While many out-of-Hollywood agencies do not offer the writer easy access to studio heads and other powerful clients, there are advantages to a new writer being represented by less mainstream agencies—more personal attention and career advice at a time when you need it most.

Some agencies accept unsolicited submissions; most will flat out hold themselves "closed to new writers." (The Guild list will indicate which is which.) It is true that few agents place a premium on finding or grooming writers. Most agents want scripts they can sell now and writers who will more than likely get work and generate fees. Yet individual agents at any agency will insist they are always open to good material (translation: a high-concept, star-castable, bidding-war spec script) and are always looking for good writers. So, how do you reach individual agents and interest them in making an exception to "policy" and considering your work?

Blanketing Hollywood with your script is both prohibitively expensive and terribly risky. You'll want an invitation. One way to get an invitation is to promote yourself in a charming, persistent (not annoying) way to the gatekeepers (secretaries, receptionists, assistants) whose mission is to keep solicitors (you) away from the door. Some may not be very polite at all. But their bosses are probably overworked, stressed out and rude also, so why fret about it. You need only reach that one person who will allow you to distract them from logging in hundreds of phone calls and responding to countless e-mails. Don't appear desperate, but do ask for help in guiding you through the Hollywood maze.

A friend from the Midwest sent a number of spec scripts through the Hollywood maze and received no response. He left phone messages; no reply. But, he was relentless. One day, when the entire writing staff of a hit TV series was at lunch, he managed to engage the receptionist in conversation. She was from a town near his and a bond was struck. She told him that his script was likely lost in a pile with other unsolicited submissions, but if he would send another, she would read it. The receptionist read his script on her lunch break, liked it, and kept putting it on writers' desks until somebody read it. Three months later, he got a call from the executive producer of the show telling him that if he planned on being in L.A. in the near future, he was invited in to pitch ideas for future episodes. Taking the next flight out, he made an appointment and pitched a bucketful of ideas, all of which were rejected. All the same, the producers liked his attitude and enthusiasm and gave him an assignment to write a show already in active development. Even though they never used that episode, they liked *him* and his style enough to offer him a staff position!

And there are other options. Find the name of a writer who has written a film similar to yours. Or, if you want an agency that has had recent success with a new writer, check the credits of recent independent films for the name of the writer. The Writers Guild's Agency Department can tell you who represents that writer. Then, contact the agent as a "die-hard" fan; tell him you have a script similar to the one he so brilliantly shepherded toward production and ask if he has interest in representing it. Or, using this method in reverse, try to locate clients the agency represents. This has the added benefit of determining if the agent works mostly in features or television and whether his client list indicates the agency is a formidable one, likely to be well-connected with buyers.

You can also connect with a writer whose work you admire by getting a contact number (other than the agency) from the WGA's Membership Department. Then call the writer and have a chat—it's not as hard as you might imagine. (Most writers don't need to protect their privacy from hoards of crazed fans.) Perhaps you can win the writer over and get him to look at your script. If he is impressed, a personal recommendation to his agent or someone else in the industry could result.

Be as enterprising as your imagination and dedication allow. But if all fails and you despair of ever getting your screenplay through the agency maze, cheer up. There is a way. It may be the weapon of last choice in the writer's arsenal, but it is still remarkably effective.

The Query Letter

If you don't have a personal contact to an agent already, the query letter is a step toward acquiring one. This is a *brief* but provocative letter introducing yourself as a writer seeking representation. Some writers have asked if it's a waste of time and postage, believing their letter doesn't stand a chance of being picked out of a pile of junk mail.

Q: I've finished my script, but don't live in LA, have no industry contacts, and don't know what to do next. Many books recommend the query letter as a starting point, but I've heard that's just a waste of postage. Does it really work?

Donald, Kalamazoo, Michigan

A: To some, sending a query letter is a mark of desperation, a last ditch shot in the dark from a supplicant begging for an audience with the Prince. I recommend changing that mindset. A query letter is the professional way of introducing you, your product, and services to a potential customer or sales representative. It is no different from letters from new attorneys or doctors or businessmen introducing their services. It's not a magic bullet, but it's had enough success stories to warrant a try.

As a member of the New Members Committee of the Writers Guild, I heard frequent accounts of query letters used to great success. One writer, now scripting for both Ron Howard and Castle Rock, told of how he got his start in the business by sending out over 400 form letters to agents. He received 40 or so requests for scripts, and out of that garnered four solid agency offers. His first screenplay sold within six days of his accepting representation. After all their talk of not accepting unsolicited manuscripts, agents still need to find new blood and producers need good scripts.

What does every agent and producer look for? Relationships with working writers who have something to sell—a concept so fresh it snaps, crackles, and pops off the page. Your query letter may set forth just such a concept— but do not expect a reply to your letter. A few may respond, most will not. This is the way things are; don't get angry or take it personally. If you do phone and successfully get anyone, even a janitor, to stay on the line with you, be nice. Treat everyone as if he were the head of the studio. And, do be sure to thank anyone who does anything to get you closer to your career goals, not only because it's the decent thing to do, but also because the one taking messages and answering the phone today may well be the head of production tomorrow (and production heads have notoriously long memories).

Here is a *seven-point strategy* for sending a successful query letter:

STRATEGY

1. **Make it brief.**

   One page tops, like any good cover letter that might accompany a resume, and don't hard sell. It should, naturally, be in proper business letter format and free of typos or grammatical errors. Use only quality paper and the clean, crisp print delivered by a laser printer.

2. **Make it good.**

   This one page letter will be the only hint as to the quality of your writing. It should be as clear, concise, compelling, original, and intriguing as the premise of your script. It is a matter of personal judgment in what detail you describe your plot, but a succinct summary is favored. As with your screenplay, cut to the heart of your premise, preferably in a single, irresistible paragraph that stamps your work as a sure-fire commercial hit and you as a writer others will want to work with.

3. **Make it easy to respond to.**

   Include a SAS postcard to help the recipient express interest and a business phone or private cell number (not your home number which your five-year-old answers).

4. **Mark it personal and confidential.**

   Address it to a person, not a company or an agency—a phone call should yield you a name.

5. **Maybe send it via messenger, certified mail, or even FedEx.**

   This increases the chances it will be read by the person you are sending it to and not tossed with other unsolicited mail.

6. **Do not send a copy of your screenplay until it is asked for.**

   Wait a reasonable period of time—two to three weeks—and follow up your letter with a polite phone call, FAX, or e-mail (a strange fact of modern life; people who screen every phone call and letter will read their faxes and e-mail). Should an agent respond positively to your letter or call and request your script, send a copy (never send an original) of your two best samples, if you have more than one. (And don't bother enclosing a self-addressed stamped envelope; you probably won't get your script back anyway. Just chalk up your copying and postage costs to the price of doing business.) You should also anticipate that an agent or producer may ask for a release form before agreeing to read your work.

7. **Above all, be creative.**

   Be quietly persistent. Be a good salesperson, able to get your foot in the door before it is slammed in your face. If you can capture the attention of an overworked assistant, your letter will be placed on the executive's desk—and he will read it.

Following is an example of a query letter that caught my attention.

Ronald Suppa Productions, Inc.
Attn: Mr. Ronald Suppa

Dear Mr. Suppa:

I understand you are a former South Philadelphia resident. I grew up in Northeast Philly, but I lived on South Street for five years before coming to California. I spent nine years as a stockbroker, but found what I really enjoy is writing. I recently finished my fifth screenplay and am working on my sixth.

I believe I have a screenplay that may interest you. I'm sure you remember Frank Rizzo; he's hard to forget. I've even read that Sylvester Stallone has said that he'd like to play Rizzo. Personally, I think that Danny Aiello fits him perfectly. My story is about boxers and politicians who get mixed up together weeks before the Philadelphia mayoral election. The character up for re-election is based loosely on Rizzo, known in the story as Ray Rombella. Ray has no reason to take his competition seriously until an old boxer comes forth with information that could bring him down. Ray collides with his past in a dramatic conclusion that involves murder, prize-fight fixing, the old-boy network... and a child caught in the middle.

Mr. Suppa, I feel good about this story. It's a world I know very well, having both boxed and been involved in political campaigns, the last being the election Frank most likely would have won had he not died just before the primary.

Please check at the bottom if you would like me to send a copy of my screenplay, along with a release. An SASE is enclosed. Thanks for your time and consideration.

Clearly the writer did his homework. Maybe he read an article that mentioned my connection with Stallone; perhaps he looked up my credits in a Hollywood resource book. The fact is, he made the letter personal.

He then outlined, in general terms, a story that interested my company in the past. He also tied in his work experience, letting me know that his script would offer an insider's view of his subject. This also made the point that he wasn't a novice writer, having taken time from a "real job" to write six screenplays. While this kind of boasting can backfire (if he's been at it a while, why is there no agent?), I knew, for example, that even Oliver Stone had written a dozen screenplays before garnering his first agent. For me, at least, the point was moot. The general tone of the letter was friendly and respectful—so few letters meet even these rudimentary rules of etiquette.

Finally, the writer made it easy for me. His willingness to supply his own release form marked him as a team player, aware of the exigencies of the industry. And that SASE is a must if you expect a reply to your query letter; some writers enclose a postcard (it calls for less postage and the agent doesn't have to lick the envelope).

I dropped the reply card in the mail. He sent the script the day after receiving my response. It was a workmanlike, professional effort, but we passed. I called the writer and explained our reasons for passing. He didn't get defensive or argumentative; he listened and asked questions to understand exactly what we were looking for. He also told me about another project which he was pursuing. His letter and serious attitude had put him into the game.

from the trenches: CHANCE FOLLOWS DESIGN

Comparing a spec sale by a new writer to winning the lottery is not so far off the mark. Sadly, talent is often not enough (though, to be fair, getting talent noticed is as difficult in almost any field of endeavor). Having respected industry contacts helps, as does the opportunity to have your work seen by someone in a position to further your career. But some say you practically need an agent to get an agent. And even then who knows what's selling this month? The hot pics are determined not by critics and cinephiles, but by the fickle crowd of pre-teens devouring endless tubs of popcorn on Friday nights down at the mall. And even that one great script does not a career make. You need success piled upon success to stay in the eye of the tiger. The prospect of going beyond breaking in and forging a long and fruitful career as a screenwriter takes an alchemist's mix of luck, timing, opportunity, contacts, and talent. It's a crapshoot. But I believe chance follows design.

First of all, there's no point in whining over how tough it may be to get that first break. Just get over it. The fact is that against all odds, people do manage it. The Writers Guild welcomes nearly 50 new writers a month into the fold. One hundred percent of them had once never been writers at all and now they were members in a fairly exclusive writers club. So it's not impossible, right? Let's all acknowledge that somehow, some way, some people—more than a few—are winning that lottery and finding a way to become paid screenwriters. And if you asked them how they did it, you'd find it wasn't any genie waving a magic wand.

The people I spoke to agree: Agents are great, get the contact and go for it—but don't waste your time waiting around for their call. Don't come to town on a one-way bus ticket and expect the film world to put you up for the night with a hot meal. Even if you have first-class representation—agents, managers, lawyers—even if your first cousin happens to be Brad Pitt, no one can be counted on to do it all for you. Success is the product of tenacious optimism. As you wrote alone, as you believed in yourself through those long days at your computer, you have to take primary responsibility for marketing yourself and your work.

First, don't rush your work to market. Before you buy that bus ticket to L.A., let your script do the walking. Give it to a couple of movie loving friends and see what they think of it. Take notes, don't be afraid to make changes you agree with. Maybe submit to a contest or two, or get feedback from a reliable script consultant. (Demand recommendations, check track records, and use common sense in choosing one.) Then, when you're confident of your material, when you believe

continued

you've done all you can with it—write another. Having two scripts proves you're not a one-shot wonder, and helps define your talent niche.

Then—and only then—send the query letter. And that doesn't mean shotgun a form letter to every address in the *Hollywood Creative Directory* or the *Hollywood Representation Directory*. Be selective and personalize the submissions. Send to individuals, not companies. Try to target newer, younger (hungrier) agents. Find agents who have represented (or producers who have produced) material similar in genre to your screenplay. (Note the writer of such a movie and contact the Guild's agency department for a contact number.) Read the trades and keep abreast of the spec script and pitch sales. Find out who is where at the studios and production companies and what agents, managers, and attorneys are representing successful writers. And never stop networking for contacts. When possible, attend events such as the L.A. Screenwriting Expo that bring writers and industry folk together. Find a seasoned writer or businessman (in the film or, frankly, any business) who may agree to provide guidance and act as a mentor.

And be prepared for rejection. Most queries will receive no response at all. Some may respond, but months later. You can call and check to make sure your letter was received (a naked excuse to connect with someone, anyone, on a personal basis) but after that first follow-up, anything more will be largely a waste of time. Should you actually get a rejection letter, mark that agent as one to whom you'll submit your next script. And be certain you have a next script—you should never submit the first before starting another.

Or you might try and raise production funding yourself. (Sometimes you have to build the road to get where you want to go.) A good crew can be had out of a local film school. And film festivals are crawling with actors, directors, and independent producers hungry to develop new material. Some can add credibility to your script or may be willing to work with you because they believe it will help their career. Be choosy though, as you don't want to attach deal-killing baggage to any future sale. (Remember that friends can be made without binding contracts.) This is not so very different from dating with the hope of finding someone to marry. You want to cover the available field and not fall for the first pretty face, but you also have to be ready to jump on a good thing when it comes up.

There is a wonderful quote from the German poet and dramatist Goethe: "There is one elemental truth, the ignorance of which kills countless ideas and splendid plans—that the moment one definitely commits oneself, then Providence moves all." You want luck? Who doesn't need it? You want the Gods to shine their light and benevolence upon you? Work for it. Success comes to the relentless who leave as little to chance as possible.

The Release Form

The release form secures your agreement not to sue if a potential buyer happens to later make a film bearing a resemblance to your submitted script, treatment, or pitch. Most producers require them as standard business practice, and most agencies now request them from new (and sometimes not-so-new) writers before considering work for representation.

This practice is not meant to condone or legalize the theft of ideas (although some release forms are so broadly worded as to appear to permit just that, and with near impunity). Rather it is a response to the increasing risk and expense of lawsuits resulting from (often spurious) claims of similarity. Generally, the release form is not used to a writer's detriment but, if you refuse to sign it, your work probably won't be considered.

"It took a little faith." That's how Microsoft founder Bill Gates viewed his decision to sign the disclosure and release forms presented to him by IBM on that fateful day when the two companies agreed to join forces in the most successful partnership in the history of entrepreneurial enterprise. Earlier that day, IBM had presented that same set of documents to a competitor of Gates, who called in an army of lawyers and ultimately refused to sign. Today, he's a footnote in computer history while Bill Gates is the richest man in the United States.

So the best advice is to sign the one they offer or supply one on your own volition. In either case, you will be expressing your desire to make it less onerous for those with legal vulnerability to read your material and establish a business relationship with you. For your use, a typical release form follows.

Literary Material Release Form

To: [company]

Re: [title of material submitted hereunder]

Gentlemen:

I am today submitting to you certain literary material, the present title of which is indicated above (hereinafter "the material)," upon the following express understanding and conditions:

1. I agree that I am voluntarily disclosing such material to you at my request. I understand that you shall have no obligation to me in any respect whatsoever with regard to such material unless and until each of us has executed a written agreement which, by its terms and provisions, shall be the only contract between us.

2. I agree that any discussions we may have with respect to such material shall not constitute any agreement, express or implied, as to the purchase and use of any such material which I may disclose to you either orally or in writing.

3. If the material submitted hereunder is not new or novel, or was not originated by me, or if other persons including your employees have heretofore submitted or hereafter submit similar or identical material which you have the right to use, then I agree that you shall not be liable to me for your use of such material, and you shall not be obligated in any respect whatsoever to compensate me for such use by you.

4. I further agree that if you hereafter produce or distribute a motion picture and/or television program or programs based upon the same general theme, idea, or situation and/or having the same setting or background and/or taking place in the same geographical area or period of history as the material, then, unless you have substantially copied the expression and development of such idea, theme, or situation, including the characters and storyline thereof, as herewith or hereafter submitted to you by me in writing, you shall have no obligation or liability to me of any kind or character by reason of the production or distribution of such motion picture and/or program(s), nor shall you be obligated to compensate me in connection therewith.

I acknowledge that but for my agreement to the above terms and conditions, you would not accede to my request to receive and consider the material which I am submitting to you herewith.

Very truly yours,

[Signature of writer, date, address, and phone]

The Agency Agreement

What does an agent look for in a client? First, something to sell: a script that will attract buyers and scream forth your writing talent. Without an available script (one that is not previously sold), most producers will decline to meet new writers or read their work. It is not the fault of the agent, then, if pitch meetings and assignments never materialize.

An agent also wants a client who will listen, take advice, and appreciate that the agency has other clients as well. Of course, should the agent want to represent you, make sure the feeling is mutual. Embarking on an agent-client relationship is like entering into a marriage, so attempt to know your agent as well as possible (either by phone or in person) before you sign.

You want an agent who is respected and connected, one who is a strong negotiator and who truly believes in your work. He should take an active interest in promoting you and your writing and be sincerely supportive of your career. He should have integrity, be trustworthy, and, when necessary, be capable of delivering a healthy dose of candor.

Agents procure employment and negotiate deals. In California, the state labor and employment code requires all agents to get a license, post a bond, and record their agreements with their clients. *An agent receives a 10 percent commission on what he sells, whether it is literary material or the writer's services. In no instance should you pay him to read your work, to attempt to sell your work, or to represent you.* In some cases, a special commission, known as a packaging fee, is taken by an agency in lieu of the agent's regular commission. This occurs when certain agencies "package" the major components (such as star, director, writer, and producer) of a theatrical film, television movie, or series and then sell the package to the studio or other production entity (which pays the packaging fee).

Should the agency press you to sign an agreement with them, by all means do so (since this formality is more to the agency's advantage than yours, you should not bring it up first). Not every agency will ask. Many agents represent a few clients without a contract (agents call these "*pocket clients*") so as not to "pad" their lists with non-producing clients and run the risk of making their more valuable clients worry they are getting short shrift and switch agencies. As a pocket client, you can expect the agent will send your script to a few potential buyers, but if an offer or measure of enthusiasm for your work is not forthcoming, they will pull back. If you then get a deal on your own, they will step in and negotiate it for their 10% fee. Of course, if you sell your work on your own you are technically free to not commission the agency on your sale. As a pocket client, you may even work with two agencies at the same time (though attempt this and you run an unhealthy risk of "never working in this town again").

If you do decide to sign, resist the temptation to haggle over the agreement. Agents are wary of problem clients and you are protected from a fiasco by the Guild's contract with the ATA (Association of Talent Agents) which allows you to exit an agent if you have not worked within 90 days. For such reasons, negotiating the agency agreement is considered bad form (akin to asking for a prenuptial agreement in the same breath as you propose marriage). Like a prenuptial contract, if the marriage works, you'll forget all about it. If it doesn't, a good lawyer can always find a way around it.

Entertainment Lawyers: Hollywood's Best-Kept Secret

Your screenwriting career does not rest solely on your ability to attract an agent. A good script will always find a home and after it does, agents will come knocking. But writers have another powerful ally in this murky world of deals and dealmakers—the entertainment lawyer.

Whether you sell a script or are hired to write one, there will be deal points to negotiate and contracts to sign. An entertainment lawyer can anticipate problems and cover the writer with protective language. Do you need to obtain the rights to a true story, novel, play, biography, magazine article, or other source material you wish to adapt for the screen? An entertainment lawyer can draw up agreements that will satisfy both the law and the sometimes more stringent requirements of networks and studios. Even major players in Hollywood—the directors, stars, and studio heads you read about over your morning bowl of Wheaties—have agents who may put the deal together, but each also has an entertainment attorney who will close the deal.

Moreover, in an industry where the name of the game is access, I know agents, producers, and executives who will put a script sent to them by a reputable film lawyer first on their list of things to read. And film lawyers always get their calls returned, promptly.

Another often overlooked advantage to having an entertainment attorney is having another friendly voice on your side (albeit a paid one). As writer Roger Simon once said, "In a town of liars, you need at least two or three people who will tell you the truth." In the short chain of those on your side, your lawyer should be one you can count on to honestly appraise the wisdom of your career choices.

In addition, an entertainment attorney, like an agent, can put a screenwriter in touch with other clients to create valuable movie packages. A package is the pooling of a group of talents whom a studio might deem desirable to work with, using their combined strength to get a project developed or produced. A lot more attention will be paid to your script if Dustin Hoffman or Sydney Pollack is attached. In providing this service alone, a good entertainment lawyer may be the most valuable gun in Hollywood's arsenal.

Attorneys sometimes replace agents altogether. A short while ago, filmmaker James Cameron (*Titanic*) gave notice to his longtime agency that henceforth he would be represented solely by his attorneys. The move sent shockwaves through the agency community. If Cameron could walk—and take all of those lucrative commissions with him—what would stop other players from following suit?

Perhaps, it is fear. In a series of now infamous letters to former CAA superagent Michael Ovitz, writer Joe Eszterhas spelled out his fear of endangering the career he had worked so hard to build after deciding to leave Ovitz for other representation. Eszterhas did leave and survived quite well. But, to be sure, few writers can switch agencies so easily, as Eszterhas did, or pick up a phone and get the head of a major studio to jump to attention, as Cameron can.

I'm sure any superstar's lawyers are quite willing to answer the phone and field offers for their client, and perhaps arrange meetings designed to lead to employment and film deals. But to be clear, entertainment lawyers most often *won't* solicit and get you a deal or get you a job. That's what agents are for—agents are licensed by the state to sell clients' work; lawyers are not (at least not in California). Without an agent, you most often must make and exploit your own contacts and do all the legwork yourself. If you are successful, a good film lawyer can then review and negotiate a deal as well as (or better than) most agents and can also help protect you from potentially ruinous lawsuits, such as libel or invasion of privacy.

If you're offered a feature deal, you may need an entertainment lawyer in addition to your agent in any case. The agent will lay out the broad strokes of a deal, most often in a short letter known as a "deal memo." But, agents rarely negotiate "usual and customary" provisions, such as sequel and remake rights, spinoffs, ancillary rights, residual schedules, reversions, warranties, and indemnities, nor do they negotiate the fine points of force majeure, droit morale, and favored nations. And, of course, you'll need an attorney to sort out the mystifying definition of "net profits" (known to run as long as 50 pages in some studio contracts).

What if your writing partner dies during development—or as a result of it, as (the now sadly deceased) John Gregory Dunne almost did during his assignment on *Up Close and Personal*? (You can read about this and other travails of the screen-writing life in Dunne's great book, *Monster* [Random House, New York, 1997].) Do you still have a deal? Your lawyer will make sure you do.

As you might expect, entertainment lawyers are not cheap. Most bill anywhere from $250 to $600 per hour. However, some will make a percentage agreement with you; five percent of your deal is the going rate (half what an agent would charge), but this percentage only applies when you have an agent that is already collecting ten percent. When an entertainment lawyer supplants your agent, a fee of ten percent of your gross deal is the practice. Should the law firm represent more than one element in a given production (the writer, producer, director, or star), it may also earn a package fee that may include a profit share. But these fees are similar to and often less than what an agent charges.

Moreover, if you *can* get an appointment with an entertainment lawyer, the initial consultation and the career advice that goes with it is usually free. Many attorneys pride themselves on their ability to develop a client base by representing new talent *pro bono* (for free). Of course, they will eventually exact payment but, usually, this will be a sum that bears a reasonable relation to funds the writer receives from the option or sale of a script (similar to a contingency fee paid to personal injury lawyers).

In your shopping for representation, remember that you want an *entertainment attorney*. If you know a lawyer who handles divorces and writes wills or is the person to see if you get into an auto accident—he is not an entertainment lawyer. And, you want a lawyer who handles more than contracts. A film lawyer is connected to the film business 24 hours a day, seven days a week. He knows the current salary quotes for a hot actor or director, the sticky points that will break a promising deal, even which two people must never be brought together in the same room, much less the same film. So highly specialized is this area that a half-dozen or so boutique law firms can lay claim to representing 90 percent of the name talent in Hollywood. This can result in one firm or even one lawyer representing both sides in a contract. Recently, this cozy arrangement has been subjected to scrutiny by the courts and has spawned a flurry of "conflict of interest" lawsuits. While it may be true that business has always been done this way, should you find yourself in such a position, separate counsel is recommended.

So how do you obtain such high-powered representation? The best and the brightest operate out of boutique firms and are as busy and elusive as top agents. As standard business practice, they are usually put in touch with new clients through referrals. A phone call to any reasonably established person in the film business will often yield you a name and a number. If you possess no such contacts, the *Hollywood Representation Directory* has an updated list of attorneys and contact information, including areas of specialization, but as a practical matter, you still may wish to call your local bar association or one of the creative guilds (SAG, DGA, WGA, PGA) for a reference to attorneys with whom they deal on a frequent basis.

Literary Managers: Who Are Those Guys?

What if you have neither an agent nor an entertainment lawyer? Is there still someone out there who knows the ropes and has your best interests, as a writer, at heart?

First, a parable. She was late-fifties, well spoken, a smart dresser, fit, with a demeanor that radiated success. An embossed card presented her as a "Literary Manager." Not an agent, mind you, not a lawyer, not a publicist, but yet another percentage drain on a writer's sweat income. Her name was reminiscent of wind, or gale or gusts, though my writing partner remembers her as "Air," an homage to her substance (as in empty, as in full of hot...).

"Air" contacted us after hearing a development executive glowingly endorse our work. Before I could pocket her business card, she won us over by pronouncing that our admittedly hard-sell political screenplay was a "slam dunk." It was "brilliant, commercial, but also literary!"—all after perusing only a short synopsis we had dutifully carried to our first meeting at the Beverly Hills café of her choice. She made four calls on her cell phone and took two more before flagging down the waiter for a second espresso—she checked her urgent messages, she rescheduled important meetings, she brokered clients. So busy was she, she zoomed out of there, leaving us with the check.

Later that day, she turned up the heat. Her first four faxes asked, in order, for our script via messenger, informed us her "very trusted assistant" was reading our work, suggested no less than ten different pitch meetings she would "immediately" set up, and pleaded with us to allow her to fire our agent for "not properly handling" us or our material. Four hours later, at 2 a.m., a frost set in. A final fax demanded that we contact her first thing in the morning. She now had "serious doubts" about the viability of our work in its present form and felt it needed "major changes" before she could consider representing us.

The next day, when we contacted her, she dodged specific questions about plot and character and admitted that her concerns were those of her assistant (whom we later learned was a 22-year-old unpaid volunteer who had been in her employ three weeks). Oh, and one last thing: she would be faxing over a document for us to sign which gave her the right to attach herself as a "producer" to any film based on our work, "in lieu of my commission, of course."

Exhausted yet intrigued, we wondered: What could a literary manager do for us and did we really want one? Also, what qualified her to be one? Or, as Sundance asked Butch: "Who are those guys?"

How Do Managers Fit into the Writer's Support Team?

It seems the agency business has overextended itself. Agents are so busy cultivating writers with proven track records and a steady income stream that they hardly have time to read work by new writers. In fact, most agencies operate a closed shop—unsolicited material is barred at the door. Especially in the new Hollywood hustle where a blockbuster mentality rules and access to the heavy hitters—the studios and big producers—is the goal of most new scribes, such a policy has proven highly frustrating for writers. The result is a black hole into which an army of untended writers have fallen. And where such a vacuum exists, someone will fill it.

Enter the literary manager. While talent management is not a novel concept, what was once hands-on career guidance for highly successful actors is now seen as a viable support base for, and income source from, writers as well. The financial carrot is there: A film agent is limited by law to ten percent of a client's gross income and cannot produce or otherwise involve himself directly in a client's film. Managers have free reign to take 15, 25, or even 50 percent if the client so agrees, and can negotiate freely for credits or employment on a client's film.

And, anyone can declare themselves to be a literary manager—no training, no tests, no licensing required. For qualifications, entertainment industry experience and contacts will do. In California, agents must be licensed and bonded to procure employment and negotiate deals, while personal managers are neither regulated nor franchised. By law, their services are strictly limited to advice and counsel. Many managers, however, ignore these regulations and solicit jobs for their clients with or without the help of an agent. And because the money is better, former agents seem to take to the management business like a fish to water. This mass exodus has ruffled more than a few feathers in the agency business.

When a key agent at United Talent Agency left the agency to form a management company, many of his writing clients went with him. Likewise, when former super-agent Michael Ovitz announced the formation of his (now defunct) management company, Artists Management Group, his former client, Robin Williams, promptly exited Creative Artists Agency (with his then agent) to join him. Such developments have left agents wondering out loud whether managers are acting as *de facto* agents. (In California, the argument has reached Sacramento, where legislation is being introduced that would oblige managers to labor under substantially the same rules as agents.)

Why Do Writers Need a Literary Manager?

What are the benefits of working with a literary manager? Simply put, writers want work. And *despite the legal constraint in California against managers seeking or obtaining work for their clients*, the *implication* of the management relationship is that the manager will help a writer find work and will build or enhance the writer's earning capacity.

In practice, a manager can gain employment for his clients and still remain within the law. For example, he can help obtain agency representation or switch the writer to an agent who will more aggressively market the writer and his work. He can prod the agent to action with calls a writer may be loath to make himself. He can "help" the agent arrange meetings with producers, production company executives, and others in order to more widely expose the writer and his work to the film community.

Managers can also help build the rest of the writer's support team, finding him a publicist, entertainment attorney, business manager, or industry-savvy accountant. He may even help a blocked writer find a writing partner to get the creative juices flowing again. Creatively, a manager can help identify the current needs of the marketplace and serve as a critical reader of the writer's work before it goes out to potential agents or buyers. A manager can even act as a test audience for a writer's pitch. And, in a business in which truth is in short supply, managers can make discreet inquiries to production companies and receive valuable feedback on what worked or didn't work at those pitch meetings. Perhaps most important for the writer who feels isolated at his computer, the manager can serve as a sounding board for the writer's concerns about the day to day activities of the film business and his place in it. A good manager keeps in constant touch with his client, unlike an agent who may speak with his client only upon the delivery of a new spec script to market.

As if all that was not enough bang for your buck, remember that the manager often toils long and hard and far in advance of any money changing hands. Many managers have small client lists and charge as little as 5 percent of the client's gross income (though 10 or 15 percent is more the norm) for developing a client's career.

Sometimes, the legal limits on the manager's role makes for curious justice. As a young lawyer, I represented a Country & Western singer who was suing her manager of ten years after a personal falling out. Her complaint, ironically enough, was that the manager had solicited bookings for her during a rough period when her agents had let her career simmer on the back burner. Though the manager's efforts were, at that time, well intentioned and encouraged, the judge ordered all of his hard earned commissions forfeited.

Managers, like agents, are best found via personal recommendations. Or try contacting one listed in *The Hollywood Representation Directory*, c/o Hollywood Creative Directory, 5055 Wilshire Blvd., Los Angeles, CA 90036; telephone: (323)525-2334 or (800)815-0503; fax (323)525-2393; or contact them online at www.hcdonline.com.

So What's the Catch?

The manager-client bond is often the closest of all professional relationships in the entertainment industry and there is much to recommend it. But, any seasoned veteran knows that where money can be made from the exploitation of talent, abuse is possible.

The manager being attached to a client's project—as a producer, for example—is a common development in the manager-client association. And not necessarily an unwelcome one. For the writer, having a manager may mean acquiring an instant producer for a new screenplay as well as a chance to be in business with a trusted ally. For the manager, having a writer for a client is like getting a free option on good screen material as well as providing a means to profit from the alliance in a way prohibited to agents (who are barred by law from involvement in the production of their client's work).

Nevertheless, this kind of close relationship can also lead to a potential conflict of interest that the writer must vigilantly monitor. Ask yourself: Is the manager working primarily for you or for him? What if a studio wants to bid one million dollars for your spec screenplay, but views your manager-cum-producer as excess baggage—can he hold up *your* deal with demands of his own? Horror stories have been known to happen, especially if a management contract expressly grants permission for your manager to act as the producer of your projects.

How Can Writers Protect Themselves?

The core of any management relationship is built on trust even though a writer will most likely have to sign a *management contract*. Ideally when the arrangement is no longer working, the parties should be able to shake hands and go their separate ways. But ours is not an ideal world; experience dictates that it's best if the terms of the association are set forth as specifically as possible.

Unlike an agency contract, which allows the writer to quit the agency if no work is obtained within a 90-day period, a typical management pact is harder to exit gracefully. A writer can find himself contractually bound to a failing relationship or to a vague notion of what services are expected on his behalf. Forewarned is forearmed; let the following *three-point strategy* serve as a guideline for your agreement:

STRATEGY

1. **Be certain that the contract clearly spells out the duties of the manager and the responsibilities of the writer over the term of the contract.**

   These duties can be so specific as to set forth the "meet and greet" contacts the manager will arrange, the number of times a week the manager will contact the writer, and the circumstances under which both parties can be released from the contract.

2. **Presumably, you will want a personal manager who is held in high esteem in the industry and who will give you the personal attention that sparked your interest in the manager to begin with.**

   Therefore, you do not want the manager to be free to delegate or assign his duties to third parties without your approval. Similarly, while you may want help in finding an agent or lawyer, you do not want to grant the manager the right to form these associations *without your prior consent.*

3. **Finally, be very wary of giving your manager power of attorney over any of your affairs, particularly the incurring of debt, the signing of contracts on your behalf, or the right to endorse and cash checks payable to you.**

   Also, be careful about granting your manager the right to act as or be credited or paid as a "producer" of your work on the screen.

Although problems can arise as in any business relationship, when a writer and manager respect and value the other's contribution to the relationship, they can form a winning combination that's hard to beat. Sadly, however, some writers may find themselves employing the very attorney the manager recommended to find a way out of the management contract that same attorney advised them to sign.

The Writers Guild: A Safe Haven

"We're a guild, not a union," Writers Guild of America, west's former President Brad Radnitz liked to tell new members when asked if the WGA can help them gain employment or lessen the competition. One can't blame the man for expertly sidestepping a direct answer; the WGA manifestly does not help writers get a job, and they do nothing to bar the door to any stranger who comes knocking. In most unions, only when the current membership has passed or is otherwise unavailable for an assignment may a prospective employer look outside the union for workers. Not so in the four top Hollywood creative "guilds"—the Screen Actors Guild (SAG), the American Federation of Television and Radio Artists (AFTRA), the Directors Guild, and the Writers Guild (the latter hereafter sometimes referred to as the Guild)—all of which are open to new members once they have rendered eligible services for a "signatory company." Yet there are definite benefits to membership.

Membership

The Writers Guild currently has roughly 8,000 members (unfortunately, less than half are employed in any given year), with animation and reality writers soon to be admitted into the fold.

In general terms, admission to the Guild is invited upon the sale or licensing of previously unpublished and unproduced literary or dramatic material or upon the completion of writing services pursuant to a contract of employment ultimately totaling 24 "units of Credit" (a motion picture screenplay or radio play or teleplay 90 minutes or longer earns 24 credits each); said sale, licensing, or employment must be with a company or other entity that is signatory to the WGA's Minimum Basic Agreement (the "MBA"). (The complete Guild rules of member eligibility are set forth at the end of this chapter.) Should you earn the right to be invited to join, the initial fee is currently $2,500, plus 1.5 percent of your gross income as a writer and quarterly dues of $25.

Nearly all of mainstream Hollywood's employers—the studios, networks, and many independent film companies—are "signatory" to the MBA, meaning they must abide by negotiated minimum standards of pay and working conditions for Guild members. The agreement is set forth in full on the Guild's web site (www.wga.org), though, as the MBA has evolved, even the current outgoing (as of this writing) WGA, west, president, Daniel Petrie, Jr., concedes that it has become "increasingly difficult to understand and interpret." However, there are the two basic edicts:

- **Only a Guild member may write for a signatory company.** The precept is deceiving. The WGA is not a closed shop. A non-member who sells a script to a signatory company will be offered Guild membership. A writer hired to write for a signatory company will have 31 days after employment begins to request membership. In either case, if you pass it up, you won't be offered membership again. But if only Guild members can work for signatory companies, how do some non-Guild members work for the majors? (George Lucas and Quentin Tarantino, two writers who have openly eschewed Guild affiliation, come to mind.) The MBA is not a perfect system; if a company wants to hire a non-union writer, it can create (although not directly control) a new non-signatory company for the purpose of making just that one picture and that company may then hire anyone it wants who is not in the Guild.

- **A Guild member cannot sell to or work for any producer or company that isn't a Guild signatory.** This rule is strictly enforced and it makes it arduous for smaller, non-signatory companies to find talented writers. It's also good news for new writers still honing their skills—work is available, if unregulated—just don't check your common sense at the door: trust your instincts, and make sure you are fairly compensated for your work.

If you and the company you're working with is not Guild-affiliated, you can still ask that the terms of your pact be subject to the MBA, thus affording you the protection, if not the enforcement power, of the Guild. You can also use the Guild *minimums* as a guideline for negotiating your deal.

Minimum wages for script sales and writing services are established by the MBA and are the most visible result of the sometimes protracted and bitter negotiations between the Guild and the signatory companies. For example, for the period 11/1/05 through 10/31/06, a signatory company purchasing an original screenplay for a photoplay costing less than $5 million would have to pay at least $36,856. If the budgeted photoplay is in excess of $5 million, the purchase price would be a minimum of $75,443. The minimum price to *hire* a writer (or writing team) for an original screenplay (two drafts) including a treatment, would be $102,980 for a film to be budgeted above $5 million. The complete and current Schedule of Minimums may be accessed online at http://www.wga.org or www.wgaeast.org.

In North America, there are two separate and distinct branches of the Guild. (Writers Guilds also exist in Canada, England, Australia, and New Zealand.) The WGA, west—largest in terms of membership—serves writers west of the Mississippi; the WGA, East serves those east of the Mississippi. The two branches usually act as one but, in 1998, a dispute over a crucial contract vote emphasized a potentially larger chasm between the two than had previously been envisioned. Then again, in 2004, a serious breach in relations between the two branches resulted in a lawsuit and an aborted attempt at mediation. This dispute was the subject of ongoing conversations between the governing boards of the two branches at the time of this writing; however, both are united in a common belief that the Guild serves the writer and it shall not be sacrificed to partisan bickering.

Benefits

There is much to recommend about membership in the WGA, not the least of which are the opportunities you'll have to hang out with other writers (at least during the strikes). Writing is a lonely experience and it's nice to know that there is always some other writer up at 3 a.m., happy to join you for a cup of coffee or engage in an Internet chat.

The more obvious purpose of the Guild is to serve its members. Clearly, the establishment of negotiated minimum payments for the various writing services performed by Guild members is widely recognized as the single most visible contribution to the financial welfare of its membership. And while the MBA makes no guarantee of job security, it has consistently and considerably improved the conditions under which those writing services are performed. In the difficult area of creative rights, for example, the Guild has managed to get employers and purchasers of original material to agree to accord the original writer (among other things) certain rewrite rights, the right to be consulted on the director's cut of the film, and promotional rights (which insure the writer will not have to crash the premiere of his own film). These rights are discussed in more detail in the Creative Rights section of Chapter 12.

Perhaps the most widely appreciated benefit is the WGA health fund. Eligibility is based on a sum of earnings tied to the Guild minimum for a one-hour, network primetime story and teleplay. As of November 2005, writers must earn the sum of $30,145 within four consecutive calendar quarters for eligibility.

The Guild also maintains a staff of attorneys to review (but not negotiate) contracts and to protect the writer's creative rights and work, even after the writer has sold it. One of the most crucial of these functions is the policing and collection of *residuals* which may become due as a film based on your work is released to various markets (such as network television, cable, video, DVD, CD-ROM, multimedia games, foreign markets, etc). Guild watchdogs monitor broadcasts and releases worldwide and bill the producing companies. Signatories delinquent in paying residuals are placed on the Guild's "Strike" or "Unfair" list.

> The prudent writer will not trust his hard-earned residuals to this process alone, but will use the Internet to check on reports of an airing in other cities and countries. This will help Guild lawyers to bolster (and often to make) their case. (**Tip:** Non-Guild writers might consider asking for an additional flat fee payable upon foreign sales, in lieu of residual payments.)

The Writers Guild Foundation Library, located on the first floor of the WGA, west headquarters in Los Angeles, was recently completely remodeled and is open to the general public. In addition to being an original movie and television script depository without parallel, it offers pleasant reading rooms and writer resources (even free coffee) that are worth a trip. The Guild also publishes a great magazine, *Written By*, which focuses on writers' issues, work, and lifestyles, and offers many inside tips. Non-members can subscribe or purchase issues at most chain bookstores and large newsstands.

For those of you who ask not what the Guild can do for you, but what you can do for your Guild, there are a wide variety of committees (such as agent and employment access, age and sex discrimination, and various writers' groups representing women, gays, blacks, Latinos, and Asian-Americans) upon which members may serve.

The Guild also administers a script registration service, a pension plan, a film society that offers first run screenings of most studio releases, a credit union (very useful for a profession marred by erratic income), a free notary service, and when requested, member *arbitration for screen credit*. This last function may be the Guild's most frequent source of interaction with its members.

Credit

In today's film climate, it is normal for many writers to work on the same script (whether to fix script problems, accommodate the budget, stars, or directors, or simply to placate a nervous studio executive). Therefore, credit on the final film—who is entitled to it and who ends up receiving it—is naturally the subject of much debate. The Guild Policy on Credits runs seven pages in the membership manual, and while it may not make the best bedtime reading, it confirms that "a writer's credits are essential to building or sustaining his/her career."

For your credits to be determined by Guild policy, you must have your work acquired by, or perform writing services for, a company signatory to the WGA Minimum Basic Agreement and be considered a "professional writer" by Guild definition. Dealing with a non-signatory company places the final credit determination beyond Guild jurisdiction.

When performing work-for-hire, be certain to inquire whether or not there is any assigned source material and whether or not other writers are employed or have been employed on the project. Also, the Guild stresses that writers "keep copies of all materials and accurate records of delivery dates." (To protect yourself, always turn in your assigned material with a cover letter setting forth the material delivered, date, and to whom delivered.)

After the movie is completed, the producer must send to the Guild and to all writers who worked on the project (or a prior produced version) a "Notice of Tentative Writing Credits" and a copy of the final shooting script. If any writer disputes the determination or if the writers cannot agree among themselves as to the final credits, the arbitration process takes place. All drafts are then submitted to an arbitration committee (composed of other Guild members) to determine the relative contributions of each writer to the shooting script. Pursuant to Guild rules:

> "Any writer whose work represents a contribution of more than 33 percent of a screenplay shall be entitled to screenplay credit, except... an original screenplay [wherein] any subsequent writer or writing team must contribute 50 percent to the final screenplay."

The percentages stated are designed as a guideline. For a second writer to receive credit, arbiters must take into consideration "dramatic construction, original and different scenes, characterization or character relationships and dialogue" and determine which elements "are most important to the overall values of the final screenplay in each particular case." Final screen credit may not be shared by more than two writers or, in unusual cases and solely as the result of arbitration, three writers or two writing teams.

There is a considerable bias in favor of crediting the original writer.

All of the hoopla over screen credit is more than a battle of egos—it can translate into a significant amount of money in residuals and much more. An appeals court recently upheld a $7.3 million verdict in favor of a writer who sued Universal Studios, claiming that the studio stole from his original teleplay the idea for the television series *Northern Exposure*. The ruling was heralded as significant for writers as a recognition by the courts of the impact a screen credit for a hit series can have on a writer's career and future earnings.

The Guild has published a *Screen Credits Manual* and *Credits Survival Guide* "to provide writers with a plain language guide to the credits determination process and practical tips writers should know to help protect their interests in credits." To obtain a copy of either, contact the Guild's Credits Department at (323) 782-4528 in Los Angeles or (212) 767-7804 in New York (or check their web site at http://www.wga.org or www.wgaeast.org).

Credit = credibility and determines fees, power and, ultimately, careers.

Careers

A common question from novice writers is whether a long-term career as a working writer is a reality. Has the Guild been remiss in its duty to act in the interest of all writers in building the *profession* of screenwriting, with its incumbent recognition, job security, and perks?

The Guild has insured broad financial gains, to be sure. But has the concentration on the short-term goal of higher pay been at the expense of the dignity, respect, and long-term future to which the average working writer aspires? In fact, is there such a thing as an average working writer? Staff writers of episodic television earn big bucks and big residuals—so long as they are able to maintain their jobs. But, less and less freelance work is available and the age at which writers are permitted to ply their trade is shrinking.

In the feature world, some screenwriters have famously garnered $1 million or more for a story outline and, though that practice seems to be on the wane, there is still much ballyhoo in the press about the occasional spec script that brings instant wealth to a new writer. But the "middle-class" screenwriter, the writer who earns a decent living wage by consistently selling his work, year in and year out, has almost disappeared. And though there are affirmative action committees within the Guild, the odds for a writing career dwindle if you are not white, male, and under 40.

In the late '90s, the Guild released a two-year study outlining the decline in employment for older writers: 73 percent of Guild writers 30 or younger were employed, compared to 46 percent of those in their forties, 32 percent of those in their fifties, 19 percent of those in their sixties, and a negligible percentage beyond that. Taking action, the Washington, D.C. law firm of Sprenger & Lang, PLLC, filed in Los Angeles a package of 23 class-action lawsuits against the networks, studios, and talent agencies on behalf of television writers claiming age discrimination. As of late 2005, these claims are still winding their way through the legal system.

In the interest of *all* writers, it was suggested that the Guild take a hard line in recent contract negotiations with the producers and studios. Besides the usual struggle over higher minimum payments to writers of film and television, the Guild was charged to demand profit participation for writers in all media in which the writers work is released, demand retention of the writer's copyright, refuse to sanction rewrites on the original writer's work, demand real creative participation for the writer in the making and marketing of the final film, and absolutely demand an end to age, sex, and race discrimination.

Chief among the issues on the table were:

1. The writers share of DVD, video, and basic cable revenue in a rapidly evolving new marketplace, one in which the distributors are receiving much higher profit margins on significantly lower manufacturing costs than were considered in past negotiations;

2. The jurisdiction over all writers and de facto writers of animated and reality-based entertainment, the vast majority of whom currently receive no DVD or VHS royalties, no residuals, and no pension and health care coverage;

3. The saving of the fragile Health Care plan by greater contributions from signatory companies (the writers have already been asked to kick in more for their part); and

4. More meaningful professional standards (formerly "creative rights") for all writers.

How does all this affect you whether or not you are a member of the Guild at present?

Consider the last time the industry labored under the threat of a strike. The Screen Actors Guild work stoppage had crippled the advertising industry and a spilloff from commercials to feature films was feared. A strike by writers threatened to further paralyze the industry. Without scripts and access to the writers that write them, producers scrambled to make whatever scripts they already had on the shelf. For months leading up to the possible strike, the producers bought everything that wasn't nailed down. Scripts that needed further development before the cameras could roll were sometimes handed over to non-Guild writers. (Many of whom would later be welcomed into the Guild.) Studios and indies alike rushed films into production to avoid a vacuum. But after the last batch of films were released, then what? The distribution monster must be fed. The fear of the machine grinding to a halt led to productive talks on crucial issues for the first time in years.

Most significantly, if only for the health of writers' morale, the strike produced some of the first real creative gains made in years, such as giving the writer the opportunity to meet with the director after he or she has been hired to discuss the script, the writer being invited to cast readings, named on cast and crew lists, invited to visit the set, to attend premieres and film festivals, to participate in domestic press junkets, and to be included in the electronic and printed press kits, the DVD version, and web sites advertising the film.

But in the real world of supply and demand, the studios can pay lip service to such demands while at the same time brushing them aside. Progress was made, but only symbolically—most gains were recommended, not mandated, meaning they were accorded the writers "unless notified otherwise by the Company." Congress, after all, via the Copyright Act, takes even the title of "author"—the very dignity of authorship—away from a writer for hire and hands it, along with the copyright to the work itself, to the studio or other employer—those who may never have put pen to paper!

As to the membership itself (the power to strike aside), the Guild has a practical mandate of maintaining employment. Yet, how often has a second writer refused to tinker with the original writer's vision or take full credit for the result? Until writers give value to their work, to their lonely but crucial role as filmmakers and to each other, no reform is possible. Because, after all, even the Guild cannot legislate respect.

REQUIREMENTS FOR ADMISSION
TO THE WGA, WEST, INC.

FILM, TELEVISION, RADIO

An aggregate of twenty-four (24) units of Credit as set forth on the Schedule of Units of Credit, which units are based upon work completed under contract of employment or upon the sale or licensing of previously unpublished and unproduced literary or dramatic material is required. Said employment, sale or licensing must be with a company or other entity that is signatory to the applicable WGA Collective Bargaining Agreement and must be within the jurisdiction of the WGA as provided in its collective bargaining contracts. The twenty-four (24) units must be accumulated with the preceding three (3) years of application. Upon final qualification for membership, a cashier's check or money order, payable to the Writers Guild of America, west, Inc. in the amount of Two Thousand Five Hundred Dollars ($2,500) is due. Writers residing West of the Mississippi River may apply for membership in the WGA, west, Inc. Writers residing East of the Mississippi River are advised to contact: Writers Guild of America, East, 555 West 57th Street, New York, NY 10019.

SCHEDULE OF UNITS OF CREDIT

Two Units   For each complete week of employment within the Guild's jurisdiction on a week-to-week basis.

Three Units Story for a radio or television program less than thirty (30) minutes shall be prorated in increments of ten (10) minutes or less.

Four Units   Story for a short subject theatrical motion picture of any length or for a radio program or television program or breakdown for a non-prime time serial thirty (30) minutes through sixty (60) minutes.

Six Units   Teleplay or radio play less than thirty (30) minutes shall be prorated in five (5) minute increments;

Television format for a new serial or series;

"Created By" credit given pursuant to the separation of rights provisions of the WGA Theatrical and Television Basic Agreement in addition to other units accrued for the literary material on which the "Created By" credit is based.

Eight Units	Story for a radio or television program or breakdown for a non-prime time serial more than sixty (60) minutes and less than ninety (90) minutes; Screenplay for a short subject theatrical motion picture or for a radio play or teleplay thirty (30) minutes through sixty (60) minutes.
Twelve Units	Story for a radio or television program ninety (90) minutes or longer or story for a feature length theatrical motion picture; or breakdown for a non-prime time serial ninety (90) minutes or longer.
	Radio play or teleplay more than sixty (60) minutes and less than (90) minutes.
Twenty-four Units	Screenplay for a feature length theatrical motion picture; radio play or teleplay ninety (90) minutes or longer;
	Bible for any television serial or prime-time mini-series of a least four (4) hours;
	Long-term story projection which is defined for this purpose as a bible, for a specified term, on an existing, five (5) times per week non-prime time serial.
A Rewrite	One-half (1/2) the number of units allotted to the applicable category of work.
A Polish	One-quarter (1/4) the number of units allotted to the applicable category of work.
An Option	One-half (1/2) the number of units allotted to the applicable category of work subject to a maximum entitlement of eight (8) such units per project in any one (1) year. An extension or renewal of the same option shall not be accorded additional units. If an option on previously unexploited literary material is exercised, the sale of this material is accorded the number of units applicable to the work minus the number of units accorded to the option of the same material.

ADDITIONAL RULES FOR THE UNIT SYSTEM

Teams: Each writer who collaborates as part of a bona fide team on the same project shall be accorded the appropriate number of units allotted to the applicable category.

New or Unique Cases: In any case not covered by this Section 4, the Board of Directors shall have the authority to convene a Committee to Review the Unit System, which Committee shall suggest specific units applicable to any such work to the Board. Such unit determinations as may be adopted by the Board shall be submitted for membership approval at the first annual or special membership meeting following the Board's action.

Writer Owned Company: In all cases, to qualify for membership, if the writer's employment, option or purchase agreement is with a company owned in whole or in part by the writer or a member of the writer's family, there must be a bona fide agreement for financing, production and/or distribution with a third party signatory producing company. Failing such an agreement, the script must be produced and the writer must receive writing credit on screen in the form of "Written by," "Teleplay by," "Screenplay by," or (audio credit) "Radio Play by."

Writers In A Managerial Capacity or Writer-Performers: A person who is employed to write or who sells or options literary material to a signatory company while:

a) serving in a managerial capacity with the company; or b) rendering managerial services relating to the project for a network, syndicated television station(s), basic cable or pay television system, a studio, or the like, or (c) employed as a player on the project, shall not utilize this assignment, option or sale to qualify for membership in the Guild unless such script is produced and the individual receives writing credit on screen in the form of "Written by," "Teleplay by," "Screenplay by," or (audio credit) "Radio Play by."

Exceptions to the Three-Year Rule: In exceptional cases, the Board of Directors, acting upon a recommendation from the Membership and Finance Committee, shall have the power and authority to grant admission to Current membership based on units earned prior to three (3) years before the membership application was filed.

Comedy-Variety: If three (3) or fewer writers are employed to write literary material for the same comedy-variety program for television, each writer shall be accorded the number of units for teleplay applicable to a program of the same duration (as may be adjusted pursuant to the applicable time period provisions in Appendix A of the MBA). If more than three (3) writers are employed to write literary material for the same comedy-variety program for television, each writer shall be accorded the number of units for teleplay applicable to a program of the same duration but multiplied by a fraction the numerator of which is one and the denominator of which is the number of writers minus two. For example, if there are five (5) writers employed, the multiplier would be one-third (1/3); if there are ten (10) writers, the multiplier would be one-eighth (1/8).

Documentaries and Informational Programming: Telescripts for documentaries and literary material for informational programming shall be accorded the number of units for teleplay applicable to a program of the same duration.

Newswriters: Any person employed as a radio or television news writer, editor, desk assistant or in another job classification cover under the "WGA-CBS National Staff Agreement" (Or successor collective bargaining agreement) may be admitted to Current Membership in the Guild after thirty (30) days of employment in such bargaining unit.

INTERACTIVE

A writers and/or designer who has worked for an employing company which has signed the Interactive Program Contract and paid the appropriate Pension and Health contributions may join the WGA as a Current or Associate member. A writer who has earned 24 units of credit—the equivalent to a full length screenplay—is eligible for Current WGA membership.

Units for interactive programs are currently interpreted on a case-by-case basis for projects covered under the Interactive Program Contract. The company you work for must sign this contract and agree to pay 12.5 percent of your gross compensation to the WGA Pension and Health Plan.

To ensure eligibility for Associate or Current membership through the writing of interactive projects you must:

- Work for a company who has signed the Interactive Program Contract and has paid the 12.5 percent Pension and Health contribution.
- You must send your signed contracts, both interactive and personal services contract, along with a completed Membership Application form, a Project Summary Sheet and the project script (and/or the project item itself, if applicable) to the Department of Industry Alliances, Writers Guild of America, west, 7000 West Third Street, Los Angeles, CA 90048.

These materials are reviewed by a subcommittee of WGA members who belong to the Creative Media and Technology Committee (CMAT). This subcommittee assigns the appropriate number of units for the project. If the writer is credited with less than 24 units, then the writer may be eligible for Associate membership. Those writers who become Associate members have three years in which to obtain the 24 units necessary for Current membership. It is the responsibility of Associate members to file additional contracts with the WGA so their eligibility for Current status may be tracked. Should a writer applying for WGA membership submit a project for which 24 units of credit are assigned, he/she must become a Current member. In this case, the writer does not have the option of Associate membership.

For further information, contact the department of Industry Alliances at (323) 782-4511 or (408) 323-1898, or Membership at (323) 782-4532.

Chapter 10

Building a Writing Career: Strategies for Marketing Yourself

"Good things happen to those who hustle."
—Anais Nin

In the complex game of selling your work, even the best agents or managers can't (and won't) do it all for you. There are two primary reasons for this. First, many agents and managers have contacts limited to the studios or major independent producers. (Unless you're associated with a very hot spec script or have previously written a hit film, those markets may effectively be closed to you.) Second, the particular sensibilities of your script or your willingness to work cheaply may appeal to less mainstream buyers. (For these markets, you are often on your own.) In both cases, you must do your homework: research the appropriate market for your work, determine what these companies are looking for, how they process and evaluate material and decide how to best present your screenplay and yourself. This requires a solid career-building strategy; here are some concrete steps you can and should take to get your career on track.

Career-Building Strategies

Rome wasn't built in a day. Any professional career, like the development of a vibrant city, requires planning. Here is a *seven-point comprehensive strategy for a long-term career.*

STRATEGY

1. Make a business plan.

- Create a one-year plan, a five-year plan, and a realistic work schedule that serves those ends. Approach the selling of your work with the same meticulous care you gave to the writing of it.

- Be attentive to your work: protect it via copyright, submit it wisely, and take good notes on who has it at any given time and what, if any, response there was to it.

- Keep a finger on the pulse of the industry. Learn all you can about the people in it—who is hot, who to contact to arrange a meeting, what a particular executive recently bought. Follow who is where and doing what by reading the trades, *Daily Variety* and *The Hollywood Reporter*. Both feature a weekly chart on films in production which track the particulars of what films are being produced (a good source of producers most likely to appreciate the movie you are scripting). Industry magazines such as *Creative Screenwriting* often list recent spec script and pitch sales along with the agents, managers, and lawyers that brokered the deals. Information is power.

- Resolve to make others see you as a fellow professional, conversant with the usual and customary way business is done. Don't know what a producer does or how a movie is actually put together? Producers, agents, managers, writers, and directors have all written memoirs that take you behind the scenes.

- Develop a plan for dealing with rejection. Not all screenplays sell, not even some very good ones—so follow this advice:

  - Start a new screenplay before trying to market the one you finished. That keeps you in the game for the long haul.
  - Keep your unsold, rewritten, polished work in circulation. (Unless *you* have outgrown it.)
  - Make lemons into lemonade. View rejection as an opportunity to become a better writer and to cement a deeper relationship with the person who rejected your work. See if you can get him to explain why the material didn't work for him. Ask him to be candid. Tell him you respect his opinion and want to gain the benefit of his insight. Any dialogue at this point should leave an open door for future work; in a business where rejection too often makes enemies, you will have employed it to make friends.

2. Build your creative team.

- A creative support team of two trusted readers, an agent, and/or manager is best. With most buyers, you only get one shot. Blow it and you're not likely to get another. You will rarely hear: "Do the rewrite and resubmit it; we'll take another look at it then." It is up to you to make sure your writing is the best you can deliver before you submit it the first time. For this, you need honest, informed, reliable feedback on your writing before you bring it to market.

- First, go to two friends—two friends who are not averse to being honest with you. Why two? One will weigh too heavily on you and more than two may confuse you. And, when they comment, listen quietly and take notes (a certain amount of humble pie goes with the territory). Their reaction (or lack of reaction) can be a good barometer of how spellbinding a story you've created. Watch for eyes glazing over as you race over the murky middle; see if they register confusion or ask questions as you try to tip-toe around the weak areas of your work ("oh that, oh well, I have to fix that, just keep listening"). The feedback will help strengthen your script (and improve your pitch) before you present it to those few precious contacts you hold in your back pocket.

- Then go to your agent or manager. If you *have* a manager or agent, and they are willing to help during the creative stage, great, though sending it to them first may seem obvious. But even for established talent, I recommend against submitting work to your marketing team before it's ready. They may not respond to your draft and discourage or turn away from you at this vulnerable stage in the writing process. And if they *hate* your script, but *you* still love it, find another agent or manager.

3. Network.

- Keep in touch with your industry contacts and do what you can to cultivate and expand them. Screenwriter Robert Towne (*Chinatown*) gives this advice: "Make movies with your friends." (Of course, that's easy when your friends are Jack Nicholson and Warren Beatty.) The point is that personal relationships are the butter that smoothes the way for business relationships to form. We all have contacts, but not all contacts are so obvious; sometimes you have to look for them. You may have friends you don't know yet. The party game known as *Six Degrees of Kevin Bacon* (connecting the actor to other actors through common films) is a variation on an old theme; with enough research, you can find someone who will connect you to just about anyone. If your great aunt has a friend with a son who knows a guy that dates a woman whose cousin works as a secretary for a small L.A. entertainment law firm—that's a contact!

▪ Build alliances with your peers; perhaps start your own writer's table. Attend film classes and writing seminars. The USC and the UCLA film schools have become Hollywood legend, but strong professional bonds have also been built at Yale Drama School, The American Film Institute, New York University, Columbia University, The University of Miami, and other academic institutions as well. For example, executive producer Stephen Bochco didn't look much further than his circle of buddies from Carnegie Tech when he began to staff and cast television shows like *Hill Street Blues*, *LA Law*, and *NYPD Blue*.

▪ Make a wish list of contacts you'd like to have—then go after them. Don't be afraid to include those "names" established in the business, even if you believe to contact them may be presumptuous. You might be surprised at how many are happy to share their experience (and their contacts) with new writers who express a sincere willing-ness to work. As local networking resources, there are university adult education courses, seminars, workshops, and showcases, all of which attract industry professionals that might be predisposed to help a new entrant. Listen intently when they speak, ask questions, quietly contribute your point of view about aspects of the business or their careers that you have researched or cultivated from reading the trade papers. This is not the time to be pitching your new script or high concept—you are that interesting party guest that others wish they knew more about.

▪ If you live in Los Angeles, the creative Guilds and their many func-tions are often open to the public and many feature screenwriters, producers, agents, and studio executives. Or you could go directly to the studios—to have lunch in the commissaries, to make contact with people there in a friendly (not overbearing) way. Brian Grazer met longtime partner Ron Howard when both were strolling across the Paramount lot to the commissary for lunch. Grazer was an assistant to an executive and Howard already a star, but they just hit it off. How will *you* get in? Perhaps take your cue from the legend of how Steven Spielberg bluffed his way onto Universal Studios—park outside and walk through the main gate, preoccupied with the contents of your briefcase and always wearing proper business attire. (Worst way: look like an aspiring actor!)

- The goal here is to make and keep connections, at whatever level they are found, with the same relentless drive, creativity, and imagination that will serve you well as a writer. And never forget: Have no script when opportunity knocks, and even the best of contacts can't help you.

4. Find a mentor.

- You can, of course, consult a professional. Any good psychologist or life or career coach, particularly one that specializes in working with creative types, can help you get over the rough spots along the road. In New York and Los Angeles, I'm told that writers make up the largest single professional group in the average psychiatric practice. But there may be a cheaper and even more effective alternative—a career guide just for you.

- A mentor can be an invaluable ally. Often someone older, but not always, not necessarily even a writer, or someone in the film business at all. Because, as you've surely learned, there is no logic to the film business—only connections and power. A mentor is someone who possesses one or both of those qualities, along with the wisdom borne of real life experiences in the trenches and the sincere desire to help *you* win.

  Steven Spielberg had a mentor—by all accounts Universal's longtime chief Sid Sheinberg, though Sid's recently deceased and powerful boss, Lew Wasserman, also lent a fatherly hand from time to time. To them, Steven was like a son. They watched over him, not in a judgmental way, but rather with all the guiding influence and patient advice of the ideal father/son relationship without the years of future therapy. Read almost any celebrity bio and you will find someone, some mother to a would-be daughter, some father to a would-be son, who took the fledgling at some crucial time under his or her arm and gave him the wings to fly.

The late Gordon Stulberg served as my mentor. He was my lawyer who brought to his practice a wealth of wisdom and experience born from his years as president of Twentieth Century Fox, CBS Films, and Polygram Films. But his legal work on my behalf was incidental. He was primarily my friend and teacher, freely dispensing advice, patronage, and contacts—dipping into his favor bank whenever necessary to help me out of yet another sticky situation in which my youth and inexperience had landed me.

- How do you find a mentor? Be proactive. Contacts breed contacts. Cultivate a network of friends who want to see you succeed because they care and because your success is in some respects a measure of theirs. Your ambitions, your honesty, your tenacity, should sooner or later steer you into the flight path of one or two people whose own desire to give back blends with your needs. Many seemingly aloof and unapproachable power brokers actually delight in using their industry savvy, born of years of in-fights, to help those with the chutzpah to ask for it. You might be surprised at the show biz pros who would be flattered to get your call—though in Los Angeles, where there are far more supplicants than mentors, don't take a brush-off to heart.

Post this advice on your bulletin board: When a group of USC film students asked Star Wars creator George Lucas how to go about breaking into the film business, he replied, "Somehow."

- If you live outside the main stream of the biz, find someone powerful and connected in almost any business. Their wisdom is often transferable and connections in one business lead to connections across the business world.

  Caveat: *Your agent, manager, or lawyer is not your mentor.* Ideally, you want a real pal, not an industry friend. Business relationships come and go, but your mentor is like family. Also, those in our employ—particularly the agents who share in our income stream—often exude a sense of class superiority toward their writer-clients. Sure there have been gentlemen and gentlewomen among their ranks, but most tend to keep close only their biggest breadwinners and rarely will one lose sleep over what could be done to further a writer's career unless it also involves a big boost to their own.

5. Enter screenwriting contests.

- The good news: Finding a contest to enter is easy. So many writing contests emerge (and disappear) each year that entire books are devoted to cataloging and updating them. A handful of such contests are a legitimate search for talent, such as those sponsored by universities and other well-established educational institutions or by large film companies or studios. Some offer the novice or unexposed screenwriter access to the movers and shakers of production, some yield agents and options or cash awards, work stipends, or workshops with established professionals.

- The bad news is that many contests are not well-established, are difficult to monitor, and may even be rip-offs. The fringe of the contest market has become infested with charlatans. Some contests are unconscionable scams that require substantial entry or reading fees but offer winners little or no film contacts, media exposure, or real prizes. Others are thinly disguised efforts by wanna-be movie producers to find cheap and plentiful material to shop with little or no option fee—while getting *you* to pay for the privilege of giving away the fruits of your talent!

A student entered (for a $35 fee) a contest based in New York that certainly sounded legitimate. She won first prize (over "close to 10,000" contestants), receiving a nice computerized announcement to that effect but nothing else. Her spec episode was to be "presented" to the producers of the show; she never heard a word. My guess is that the promoter (richer by $350,000 if the entrance figures are accurate) mailed her winning script to the producers who tossed it in the bin along with all other unsolicited manuscripts.

- Who are these "judges?" In such an unregulated environment, anyone can anoint himself a judge of writing talent. But what are their credits and what is their motivation? Gaining access to new talent can be a noble purpose; collecting fees for the chance to "borrow" material from writers is not. How does your entrance fee differ from paying any stranger to read your work? (It is considered unethical for an agent or production company to charge a fee to offset their reader costs, a practice I find particularly abominable, even as part of a contest.)

- What do the judges look for? Unless the contest targets special genres or select entrants, the answer is usually the "very best of which you are capable." That aside, the most important aspect to entering a contest is to determine how winning the contest will benefit the entrant. If the prize is money, is there proof bona fide winners were actually paid? If it's industry access or recognition, is there a list of prior winners and their accomplishments that resulted from winning the contest? If it's the promise of an option or sale, be especially cautious: One well-publicized contest requires "potential" finalists to sign a long and onerous legal document effectively transferring, in advance, all rights to their work for an unconscionably low purchase price—which in fact may never be payable and which compels the writer to perform substantial additional writing services over an unspecified period of time at no additional compensation.

The well-established Worldfest—Houston International Film Festival (P.O. Box 56566, Houston, TX 77256; 713-965-9955; Deadline December 15) charges outrageous fees ($85 for screenplays) in order to discourage contest shopping and limit entries to 400, but brags that Hollywood heavyweights like Spielberg, Lucas, and Ridley Scott received their first filmmaking award from Worldfest—and still take their recommendations!

- How do you choose a contest? Track records are your best barometer. Why submit to contests that hold little industry cache when established contests may cost the same to enter? Granted, it may be difficult to know which is which. One sure finger on the pulse of the contest beat has been Patricia B. Smith's column in *Creative Screenwriting* magazine. Noting that contests have sprouted like mushrooms, she cautions writers to:
    - Look at the relative cost of the entry fee versus the value of the prizes;
    - Be wary of contests that list awards as to be announced or to be determined;
    - Read contest report cards on moviebytes.com; and
    - Check out where the contest is headquartered and how long it's been in business.

I would add that you should check the track record of success for prior announced winners. You can choose (do so judiciously—five is a lot) among the many new contests opening up yearly (some have monthly competitions), but the following seven (plus two wild cards) are my consistent favorites:

(Note: Application deadlines, fees, procedures, awards, and contact names and numbers are subject to change—and do so frequently. So send a self-addressed, stamped envelope (SASE) for an application, specific guidelines, and rules of eligibility.)

- **American Zoetrope Screenplay Contest: 916 Kearny Street, San Francisco, CA 90291; 415-788-7500. Entry fee: $30 by 8/1, $40 thereafter. Deadline: September 1.** Coppola himself serves as a judge for this (currently) three-year-old contest awarding a $5,000 grand prize, wide industry exposure, and all finalists are considered for development by Zoetrope.

- **Nicholl Fellowships in Screenwriting: Academy Foundation, Academy of Motion Picture Arts and Sciences, 8949 Wilshire Blvd., Beverly Hills, CA 90210-1972; 310-247-3059. Entry fee: $20 for entry by 4/1, $30 thereafter. Deadline: May 1.** The nation's most prestigious screenwriting contest, it awards up to five $30,000 fellowships and promises publicity and industry contacts. Caveat: With up to 6,000 entries per year, only well-crafted scripts which demonstrate writing ability will make the finals.

- **Screenwriting Expo Screenplay Contest: 6404 Hollywood Boulevard, Suite 415, Los Angeles, CA 90028; 323-957-1405. Entry fee: $50. Deadline: August 22.** An arm of the annual Screenwriting Expo in Los Angeles, sponsored by *Creative Screenwriting* magazine, over $80,000 in prizes will go to over two dozen winners and runners-up, plus a $50,000 production deal—more than any other non-fellowship contest. Access to production companies, agents, and managers is also a part of certain winning packages.

- **Scriptapalooza: 7775 Sunset Boulevard, Suite 200, Hollywood, CA 90046; 323-654-5809. Entry fee: $45 by 3/10, $50 thereafter. Deadline: April 15.** Held in association with The Writers Guild, this contest has bloomed with over 4,000 entries per year, serious industry recognition and promotion of winners, and a $10,000 first prize.

- **Sundance Screenwriters Lab: The Sundance Institute, 225 Santa Monica Blvd., 8th Floor, Santa Monica, CA 90401; 310-394-4662. Entry fee: $25. Deadline: June 28 and November 15.** Offers a chance to work at Robert Redford's Utah ranch with some of the best writers and other creative talent available and promises publicity and travel expenses.

- **Walt Disney Studios Fellowship Program: Fellowship Program Administrator, 500 South Buena Vista Street, Burbank, CA**

91521-0880; 818-560-6894. **Entry fee: None. Deadline: June 3.**
Preference given to women and minorities; WGA members not
eligible; 12 writers (8 television and 4 screenwriters) are awarded
$50,000 fellowships; out-of-state winners are afforded airfare and
some expenses. Industry exposure and career boost: priceless.

▪ **Warner Bros. Television Writers Workshop: Warner Bros., 4000
Burbank Blvd., Burbank, CA 91522-0001; 818-954-7906. Entry fee:
$25, $450 to participate in the workshop. Deadline: Fall (call for
exact date).** Professional training, development deals, possible staff
positions, and assignments are offered.

▪ **Two lesser-known contests—the Wisconsin Screenwriters Forum,
5747 North 82nd Court, Milwaukee, WI 53218 (not limited to
residents of Wisconsin) and the Austin Film Festival Screenplay
Competition, 1604 Nueces, Austin, TX 78701; 512-478-4795)—**
have not only consistently increased their prizes and the profile of
their winners, but offer serious bragging rights to winners who
aggressively market their work to agents and buyers.

▪ Finally, the trades, other film publications and state and local film
commissions are sources of information or advertisements for
contests. Investigate carefully, use good common sense, and make
inquiries on the Internet before committing your hopes, entrance
fee, and postage. And *never*—under any circumstances and not
withstanding flattery or rosy promises—sign anything that could
be construed to sell or transfer the rights to your "winning entry"
without first consulting a good contract lawyer.

Most large cities and all states have a strong economic interest in promoting local
film production. Many sponsor screenplay competitions expressly for the purpose
of targeting good scripts which can be shot locally. (See for example, the "Set in
Philadelphia" Screenwriting Competition; 3701 Chestnut Street, Philadelphia, PA
19104; 215-895-6593; or, the Arizona Screenplay Search; 2345 E. Thomas Rd., Suite
300, Phoenix, AZ 85016; 602-955-6444.) If the setting of your story lends itself to
a particular location, write the appropriate state or local film commission for a list
of contests for which your script may be eligible.

---

6. Consider consultation services.

▪ A first-rate second opinion from a seasoned pro can be a wise
investment. But make sure you choose someone with an objective

perspective and a sincere desire to offer both script and career-building advice. Unfortunately, that is not always what the writer will receive for his money. Some well-intentioned industry readers, story editors, writing teachers, and screenwriters have taken to moonlighting as consultants. Ads are placed offering first-rate, insider analysis of submitted work. Nothing wrong with that. Some promise to connect you to agents or buyers or even to produce selected work themselves. Some *are* competent, well-intended, and reasonable. A positive experience with a consultant can net professional feedback and an industry contact. But here's the rub: Many so-called consultants may be out of steam, out of work, out of touch, disgruntled, bitter, and in need of exorcising their own demons. These consultants should be avoided, no matter the bargain they may seem to be.

■ Demand recent references. Also, examine your own motivations. At this point in your career, do you need help with the mechanics of the writing process or an objective critique of your finished work? Or, perhaps you desire advice on how to market your screenplay, including personal recommendations to agents or production companies. In either case, will you be getting individual attention and advice superior to that you could access yourself (often for less money) through university courses, screenwriting seminars, Internet web sites, and various publications?

Caveat: *The same warning for contests applies here.* Phone and actually talk to any references offered, check track records, and ask questions that go to the heart of your expectations before placing your money and dreams on an opinion that may carry little weight with mainstream Hollywood. And note: Whether you submit a concept, outline, treatment, or screenplay, whether it is for evaluation by a producer, agent or for entry into a contest, whether for grant or scholarship consideration or for professional consultation or analysis—register and/or copyright your work and maintain a good paper trail of all correspondence relating to your submission. The operative phrase here is "buyer beware."

It is best to steer clear of mass-marketed consultation services. Find out whom, exactly, will be doing the reading—the consultant or a paid reader? Will the service include a personal phone consultation or will it be conducted entirely by mail? Will you be paying for a glorified reader report—or a line-by-line script analysis and in-depth, truthful advice to make you a better writer? Or will you receive an adapted form letter on the general principles of screenwriting?

Q. I have access to script classes in L.A.; are they a better financial investment than a consultant? And what is a fair price for a consultant?

Mark, Tempe, Arizona

A. Start by comparing apples with apples. Ask yourself what you really want. An education in the basics of the craft? A social atmosphere? A mentor? A contact? A writing partner? Classes, seminars, and workshops can offer all that, as well as more learning time for less money. But other bodies also mean less time available to be spent on your script. That's why if you have a full script and a desire to invest in a professional approach to rewriting it, a consultant is often a worthwhile option. The one-on-one mentoring alone can give you confidence and direction in your new career.

But consultants vary in price and quality. The good ones are worth their weight in diamonds and the poor ones are expensive at any price. So do your homework. First, check credentials. Does he/she teach screenwriting, practice it, have a track record as a produced screenwriter, or solid experience in the production, development, or agency ranks? What qualifies their advice over your best friend's? Next, define your needs. Do you want a line-by-line edit with detailed suggestions for rewriting or notes akin to basic script coverage? An honest, professional appraisal of your work and talents? Or a shoulder to lean on, a supportive mother/father figure who will tell you what you want to hear?

A free five-minute phone call testing the vibes should be your first step.

7. Publicity and public relations.

- In Hollywood, the writer can be as invisible as a polar bear in a snowstorm. Out of sight, out of mind. If they can't see you, how can you expect them to respect you? ("They" being the agents, producers, and studio honchos.) The challenge, as in any business, is to get brand name recognition. What will entice the buyers to call on you in their search for good screen material? What will separate you from the ever-swelling mass of writers registering screenplays with the Writers Guild? In a town where perception is everything, the answer is the power of marketing, promotion, publicity, and public and media relations.

from the trenches: THE ART OF SELF-PROMOTION FOR WRITERS

Much is made about the value of toiling for years in the Hollywood trenches before "making it." Those at the top call it "paying your dues." Baloney. Directors become directors by directing, producers by producing. They don't work their way up the food chain. There is no glory or career edge gained by laboring in obscurity while honing your craft. Hone it right out there in the limelight like everyone else. After all, you're already a good writer. You know it and your family and friends do too. Now is as good a time as any to let the secret out. And who is going to do that? You, that's who. You must be the agent that gets you an agent, the manager that gets you noticed. It's as much your job as the writing itself. I learned this in my salad days as a producer. Sure, I carried good scripts under my arm, some with name talent attached, but so did lots of wanna-be producers. In the end, it wasn't the scripts or my agents that helped me along; it was my decision to hire a publicist. I had a coming out story in the trade papers, listing my projects and goals. My presence at premieres or parties was regularly noted in columns in *Variety* or *The Hollywood Reporter*. Producers and development executives I'd never met began greeting me like we were old friends. I became a member of the club by giving the impression I already belonged. I had a three-picture deal and offices on the Universal lot within the year.

The goal is visibility. Name recognition can lead to industry awareness, respect, writing assignments, higher pay, and greater creative control over your career. Think: what can I do today; what friends can I make? Put yourself out there. It's not why you became a writer, I know. You want your work to speak for itself, of course. It's unseemly for an artist to promote himself, right? But while the meek may inherit the earth, strict adherence to that philosophy won't get you very far in Hollywood. The image of the writer as a shy, retiring recluse no longer fits our job description. It's a new century, one of information overload and celebrity worship. And we writers would do well to modify our battle plan to better equip ourselves for life in this hostile and alien environment.

First, accept the lesson of corporate America: *do only that which only you can do!* The more business-savvy among our lot have gone way beyond the age-old support group of agents and lawyers and now regularly employ researchers, assistants, personal managers, and publicists. They issue press releases to keep the rest of the business informed of their battles and triumphs. This isn't just ego. It's smart business.

continued

Take Joe Eszterhas. He was always a good writer, but he entered the public consciousness when he leaked his private war with then agent Mike Ovitz onto every fax machine in town. He stayed in the scandal sheets by marrying the cast-off wife of the producer of his movie who had dumped her for the star, Sharon Stone (who subsequently dumped him). Makes good copy, doesn't it? That's the point. His brand name value contributed to multi-million dollar deals for his pitches and treatments, even in the face of downright flops for some films he eventually penned.

Or how about the prolific and talented David E. Kelley? Why is he such a magnet for the camera during award telecasts—bypassing other talented showrunners, such as Aaron Sorkin, Steven Bochco, David Milch, or John Wells, seated nearby? Could it partially be due to his wife, the beautiful Michelle Pfeiffer, next to him? That's publicity value. That makes for ratings. That almost makes writers seem glamorous. And it doesn't hurt when he walks into a room to negotiate a new series concept.

Bruce Vilanch, a writer previously unknown outside limited show biz circles, wrote a documentary film called *Get Bruce!* starring himself as a talented gag writer for the stars. He was booked on talk shows. His asking price as a writer soared. He got his own square on *Hollywood Squares*.

So, okay, you're convinced. But you also can't produce award-winning television, write jokes for the Oscars, or marry a movie star—at least no one yet will let you. Hang in there. A little personal makeover is in order. I'm not saying shell out $75,000 for a full-page ad in the Sunday *New York Times*. There are baby steps you can take to get started. But before you rush out and hire a publicist or invite reporters from the trades to lunch at the Four Seasons, remember it helps if you have done something worth shouting about. While a little media coverage is priceless (literally), journalists usually require something newsworthy to write about.

Even if you have done something of interest, you may have to stand up and wave your arms around until somebody notices you. All journalists love a good story, but don't expect them to come hunting you down for one. Fame comes most often to those who seek it. Of course, you have to give them something to write about. There is no marketing magic that can turn a mediocre talent into a hot ticket. You've got to have the goods. Your talent is your best selling point, but communicating that talent to others will help you get the assignments and recognition your work deserves. If you were profiling yourself, what's impressive about you? What is your image, your signature accomplishment? You're a writer, find a good story hook, like the real-life trials that inspired your film or MOW. Maybe you have a personal story that complements the one you've written. Or perhaps you've taken a maverick approach to your craft or sold your script in an unusual way.

Have a script in production? Ask the unit publicist for your film or the studio or network publicity department to be sure and include you in their electronic press kits, press junkets, and on-set interviews (they may forget about you if you don't). Make their job easier by providing any interesting story history, film biz anecdotes, or heart-warming personal vignettes that make for good copy. If your film makes it to a film festival, be there, hobnob, and offer yourself for interviews and seminar panels. Be animated, positive, and quotable. Create a little controversy when you speak. Be a devil's advocate. Create your own news; the networks do it all the time.

Maybe you can send a ready-to-print press release of your recent sale to your alumni newsletter or to a publication that focuses on the subject matter of your script. Be sure to accompany it with a bio and a nice black and white 8x10 (an informal photo with you and the star or director is best). See if your school or university can use a luncheon speaker from the film world for one of their scheduled functions. Book yourself as a celebrity guest on a local cable talk show. Offer your services for a charity affair or participate in a community or industry panel that addresses issues you may have drawn on for your script. Testify before a congressional committee!

Knock yourself out, but move fast. The time to act is when your story is still a current event—a week after your cable movie has aired or your film has left the theater is often a week too late.

The ABC's of Producing It Yourself

The cold truth is that nobody curls up at night with a good screenplay. The goal, the only goal for a script, is to be made into a movie. Yet it sometimes seems that anyone who is anyone or connected to anyone who can do anything for you apparently has something better to do than read your script. And nobody seems to want to give a new writer a break. So why not cut out the middlemen, pick up a hand-held camcorder, cash in those savings bonds, and do it yourself—make your movie, from your script, done your way. You can even hire yourself to direct! (Or to star, sing, edit, or wheel the camera around on those little tracks!) At long last, you'll have some control over your destiny as a writer.

You've read the Sunday movie section, you know the drill: A new writer had a passion that grabbed her by the throat and wouldn't let go. But her spec never made it out of the slush pile of a top agent. So the writer decides to make her movie herself. She hangs around film festivals, interests a TV star in the charms of her screenplay, and attracts a small investment in the film's production. A first-time director is brought on board. Together with a rag-tag crew, they create some wonderful shots and memorable moments on film. A good editor assembles a cohesive story that hits its audience with the impact of a freight train. Later a distributor is found, a marketing campaign launched, and another writer wins the spec script lottery!

Careers are made of less. But producing isn't for the feint of heart. Seeing one's words spoken by actors on a sixteen-foot high screen in a theater near you takes luck, money, and the willing participation of a lot of people. Your first move should probably be to partner with someone who has a track record as a producer.

But who is a producer, anyway? One answer is that a producer is someone who knows a writer. Only with a script or some other story material in hand can the rest of the business of movie making proceed. So you're already one giant step ahead of the game—you have a script. (You are also in the unenviable position of having to shout, "Eureka! I've scoured the world and read a thousand scripts and here, I swear, is the best—and, surprisingly, I wrote it!".)

Studios can afford to take on the challenge of developing scripts into movies; they may be driven by the interest of talent they wish to be in business with or by the power of the concept. Most independent film companies (with less time, money, and staff) cannot afford the same luxury. They look for a finished screenplay strong enough to attract talent, or one with money or talent (especially a star) already attached. So the best way to attract these companies to your work is to help raise the money to film your screenplay and to link your work to talent. This definitively qualifies you as a producer.

Raising Financing

Novice or pro, once you decide to go it on your own, the artist in you must give way to the salesman. Making a movie is never cheap, and your primary job as a producer will be to *find the money*. That means selling yourself and your script to people to whom a whole lot of other people are trying to sell things to. And there are certain basic questions which any investor will ask and which you must be able to answer:

1. What is the "package" for this film? Who have you assembled with a reputation for delivering a film on time and on budget? Do you have a shootable screenplay, a director (if that's you, that's two key pieces

of the puzzle right there), a co-producer or production manager, and any recognizable (sometimes called bankable) acting talent?

2. What are the primary locations, shooting schedule, and final budget for your film?

3. Are there any product promotions, discounts, or tax rebates which the film can take advantage of? Any potential marketing tie-ins such as a top musician performing the score or a script based on some newsworthy topic or person in the public eye?

4. Do you have any presold markets, a distributor, and/or a completion bond?

5. What are your income sources and projections for how the investment will be secured and recouped?

In this last regard, you'll need a *marketing plan*. Who is your target audience? Is it a film that appeals primarily to families or teens or to an ethnic or special interest group, or is it truly that rare film with universal appeal? Can the film's premise be easily expressed in a log line or is it a concept that's new to a paying audience and therefore a challenge to promote?

Once, in a theater in Houston, the lights went up on a preview screening of a movie I had produced. The distributor's representative sitting next to me said, "Get ready, they're going to ask you what this movie is about." "Didn't they just sit through the same film we did," I replied, nonplused. "Yeah," he said, "but that doesn't mean they have any better idea of how to reduce it to a log line than I do. You made this *facacada* movie; now you've got to help us sell it."

It wasn't an easy sell. It fit no easily identifiable category or genre. This made marketing to or even pinpointing its potential audience difficult. For this reason, most low-budget films *do* fit an easily identifiable genre. It's axiomatic that the budget of your film should never exceed the film's likely profit potential. The cost of production for different genres can be weighed against that genre's audience to form at least a preliminary measure of potential success. Certain genres, like costume dramas or those that require elaborate action sequences or special effects, are not cheap to produce. Horror films or slice-of-life teen comedies or most adult drama, on the other hand, can usually be mounted for an affordable price. Yet quality cannot be sacrificed. Even a homegrown film like The *Blair Witch Project* jousts for screen space with mega-budgeted, television advertised, commercially tied-in, star vehicles—and the price of admission is the same.

Or maybe you can raise just a little money—known as *seed money*—to build a package that can attract more deep-pocketed investors to pony up. Traditionally, seed money is spent optioning and developing books or scripts. It can be used to hire writers to write original material or do rewrites. It's also useful in attracting talent to your project. An escrow fund can be set up to lock in a "name" director or star by guaranteeing them a *"pay or play"* fee (they keep open a period of availability in exchange for your promise to pay them whether or not you actually use their services during that period). And even though your personal payday may have you on a tuna fish and macaroni diet, at least seed money can help keep the lights on. Ultimately, a producer must make a lot of pitches to raise the full production financing for his film.

Seed money can be useful there too. You can use it to develop marketing materials to sell your project to investors, such as a movie poster—a mock "one-sheet" to convey the excitement of your potential film—or even produce a short video or film "trailer" of your film to really sell the sizzle. You may print up glossy brochures showing how similar films to yours have fared in the marketplace (choosing only the more successful ones of course). You'll host dinners with the director or the star. You'll have your attorney draft a limited partnership agreement to insulate investors from liability or personal exposure beyond their investment. All this requires a funding source.

Private money sources are the low-budget film's best bet. Your local dentist or doctor can brag about their involvement at cocktail parties, and are too busy making their own money to closely oversee how you spend it. Still, it takes more than a casual millionaire to invest in anything much beyond a student-quality production. Remember this: *Your best intentions noted, these people are very likely to lose some if not all of every penny they invest in your film.* Never forget that fact when you are knocking on the doors of your neighbors and relatives.

For this reason, traditional investors are often best. A number of markets exist primarily to expose distributors to new (even unproduced) product for which the theatrical, television, video/DVD, or cable rights are available. At such popular industry conventions as MIFED or Cannes in May or the American Film Market in Los Angeles in February, producers (or the seasoned sales reps they hire) attempt to sell those rights to distributors worldwide. These are called *presales* since rights are sold to a movie that doesn't yet exist. If your package includes a recognizable star or a producer or director with an identifiable track record in making and delivering similar films, you may be able to raise most or all of your budget this way before you expose even one frame of negative.

You may also be able to finance your film by preselling it to a studio via a *negative pickup*. A negative pickup is a contract that guarantees you a negotiated sum upon delivery of your completed film in exchange for the right to distribute the film domestically and/or in specified foreign territories. Assuming you make the same film you scripted, with the elements you promised, you could fund your entire budget this way. The studio saves their overhead and avoids the bloated fees that attach to any studio production. Your guerrilla production, meanwhile, is able to proceed without the headaches of a studio's daily oversight. The negative pickup is often one-stop shopping. You take the studio's (or other distributor's) contract or promissory note to a bank, which discounts the note (sometimes by as much as half!) before giving you the balance to make your film. The bank is repaid when the movie is made and the studio pays the agreed price to the producer upon delivery. Having made a significant investment in your film, the studio is likely to put their full weight behind the promotion and marketing of it. A win-win situation all around.

Except if you produced a sleeper hit. Each year a few "small" films reap huge publicity playing at film festivals, such as Robert Redford's Sundance festival in Utah in January. The award winners (and even some also-rans) are often the subject of heated bidding wars by the boutique distributors and major studio reps in attendance. If you presold the rights to your film *before* the festival, you've already made your pact with the devil. But then again, if your film was a turkey, at least the relatives will still be talking to you.

Packaging Talent

You need to get a cast and secure a director if your movie is going to be made. Your wish list has only stars on it. That's okay. Stars seek the artistic freedom of more intimate productions, character-driven stories, and the chance to link up with emerging writers. (Note Harvey Keitel's work in Quentin Tarantino's directorial debut, *Reservoir Dogs*, and the resurgence of John Travolta's stalled career when Tarantino interested him in *Pulp Fiction*.) Even hot directors need to find a great script or they have nothing to direct. See how easy this can be? Of course, attaching talent to your screenplay can be a double-edged sword. A desirable name can create instant heat on your project, but a prospective buyer may see that person as more of a burden than a benefit. Attach more than one person and you increase the odds of that happening. Multiply this by 10 for any notion you may have of attaching *yourself* as a producer, director, or principal actor. But, if you have a proven track record in the slot you wish to fill, that's different—or, if your screenplay is so hot you have negotiating leverage, go for it!

More power to you if you've managed to raise the production financing yourself while retaining the authority to cast yourself as director or star. Or, if you would rather burn your screenplay (really, not just bluffing) than sell it without directing or starring in it, etc., then you must follow the dictates of your heart. But, attaching yourself in such a key capacity is bound to do more than just raise eyebrows; it may be a deal breaker. Before you dash a promising career on the rocks of your own ambition, seek the advice of others who have your professional interests at heart, your agent, lawyer, manager, or all three.

---

from the trenches: GETTING TO DIRECTORS AND STARS

Look into your crystal ball to see what your poster (movie folk call it a one-sheet) might look like if you were to make the movie. What is the hook in that poster to attract an audience to your film? An intriguing logline and a recognizable star? That's exactly what you need to make it. But scripts and actors cost money—so that's top of the shopping list.

Not your money, of course. Even the most successful (filthy rich) producers—Bruckheimer, Grazer, or Silver, for example—never put a dime into their pictures. The nature of making movies—its costs and its risks—makes using other people's money axiomatic. Fortunately, just about everybody wants to be in the film business, even if they have to buy their way in. First, you may have to dig into your own wallet, buy a plate at civic events or fund-raisers, and mingle. But since all kinds of pitches are dangled in front of anyone with deep pockets, you'll have to set your hook with tempting bait.

The costs of talent and production look ridiculous to folks in the real world and the audience is fickle. No one has the inside track on what makes a good film, any more than development execs really know what makes a winning script. A prospectus boasts a budget and possible revenue sources (box office projections, ancillary markets, etc.) to recoup that budget, but everyone knows those add up to little more than predictions, guesses, hopes, and dreams. Fortunately, money isn't put into films as a prudent investment, especially given the creative

continued

accounting of distributors. Money is attracted by the sizzle: celebrity power, track records, and all those award parties. In a world where there are no guarantees, sharing the risk with known talent is a step in the right direction.

In film parlance, that means packaging an element. An element is any actor, writer, director, producer—anyone really—attached to your script who makes an investor more comfortable putting their money and reputation on the line for your film. As for whether your movie will need a big element or a modest element (translated: little bucks or big bucks), let's use the one-sheet test. Do you see a bona fide movie star on it? That means big bucks. Three character actors in front of a rural train station? Little bucks. An epic, period adventure on water? Big bucks. A guy videotaping women revealing their sexual fantasies? Little bucks. See how easy it is?

Now a good production manager will tell you that you can make a budget fit just about any script and vice-versa. Film and processing are the only hard costs and you can eliminate those by going digital. You can even get talent and crew for next to nothing. Those starting out need to pad their resume. And established actors and directors are starved for good scripts and are willing to sacrifice their "quote" to be associated with them. Fortunately, the creative guilds are very cooperative, allowing talent to work on low-budget films for drastically reduced fees. (Check guild web sites for information regarding guidelines on how to qualify your production.)

The Writers Guild recently did the same for its high-priced—though often creatively frustrated—members. The sacred code of "no work for less than our hard-earned contractual minimums" had effectively barred Guild writers from a place at the low-budget table. No longer. Now, under a groundbreaking Guild concession to the realities of the marketplace, an exception to the MBA minimums has been carved out. As long as the total budget is not more than $750,000 on a feature-length motion picture with an initial theatrical release, Guild writers can defer their minimum fees. If the film is over $500,000 but under $750,000, they pick up a $10,000 fee when the picture shoots; otherwise, they defer their entire minimum guarantee until first revenues pour forth from any film based on their writing. This allows Guild writers to pen riskier, perhaps more mature, material and see those scripts produced without producers being asked to fork over sums that would price their script or writing services out of the low-budget ballpark.

But with poverty comes sacrifice. The smaller the budget, the greater the number of artistic compromises and the greater likelihood that the final film may be compared to horse pucky. Sure you can make a film for just about any price, but getting any-one to actually see it may be another thing entirely. Not only a paying audience, but sales agents, film distributors, even your friends and family won't enjoy squirming through two hours of bad acting, uninspired direction, poor sound, choppy editing, and needle-drop music. And *no stars*—that's the final turn-off. If they have to sit through a budget version of *Gigli*, at least they should get to see a few celebrities struggle to make some sense of it. The good news is, packaging a real element is a lot easier than you might expect.

Most "working actors and directors" are out of work much of the time. Many have cash flow problems. That's why famous film actors, directors, and award-winning cinematographers regularly toil in television commercials. Some, like Bill Murray's character in *Lost in Translation*, despite a fee of two million to do a commercial, have bouts of conscience: "I could be doing a play somewhere." A lot of hard-to-reach people tend to return their calls when the post-it says it's about a movie with a real chance of being made. And packaging a *movie* instead of selling a script makes it all seem that much closer to fruition. (The danger comes in packaging elements that detract from rather than add value to the little company you are putting together to produce your script. That's called adding baggage to the script and can be a deal killer. But it's a risk you may have to take.)

Sometimes, consciously or not, you may write a character that mimics the peculiar physicality, mannerisms, or voice of a particular actor (this happens a lot with actors such as Robin Williams, Jim Carrey, or Harrison Ford). Should you get the script to that actor first? You bet you should. You may not only get the actor "interested" (if not officially attached—that's always a dance involving who the director is, who the co-star is, and where the money is coming from to pay the actor's asking price), but if you have demonstrated a knack for exploiting the actor's larger than life persona and unique talents, you may find yourself being the writer of choice on the actor's future films or pet personal projects.

Where do you find an element? In Los Angeles and New York, you can hardly avoid them. If they don't push their cart into yours at the market you can boldly knock on their door by using one of those handy celebrity maps. I met Richard Harris by approaching him on the sidewalk in Beverly Hills one afternoon while he was walking with his wife, Anne Turkel. After politely informing me they were rushing to a lunch date, I accompanied them to the restaurant where they kept their appointment with Steve McQueen and the late director, Sam Peckinpah. Coincidentally, as a neophyte lawyer for a big firm, I had represented both. I ended up joining them for lunch.

Wherever you live, it's all about contacts. If you don't have them, make them. Your local Film Commission can turn you on to crew and cast in your area and your good script can attract them to you. Attend stage readings and local theater performances and connect backstage with actors respected by their peers. Seen a good film lately? Get the director's contact number through the DGA and ask if you can send a script. Do the same with SAG actors, especially character actors that don't get nearly the attention or salary you might think. Each year Robert Redford lures such actors and veteran writers and directors to his workshop in Sundance with only the promise of helping talented writers hone their craft. Some great films and filmmakers got their start there. Why not send a script and apply?

A host of name actors fell over themselves to commit to the pitch-perfect *Pieces of April*, made digitally in 16 days on a shoestring budget. The $3 million *The Cooler* attracted William H. Macy, Alec Baldwin, and Maria Bello. *Blue Car*, another low-budget critical hit, had one recognizable face, David Strathairn, but that and a taut script garnered a deal from Miramax for its first-time writer/director. Even stars such as Sylvester Stallone, in his character turn in 1997's *Copland*, and Tom Cruise, as part of an ensemble cast in *Magnolia* for director Paul Thomas Anderson, have been known to take carfare for a chance to tie their future to a hot new talent.

To play in the big leagues, you need to attract the big players. To play sandlot ball, you still have to field a team. So conjure up that one-sheet and act like George Steinbrenner.

Chapter 11

The Marketplace

Part One: The Players

"The writer is the only absolutely essential element of Hollywood, and he must never find out."

—*Irving G. Thalberg, legendary studio boss*

The Reader: The Gatekeeper

Agents, independent producers, and development executives simply don't have the time to read all the screen material that comes to them; they depend on the formidable first defense of any company—the reader. To "cover" this mountain of material, studios and larger independent companies have "Story Departments" staffed by skilled, full-time readers, adept at plucking the one script out of many that has the attributes the executives they serve are seeking. These jobs are often unionized—Story Analysts Local 854 serves Los Angeles—with a going rate of about $25 an hour plus benefits. But even at the studio level, outside help must be employed to read and critique not only spec screenplays, but also the galleys of soon-to-be-published novels that might be candidates for adaptation to film. To meet this demand, a veritable army of freelance readers has risen up—some only part-time interns with little training, others highly educated and industry-savvy, for whom being a reader is a full-time job (at least temporarily; most readers see their job as a stepping stone to a career as a screenwriter or creative executive).

The going rate for freelance readers is about $50 per screenplay (as high as $75 if the reader must pick up and deliver). With more than 60,000 scripts making the rounds each year, getting them read can prove prohibitively expensive, especially for smaller production companies.

To put this process into perspective, let's use my old agency, CAA, as an example. As a large full-service agency, they currently employ about two dozen readers; a few are on staff and receive a salary, but most come in and pick up a handful of scripts from the submission slush pile and bring them home to read and report upon. These readers may have never written anything approaching a screenplay themselves. They skew at around 22 years old, a mix of former college lit majors, agency or film hopefuls, a few "friends of the family" (of agents, clients, their dentists, etc.). They will be paid $40 or $50 per script to read and submit *coverage* (as it is known in the trade). Coverage typically consists of a brief "log line" of the story (a one-sentence description); a one or two page plot synopsis; and a short critique of its merits and faults. The report usually concludes with a "Recommend," "Consider," or "Pass," which is based on story, characters, and the company's specific needs. Some companies use a final grading system (known as the "box score") which assigns marks to aspects such as idea, storyline, characterization, dialogue, and production values, and sometimes asks the reader to hazard a guess on the budget needed to produce the film. The coverage determines whether a screenplay moves up the ladder at the agency and also enables the agent to discuss the work knowledgeably with the writer or others without actually having spent hours reading the material. (The importance of this function increases in direct proportion to the growing number of script submissions.) A pass from the reader usually represents a dead end for a script at that agency.

The reader process awaits not only scripts by new writers but also those of established writers with produced credits and agents in tow. Thus, in effect, the reader becomes the writer's target audience. The writer's task is to put the movie into the reader's head, to create a powerful curiosity in the reader which makes him want to go forward, and to avoid turning off a reader by profane, racist, or sexist characters or situations.

A sample of actual development coverage for the screenplay of *My Best Friend's Wedding*, written by one of Hollywood's most highly paid and well respected screenwriters (a fact which the reader was fully aware of), follows:

DEVELOPMENT COVERAGE

Type of Material: SP

Number of Pages: 128

Publisher/Year:

Submitted to: Confidential

Submitted to: Hollywood Pictures

Analyst:

Coverage Date:

Elements: Julia Roberts

Title: My Best Friend's Wedding

Author: XXXXXXX

Draft: 1

Circa: Present

Location: New York/Chicago

Genre: Romantic Comedy

1 November 1995

LOGLINE: Upon hearing of her best friend's wedding, a young woman sets out to stop the wedding and marry the man she has decided should be hers.

SYNOPSIS

When JULIANNE POTTER hears that her best friend, MICHAEL O'NEAL is getting married, she sets out to change his mind. She is invited to act as the "best man" in helping her nervous friend get through the ordeal. Julianne discovers that her heart belongs to Michael, that the nine years that they have been friends outweighs his commitment to KIMMY, who is described as rich, beautiful, young, and smart. Michael and Kimmy meet Julianne at the airport and Kimmy immediately embraces her as a sister and asks her to replace her injured best friend as the maid of honor. Julianne continues all efforts to sabotage the wedding which is due to take place in two days. She even goes so far as to try to convince Kimmy's father, WALTER, that the marriage is not a good idea. In her last effort, she addresses an e-mail to Michael's employer asking him to interfere. In the end, nothing can stop the wedding from taking place and Julianne returns home to New York to her gay friend and confidant, DIGGER.

DEVELOPMENT NOTES

My Best Friend's Wedding is an obvious star vehicle, having a majority of the screenplay revolving around JULIANNE and her comedic efforts to put a halt to her best friend's wedding. The storyline, dialogue, and characters all have the potential for a delightful romantic comedy. There are, however, several issues that need to be addressed in the rewrite process.

274 Chapter 11 ■ The Marketplace

CHARACTERS

Julianne is not interesting, sympathetic, or believable as a renowned food critic. The first 8 pages tell us of a character that is completely inconsistent with that we see on the following 120 pages. We also don't like her very much for attempting to break up this seemingly perfect marriage. She becomes selfish, childish, and we don't see her as learning or growing from her experience. We see a character that will fall short of winning the hearts of the audience.

Michael is not given enough meat to identify him as realistic in his ability to win Kimmy and Julianne. His temper tantrum midway through the screenplay is obviously rewrite material. He appears shallow and self-centered throughout the screenplay. Also, he is described as "smelly" and "rumpled." This is not good. We need to see a Michael that is a trusted and faithful friend and fiancé, with the sex appeal that would transcend Kimmy's economic expectations and Julianne's personal limitations. We might get a sense of how wonderful he is by how much her family adores him, how he calmly handles Kimmy and Julianne, or how committed he is to providing Kimmy with a wonderful future together. The point is, the guy should appear too good to be true.

Kimmy needs a little reworking. When we meet her at the airport, she appears insincere. She should be a little more reserved, not a fast car racing, calculating debutante that wouldn't mind a ménage on her wedding night. Either she needs to be totally calculating or totally oblivious; she cannot be both and have us trust her.

Digger is wonderful and delightful. He borders slightly too colorful, which may detract from our more subtle main characters.

Walter is a bit too likeable and not stuffy enough to portray the "stuffed shirt" that Michael believes represents the "establishment." We also wonder if Walter really approves of this marriage. Certainly, Michael is not the ideal partner for his economic position in society. Wouldn't he be better as the adversary pulling the couple apart? An ally for Julianne?

The twins, Mandy and Sammy are crude and not worthy of the "Southern Belle" title they are given. Either they should be a disgrace to the family, or the ideal representation of what this rich family stands for. All their sexually explicit talk has to go, replaced, perhaps, with an obsession for getting married and the money they will marry into. Shallow would work better than sexy for these two.

Joe has the potential to be a delightful character who can shake Julianne to her senses; however, the underdeveloped character falls into the background and becomes unnecessary. He either needs to be dropped or put to good use.

DIALOGUE

The dialogue is quite good at times, however, the characters do not speak consistent to their nature, i.e. Michael's temper tantrum when Kimmy says he should take a job with her father. Also, many of the scenes ramble on and on. As an example, the first scene is eight very long pages of talking at a dinner table. Throughout the screenplay, the issue of less is more should be taken literally.

STRUCTURE

Because we spend the entire screenplay on Julianne's plight, we never get to see any of the other stories and we feel cheated. Also, this makes for very choppy writing, When a second story is followed, there is a sense of time passing before we get back to the main story. In this case, we see chop, chop, chop as we go from one Julianne scene to the next. The story is too long to have just one story going on. The repetitive nature of Julianne's futile attempt to break up the couple is a bit boring, especially when the couple continues to reconcile. We lose interest in Julianne and her desires by page 90 and are left with a third act that is less than satisfying.

STORY

I am not sure that we can like the story as it is delivered. It seems as if none of the characters learn anything from the experience, although some would argue that she learns to give up on winning the gold ring, it really isn't clear that she learned anything. Although a gal realizing that she is losing the best guy she has ever known is a good reason to go chasing after him, we really aren't sympathetic to her cause because the family he is getting into and the girl he is marrying are perfect. There is no villain, except our hero.

PAGE BY PAGE

1-8   Too long

2   "ass chapped" line is a bit crude for such a high-powered writer.

5   "He's nothing like me, he's like you" is in direct conflict with what she is saying from the second act on, which is how much alike she and Michael are.

8   When she is brushing her blackened tongue in the bathroom, we need something said at the restaurant which will let us know this will happen. Uneducated audiences will not be able to put the two events together and they will wonder why their hero has this tongue problem.

12   When Julianne talks to her gay friend's machine, she implies that they are having sex. This line is offensive to the gay population who might feel that the general public believes their relationships to be nothing more than sexual relationships.

13   Julianne wouldn't refer to her friend as an "asshole."

16   Kimmy's statement that a ménage would be alright on her wedding night gives us reason to suspect that she might not be the perfect person for Michael.

19   "Rumpled, smelly, old Michael" as used as a description for the guy both women are in love with is not realistic.

25   Does the elevator stop? Is that why Julianne begins to panic inside the elevator? The entire elevator scene does not drive the story further. CUT

26   The twins greeting Kimmy and Julianne at the elevator door instantly sets us to a position of not liking these girls. They are not enough of anything to be interesting.

28   The scene where Julianne is getting the guys beer. Totally irrelevant to the script.

30   When Julianne shows that she can dance to an astonished Michael, it might be nice if she said something to the effect that there is a lot he doesn't know about her.

38   The "hold on I'm coming in for you" line won't work, no matter how it is shot.

46   The "long and hard" cigar stuff needs to be a lot more innocent to keep the audience in love with Julianne. She cannot appear to be as sexually provocative as this portrays her.

In lieu of continuing with page by page notes throughout the screenplay, I make the aforementioned suggestions with full knowledge that the balance of the screenplay will fall into place once the fine points are addressed in the first 50 pages.

This is a wonderful star vehicle and, with the proper modifications, will allow the audience to fall in love with the lead actress. It is highly recommended that the character of Julianne be given a more sympathetic nature. This can be achieved by raising the stakes of the marriage. It is possible to have Michael be the love of her life since she was a child and having her fighting for him since she was a kid. This would allow us to accept her blatant lies and deception more readily. Also, we must see how much she does not want to lie, cheat, and steal, but she HAS to get her man. She cannot appear to be as fumbling and clumsy as she is written. We could understand her tripping when she was excessively nervous, but to have her ripping dresses and falling all over the place makes the viewer wish she were tied up in a strait jacket. Michael, of course, needs to be worth chasing after. He needs to be everything every girl could ever imagine in a man. He has to say the right things at the right time and dress the right way. Once those two characters are given proper direction, the humor will emerge out of the situation, not out of their weaknesses.

Some development executives use the reader report as a quick summary from which they can determine whether a script is worth their personal attention, rather than relying on the reader's critique or recommendations. In fact, most readers will admit that factors beyond their control will go into the ultimate decision of any executive as to what material is pursued to production—such as their employer's connection with or commitments to talent. If a script comes with a hot director or a Julia Roberts or Harrison Ford attached, or even has their strong interest, you can be certain it's going up the ladder regardless of any negative reader report. Similarly, a script that "goes out" with agency supplied "heat" as a potential bidding war script is going to be read by the top honchos at the production company or studio given it to read. Though many screenplays die at the gate due to a reader's negative impression, very few produced screenplays can attribute their start to a reader's recommendation; it is a testament to the professionalism with which most readers approach their job that this reality does not permanently discourage them.

In fact, the opposite is true—all readers share the desire to find something truly wonderful. The hope is to be the first to discover the hot, new talent—to unearth the jewel hidden in the pile of often poorly executed and formulaic writing. Take the reader on an emotional thrill ride and he or she will champion your screenplay to executives further up the chain of command. The irony is that—though all are loathe to admit it—like any good gatekeeper, the reader's primary job is to pass. He must limit the reading load of his boss, not increase it.

One reader I know has this motto taped on her bulletin board: "It is easier and cheaper to pass." Do not make it easier still for the reader to say "no"—your script must be technically flawless, have a clear story "hook" in place, and be imminently castable (i.e., with lead characters that scream "star turn"). To have a solid reason to contact stars and institute a working relationship is the stuff of a development executive's dreams.

The Independent Producer: The Gray Knight

A lot of film has passed through the projector since independent producers such as David O. Selznick and Mervyn LeRoy manipulated and controlled writers, directors, and stars in bringing us such screen classics as *Gone with the Wind* and *The Wizard of Oz*. Yet, the way business is done in Hollywood has not changed all that drastically. It's still the indie producer, the savvy insider with a vested interest in finding projects that will make good movies, upon whom studio executives rely to feed the public's fickle and seemingly insatiable appetite for product.

Who is the independent producer? Someone who puffs long, Cuban cigars and escorts prepubescent girls to decadent Hollywood hot tub parties? How about money mavens who count ciphers rather than sheep to fall asleep at night? Those are the popular myths. In reality, the independent producer is often a hustler and a scapegoat and the unsung hero of film history. (How many producers of award-winning films can you name?) He is most often the person who seeks out fresh material and new talent, develops it by supervising the writer through various screenplay drafts, packages it with other creative elements (such as a director or stars), pitches it to the powers on high, garners the necessary funds to film it, and nurtures it through its premier to the film festivals and its appearance at your local multi-plex theater.

The producer (not the Executive Producer) is considered the architect of the movie project and the one who carries off the Oscar if the film wins for "Best Picture."

Yet—and here's the important part—after all of it, a producer is still just someone who knows a writer. For no matter how many awards a producer may have on his mantel, no matter how long his list of credits, his future credibility in Hollywood rests on the quality of the material he controls. It is only on the strength of a well-crafted screenplay that the producer can gain admission to those few, powerful executives, directors, or stars whose nod of approval can coax millions of dollars to be gambled on a film's production and success in the marketplace.

As in a genre love story, the writer chases the indie producer until he catches you!

Today, a growing list of actors and directors have their own production companies (many consist of one executive and an assistant), often funded by a major studio. Television networks fund such companies for a series creator or star. The mandate is to find material suited to the talents or ambitions of the owner-star. Writers often complain that dealing with such companies almost assures a turn in "development hell," but some "star" companies should be applauded for using their clout to develop and champion many scripts that the studios or networks would be reluctant to adopt, even (at times) providing production financing from their own pocket.

Many independent producers work on a limited budget, offering little option money and asking for free rewrites. The quid pro quo is the tenacity with which he will promote your material and the exposure he can offer you in the marketplace. You should also receive a sizable back-end payday (purchase price and profit share) to compensate you for the trust and good faith you've demonstrated in working for less.

When seeking a producer for your script, integrity and current business relationships should be high on your list of desirable qualities. If the producer has an office, try to wrest an invitation to discuss your script there. See if the phone rings, if activity is in the works. Does the producer have a director or star in mind? Can he set a meeting with you that includes that director or star? Since anyone can call himself an independent producer, legitimacy is judged by a provable track record or a contract accompanied by a check. But danger lurks for the writer who does not take early steps to protect himself.

The Problem: The Producer's Home Shopping Network

Sometimes, an unscrupulous producer will ignore the step of paying you to acquire the rights to your work. Instead, he may pitch your story over the phone to his contacts at studios or networks or even to actors with whom he has a relationship—all without a paid option giving him the right to do so. Unless great enthusiasm is expressed on the other end, the producer can simply drop the submission in the wastebasket and no one is the wiser.

Even experienced writers have been known to cave in to a producer's request to "let me just have it for a week, to see what I can do with it." A well-connected producer can "cover" the studios and other major markets for a script in a series of phone calls. The writer's script, never having been properly prepared for the marketplace or pitched with the proper degree of thought or energy, is considered "shopped" and may be dead in a weekend.

Later, the writer, unaware of the producer's illicit activities, may find a legitimate producer willing to buy the material or an agent willing to represent the work, but upon submission to those networks or studios already contacted by the unscrupulous producer, he will receive a curt reply that the material has already been "covered" and rejected. The agent may end his representation of the writer and the honest producer (who paid money in good faith for an option) may sue for return of his funds. Unless the writer attaches a new, marketable element (more than a new title is necessary), the screenplay will be history—and the writer will have a near to impossible task identifying the culprit who did him wrong. In this risky atmosphere, made more perilous by the growing (and, by me, strongly discouraged) practice of sending stories over the Internet, ethical producers will find themselves "chilled" from paying options unless they can receive convincing assurance that the material has not "been around."

The Writers Guild of America prohibits shopping in its agreement with producers, levying substantial fines on abusers, but the practice continues to be widespread.

The Solution: Control Your Submission List

If possible, submit through established channels—agents, attorneys, managers. Do not "shotgun" your material all over town. (Producers you may never be able to trace may take a liking to your work and shop it without contacting you.) Court producers one at a time. Don't give anyone a lot of time to decide about his interest in your work—let him know that you are actively pursuing other contacts.

Then make other contacts. Publications such as *The Hollywood Creative Directory* can provide the names and titles of individuals you may wish to contact. Internet services also list production companies and their current needs—many like to circumnavigate agents and managers and want to deal directly with writers.

A query letter will keep you from sending your screenplay to parties who do not accept unsolicited material. A good telephone personality can help you through the first line of defense—the protective assistant—and perhaps receive an offer to submit your work. Follow up any contact with a letter, fax, or e-mail confirming the substance of the contact.

However you contact a producer, be cautioned: Clear title (ownership of rights) to your work can be clouded if a producer (or other third party to whom you have submitted your screenplay) later claims that an "oral transfer of rights" was made or a courtesy period of time was extended in which he could consider your script for production. This cloud must be cleared up before any production company can obtain the "E & O" (Errors and Omissions) insurance policy necessary to begin production. So take good notes and keep meticulous records; make it a business practice to follow up all meetings with letters which clearly document any understandings reached. And don't forget to review Chapter 8, "Protecting Your Work."

The Studio Executive: The Suits

"How do all these bad movies get made?" we ask. The "suits," as studio executives (male and female) are nicknamed around town, do not always deserve all the blame. After all, they face a revolving door (most executive jobs last only a few years) and during their short tenure they are under great pressure to find a blockbuster that will guide them up the ladder of success before they are knocked off. Since movies have long gestation periods (two years or more from development to release), job pressure begins on day one: The executive must establish and nurture relationships with people who can help find or develop unique stories that will attract the same few major stars or directors being besieged daily by the competition.

To many studio executives, in the immortal words of critic Pauline Kael, "A good script is a script to which Robert Redford will commit himself. A bad script is a script which Redford has turned down. A script that 'needs work' is a script about which Redford has yet to make up his mind."

Preying on these fears and needs is a cadre of agents, lawyers, and managers who profess to have the hot script to put the executive's career into orbit. If you go to enough Hollywood movies, you know there just aren't that many hot scripts around. But the executive cannot shut his door on these people—one of whom may actually have that blockbuster-to-be. So bad decisions are made, good scripts are mangled, outrageous budgets are greenlighted for production, and superstar salaries rise—and the executive is the scapegoat when that potential blockbuster is a big-budget flop. (Of course, few actually have greenlight power; those that do have a survivor's knack for distancing themselves from failure and those that don't—but act as if they do—claim *too much credit* when one film out of many at their studio does find an audience.)

"An old studio head... said to me, shortly after being fired from Paramount, that if he had green-lighted the movies that he had passed on, and canceled all the movies he had agreed to make, he would have ended up in the same place."

—Art Linson, *What Just Happened*

But what is the writer to do when faced with story conferences called because the executive felt lonely, when two years of work is jettisoned for an idea hatched at a 2 a.m. House of Blues concert? Remember that you labor in a collaborative art; maybe all those notes will help the work to get better. Or not. And don't despair: Any executive with a history in the business knows, in his gut, that it is the power of the word—the script—that spawns any blockbuster and not the actor or the director or the mega-budgeted special effects.

As Robert Towne recently reminded an awards audience studded with stars, star-directors, and studio honchos: "Only when the writer has done his or her job can anyone else here begin to do theirs."

It is the responsibility of every writer to not let the exec forget that—especially in the beginning, when he needs you most. That's your chance to make him respect you. Have your agent extract more money for that dialogue polish, or perhaps some future perk that involves you in casting and location scouts. If the studio is to get first crack at future scripts, make them honor both the letter and the spirit of those rewrite commitments. Do all this and you may not feel (at least for a time) the inevitable need to direct in order to preserve the integrity of your artistic vision.

Should you manage a face-to-face with any development or production executive, it may help to remember that the meeting is not, in the final analysis, about you or your script—it's about how making a deal with you will help further that person's own career ambitions. As writer David Mamet said: "Your business is writing movies, theirs is to get ahead in the movie biz."

from the trenches: LIES OF THE ARTLESS AND CRAFTY: PART THREE

- **Lie number 5:** *If you work hard enough at it, your good script will always find a home.*

Do you believe in the Tooth Fairy? There is no justice in the world of art. Accept that fact and get past it. Despite your unfailing faith in yourself, you may have no talent. Or you may have talent, but what you write may not be particularly commercial. Or it may be wildly commercial, but you may be unable to get anyone to read it. Or they'll read it, but they won't get it because they're idiots. All creative art from the beginning of time has labored under the need for a receptive audience. Tastes, like fashion, change. You may have written what's hot this month, what's not the next. There's no proven correlation between how hard or long you work and your ultimate success or failure. If you must be a writer because that's who you are, then it won't matter all that much. You write to please yourself first. Do your best, believe in yourself, have something to say, write, write, write, and don't let rejection stand in your way.

Part Two: The Markets

"Do you know what the monster is?"

The writer shook his head.

The executive said, "It's our money."

—**John Gregory Dunne,** *Monster*

The Major Studios

The movie business is not for the faint of heart or the poor of pocket. It's a risky business and most of the players in it do not wish to, nor will they, risk their own money. It is a fact that the great majority of the movies we see at our local theater or rent at our video/DVD store are financed, produced, marketed, and distributed by a handful of major motion picture studios. It is they who finance our art, our dreams, and, if we are lucky and talented enough, our careers. For that, we must be grateful to them. Sure, it's a business and the studios are in it more for the money than for the art, but to complain is to bite the hand that feeds us. Yet no less a player than William Goldman recently denounced the mainstream studio system as having finally crushed art beneath the boot of commerce—as a system where, "the studios are making movies for mouth-breathers in foreign lands, testosterone-filled young men who get off on the violence." To which highly-regarded Newsday film critic Jack Mathews added, "If [Hollywood is] going to spend $80 million to $140 million on a picture, why not include a compelling story as well as a tricky premise? Why not characters as well as stars? Would a few subplots and a little relevance—just the least food for thought is all we ask—really cost them at the gate?"

Therein lies the problem. The gate. The box office. The big bucks. Films like *Titanic*, or any franchise, tentpole movie in the series of *James Bond, Lord of the Rings, Harry Potter, Star Wars, Spider-Man, Shrek, Batman*, and others, some of which cost close to $300 million to make and market, prove to the Wall Street mentality behind the studio gates that a very expensive film can be a sound investment after all. And in the wake of billion dollar-plus worldwide grosses for epic adventures, comic book movies, and flights of teen fantasy, the major Hollywood studios (Warner Bros., Twentieth Century Fox, Disney, Sony Pictures, Paramount, MGM/UA, and Dreamworks) can be counted on to continue to greenlight "event" movies, based on bestsellers and high-concepts, some of which will become classics, but many others of which—saddled with dumb plots and dumber dialogue—will be lost to film history.

In that great gamble that is movies, the best bet for a big hit in the world marketplace today still points to big stars, bigger budgets, and high (and higher) concepts from the writer. This requires the big paychecks only the studios can deliver. To be sure, Hollywood has taken notice of the resurgence of the independent film (and its tendency to carry off most of any year's Oscar nominations) and has set up its own "art" divisions to compete. Still, at the cost of making films today, downside risk (potential financial disaster) is limited in the only way the studios trust—by delivering what has been successful in the past. In a sense, then, the audience may have itself to blame for getting the same old stuff: mindless action, bathroom humor, recycled plots, and aging stars. But the audience may be rebelling at long last. Summer 2005 tallied the worst record of film attendance since 1997, down 12% from a year earlier. The studios have reason to be nervous; it remains to be seen if or how that will affect their production decisions.

For the time being, however, should you desire to write for mainstream Hollywood, the guideposts are the same as they have been for years: write a high-concept or character-driven genre film that sports a strong starring role (preferably for a male). The financial rewards for success are considerable. But if this doesn't sit well with your passions or your soul, consider the following alternatives:

The Independents

For personal stories with morally ambiguous points of view, for stories that challenge established filmmaking formats—the daring, often controversial stories that many screenwriters must tell—you may wish to court smaller production companies with the freedom to produce product for select, target audiences. (The nurturing of and marketing to such audiences has become an art unto itself.) In the eyes of the critics, audiences, and even the venerable voting members of the Academy of Motion Picture Arts and Sciences, a good portion of these small, independent pictures have finally matured to A-list status.

The box office dominance of animated extravaganzas and comic book franchises does not obliterate the lessons of recent history. The offbeat, diverse, and independently produced films continue to touch audiences like no others in recent years. Even a *National Geographic*-type documentary about penguins crossing the frozen wasteland of Antarctica may yet reach $100 million worldwide gross. Why? Dare I suggest that it is because it demonstrates genuine heart? And where have these ideas, once celebrated only in the underground cinema, and these unsung talents, often laboring for years on projects financed from their savings and credit cards, where have these stories so anathema to the mega-budgets, formula heroes, and calcified story structures of the majors, been nurtured? Through *the festival circuit.*

Film festivals have become an increasingly important component to the nurturing and discovery of new talent. Producing your own work or having it produced by film students (or even former video store clerks) may not pay much, but if your film is then accepted into one of the premiere festivals, it can bring you exposure, honor, and perhaps even turn you into a hot commodity.

At festivals such as Sundance, Toronto, Telluride, Cannes, New York, MIFED, The Los Angeles Independent Film Festival, and the American Film Market, independent film producers, studio executives, and distribution companies (large and small) fan out in search of the daring, the unconventional, and the unsigned. Even the unproduced, first-time writer can attend and rub elbows with those creative talents, producers, and executives that would be near-to-impossible to get on the phone back in Hollywood.

For a comprehensive list of festivals, deadlines, awards, and tips from those who run them and those who have been there, Chris Gore's *The Ultimate Film Festival Survival Guide* (Lone Eagle Publishing, Los Angeles, 1999, as recently updated) will serve as an excellent resource.

The Alternative Markets

Writers need not labor only in the more glamorous fields of the entertainment business—feature films and network series television. There are, in fact, significant advantages to writing for what have been labeled "alternative" markets.

For years, alternative markets such as animation, cable, and first-run syndication, to name a few, suffered a "poor cousin" reputation. Often low-paying and unmonitored by the Writers Guild, many mainstream agents shied away from actively representing writers in these markets. But the Writers Guild has recently legitimized many such markets by creating and monitoring specific guidelines for employment. An increasing number of writers are now availing themselves of the higher pay, creative freedom, and job security these markets may offer.

Should you aspire to write for a particular market, identify a current show in that market and try to obtain and then study writing samples of that show to familiarize yourself with the style and format. Then submit writing samples appropriate to that market. Be forewarned: writing required for these markets is often very specific. A sample for one market may not be effective as a sample for any other market. Helpful material for breaking into any specific show/market may be available in your local library or through the Internet—or from a contact within such show/market, the best way to plug yourself into any new area of employment.

Caveats in place, here are some fields that may capture your interest:

- **Animation.** Once a "Disney thing," virtually every studio now has a long-term commitment to develop and produce animated features and television. Is it any wonder? One glance at the list of the highest grossing box office successes in the last five years and it is clear that animated features lead the pack. The movies being produced from the artists, animators, and computers of Pixar and other animation studios have so charmed critics and audiences alike that the Motion Picture Academy was forced to create a separate category for "Best Animated Feature" lest they watch the top honors for "Best Picture" go to films about lions, ogres, and fish. Equally significant for writers is the animation industry's recent recognition of the importance of writers to develop that programming. Previously, characters were conceived by the cartoonist and plots were often devised by what was possible in the medium or simply fun to draw. Today—sometimes before a drawing is rendered—writers are working in consort with the animators in applying the principles of the three-act film structure, defining character arcs, and developing full storylines.

In a recent, two-day course on structure and characterization for Disney Television's animation team, it was encouraging to witness animators' desire to learn how to better work with writers on story and character development from the early concept stages. The Writers Guild has taken notice: The WGA Animation Writers Caucus was formed to advance and protect the rights of writers working in animation and has begun the process of bringing animation writers fully under the Guild's jurisdiction. Currently, writers on every network primetime animated TV show, including *The Simpsons* and *King of the Hill*, are covered by the Guild's MBA.

- **Children's Programming.** Shows like *Sesame Street, Barney, The Puzzle Place, Rugrats, SpongeBob SquarePants,* and *Teletubbies* have become staples on morning television. Entire family-oriented cable networks like The Discovery Channel, The Animal Channel, or The Disney Channel also provide a platform for children's programming. There are also children's afternoon specials which focus on issues of interest to teens and preteens and a burgeoning market in children's and young adult direct-to-video films. (The Olsen twins, those loveable girls who began on the television series *Full House*, have turned their unique personalities into a $50 to $100 million enterprise, releasing everything from shorts and direct-to-video movies to more ambitious feature films.)

- **Cable Television.** Cable television has fully matured into a viable full-service market in need of original programming to supply the explosion of new channels and the flood of new subscribers. Made-for-Cable films and episodic series (e.g., *The Sopranos, Entourage, Curb Your Enthusiasm*) are not only proliferating, but are offering writers some of the purest and unimpeded creative experiences available in film and television. The major suppliers like Home Box Office, Showtime, The Movie Channel, The Disney Channel, Turner Broadcasting, etc. usually require agency submissions; however, a contact or good query letter and writing sample may make breaking in a lot easier. And the pay is quickly catching up to the standards of the networks.

- **Non-Dramatic Programming.** This wide category includes documentary (e.g. *Biography*), musical/comedy/variety (e.g., *Late Show with David Letterman, The Tonight Show with Jay Leno*), quiz and audience participation shows (e.g., *Jeopardy, Wheel of Fortune*), award shows (e.g., *The Academy Awards, The Grammy Awards*), and even news programming (e.g., *Nightline, Dateline*). Never forget that it is writers who research and fill the categories for *Jeopardy*, draft David Letterman's "Top Ten List," and compose those short, seemingly informal exchanges the presenters at an award show squint to read off a monitor.

■ **Syndication.** There are many first-run syndication shows, including talk shows (e.g., *Oprah, Larry King Live, The Jerry Springer Show*), game shows—soon to get their own cable channel (e.g., *The Dating Game, Hollywood Squares*), magazine shows (e.g., *Entertainment Tonight, Extra*), and reality programming (e.g., *Unsolved Mysteries, Doctor 90210.*) Add to that the almost daily bombardment of the "news as entertainment" shows on CNN and the Fox Network and the real action in syndication—first-run one-hour dramatic series programming.

Aided by an expanding number of foreign broadcast companies and a burgeoning market for supplying cable and satellite delivery systems, there are currently more than two dozen first-run, one-hour syndicated dramatic shows on the air. Following the hugely-successful *Star Trek* franchise (which has yielded billions of dollars to Paramount) and *Baywatch* (a network-canceled show currently well in its third billion of worldwide revenue for Pearson All American Television), virtually every major studio or cable supplier are flexing their programming muscles in the same market.

The writing staff of a syndicated show is usually leaner and more restricted by budget and time, but usually receive greater responsibility for the creative direction of the show, from writing a greater number of episodes to being consulted during production and post-production. This kind of experience pays off in producer positions on their next network post. On the downside, less staff and more episodes translates to long work hours (six or seven days to churn out one episode), less pay (about two-thirds of the network fee), and fewer residuals (about one-third of the network rate). Still, for now at least, according to a *Written By* article, "the reality of producing 22 episodes in one season in syndication puts the writer in the driver's seat."

■ **Interactive Multimedia.** Studios, animation and special effects companies are escalating the production of electronic programming, including feature films, direct-to-video films (including cassettes,

CDs, and laser discs), video games, interactive programming, multimedia, and CD-ROMs. While the majors briefly shied away from the "Third Screen" market in the late '90s (they frankly didn't understand how to fully exploit it), they have now jumped in with both feet, and big-name writer/directors like John Milius, Clive Barker, John Carpenter, and John Singleton have all signed on to write and develop interactive games. Even new writers can gain direct access to the leading producers of these media without an agent—usually all that's required is a solid concept, sometimes augmented by a flow chart and/or a treatment that is three to ten pages in length. But caution: essentially unregulated and in a state of evolution, abuses are frequent. Non A-list writers still report doing three times the work for one-third the pay and being denied credit arbitrarily. You should query the WGAw New Media Committee for guidelines in accepting employment in this market.

- **The Foreign Markets.** The foreign market for feature films (for both theatrical and video consumption) gobbles up all the majors can deliver and hungers for more. This hunger for American product has created a universal respect for the way American movies are made, i.e. with writers. Foreign productions were historically the product of an auteur system in which scripts were improvised by actors under the guidance of a director usually working from a fleshed out treatment at best. Today, writing conferences are popping up all over Europe and Asia and the invited stars are American writers. Just following American principles of structure and character development can almost automatically raise your screenplay to a competitive level in such markets. And submission there is more a matter of contacts than credits.

- **Daytime Serials.** Employment opportunities abound in the area of daytime soaps due to high staff turnover (long hours, low pay). And, new writers can submit writing samples outside the soap arena (almost any dramatic piece will suffice) since the plot lines of soaps are planned a year in advance and are folly to predict.

- **PBS.** Produced by local stations or independently by producers or documentary filmmakers, PBS airs shows (such as *American Playhouse*) which attract CPB (Corporation for Public Broadcasting) and corporate funding, and grants from such foundations as the National Endowment for the Arts. After having queried programmers on their interest in your proposed project, contact appropriate funding sources. Many writers consider the low fees and small production budgets a fair trade for creative freedom and the chance to contribute to quality programming.

- **Documentaries, Industrial, Educational, and Training Films.** The non-broadcast audio-visual industry may employ more writers than the film and television industries combined. Research the industry of your interest and contact local production facilities for lists of producers working in that area. Local film commissions may also have a detailed list of such companies. Some schools and corporations have video or in-house educational managers you can contact. Access is surprisingly easy (a premium is placed on enthusiasm and almost any writing sample will do) although the pay is usually low.

The WGAw has approved a basic cable nonfiction contract designed to help writers working on low-budget documentaries on basic cable. It can be downloaded from the Guild's web site.

- **Public Access Television.** Every citizen (writers included) has the right to take advantage of the public access station in his particular city to create his own programming. For your 15 minutes of TV fame, check your phone directory for the cable companies in your area and inquire about their public access programming. Many provide training, equipment, and even technical support.

- **Radio.** Radio has enjoyed a proud history of drama, comedy, horror, and suspense programming long before television was invented. Contact your local radio stations for employment guidelines and opportunities. For minimum terms and conditions of the Writers Guild Radio Agreement, contact the Guild Contracts Department.

  And last, but most certainly not least…

- **Reality Television.** Reality television is here to stay—it's cheap to produce, draws big advertisers and audiences, and holds its own with scripted and cast shows that can cost millions more. Michael Moore's blockbuster documentary *Fahrenheit 9/11* and the recent success of *March of the Penguins* and *Grizzly Man* set the bar for shaping character images and finding compelling storylines through careful writing and editing. Sure, documentaries have always done that. But as Charles B. Slocum of the WGAw points out, this new genre goes further to engage the audience, with the camera moving "from mere observation to storytelling in a way traditional documentaries have not."

As reality writer J. Ryan Stradel put it: "Just because something is real doesn't make it a story. Hundreds of hours of footage are shot to make a single hour of reality television and the final cut is very similar in its narrative structure to scripted television. There is a beginning, middle, and end, with character development, goals, conflict, and resolution. If you've ever been pulled into watching a reality series, it's for the same reasons you get invested in scripted TV: sympathetic characters, interesting settings, and a sequence of events that inspires curiosity."

I recently had a reality TV experience of my own to validate that.

from the trenches: THE REALITIES OF WRITING FOR REALITY TV

Night was fast approaching and I could feel the tension crawling up my spine. I should have been out of my cage hours ago, but this tiger just didn't want to cooperate. She was a little skittish all day, nervous on set, wouldn't take direction. But nothing goes the way you plan with kids and animals. The long day was probably wearing on her or maybe the wind picking up spooked her. Wind raises the serotonin levels of some cats; they get agitated, emotionally high. It brings out their hunt instincts. Just because she could come to a mark and stand and snarl on command didn't mean she was a pussycat. With my abominable night vision, I couldn't tell if she was baring her teeth (a sign she was likely bluffing), or curling her lip down to hide her teeth, in which case I had only a safety pin between me and this 450 pound animal in full attack mode.

Visions of *Grizzly Man*, me being devoured by the object of my fascination, played in my head.

Just two months earlier, I was hired for my dream gig: writing and producing my very own television pilot. Total creative license. Actually I had begged for this job—the year was closing down and I had yet to attain my health fund "minimum earnings." I needed just a bit more. So I phoned a friend, a producer working with a hot young director, and to my surprise, as I was about to grovel for a dialogue polish, he blurted out that he had been getting ready to call me. He had this concept for a show kicking around on his desk and the option was running out and now he was being sent halfway round the world to set up a major studio feature for his director partner and so he thought he could use a little help. He was willing to do (within reason) whatever it took to land me. (Just then, what it took to land me

continued

was pitiful little, but my lips were sealed.) And so it happened, my baptism into the wacky world of reality television.

A working writer can hold his nose in the air for only so long. Besides, I wouldn't be doing another *Bachelor* or *Survivor* or *Big Brother* or *Fear Factor* or *American Idol* rip-off. Mine would be more like a classy nonfiction documentary—which was cool, right? Just ask Ken Burns. Except that there would be a scripted "story." (As in fully scripted television shows, the writer would produce too. My title was "story producer.")

There are differences though. In reality shows, the script is more of a template, a plan for the show, rather than the show itself. The premise of our show was filming wild animals being trained to do movie stunts. This was, of course, all very real. There is something about the thrill and danger of wild animals that keeps writers putting them into scripts. And since no actor is going to risk life and limb to work next to killer beasts, we would give an up close and personal peek behind the scenes, with a world-famous wild animal stunt coordinator as our guide, to show how such stunts are accomplished safely. Of course, the audience deserves an adventure ride—not only the stunts themselves, but the tension and drama that comes when the stunts fail or nearly fail and lives are at risk. That's the voyeur experience that makes for great reality TV.

And that's where a script comes into play—planning events and narrative flow before the hours of shooting begin, staging segments of animal footage and inter-cutting contrived circumstances with their human handlers to provoke, manufacture, or capitalize on whatever action or conflict is possible within the stunt. Scripted narration would accompany the footage as well as the banter between the stunt persons and the animal trainers in filming the actual stunts (much of those being written and filmed in "behind-the-scenes" interviews after-the-fact to match the footage actually assembled). Even the choice of locations and the "casting" of camera personnel who would be filmed filming the stunts (there would be at least three camera crews working most times) is done to facilitate story and audience identification with the principals on the show.

We filmed on location in British Columbia. We had to plan the field shoot, the setups, the responses we wanted to coax out of the tigers. The actors, stuntpersons, and cameramen had to be briefed by the trainers on the personalities of the animals, safety precautions, drills for reacting in an unplanned crisis. There were character arcs for the animals, believe it or not, as well as the trainers, story beats on how the training sessions could be most dramatically presented. This would prepare the crew for what specific actions or reactions of humans and animals to be sure to capture or provoke. Though the stunts were filmed as they occurred, they ultimately had to be edited into a cause and effect storyline that would keep the audience wondering what would happen next. Audience empathy had to attach, tension too, and turning points had to be created in the arc of the show. Which means there had to be an emotional spine to the story and a journey of discovery for the actors playing opposite (even on blue screen) these magnificent but unpredictable beasts. (Editors call it "storytelling on an Avid.")

We worked 14 long days in a North Vancouver winter to get 30 minutes of usable film. Everyone, from the big cats to the crew, was cold, wet, and exhausted—and "script" changes were necessitated on nearly an hourly basis.

It was as hard a shoot as I had encountered in scripted drama, harder maybe, but I was lucky. The company I was working for was a Writers Guild signatory and so my writing services and working conditions were covered under the Guild's minimum basic agreement (the MBA). Most reality shows are not. The networks and cable stations often subcontract out the content to production groups not signatory to the MBA. These companies do not pay union wages, offer pension or health plans, or observe union mandated working conditions (often working producer/writers like slaves—16-hour days for weeks on end). If they do pay union scale, driving up the cost of the show, the networks can simply go to those non-signatory companies who can provide cheaper content—the writer/producer paying the price of the competition.

For this reason, organizing reality and animation writers, producers, and editors (the real storytellers in reality TV) has been a recent Guild priority. In fact, in mid-2005, nearly 1,000 reality TV writers (and editors—a recognition by the Guild of the "crucial collaborative role they play in crafting reality storylines") signed authorization cards giving the WGA "the legal right to demand industry recognition of the union as their representative in collective bargaining."

The finished script I originally submitted, after a thoughtful rewrite by my producer friend (okay, not total creative license), was made into that test pilot we shot and also used as a "bible" which we brought to the "Cable" Channel as a template for a possible series. The meetings went well—everyone was on board—it was a go from all I could read into the inner workings of the network. In fact, they wanted two shows—a two-hour special for the "Cable" Channel and a one-hour pilot for "The Other Channel," their subsidiary.

That was six months ago.

We're still waiting.

Just like in fully scripted television.

PART IV

SELLING YOUR SCREENPLAY OR TELEPLAY

Chapter 12

The Deals

"No man but a blockhead ever wrote, except for money."

—Samuel Johnson

Part One: Feature Films

In February 1999, Sony-owned Columbia Pictures made an announcement: henceforth, it would grant a select group of top screenwriters a share of the gross revenue of the movies they scripted. "Without writers, we'd have nothing," Columbia President Amy Pascal was quoted as saying. "They're the foundation of the movie business." Industry reaction was swift: "First, they broke the $20 million mark for actors and now this—and for writers; please, not for writers!" Of course, nobody said that out loud; rather, the competition rushed to point out that writers *deserved* to share in the success of their blockbusters, along with the many stars, directors, producers, and studios that have been gross profit participants for years. It was just that, well, these are rough times in Tinseltown; there's not all that much profit to go around, is there?

One high-ranking studio executive threatened that Columbia's deal with the writing elite "is going to force us to take more chances on newer, less expensive writers." From his mouth to God's ear.

To be sure, Hollywood is feeling the worldwide recession just like everyone else. Attendance is down dramatically and once sure-fire genres are sputtering at the gate. Development deals are also down (80 percent at some studios). Production companies may still promise big bucks for a "high-concept" screenplay, but, in reality, the producers only pay off when—and if—they can get a studio to pick up the tab. And although the trades still report million dollar spec sales on the front page, the actual purchase price is usually pared down considerably before the deal closes (though it's in no one's interest to relay that bit of news to the public). To be sure, good material will always command a price. As proven by the last writers' strike, the industry would grind to a halt without it. If your screenplay is hot enough to attract a bidding war among eager buyers, the sky is the limit. If not, even if they love your script, a new writer can usually expect not much more than Writers Guild minimum, plus 10 percent (to cover the cost of your agent).

The current Schedule of Minimums of the Writers Guild of America, for both features and television, can be accessed through the Guild's web site, www.wga.org. Of course, if your screenplay is sold to or written for a non-WGA signatory, those minimums do not apply—only the laws of contract will govern such a transaction.

Not that that's chump change. Effective November, 2005, the minimum payment for an original screenplay, for a film budgeted in excess of $5 million, is $75, 443. (To hire a writer to write an original screenplay, *including* treatment, for a similarly budgeted film is $102,980.) Of course, after splitting that with your writing partner and after paying your attorney, Guild, IRS, and other taxes, your windfall may not be enough to retire on. You also may not get it all at once; outright purchases are becoming as extinct as the T-Rex.

Joe Eszterhas can claim some credit for the former excesses of the spec script market. He wrote *Basic Instinct* on a manual typewriter in three weeks and sold it to Carolco for $3.5 million. Later, he was handed $4 million in cash by a Las Vegas investor and an equal amount by a major studio for verbal pitches of high-concept ideas (both films were bombs: *Showgirls* and *An Alan Smithee Film: Burn Hollywood Burn*). Is this business great, or what?

This makes it all the more important for you to have your deal clearly set forth in a writing signed by all parties—especially noting what you are entitled to should an option taken on your work not be exercised, or should your writing services be terminated or should the movie you've written never be made. *The first written agreement among buyer and writer (or employer and writer) that delineates these and other crucial bargaining points is usually set forth in a brief "deal memo."*

The Deal Memo

The deal memo is a written confirmation of the fundamental terms of any purchase or employment agreement. While giving the appearance of an informal letter (often only one or two pages long), the deal memo is a binding agreement between the parties and governs all later writings on the subject. In practice, it is sometimes the only document the parties will ever actually sign. It should, therefore, be as complete as possible and fully executed, with all essential deal points in place and purchase monies or commencement monies paid before any submission of original material is permitted or writing services are begun.

If the deal memo is for the purchase of literary material, it should clearly set forth the rights being granted, the purchase price, any bonus or contingent payments that apply, provisions for screen credit and other creative rights, including any turnaround provisions or rewrite obligations to the original writer on the part of the buyer.

If the deal memo sets forth an employment agreement, it should clearly state the services to be performed, the payment due for those services, exactly what you are required to deliver in order to get paid, to whom, where, and when such delivery is to be made, and a complete payment schedule. The writer should also be made aware of any other writers on the project—whether previous, simultaneous, or subsequent to the writer's contribution—and the ownership status of any source material supplied to the writer.

Most deal memos contemplate further, more detailed written agreements by the parties.

Following are the two basic contractual formats all screenwriters should become familiar with: the *option/purchase agreement* (whereby the rights to your literary work are acquired by a third party), and the two most common *writer employment agreements*—the development deal and the step deal. (Note especially the various forms of compensation payable under either contractual arrangement and the provisions affording writers greater creative control over their work product.)

Option/Purchase Agreements

A Literary Purchase (or *Assignment of All Rights*) agreement can be lengthy, but it is fairly self-explanatory. Pared down to its essentials, the writer sells the motion picture, television, and allied rights (or other negotiated rights) to his screenplay and receives money in exchange. If the writer is a member of the WGA or dealing with a company signatory to the Minimum Basic Agreement, applicable minimum terms and purchase prices are set. However, most producers (and even studios) are reluctant to lay out the full price for material only to find out later that their enthusiasm has waned or is not shared by others (such as bankable stars). They'll "option" it instead.

The Option Agreement

In an option agreement, the writer receives a fraction of the agreed-upon purchase price in exchange for granting the producer the exclusive right— over a given period of time (the option period)—to rewrite, package, and/or make the financial arrangements for the production of the material. At the end of the option period, the option owner can:

- Exercise the option by paying the balance of the purchase price— thereby gaining ownership of the material, in which case the writer has no more control over it (subject to contractual exceptions); or

- Pay an additional fee to extend the option (if the deal allows for that); or

- Allow the option to lapse, in which case all rights to the material revert back to the writer, who keeps the option fee.

An option agreement must be in writing executed by all parties, and is customarily attached to a fully negotiated and detailed Literary Purchase Agreement which becomes effective when the option is exercised. Without an already agreed-upon price and definite terms for the purchase of the movie rights, the option is, on its face, too vague to be enforceable.

For years, this was business as usual in Hollywood; option fees kept a writer going between sales or assignments. Today, despite yearly theatrical box office grosses totaling $9.5 billion and climbing, studio chiefs worry about runaway costs and look for ways to tighten the belt; one casualty has been the slow death of the option fee. Today, producers want a *free* option— maybe even a free rewrite in the bargain. And it isn't that they are necessarily cheap; the real cause lies with the changing nature of the business itself.

Many screenplays are developed but few are produced. Since the average cost of an MPAA production (the *negative cost*—the physical cost of production, not including interest or marketing expenses) hovers around $63.6 million, studio executives in charge of giving the green light to films tend to get picky—they like to window shop but they rarely buy. When the deep pockets cut back on their development slate, it is the independent producers who feel the pinch. Option fees and script development costs—if unreimbursed—can quickly drain the resources of the most well-heeled production company. Even established producers will offer only a small sum against a set-up fee payable when a studio or other financier signs onto the project.

Unsolicited submissions to opportunistic producers willing to "shop" a project they do not own—a clear contravention of Writers Guild policy—has been a key factor in the serious decline in option payments to writers, particularly new writers without representation. To protect yourself from this practice, see the methods outlined in the section on the Independent Producer in Chapter 11.

Standard Terms

If an option agreement is proposed to you, terms might involve an *option payment* of perhaps 10 percent of the purchase price (as a rule of thumb), although options have been had for as little as a dollar or for as much as several hundred thousand dollars. The payment covers an *option period*—typically one year with the right to renew for a second year at a similar payment. The first option payment is often expressly *applicable* against the purchase price, while any subsequent option payment should be made *not applicable* to the purchase price. (There would otherwise be no incentive for the option owner to exercise and pay the full purchase price; he could just keep his money in the bank and pay the writer off in small yearly option amounts until a film based on the work is made.)

Following is the compensation package of a recent option of a spec screenplay written by a first-time writer as set forth in a deal memo executed by a well-known producer. The array of payments possible in negotiating for the rights to an original screenplay are well represented:

> $5,000 for a one-year option from the date of execution against an $85,000 purchase price, with an option to renew for another year for an additional $5,000, non-applicable against the purchase price, plus a contingent payment of 3 percent of 100 percent of the net profits of any film based on the work, the definition of net profits to be no less favorable than any other net profit participant in the

film, plus a bonus of $50,000 payable upon the commencement of principal photography of any film based on the work in which the writer receives sole screenplay credit or $25,000 payable upon the commencement of principal photography of any film based on the work in which the writer receives screenplay credit shared with not more than one other person, plus an additional $50,000 bonus, payable upon the commencement of principal photography, if the final budgeted cost of the film exceeds $20 million, plus $100,000 deferred, payable out of first profits, *pari passu* with any other deferred profit participant.

Naturally, if the option is never exercised, the writer keeps the initial $5,000 (on the low side in this deal, but in keeping with the trend) and the rest of the paperwork is moot.

On the following pages is an option agreement, in letter form, which was recently negotiated by a literary agency for a respected writer/client. In this instance, the writer desired a working relationship with the producing company and was willing to forego an initial option payment in exchange for other concessions; terms included or excluded may, therefore, be peculiar to this particular bargain. For space considerations, exhibits are not reprinted here, but all were consistent with "boiler-plate" language typically found in such option/purchase agreements.

In the event the option is exercised, the result is the same as if the work is sold outright: the writer loses all control over it, subject to contractual exceptions. This means that the new owner of the material can change it, sell it, film it, or discard it. And, the writer may never see or hear from the producer again.

Fortunately for the writer, there is one very common exception: the turn-around provision.

OPTION AGREEMENT

Date _____

Dear _____ :

In consideration of the mutual covenants and undertakings set forth herein and for ten dollars and other good and valuable consideration, receipt of which you hereby acknowledge, we mutually agree as follows:

1. You grant to the undersigned (hereinafter "Producer") the exclusive and irrevocable right and option (hereinafter the "Option") to purchase, exclusively and forever, the motion picture, television, and allied rights (all as are more particularly set forth in Exhibit "A" [Assignment Of All Rights] attached hereto and made a part hereof) in and to the unpublished, original screenplay written by you currently entitled "X" (hereinafter the "Work"). In the event Producer shall exercise such Option in accordance with the terms hereof, Exhibit "A" shall become a binding and valid agreement between us.

2. Producer may exercise said Option at any time during a period of one year commencing on the above date, and may extend the period during which said Option may be exercised for an additional one year term only by payment to you of the sum of Fifteen Thousand Dollars ($15,000) on or before the expiration of the initial one year option period, time being of the essence to both any extension and exercise of the Option. You agree that Producer may during the option period, as the same may be extended, at the sole risk and expense of Producer and without prejudice to your rights if the Option should not, for any reason, not be exercised, undertake or cause others to undertake production and pre-production activities, including but not limited to changing, altering, rewriting or in any other manner adapting the Work, in connection with all or any of the rights granted by you hereunder.

3. Producer shall exercise the Option granted to it hereunder only by giving you written notice of its election so to do and by paying to you as full consideration for all rights granted or conveyed by you to Producer the following:

    (a) As fixed compensation, the sum of One Hundred and Fifty Thousand Dollars ($150,000), less the option payment, if made, set forth above, such sum to accrue and

continued

be payable to you, one-half concurrently with the exercise of such option and one-half upon commencement of principal photography of the first feature motion picture or movie-for-television based upon the Work (hereinafter the "Film");

(b) As deferred compensation, the additional sum of Seventy-Five Thousand Dollars ($75,000) payable only out of and against first profits, if any, from the production and exploitation of the Film, and payable pari passu with any and all other deferments out of first profits of the Film, it being understood that first profits shall be computed and deducted prior to the computation of any other participation in profits; provided, however, that any participation in box office or distributor's gross proceeds shall not be deemed a participation in profits for the purposes hereof;

(c) As contingent compensation, an amount equal to ten percent (10%) of one hundred percent (100%) of the "Net Profits" of the Film, which amount Producer may reduce, at its option, to seven and one-half percent (7-1/2%) of one hundred percent (100%) of said Net Profits by making payment to you of the Seventy-Five Thousand Dollar ($75,000) deferment as set forth in sub-paragraph (b) above as a cash payment upon commencement of principal photography of the Film. "Net Profits" shall be defined, computed, accounted for, and paid without deduction of any participation in profits except for first profits and on terms no less favorable to you than those accorded Producer or any other participant in profits in any agreement relating to the financing and distribution of the Film; provided, however, that any participation in box office or distributor's gross proceeds shall not be deemed a participation in profits for the purposes hereof;

4. You agree to render your services in good faith to Producer at its written request, and at two times (2X) the appropriate Writers Guild Minimum therefore, for one rewrite and/or one polish of the Work in accordance with the instructions of any director contracted to direct the Film.

5. You agree that all representations, covenants, warranties, and indemnities set forth in Exhibit "B" attached hereto shall be deemed incorporated herein and made a part hereof as if the same were set forth in full herein.

6. In the event Producer exercises the option set forth above, the following additional terms shall be contained in the formal documentation by which Producer shall acquire the rights in and to the Work as set forth above:

(a) Retained rights. You will retain live television, radio, stage, and publication rights, subject to standard exceptions and holdbacks which shall be accorded to Producer, its heirs or assigns, including the following specific terms:

   (i)   Publication rights subject to a 7,500 word exception;

   (ii)   Radio rights subject to a holdback of five (5) years from the exercise date of the Option or three (3) years from the release of the Film, whichever should first occur, and subject to a fifteen-minute exception;

   (iii)   Live television rights and dramatic stage rights subject to the standard five (5) and seven (7) year holdbacks.

(b) Remake and Sequel Rights. You grant to Producer the right to produce remakes and sequels of any Film, and Producer agrees to pay to you an amount equal to thirty-three and one-third percent (33-1/3%) and fifty percent (50%), respectively, of the purchase price, including deferments, but not including contingent compensation as set forth above, upon each separate exercise of the applicable rights.

(c) Television Series Rights. You grant to Producer television series rights, provided that these rights may not be exercised unless the Film has been made and released first. Should Producer exercise such series rights, a per segment royalty shall be paid to you as follows: Fifteen Hundred Dollars ($1,500) for each segment thirty minutes or less in length, Two Thousand Dollars ($2,000) for each segment more than thirty minutes but not more than sixty minutes, and Two Thousand Five Hundred Dollars ($2,500) for each segment over sixty minutes in length. Additionally, One Hundred Percent (100%) of any such royalties shall be paid and spread equally over the first five (5) reruns of any such segment. Additionally, you will receive ten percent (10%) of one hundred percent (100%) of the net profits from any television series and for any spin-offs one-half (1/2) of the royalties and rerun payments plus five percent (5%) of one hundred percent (100%) of the net profits from any such spin-off. Also, you retain rights of first negotiation and first

continued

refusal to write any pilot for any such television series, such rights to be exercisable by you in writing within fourteen (14) days following written notice to you by Producer or its assignee of any such contemplated pilot.

(d) Credit. You shall receive credit in accordance with The Writers Guild Basic Agreement, as the same may from time to time be amended or modified (herein the "WGA Agreement"), on all positive prints of the Film and on all paid advertising issued by or under the control of Producer, subject to normal exceptions and exclusions; provided that in any event you shall receive exclusive story credit on the Film. On any television series or spin-off, you, alone or with no more than one other author, shall be accorded separate card credit as Creator or Creator of the characters on which the series is based.

(e) Health, Pension and Welfare. Producer shall, in a timely manner, pay the Employer's share of all health, pension, and welfare benefits to which you may be entitled hereunder in accordance with the WGA Agreement.

7. If Producer shall resell the Work to a third party, you shall participate in any profits derived from such sale as follows: The sum paid to you for the Work shall be deducted from any such sales price and you shall receive ten percent (10%) of the remainder. In addition, any such third party shall be made to assume all obligations to you hereunder and no such sale shall relieve Producer of its obligations to you hereunder unless such sale is to one of the so-called majors in the field of motion picture distribution, in which case Producer shall be relieved of its obligations to you hereunder.

It is contemplated that we shall enter into more formal agreements reflecting the terms set forth above as well as all other usual terms and conditions not inconsistent herewith as are customarily contained in agreements of this nature. In the interim, this letter shall constitute a binding agreement between the parties and may only be modified by a subsequent writing between the parties.

If the forgoing reflects our understanding and agreement, please sign in the space provided below.

_____

The Turnaround Provision

There are a variety of reasons why many scripts are developed and so few made. Quality isn't the only factor. The "heat" may be off a story genre or an actor for whom the project was developed; executives or producers who championed the project may have changed studios or agendas or just lost interest in "trying to make the story work." Or the top reason—they were unable to commit (and hold) major talent to doing the film. In any case, many such projects are placed in a state of limbo the studios call "turnaround" (and many writers call an early grave).

A typical turnaround clause in the sale of literary material allows the writer only a set period of time—at some future date and under certain conditions—to "buy back" his abandoned work. Though not every contract allows this second chance, a good lawyer will usually negotiate this reversion provision for his client. The writer may then try to set up the script with some other buyer, subject to reimbursing the original buyer for an agreed upon price. (Usually, the reimbursement is for the purchase price paid to the writer plus, if a film is made, all other expenses and fees attributable to the project, including rewrites, overhead, interest, etc.)

As this can sometimes be prohibitively expensive, the Writers Guild has built into its agreement with producers a little known provision that allows a writer of original material a two year window of opportunity in which to buy back a script at *the original purchase price* from the current owner who, after a five-year period, does not have the work in active development. And the writer does not have to dig into his own pocket for the cash; the re-purchase monies can be from any buyer the writer has solicited.

Employment Contracts

In one type of employment agreement known as a *flat deal*, a writer is hired to write for a specified period of time; usually a weekly paycheck for a week's work. The Writers Guild has set minimum amounts payable for this labor and non-members can use the figures as a guide for their negotiations.

In the more common type of employment agreement, the writer must deliver a certain work (outline, treatment, screenplay, rewrite, or polish) within a specified period of time. Typical delivery periods might be 6 weeks for a treatment or beat outline, 12 weeks for a first draft, 6 weeks for a rewrite, and 3 weeks for a polish. While this employment agreement is often known as a "development deal," there are actually two distinct types of arrangements.

The Development Deal

As the name implies, this is an agreement by a producer to pay a writer to develop an outline, treatment, or script from material or concepts initiated by the writer or some third party, or to adapt a novel, true story, or some other work already owned by the studio/producer. The writer is guaranteed payment whether or not the producer is satisfied with the work and whether or not the work makes it to production. If the employer is dissatisfied, his only recourse is to not hire the writer again.

It is also common for a development deal to be made part of an outright purchase agreement for original material. In fact, should you sell your story, treatment, screenplay, or other work for screen or television, it is prudent to also include in the same agreement an assignment to further develop or rewrite such material. This will keep you in the process for as long as possible, ideally enabling you to champion your original vision and see it fully realized.

For WGA members, an automatic first rewrite must be offered to the writer of original material. In addition, subject to certain exceptions, such writer must also be offered the opportunity to perform an additional set of revisions if a new director or principal actor is later assigned to the project. And, this employment mandated by the Guild has a further added benefit: It not only allows the writer to qualify for pension, health, and welfare benefits (all such benefits being tied to employment), but pursuant to a recent ground breaking change secured under the latest Guild contract, contributions to the writer's pension plan and health fund will also adhere to the underlying purchase of "literary material" (as defined by the WGA MBA)—provided the purchase is from a writer also employed to perform at least one rewrite or polish of such material. For this reason, if for none other, every WGA writer is strongly advised not to waive his right to perform such additional writing services.

Should you be assigned to rewrite your script, be forewarned: Should the option on your screenplay expire and the rights revert to you, or should the buyer of your screenplay fail to produce it and you are able to reacquire it, you will get your screenplay back—but not the rewrite. The producer (or studio) will keep your work-for-hire. Thus, some of your best work and brightest ideas on your own screenplay may be lost to you. A solution is to put a provision into your contract that ties your rewrite to your original work as part of any reversion of rights agreement. Of course, you or a subsequent buyer of the screenplay may need to reimburse any monies paid for the rewrite (or some other mutually agreed upon sum).

Regrettably, some development deals do not carry the prospect of being paid at all. Producers may concoct all sorts of arrangements to lock up rights to a screenplay or the writer's most inventive creations, while the writer is made to execute endless rewrites (often for a nominal fee or no fee at all!—sometimes accomplished with the lure of a producing or directing gig should the film move forward). Hence, the creation of the phrase "stuck in Development Hell!"

Beware of producers who promise you big things down the line under the proviso that you do a "little" work on your screenplay (or someone else's)— "just polish it up a bit for me—c'mon, it's as easy as filling in the dots." Of course, you're flattered someone wants your work and you want to please him. To be fair, most first dealings with indie producers may involve no money at all changing hands—the producer may ask you for a free option period or want you to fix "that problem in the second act." Particularly if you're a newcomer desperate to break in, you may not want to thumb your nose at someone who shows sincere interest in your work.

Sometimes passion is a worthwhile trade-off for money. But what else do you get in the bargain? Does the producer have a star or director they plan to attach to your project? If you believe that the producer has connections that can increase your script's chances of gaining attention in the market-place, and if you believe that the producer will actively promote you and your work, maybe you'll choose to do a rewrite if necessary—as long as it's on your material.

But, *never write for free when it involves rewrite services on someone else's work or on ideas supplied by a producer* (who can then claim he owns the underlying material and thus leave you with nothing). That is, no free rewriting, for anyone, *except yourself.* Tell the producer to have his secretary "fill in the dots" if it's so easy.

The Step Deal

This is a development deal in which the writer is paid for the work in stages (story, treatment, first draft, etc.), with the producer having specified reading periods (typically ranging from one week to one month) in between each step to consider the work; this also gives the producer the concurrent right to exit the deal at any stage. It is the writer's responsibility to clarify the exact writing services to be performed, how many "steps" are guaranteed, and the monies to be paid for each step.

A professional writer is a paid writer. "If we work for hire, we are hacks. If we work for nothing, we are chumps," noted one contemporary pundit. All too often, the value placed on your work is the price paid for it.

The step deal is usually a flat deal; the monies payable to the writer *for each step* are guaranteed for work actually performed through that step. (The Guild's sample Writer's Theatrical Short-Form Contract appears at the end of this chapter; a version for use by writers with loan-out companies is also available on the Guild's web site, www.wga.org.)

For example, the writer may be hired to write and deliver an original story (perhaps based on a pitch he previously made) for a fee of $10,000. In the next step, the writer is employed to write a treatment or long outline based on his story for an additional fee of $20,000. Perhaps an additional fee of $30,000 will be payable for a first draft screenplay, with a balance of $30,000 upon delivery of a final draft. There may even be a polish step—a sort of mini rewrite in which dialogue is improved or scenes paired down to meet budget restrictions—for an additional $10,000. That's $100,000 altogether for the final polished script—a fair sum.

But the writer must be vigilant: In a typical step deal, the writer is only entitled to be paid for work performed for a particular step in the writing process. The WGA has minimums ("scale") that must be met for every step and encourages writers to make "overscale" deals whenever possible. However, this is no protection for the writer who provides, in the initial story step, the core of the plot, character, and structure, only to find himself cut off from other writing services (and money) and replaced by another writer in the later stages. The writer must always keep in mind how much money will be due him if the employer chooses not to renew his services beyond a step in the deal—this is the only money the writer can count on.

You may wish to build in safeguards against being cut too early from a project, especially one born from your concept or your particular take on a producer's concept. For example, while the producer can choose not to use you beyond the treatment stage, your contract can require him to pay you through the first draft stage (or perhaps pay some percentage of what would be owed you). This is known as a "pay or play" deal and it gives employers a strong incentive to keep you on the project.

Also, as you move through the development steps, you can anticipate that you will receive "notes," those helpful suggestions from executives and producers (and just about anyone else). Notes can be valuable or they can be the death of a project (if given by an insecure and fickle employer). You may wish to suggest that all persons give their notes at the same time. Also, if you are asked to change the plot or characters substantially from your pitch or initial story conference, get the executive to initial the requested changes before embarking on the next step. Later, if he claims that the script you delivered wasn't the script he bought, show him the initialed changes. Absent such precautions, you may find yourself the scapegoat in a development process that has slipped out of control.

Compensation: Fixed, Bonus, Deferred, Royalty, and Contingent

> "A bird in the hand is worth two in the bush."
>
> —*Anonymous*

Fixed Compensation

Every writer has heard the refrain: "Get what you can up front." Up to now, that's what we have been discussing: the *fixed compensation* that a writer receives for the sale of his work. These are the monies payable as option fees, purchase fees, and whatever other monies are contractually due and payable even if a movie is never made. For example, all Writers Guild minimum payments must be met by a purchaser or employer whenever a screenplay is sold or writing services performed. All work-for-hire is payable upon the delivery of the material contracted for and may not be withheld for any reason.

A contract for the sale of film rights may also provide for *bonuses, deferments, royalties, and/or contingent payments*; however, these are usually (but not always) tied to the actual production of a film based at least in part upon the writer's material.

Bonuses

There are as many bonus possibilities in a contract as the writer's agent or attorney can envision. For example, if a novel is purchased as the basis for a movie, the author could receive a bonus for each week the book appears on the *New York Times* Best Seller list. For a musical, sales of the soundtrack may trigger writer bonuses. Production bonuses are often offered to a writer who receives sole screenplay credit on the final film; a smaller bonus could apply if the final screen credit is shared by not more than one other writer or writing team or perhaps a sum smaller still if the credit is shared with not more than two other writers or teams, and so on.

Deferments

A deferment is a fixed sum payable out of the first net profits in the film, just before other net profit participants begin to collect their percentage share. When all possible fixed sums have been demanded from the buyer, why not ask for a substantial deferment? Since it is payable only out of the profits of the film (which means the film must be hugely successful), the producer doesn't expect to pay it anyway and he may well grant a deferment to close the deal. If you have a deferment in your contract and the film should become a blockbuster (in terms of revenue in relation to cost), you'll have an easier time getting a settlement of the sums due you than you would in a straight lawsuit over net profits.

Royalties

Residual payments, sometimes called royalty payments, are due when a film the writer has authored (at least in part) is broadcast in another medium, such as home video or foreign television. Collection of such payments is monitored and administered by the Writers Guild. If you are not a member of the Guild, provision for this payment will be hard to include—it is rare for any contract with a non-signatory employer to provide for the payment of residuals and it is rarer still for a non-Guild writer to actually collect these residuals.

However, all writer's contracts should provide for royalty payments or fixed bonuses should any film based in whole or in part upon the writer's work be used as the basis for a TV series (a "spinoff"), a *sequel* motion picture (following the characters through a new story), or a *remake* motion picture (essentially, the same characters in the same story). These payments are due whether or not the writer is involved in the actual writing of the spinoff, sequel, or remake (if the writer is involved, a new payment for new work is negotiated). The royalty fee for spinoffs and sequels is typically 50 percent of the original purchase price, including bonuses; the norm for remakes is 33-1/3 percent.

Contingent Compensation

Contingent compensation can be based on:

1. gross receipts;
2. adjusted gross receipts (including gross after breakeven);
3. net profits.

True gross participation (that is, a percentage share of the actual monies collected at the box office) is rare, even for superstar male action heroes. When those in the film business speak of someone getting a gross participation, they are usually referring instead to the payment of an agreed percentage of the gross monies that a distributor receives from the exhibition and exploitation of a film—this is known as "first dollar gross;" no distribution fees are chargeable and either no costs or only selected hard costs of distributing the film are taken "off the top." In practical terms, this category is reserved for very powerful stars whose salaries are too large for the production budget or for whom this method of payment is deemed a more accurate determination of their worth. Jack Nicholson, for example, got very wealthy from his gross participation in *Batman*, as did Tom Hanks for his performance in *Forest Gump*.

Deals based on *adjusted gross* receipts provide for gross profits less specified distribution expenses (and perhaps a lower distribution fee than would be customarily chargeable). Once the sole prerogative of superstar directors and actors (or some of Hollywood's most successful producers; e.g. Scott Rudin or Brian Grazer), only a few writers (typically writer-producers or writer-directors; e.g. Michael Crichton or Woody Allen) have managed to negotiate gross participation—until Sony-Columbia's recent announcement stunned the movie industry. Pursuant to Columbia's deal, certain screenwriters will receive 2 percent (1 percent for those receiving shared screen credit) of the studio's distribution receipts after it has recouped all of its production and marketing costs. So, for example, if a film has a negative cost (the cost of production) of $50 million and marketing expenses of another $50 million, and the studio's income from all sources of exploitation (including theatrical, television, and video) amounts to $200 million, the writer will get 2 percent of $100 million, or $2 million.

Initially, Columbia extended its deal to a select "power list" of more than 30 top screenwriters (known informally as "The Thursday Night Gang," for the night they met for the purpose of devising a plan to net writers a greater profit share in their movies)—getting in exchange a one-script commitment from each over the next four years. Other writers can "qualify" for the deal if they've received $750,000 for any one writing assignment or $1 million for the sale of a spec script or have been nominated for an Oscar or Writers Guild of America award. According to attorney Alan Wertheimer, who helped negotiate the details of the Columbia deal, approximately 300 writers currently qualify.

A popular adjusted gross calculation defines the point of profit sharing as occurring after "*breakeven*" has been reached. Breakeven can range from recovery of the distributor's out-of-pocket costs, including the cost of production, to any other cost the distributor can fathom. In a gross-after-breakeven deal, costs accumulate but cease to be chargeable to the profit participant after the point of breakeven. This differs from "net profits," wherein fees and expenses, including interest, continue to accrue even after the film has attained a profit position.

It is standard practice to calculate net profits *after* first deducting any gross participation. Thus the very payment of adjusted gross profits to a profit participant can single-handedly ensure that "net" profits are never reached. So it was that Eddie Murphy's gross profit participation in *Coming to America* kept that megamillion dollar box office smash technically and legally in the red for years.

For most writers, a net profit participation is the contingent payment they can expect—(the back end, or "points" as they are known in the business). The actual definition of "net profits"—the legal calculation of what receipts from the exploitation of the film are considered "income" and what charges to the film may be deductible as fees and "expenses"—has been known to run to 50 pages in a writer's contract. Yet, as notoriously difficult as net profits are to achieve, they are routinely granted. Therefore, certain negotiating points should be kept in mind.

1. Even a new writer, if he demands it, will probably be accorded a percentage of net profits. Percentages from 1 percent to 5 percent are customary, the amount depending on such factors as whether the script is written-for-hire or is an original spec screenplay sale, the bargaining power of the writer, etc.

2. Net profits should always be calculated as a percentage of 100 percent of net profits from the picture (e.g. 5 percent of 100 percent), as opposed to owning a share of just "net profits." In the latter case, net may be read as "producer's net," and if the producer receives 50 percent of net (the financier/distributor getting the other half) and then shares that portion with various other net profit participants, such as stars or director, the writer may end up with a part of only 25 percent or less of the actual "net profits" on the film. (In a worst-case scenario, the percentage may be that of a production company later discovered to be a shell corporation which is not entitled to any profits on the picture.)

3. It is sound business practice to tie the writer's definition of net profits and rights of accounting to those of the producer's. There is even a notion of "favored nations" whereby the writer shall be entitled to no less of a favorable definition of net profits than any other participant (director, star) in net profits on the film.

Unfortunately, whatever the writer's definition of net profits, and despite the ever expanding profit base from the worldwide marketing and exploitation of a film, it will take a hugely successful picture for a net participant to ever see an actual distribution of monies.

The notion of any film actually achieving "profit" continues to be an ethereal concept. Screenwriter William Goldman in his book, *Hype & Glory*, tells of a famous producer who likened film profit to the horizon: "It always recedes as you get closer."

A typical net profit scenario might unfold something like this:

Begin with a $30 million film (well below average cost for a studio picture)—that's the cost of physically making the picture (called the *negative cost*). Now, say there are no gross profit participants on the film and it grosses $300 million at the box office. You're rich, right? Wrong.

Only about half that money—$150 million—is returned to the distributor of the film (e.g., Paramount) as "*rentals*." The other $150 million is the *exhibitor's share* for running the print in the theater (the popcorn sales are like a tip). Then, the distributor takes a *distribution fee* for renting the film to the exhibitor. This fee is based on gross receipts of the film (including video, merchandising, and soundtrack income, for example), and is calculated as a percentage of that income, usually averaging

35 percent, but as high as 40 percent for foreign exploitation and for licensing the film to television. (A full distribution fee is often charged even where a subdistributor is employed that charges a fee for its services, even if the subdistributor is the distributor's own affiliate—resulting in double fees being charged to the film!) Even under a conservative calculation, with only a single fee of 35 percent charged, we are left with $97.5 million.

Then comes *distribution expenses* (in studio legalese "all costs relating to the distribution of the film, including without limitation… "). These costs will be detailed to include every cost the distributor has incurred, including multiple prints of the film, trucking the prints to theaters, trade shows, festivals, long-distance phone calls made when promoting the film overseas, residual payments to talent, checking costs, collection fees, taxes, etc. The most important of these expenses is *advertising* (trailers, television, print, computer network services). While some distributors try to contain expenses to about one-third the cost of production, aggressive marketing campaigns and promotional tie-ins can easily see the marketing costs exceed the cost of the film itself. And these expenses are not fixed. The more markets to which the film is sold (television, foreign, video, etc.), the more money the film earns, the more costs increase (causing a "*rolling breakeven*"). Hence, there is never a point when the film is *clearly* in profit. (After *Forrest Gump* had grossed more than $300 million at the box office, Paramount Pictures had it on the books at $62 million *in the red* and losing more every day! This was due primarily to the *gross profit participants* whose early profit share siphoned off the income before it could be applied to net profit.)

For the sake of argument, let's say that the distributor spent $30 million for prints and advertising and all other expenses. That leaves $67.5 million. Except now we have to deduct that $30 million negative cost. That should still leave $37.5 million to divvy up, right? Wrong again.

The studio adds *overhead* to the actual cost of making the picture (somebody has to pay for all those executives, secretaries, parking spaces, and paper clips). A typical overhead charge can run from 15 percent to 25 percent of the negative cost. Taking the latter figure, that's another $7.5 million. (Expensive paper clips.) There are also "penalty" situations (to keep the production team more budget-conscious) in which—for purposes of calculating profits—the actual cost of production may be doubled when the budget is exceeded by more than 5 or 10 percent. (Since the writer is typically not present during production or post-production, it seems unfair to charge this against his participation—but that's the one place, of course, where the writer can count on equal treatment.)

Now we have to factor in the interest—at a given percentage over the bank's prime lending rate (higher than the distributor's actual cost of funds) for all the production costs committed to the film. (You never realized they were just *lending* the money, did you?) As a final kicker, interest is often calculated from the time, years before, when the studio first decided that this might be a good project to undertake. If you know anything about compound interest, you know it could easily exceed the $30 million left. But, just in case it doesn't, the studios might include a clause that charges interest on overhead, and then overhead on interest! (It takes a good lawyer to crawl out from under that one.)

Creative Rights

In early 1933, a group of screenwriters met at a social club "for the purpose of discussing the betterment of conditions under which writers work in Hollywood." They sought higher wages, better working conditions, fair credit, and—crucial to all of them—industry recognition and a modicum of dignity for their art, otherwise known as "creative rights." The fruits of that meeting led to the founding of the Screen Writers Guild, known today as the Writers Guild of America, with branches in both the east and the west. Many personal sacrifices and tortuous strikes later, great strides indeed have been made on behalf of writers: minimum fees for services, millions in residuals secured, better working conditions and fair credit, with disputes resolved by members of the Guild itself.

But, writers are still a long way from being viewed as a partner among equals. Studios still hold the copyright to the work of writers, directors still receive the possessory credit "A Film By," and original work is rewritten by our peers, with lines, scenes, and whole plots ordered changed at the whim of executives or others who may never have wielded a pen. Ironically, to this writer at least, the Guild marked a major "creative rights" victory in its last contract negotiation—a victory that the Guild felt to be no less than "the beginning of a cultural sea change" in the way writers are viewed by producers and the general public. The way was paved for theatrical and long-form writers to be listed on the cast call sheet, to be invited to the set and to attend cast/crew events, and to be allowed to attend premieres, festivals, and press junkets for the film they authored. Those privileges, however, are theirs only "unless notified otherwise by the company."

So it is that the battle stubbornly continues for those elusive creative rights. The novice writer who works for or sells his work to a non-signatory company must depend on the negotiating skills of his attorney or agent to remain involved through the rewrite stage.

The WGA has made steady progress, however, and the fruits of its labor have been summarized in a checklist (available through the Guild) for use by its members as a reference guide to some of the rights to which they may be entitled under the WGA 2004 Theatrical and Television Minimum Basic Agreement (the "MBA"). While the provisions of the MBA may not always be enforced and while they certainly offer no protection to anyone working for a non-signatory company, that checklist may be used by *all* writers as a bellwether when making deals for their material or their services.

The following are possible deal points for writers to codify in their writing agreements if seeking greater control over their work. They are suggested in part from those gains made by the MBA; they are not intended, however, as a creative rights bible nor should Guild members rely upon them as a substitute for reviewing the actual protection afforded by the MBA.

1. For the sale or option of an original screenplay or teleplay, the writer should be granted the first reasonable opportunity to rewrite the material. In addition, if a new element (e.g., director or star) is added within three years of the rewrite and a new writer has not been assigned, the original writer should get an opportunity to make another set of revisions.

2. If a writer sells or is employed to write an original screenplay or teleplay and the purchaser or employer contemplates replacing that writer, a reasonable opportunity should be provided for all parties to meet and discuss the continuing services of the writer.

3. The writer should have an opportunity to view the director's cut of the film in a time sufficient to allow for any approved suggestions by the writer to be incorporated into the film.

4. Credit, if due, should be included in all publicity and advertising of the film wherever the director of the film receives such credit, in a size and placement no less prominent than that of the director.

5. A credited writer should be included in all aspects of publicity and promotion of the film, including press kits, previews, premieres, film festivals, and press junkets—without any option given to the producing company to disinvite them.

Part Two: Television

As noted, movies for television are often begun with a pitch and are developed through many drafts in order to meet the requirements of the network. As the programmer's needs are much more immediate than in feature films, work schedules are shorter and the pay accordingly less. To the extent possible, payment is made upon delivery or when the network pays its license fee to the employer, the Executive Producer (*aka* the supplier-producer). However, in no instance should payment be made contingent upon delivery to or acceptance by a network, or upon payment being made by the network.

Under such intense writing pressure and close supervision, it is less likely than in features that a writer will be replaced. If replacement is contemplated, pursuant to Guild rules, the creative executive or producer must give the writer an opportunity to meet and discuss his views and attempt to work things out so the writer may continue on the project.

The Writers Guild Schedule of Minimums is a fair barometer of compensation levels for most television writing and can be accessed through the Guild's web site at www.wga.org. The Guild's sample Writer's Television Short Form Contract is also online (and printed, for your convenience, at the end of this chapter). By clicking on "For writers" you can also access a version for use by TV writers with loan-out companies.

Additionally, bonuses discussed above for feature writers can also, by contract, apply to television writers credited with sole or shared credit. And, there is almost always a special bonus payable should a proposed Movie of the Week be released as a feature film (often, a sum equal to the total amount the writer was paid for the TV movie).

By way of example, here is a typical writer's deal for a story, first and final draft teleplay for a network primetime television movie:

> $75,000 (30% payable upon delivery of the story, 40% upon delivery of the first draft, and the remaining 30% upon final delivery of the teleplay), *plus* a 20% production bonus for sole teleplay credit, or a 10% bonus for shared teleplay credit, *plus* a 100% theatrical release bonus should the film be exhibited first as a feature film domestically or internationally, or 50% should the film play as a feature following its initial television exhibition, plus a 2% net profit participation from all markets.

If a TV movie that was originally intended to stand alone is used as the *pilot episode* for a series (called a "back door pilot"), another set of bonuses is incorporated for the writer as the creator of the characters and situation which is now the prototype for the series. (This is similar to the per episode royalties and series production bonus to which the creator of any series—receiving the coveted "*Created By*" credit—would be entitled.)

To be credited as the creator of a television series usually translates to a hefty net profit (or adjusted gross) participation. But these writers may face the same futile scenario as feature writers when it comes to actually seeing payment. *Hundreds of millions of dollars* in profit can be realized by a successful series (i.e., one that enters its fourth year of original programming) if it is sold to syndication (local programming for each U.S. city or territory and other off-network venues—each of which pays a price per episode rivaling the original cost to produce the show). However, significant per-episode deficits (the difference between what it costs to produce the show and the license fee the network pays for the right to air the show) and years of mounting interest often make such dizzying profits a fantasy.

For this reason, most series creators or other writers with the power to demand it, usually ask for a *guaranteed advance* against any profit participation to which they may be entitled. Meaning, whenever the production of the show hits a certain point (e.g., the fourth year, the fifth year), a bonus is payable regardless of where the series stands in the profit picture.

If you've simply written an episode of a television series as a freelance writer (and thus lack the negotiating clout that attaches to an A-list writer, creator, or producer), you can expect WGA minimum and an episode *rerun bonus* equal to the minimum payment, but no profit participation. These deals are so standard that they are almost always negotiated on a short form directly with the writer's agent. If a multiple episode assignment is negotiated (a guaranteed number of episodes), a *staff position* may follow. Staff writers of series television, whether sitcom or hour drama, begin at a salary level close to six figures, and can earn substantially more as their tenure and sphere of influence on the show expand.

The position of staff writer is, of course, nothing new. Screen literature expert, Tom Stempel, in his book *Framework: A History of Screenwriting in the American Film*, traced its roots to 1898, when Roy McCardell became the "first person to be hired for the specific job of writing for motion pictures." A journalist, McCardell began by writing ten scenarios (as the one to four page scripts were then called) a week for $15 apiece. When word got around to his fellow scribes (averaging 25 bucks a week as reporters), "the flood of newspapermen turned screenwriters had begun." It was an easy and lucrative sideline. Films ranged from a minute long to "one-reelers" that ran up to 15 minutes long. And everything was fair game as movie material. Stempel quotes early actress/writer Gene Gauntier:

"The woods were full of ideas... A poem, a picture, a short story, a scene from a current play, a headline in a newspaper. All were grist [for the] mill. There was no copyright law [then] to protect authors."

Soon, most film companies could boast of full-time "story departments" to fill the pipeline with product. A veritable flood of ideas from filmgoers who decided that they too could write movies (sound familiar?) followed. The film companies were forced to utilize the time of their staff writers to sift through the thousands of amateur submissions that arrived in the post. Stempel found a letter from early scripter and story editor, P.B. Schulberg, to his son Budd:

"They came pouring in, mostly illegible scrawls, written on everything from post-cards to butcher paper. Everyone who paid his nickel to see one of our shows thought it was easy money to dash off a movie. Most of them were illiterate. Nearly all of them were godawful."

As with blind submissions today, only one or two out of every ten thousand was found to be viable for screen stories; of the few that were made, most flopped! The moguls soon realized it was smarter and cheaper in the long run to hire real writers—experienced dramatists and novelists—and lure them to Hollywood with offers of rich paydays, if not artistic fulfillment. No less eminent authors than F. Scott Fitzgerald, William Faulker, Bertolt Brecht, Clifford Odets, Aldous Huxley, George S. Kaufman, and Moss Hart were brought west to labor in the Hollywood trenches. Most also left as quickly as they arrived; then as now, notes and directives from those who had not bothered to read the material first, multiple writers assigned to the same film, and the rigors of collaboration brutalized writers unable to adjust. The job of screenwriter was to evolve into a highly specialized field—not everyone need apply. While it's true that movie studios no longer keep writers on staff to churn out their modern serial features, the TV series staff writer has kept the tradition alive and flourishing and accounts for nearly all series television written today.

Television staff writers are also among the hardest working people in Hollywood. The daily grind of turning out a weekly show—from the "table readings" where as many as 20 or more writers, producers, cast, and network spies "fine-tune" your first draft to the frequent all-night rewrite sessions—may be one reason why many highly compensated television writers are secretly banging out spec screenplays on the side.

The possibility of becoming a "hyphenate," a quest of all television series writers, is a perk most staff writers will attain after little more than a year on the job. The term refers to the combination of jobs and titles (with commensurate fees) earned by many series staff writers—such as writer-story editor, writer-supervising producer, writer-producer, etc. The goal in television is to eventually make it to *executive producer* or *showrunner* of the series. This is where real money from television writing is made.

Remember, in series television, the producing jobs are all held by WRITERS! Besides salaries (which can run from a low of $5,000 per episode for a "consultant" to as high as $50,000 per episode for a series producer or executive producer), the writer-producer is responsible for the look, feel, and growth of the show that grants him a creative participation unknown by his counterpart in feature films. Also, guaranteed production bonuses and profit participation on a hit series can ultimately put a writer on an earnings par with such well known series executive producers as John Wells, Aaron Sorkin, Steven Bochco, David Chase, David E. Kelley, and Larry David, to name a few.

WRITERS TELEVISION SHORT-FORM CONTRACT
(FOR MOVIES OF THE WEEK AND MINI-SERIES)

DATE: _____

1. NAME OF PROJECT: _____PROJECT')

2. LENGTH OF PROGRAM: _____ MINUTES (OVER _____ BROADCAST PERIODS/NIGHTS)

3. NAME/ADDRESS OF COMPANY:

   _____("COMPANY")

   _____

   _____

4. NAME OF WRITER: _____("WRITER")
   SOCIAL SECURITY NUMBER _____

5. WRITER'S REPRESENTATIVE: _____

6. CONDITIONS PRECEDENT:
   _ W-4   _ I-9   _ OTHER, IF ANY

7. COMPENSATION:
   A. GUARANTEED COMPENSATION (SEE 15, BELOW): $ _____
   B. CONTINGENT COMPENSATION (SEE 15, BELOW): $ _____
   C. PROFIT PARTICIPATION: IF SOLE WRITING CREDIT, ____% OF (NET/GROSS) PROCEEDS; REDUCIBLE FOR SHARED CREDIT TO ____% (SEE 33, BELOW)

8. SPECIFIC MATERIAL UPON WHICH SERVICES ARE TO BE BASED, IF ANY (A COPY WILL BE SENT TO WRITER UNDER SEPARATE COVER):

9. OTHER WRITERS EMPLOYED ON SAME PROJECT OR FROM WHOM MATERIAL HAS BEEN OPTIONED/ACQUIRED, AND DATES OF MATERIAL, IF ANY:

10. COMPANY REPRESENTATIVE AUTHORIZED TO REQUEST REVISIONS:

continued

11. COMPANY REPRESENTATIVE TO WHOM/PLACE WHERE MATERIAL IS TO BE DELIVERED:

12. ANNOTATIONS WILL ❏ WILL NOT ❏ BE REQUIRED (IF YES, COMPANY'S ANNOTATION GUIDE WILL BE PROVIDED TO WRITER IMMEDIATELY)

13. PRODUCER IS ❏ IS NOT ❏ AUTHORIZED BY THE NETWORK/ LICENSEE TO REQUEST ADDITIONAL REVISIONS BEFORE SUBMITTING DRAFTS TO THE NETWORK/LICENSEE.

14. PRODUCER IS ❏ IS NOT ❏ A SIGNATORY TO THE NETWORK WGA MBA (WHICH REQUIRES THE COMPANY TO NOTIFY THE NETWORK/ LICENSEE IN WRITING WHEN WRITER HAS DELIVERED TO THE COMPANY).

15. SERVICES TO BE PERFORMED, INCLUDING NUMBER OF STEPS (e.g., story and first draft, two rewrites and a polish)

[**Note:** not less than 10% of agreed compensation for the first delivered material is due upon commencement, not less than 30% of agreed compensation is due on delivery of story, not less than 40% of agreed compensation on delivery of first draft teleplay, not less than 90% of WGA minimum shall be paid by delivery of first draft teleplay. The balance is due on delivery of final draft teleplay. In addition, if the writer is employed for story and teleplay, not more than 14 days shall elapse between the first submission of the story and the commencement of the preparation of the teleplay. For teleplay, the applicable time limits for teleplay in Article 13.B.8. shall control.]

A. FOR STEP 1: _____(EXAMPLE: STORY/TELEPLAY/REWRITE)
       ❏ GUARANTEED
       ❏ OPTIONAL
       WRITING PERIOD: _____ WEEKS
       READING PERIOD: _____WEEKS
       PAYMENT DUE: $_____
       (50% DUE ON COMMENCEMENT, 50% WITHIN SEVEN (7) DAYS OF DELIVERY)

B. FOR STEP 2 (IF APPLICABLE): _____
       ❏ GUARANTEED
       ❏ OPTIONAL
       WRITING PERIOD: _____ WEEKS
       READING PERIOD: _____WEEKS
       PAYMENT DUE: $_____
       (50% DUE ON COMMENCEMENT, 50% WITHIN SEVEN (7) DAYS OF DELIVERY)

C. FOR STEP 3 (IF APPLICABLE): _____
           ❏ GUARANTEED
           ❏ OPTIONAL
           WRITING PERIOD: _____ WEEKS
           READING PERIOD: _____WEEKS
           PAYMENT DUE: $_____
           (50% DUE ON COMMENCEMENT, 50% WITHIN
           SEVEN (7) DAYS OF DELIVERY)

D. FOR STEP 4 (IF APPLICABLE): _____
           ❏ GUARANTEED
           ❏ OPTIONAL
           WRITING PERIOD: _____ WEEKS
           READING PERIOD: _____WEEKS
           PAYMENT DUE: $_____
           (50% DUE ON COMMENCEMENT, 50% WITHIN
           SEVEN (7) DAYS OF DELIVERY)

E. FOR STEP 5 (IF APPLICABLE): _____
           ❏ GUARANTEED
           ❏ OPTIONAL
           WRITING PERIOD: _____ WEEKS
           READING PERIOD: _____WEEKS
           PAYMENT DUE: $_____
           (50% DUE ON COMMENCEMENT, 50% WITHIN
           SEVEN (7) DAYS OF DELIVERY)

F. ADDITIONAL STEPS (IF APPLICABLE):
    _____
    _____

16. COMPANY SHALL PAY THE ABOVE GUARANTEED AMOUNTS DUE IF READING PERIODS PASS AND COMPANY DOES NOT REQUEST SERVICES. THE READING PERIOD FOR A POLISH SHALL NOT IN ANY EVENT EXCEED THIRTY (30) DAYS. IF THERE HAS BEEN NO INTERVENING WRITER(S), HOWEVER, SERVICES SHALL BE DUE, SUBJECT TO WRITER'S PROFESSIONAL AVAILABILITY, FOR A PERIOD NOT TO EXCEED _____ MONTHS. IF COMPANY AT ANY TIME GIVES WRITER NOTICE THAT NO FURTHER SERVICES ARE REQUIRED, THEN ANY REMAINING UNPAID INSTALLMENTS OF THE ABOVE FIXED COMPENSATION SHALL BE PAYABLE AT SUCH TIME AS COMPANY NOTIFIES IN WRITING THAT NO FURTHER SERVICES ARE REQUIRED.

continued

17. BONUS:
   A. For sole writing credit: $_____
   B. For shared writing credit: $_____
      Shared credit bonus will be paid on commencement of principal photography if no other writer has been engaged; balance to be paid on determination of writing credit.
   C. For "green light" or engagement of an "element": $_____
      If Writer is writer of record or is most recent writer on the Project at the time the Project is given a "green light" by a network or an element is attached on a pay-or-play basis, Writer shall be given a bonus of
      _____ Dollars ($_____) which ❑ may ❑ may not be applied against the bonus in A. or B., above.

18. CREDITS AND SEPARATED RIGHTS:
   Per WGA MBA. It is understood that writer has not sold any reserved rights by virtue of this agreement. If company wishes to acquire any reserved rights, or the compensation above is equal to or in excess of the "upset price," writer and company will negotiate separately regarding such reserved rights, subject to the wga mba.

19. EXISTING CREDIT OBLIGATIONS REGARDING ASSIGNED MATERIAL, IF ANY (SUBJECT TO WGA MBA):

20. VIEWING CUT:
   Per WGA MBA: Company shall invite Writer to view the "Director's Cut" within forty-eight (48) hours after the Company's viewing. If, in lieu of a viewing, the Company is provided with a videocassette copy of the cut, the Company shall simultaneously provide the Writer with a videocassette copy of the cut. Writer shall also be invited to [_____] other screenings.

21. PREMIERES:
   If writer receives writing credit, Company shall ❑ shall not ❑ provide Writer and one (1) guest with an invitation to the initial celebrity premiere, if held, with travel and accommodations at a level not less than the director or producer of the project.

22. VIDEOCASSETTE:
   Per WGA MBA.

23. TRANSPORTATION AND EXPENSES:
   If Company requires Writer to perform services hereunder at a location more than ____ miles from Writer's principal place of residence, which is _____, Writer shall be given first class (if available) transportation to and from such location and a weekly sum of $_____ ($_____ per week in a high cost urban area). If Company requires Writer to perform services at such location for two (2) weeks or more, Writer shall be given one (1) additional first class round trip transportation for Writer's companion.

24. SEQUELS/REMAKES:

If separated rights,

- Series Payments: $ _____ per 1/2 hour episode; $ ___ – per 1 hour episode; $ ____ per MOW (in network primetime or on pay television, otherwise $ ____ per MOW); $ _____ per sequel produced directly for the video-cassette/videodisc market; $ _____ per product produced for the interactive market based on the Project; _____ [other, e.g., theme park attractions based on the Project].
- Spin-offs: Generic – 1/2 of above payments
                    Planted – 1/4 of above payments
- Sequel Movies for Television: If Project is ninety (90) minutes or longer, Writer shall be offered the opportunity to write any sequel Project ninety (90) minutes or longer, at not less than the Writer was paid to write the Project.
- Other Sequels: If Writer is accorded sole "Written by" or "Screenplay by" credit, Writer shall have the right of first negotiation on all audio-visual exploitation, including, but not limited to remakes and sequels and MOWs, mini-series and TV pilots (or first episode if no pilot) for a period of seven (7) years following release.

25. THEATRICAL EXHIBITION: 100/50/50 (BUT NOT LESS THAN WGA MINIMUMS):

If the Project, or any edited version thereof, either in whole or in part, is released theatrically, then Company will pay Writer the following compensation in addition to all other compensation provided for in this Agreement.

(a) If the Project, or any edited version thereof, either in whole or in part, is released theatrically anywhere in the world prior to its initial telecast in the United States, then Writer will receive the greater of: (i) an amount equal to 100% of Writer's compensation specified in Paragraphs 15 and 17 of this Agreement, or (ii) WGA minimum for such theatrical release.

(b) If the Project, or any edited version thereof, either in whole or in part, is released theatrically subsequent to its initial telecast in the United States, then: (i) upon such theatrical release in the Domestic Territory, Writer will receive an amount equal to 50% of Writer's compensation specified in Paragraphs 15 and 17 of this Agreement, or WGA minimum for such theatrical release, whichever is greater; and (ii) upon such theatrical release in the Foreign Territory, Writer will receive an amount equal to 50% of Writer's compensation specified in Paragraphs 15 and 17 of this Agreement, or WGA minimum for such theatrical release, whichever is greater. For purposes hereof, the "Domestic Territory" means the United States and/or Canada; the "Foreign Territory" means any area(s) of the world outside the Domestic Territory.

continued

(c) It is understood that regardless of the number or sequence of theatrical releases of the Picture, Company will not be required to pay Writer a grand total of theatrical release payments under subparagraphs 25(a) and 25(b) above in excess of 100% of Writer's compensation specified in Paragraphs 15 and 17 of this Agreement, or the aggregate WGA minimum for all theatrical releases, whichever is greater.

(d) All theatrical release payments will be made within 30 days following the applicable theatrical release to which the payment relates.

26. NOTICES:
All notices shall be sent as follows:
TO WRITER: TO COMPANY:

27. MINIMUM BASIC AGREEMENT:
The parties acknowledge that this contract is subject to all of the terms and provisions of the Basic Agreement and to the extent that the terms and provisions of said Basic Agreement are more advantageous to Writer than the terms hereof, the terms of said Basic Agreement shall supersede and replace the less advantageous terms of this agreement. Writer is an employee as defined by said Basic Agreement and Company has the right to control and direct the services to be performed.

28. GUILD MEMBERSHIP:
To the extent that it may be lawful for the Company to require the Writer to do so, Writer agrees to become and/or remain a member of Writers Guild of America in good standing as required by the provisions of said Basic Agreement. If Writer fails or refuses to become or remain a member of said Guild in good standing, as required in the preceding sentence, the Company shall have the right at any time thereafter to terminate this agreement with the Writer.

29. PLUGOLA AND PAYOLA: Writer acknowledges that it is a crime to accept or pay any money, service or other valuable consideration for the inclusion of any plug, reference, product identification or other matter as a part of a television program unless there is a full disclosure as required by the applicable sections of the Federal Communications Act. Writer will not accept or pay any such consideration or agree to do so, and any breach of such undertaking will be considered a breach of this Agreement.

30. RESULTS AND PROCEEDS:
Work-Made-For-Hire: Writer acknowledges that all results, product and proceeds of Writer's services (including all original ideas in connection therewith) are being specially ordered by Producer for use as part of a Motion Picture and shall be considered a "work made for hire" for Producer

as specially commissioned for use as a part of a motion picture in accordance with Sections 101 and 201 of Title 17 of the U.S. Copyright Act. Therefore, Producer shall be the author and copyright owner thereof for all purposes throughout the universe without limitation of any kind or nature. In consideration of the monies paid to Writer hereunder, Producer shall solely and exclusively own throughout the universe in perpetuity all rights of every kind and nature whether now or hereafter known or created in and in connection with such results, product and proceeds, in whatever stage of completion as may exist from time to time, including: (i) the copyright and all rights of copyright; (ii) all neighboring rights, trademarks and any and all other ownership and exploitation rights now or hereafter recognized in any Territory, including all rental, lending, fixation, reproduction, broadcasting (including satellite transmission), distribution and all other rights of communication by any and all means, media, devices, processes and technology; (iii) the rights to adapt, rearrange, and make changes in, deletions from and additions to such results, product and proceeds, and to use all or any part thereof in new versions, adaptations, and other Motion Pictures including Remakes and Sequels; (iv) the right to use the title of the Work in connection therewith or otherwise and to change such title; and (v) all rights generally known as the "moral rights of authors."

31. WARRANTY AND INDEMNIFICATION:
    A. Subject to Article 28 of the WGA Basic Agreement, Writer hereby represents and warrants as follows:
        1. Writer is free to enter into this Agreement and no rights of any third parties are or will be violated by Writer entering into or performing this Agreement. Writer is not subject to any conflicting obligation or any disability, and Writer has not made and shall not hereafter make any agreement with any third party, which could interfere with the rights granted to Company hereunder or the full performance of Writer's obligation and services hereunder.
        2. All of the Work (and the Property, if any) shall be wholly original with Writer and none of the same has been or shall be copied from or based upon any other work unless assigned in this contract or in the public domain. The reproduction, exhibition, or any use thereof or any of the rights herein granted shall not defame any person or entity nor violate any copyright or right of privacy or publicity, or any other right of any person or entity. The warranty in this subparagraph shall not apply to any material as furnished to Writer by Company (unless such furnished material was written or created by Writer or originally furnished to Company by Writer) or material inserted in the Work by Company, but shall apply to all material which Writer may add thereto.

continued

3. Writer is sole owner of the Property together with the title thereof and all rights granted (or purported to be granted) to Company hereunder, and no rights in the Property have been granted to others or impaired by Writer, except as specified, if at all, in this Agreement. No part of the property has been registered for copyright, published, or otherwise exploited or agreed to be published or otherwise exploited with the knowledge or consent of Writer, or is in the public domain. Writer does not know of any pending or threatened claim or litigation in connection with the Property or the rights herein granted.

4. Writer shall indemnify and hold harmless Company (and its affiliated companies, successors, assigns, and the directors, officers, employees, agents, and representatives of the foregoing) from any damage, loss, liability, cost, penalty, guild fee or award, or expense of any kind, including outside attorney's fees (hereinafter "Liability") arising out of, resulting from, based upon or incurred because of a breach by Writer of any agreement, representation, or warranty made by Writer hereunder. The party receiving notice of such claim, demand or action shall promptly notify the other party thereof. The pendency of such claim, demand, or action shall not release Company of its obligation to pay Writer sums due hereunder.

B. Company agrees to indemnify Writer and hold Writer harmless from and against any and all damages and expenses (other than with respect to any settlement entered into without Company's written consent) arising out of any third party claim against Writer resulting from Company's development, production, distribution and/or exploitation of the Project.

32. NO INJUNCTIVE RELIEF:
The sole right of Writer as to any breach or alleged breach hereunder by Company shall be the recovery of money damages, if any, and the rights herein granted by Writer shall not terminate by reason of such breach. In no event may Writer terminate this Agreement or obtain injunctive relief or other equitable relief with respect to any breach of Company's obligations hereunder.

33. PROFIT PARTICIPATION:
Terms to be negotiated in good faith. If the parties fail to reach agreement within [ ] months after execution hereof, either party, upon 30 days notice to the other, may submit the matter to what is known as a "baseball arbitration," in which each party presents one profit proposal and the arbitrator is required to adopt one of the two proposals. The arbitrator shall be selected and the arbitration conducted pursuant to the Voluntary Labor Arbitration Rules of the AAA.

34. WRITING TEAMS:

In the event two (2) or more writers are named as parties hereto, the word "Writer" whenever used herein shall be deemed to mean "Writers," and such writers shall be treated as a unit for purposes of compensation hereunder, and, the compensation payable hereunder shall be payable to them in equal shares unless they otherwise direct Company in writing signed by both such writers or unless otherwise required by the WGA MBA. The writers signatory hereto represent and warrant that they agree with the other in good faith (and without suggestion or direction by Company) prior to offering themselves for employment hereunder to collaborate as a team and that they have obtained or will obtain any necessary WGA waivers with respect to their employment hereunder as a team.

35. AGREEMENT OF THE PARTIES:

This document [including Attachment 1, if any] shall constitute the agreement between the parties until modified or amended by a subsequent writing.

BY: _____
       [NAME OF WRITER]

BY: _____
              TITLE

CC: WGA CONTRACTS DEPARTMENT
     ATTACHMENT 1

ADDITIONAL PROVISIONS, IF ANY:

_____
_____
_____
_____
_____
_____
_____
_____

WRITERS THEATRICAL SHORT-FORM CONTRACT

DATE: _____

1. NAME OF PROJECT:_____("PROJECT")

2. NAME/ADDRESS OF COMPANY:

   _____("COMPANY")

   _____

3. NAME OF WRITER:

   _____ ("WRITER")

   SOCIAL SECURITY NUMBER _____

4. WRITER'S REPRESENTATIVE:

   _____

5. CONDITIONS PRECEDENT:
   ❏ W-4 ❏ I-9   ❏ OTHER, IF ANY

6. COMPENSATION:
   A. GUARANTEED COMPENSATION (SEE 11, BELOW): $ _____
   B. CONTINGENT COMPENSATION (SEE 11, BELOW): $ _____
   C. PROFIT PARTICIPATION: IF SOLE WRITING CREDIT, ____%
      OF (NET/GROSS) PROCEEDS; REDUCIBLE FOR SHARED
      CREDIT TO ____% (SEE 27, BELOW)

7. SPECIFIC MATERIAL UPON WHICH SERVICES ARE TO BE BASED,
   IF ANY (A COPY WILL BE SENT TO WRITER UNDER SEPARATE
   COVER):

8. OTHER WRITERS EMPLOYED ON SAME PROJECT OR FROM
   WHOM MATERIAL HAS BEEN OPTIONED/ACQUIRED, AND DATES
   OF MATERIAL, IF ANY:

9. COMPANY REPRESENTATIVE AUTHORIZED TO REQUEST
   REVISIONS:

10. COMPANY REPRESENTATIVE TO WHOM/PLACE WHERE
    MATERIAL IS TO BE DELIVERED:

11. SERVICES TO BE PERFORMED, INCLUDING NUMBER OF STEPS
(e.g., story and first draft, two rewrites and a polish):

    A. FOR STEP 1:   ❏ GUARANTEED

                    ❏ OPTIONAL

        WRITING PERIOD: _____ WEEKS

        READING PERIOD: _____WEEKS

        PAYMENT DUE: $_____

        (50% DUE ON COMMENCEMENT, 50% ON DELIVERY)

    B. FOR STEP 2 (IF APPLICABLE): ❏ GUARANTEED

                    ❏ OPTIONAL

        WRITING PERIOD: _____ WEEKS

        READING PERIOD: _____WEEKS

        PAYMENT DUE: $_____

        (50% DUE ON COMMENCEMENT, 50% ON DELIVERY)

    C. FOR STEP 3 (IF APPLICABLE): ❏ GUARANTEED

                    ❏ OPTIONAL

        WRITING PERIOD: _____ WEEKS

        READING PERIOD: _____WEEKS

        PAYMENT DUE: $_____

        (50% DUE ON COMMENCEMENT, 50% ON DELIVERY)

    D. FOR STEP 4 (IF APPLICABLE): ❏ GUARANTEED

                    ❏ OPTIONAL

        WRITING PERIOD: _____ WEEKS

        READING PERIOD: _____WEEKS

        PAYMENT DUE: $_____

        (50% DUE ON COMMENCEMENT, 50% ON DELIVERY)

    E. FOR STEP 5 (IF APPLICABLE): ❏ GUARANTEED

                    ❏ OPTIONAL

        WRITING PERIOD: _____ WEEKS

        READING PERIOD: _____WEEKS

        PAYMENT DUE: $_____

        (50% DUE ON COMMENCEMENT, 50% ON DELIVERY)

    F. ADDITIONAL STEPS (IF APPLICABLE):

_____

_____

12. COMPANY SHALL PAY THE ABOVE GUARANTEED AMOUNTS
DUE IF READING PERIODS PASS AND COMPANY DOES NOT
REQUEST SERVICES; HOWEVER, IF THERE HAS BEEN NO INTER-
VENING WRITER(S), SERVICES SHALL BE DUE, SUBJECT TO
WRITER'S PROFESSIONAL AVAILABILITY, FOR A PERIOD NOT TO
EXCEED _____ MONTHS.

continued

13. BONUS:
    A. For sole writing credit: $_____
    B. For shared writing credit: $_____
       Shared credit bonus will be paid on commencement of principal
       photography if no other writer has been engaged; balance to be
       paid on determination of writing credit.
    C. For "green light" or engagement of an "element": $_____
       If Writer is writer of record or is most recent writer on the Project
       at the time the Project is given a "green light" by a studio or an ele-
       ment is attached on a pay-or-play basis, Writer shall be given a
       bonus of _____ Dollars ($_____) which
       may ❏ may not ❏ be applied against the bonus in A. or B., above.

14. CREDITS AND SEPARATED RIGHTS:
    Per WGA MBA.

15. EXISTING CREDIT OBLIGATIONS REGARDING ASSIGNED
    MATERIAL, IF ANY (SUBJECT TO WGA MBA):

16. VIEWING CUT:
    Per WGA MBA: Writer shall be invited to view a cut of the film in time
    sufficient such that any editing suggestions, if accepted, could be
    reasonably and effectively implemented. Writer shall also be invited to
    [_____] other screenings.

17. PREMIERES:
    If writer receives writing credit, Company shall ❏ shall not ❏ provide
    Writer and one (1) guest with an invitation to the initial celebrity
    premiere, if held, with travel and accommodations at a level not less than
    the director or producer of the project.

18. VIDEOCASSETTE:
    Per WGA MBA.

19. TRANSPORTATION AND EXPENSES:
    If Company requires Writer to perform services hereunder at a location
    more than ____ miles from Writer's principal place of residence, which is
    _____, Writer shall be given first class (if available) trans-
    portation to and from such location and a weekly sum of $_____
    ($_____ per week in a high cost urban area).

20. SEQUELS/REMAKES:
    If separated rights,
    - Theatrical sequels = 50% initial compensation and bonus; remakes = 33%.
    - Series Payments: $ _____ per 1/2 hour episode; $ ____ per 1 hour episode; $ _____ per MOW (in network primetime or on pay television, otherwise $ _____ per MOW); $ _____ per sequel produced directly for the videocassette/videodisc market; $ _____ per product produced for the interactive market based on the Project; _____ [other, e.g., theme park attractions based on the Project].
    - Spin-offs: Generic – 1/2 of above payments
      Planted – 1/4 of above payments
    - If Writer is accorded sole "Written by" or "Screenplay by" credit, Writer shall have the right of first negotiation on all audio-visual exploitation, including, but not limited to remakes and sequels and MOWs, mini-series and TV pilots (or first episode if no pilot) for a period of seven (7) years following release.

21. NOTICES:
    All notices shall be sent as follows:
    TO WRITER: TO COMPANY:

22. MINIMUM BASIC AGREEMENT:
    The parties acknowledge that this contract is subject to all of the terms and provisions of the Basic Agreement and to the extent that the terms and provisions of said Basic Agreement are more advantageous to Writer than the terms hereof, the terms of said Basic Agreement shall supersede and replace the less advantageous terms of this agreement. Writer is an employee as defined by said Basic Agreement and Company has the right to control and direct the services to be performed.

23. GUILD MEMBERSHIP:
    To the extent that it may be lawful for the Company to require the Writer to do so, Writer agrees to become and/or remain a member of Writers Guild of America in good standing as required by the provisions of said Basic Agreement. If Writer fails or refuses to become or remain a member of said Guild in good standing, as required in the preceding sentence, the Company shall have the right at any time thereafter to terminate this agreement with the Writer.

continued

24. RESULTS AND PROCEEDS:

<u>Work-Made-For-Hire:</u> Writer acknowledges that all results, product and proceeds of Writer's services (including all original ideas in connection therewith) are being specially ordered by Producer for use as part of a Motion Picture and shall be considered a "work made for hire" for Producer as specially commissioned for use as a part of a motion picture in accordance with Sections 101 and 201 of Title 17 of the U.S. Copyright Act. Therefore, Producer shall be the author and copyright owner thereof for all purposes throughout the universe without limitation of any kind or nature. In consideration of the monies paid to Lender hereunder, Producer shall solely and exclusively own throughout the universe in perpetuity all rights of every kind and nature whether now or hereafter known or created in and in connection with such results, product and proceeds, in whatever stage of completion as may exist from time to time, including: (i) the copyright and all rights of copyright; (ii) all neighboring rights, trademarks and any and all other ownership and exploitation rights now or hereafter recognized in any Territory, including all rental, lending, fixation, reproduction, broadcasting (including satellite transmission), distribution and all other rights of communication by any and all means, media, devices, processes and technology; (iii) the rights to adapt, rearrange, and make changes in, deletions from and additions to such results, product and proceeds, and to use all or any
part thereof in new versions, adaptations, and other Motion Pictures including Remakes and Sequels; (iv) the right to use the title of the Work in connection therewith or otherwise and to change such title; and (v) all rights generally known as the "moral rights of authors."

25. WARRANTY AND INDEMNIFICATION:

    A. Subject to Article 28 of the WGA Basic Agreement, Writer hereby represents and warrants as follows:

        1. Writer is free to enter into this Agreement and no rights of any third parties are or will be violated by Writer entering into or performing this Agreement. Writer is not subject to any conflicting obligation or any disability, and Writer has not made and shall not hereafter make any agreement with any third party, which could interfere with the rights granted to Company hereunder or the full performance of Writer's obligation and services hereunder.

        2. All of the Work (and the Property, if any) shall be wholly original with Writer and none of the same has been or shall be copied from or based upon any other work unless assigned in this contract. The reproduction, exhibition, or any use thereof or any of the rights herein granted shall not defame any person or entity nor violate any copyright or right of privacy or

publicity, or any other right of any person or entity. The warranty in this subparagraph shall not apply to any material as furnished to Writer by Company (unless such furnished material was written or created by Writer or originally furnished to Company by Writer) or material inserted in the Work by Company, but shall apply to all material which Writer may add thereto.

3. Writer is sole owner of the Property together with the title thereof and all rights granted (or purported to be granted) to Company hereunder, and no rights in the Property have been granted to others or impaired by Writer, except as specified, if at all, in this Agreement. No part of the property has been registered for copyright, published, or otherwise exploited or agreed to be published or otherwise exploited with the knowledge or consent of Writer, or is in the public domain. Writer does not know of any pending or threatened claim or litigation in connection with the Property or the rights herein granted.

4. Writer shall indemnify and hold harmless Company (and its affiliated companies, successors, assigns, and the directors, officers, employees, agents, and representatives of the foregoing) from any damage, loss, liability, cost, penalty, guild fee or award, or expense of any kind (including attorney's fees (hereinafter "Liability") arising out of, resulting from, based upon or incurred because of a breach by Writer of any agreement, representation, or warranty made by Writer hereunder. The party receiving notice of such claim, demand or action shall promptly notify the other party thereof. The pendency of such claim, demand, or action shall not release Company of its obligation to pay Writer sums due hereunder.

B. Company agrees to indemnify Writer and hold Writer harmless from and against any and all damages and expenses (other than with respect to any settlement entered into without Company's written consent) arising out of any third party claim against Writer resulting from Company's development, production, distribution and/or exploitation of the Project.

26. NO INJUNCTIVE RELIEF:
The sole right of Writer as to any breach or alleged breach hereunder by Company shall be the recovery of money damages, if any, and the rights herein granted by Writer shall not terminate by reason of such breach. In no event may Writer terminate this Agreement or obtain injunctive relief or other equitable relief with respect to any breach of Company's obligations hereunder.

continued

27. PROFIT PARTICIPATION:

Terms to be negotiated in good faith. If the parties fail to reach agreement within [ ] months after execution hereof, either party, upon 30 days notice to the other, may submit the matter to what is known as a "baseball arbitration," in which each party presents one profit proposal and the arbitrator is required to adopt one of the two proposals. The arbitrator shall be selected and the arbitration conducted pursuant to the Voluntary Labor Arbitration Rules of the AAA.

28. AGREEMENT OF THE PARTIES:

This document [including Attachment 1, if any] shall constitute the agreement between the parties until modified or amended by a subsequent writing.

BY: _____

[NAME OF WRITER]

BY: _____

TITLE

CC: WGA CONTRACTS DEPARTMENT
ATTACHMENT 1

ADDITIONAL PROVISIONS, IF ANY:

_____

_____

_____

_____

_____

_____

_____

_____

Chapter 13

What Happens After You Sell It?

"The main thing about screenwriting is learning how to fight without making enemies."

—Frank Pierson, screenwriter (Dog Day Afternoon)

The time comes when you have been compensated for your work and released from further writing services. Like any good parent, it is with more than a little dread that you watch the child you bore, raised, and protected through its difficult gestation finally being turned out into the world. But assume this once at least, all the hard work and sleepless nights and families growing up without you have paid off. Your agent phones—your screenplay has been "greenlighted" for production by the head of the studio!

What can you expect now? What will happen to your script from this point on? Will you be involved with further writing or other aspects of the production? What is the process? Well, here's a news flash: whatever you had to contribute, it's already in the script. At least that's what they believe. Now it's time for others to make their contribution. If there are any new ideas to be explored, they're going to be exploring them, not you.

Your script, meanwhile, is already at work. The first order of business in pre-production is to have your script "broken down" for production, a task often delegated to the production manager or the first assistant director. That means retyped with scenes numbered and all sound, special effects, and prop cues highlighted. This will help the producer to estimate the cost of filming your screenplay. A director, if not already attached, must be found and a preliminary budget agreed upon. Then comes the crucial, concentrated attempt to attract stars to the lead roles. A casting company will be assigned the job of filling principal roles by matching desired talent to budget and availability.

Simultaneously, the key production team is assembled: The director will need a director of photography, a production designer, and an editor, and the producer will want a production manager (if one has not already been brought on board) to fine-tune the budget and hire the rest of the crew. Locations must be scouted, permits obtained, insurance binders executed. Similarities between fictitious names and actual persons or entities will be researched; if deemed necessary, names may be changed. Rights to existing music and art work must be cleared as well.

Then, whether or not everyone and their brother have already tinkered with your script, there will be more rewrites. Perhaps these will be done by you, the original writer, perhaps not. By this time, the director and the stars all have their own movie in mind, their own careers to nurture, their own favorite writers to lean upon, to deliver for them just a few more perfect lines. There will also be increasing pressure to lower the budget; certain writers are known for being "budget conscious" in paring down scenes and camera moves and in losing characters and dialogue—all designed to save time in production. (Time is money; principal photography can cost a half million dollars a day or better.) From here on, the screenplay will not necessarily get any better, just different.

Since production personnel are already hard at work implementing the needs of the script in its current draft, all changes will be put on colored pages, a different color for each new, dated set of revisions. The producer and director will both be calling it "my script."

As the start of production approaches, there will be round table readings of the script by the cast, after which a "polish" of the script may be required. This may be the last time a writer's hand is permitted to touch the material to be filmed. Movie making is a lesson in harmony; if they like you, you'll be asked to hang around a little longer. If the logistics and planning of pre-production go well and the budget has not skyrocketed out of control, the magical first day of principal photography will, miraculously it may seem, arrive.

And that's the day you must learn to let go. It's not about you or your script anymore. The production, not the script, is the new priority. The focus will be on the director and the stars; any journalist sent to cover the production will write of it as the director's film or the star's next big hit and the producer has long since thought of it as "my movie." As for the writer's vision, make no mistake: Directors are sturdy individualists known to adapt the very structure of the film to suit the way the wind may be blowing on any given day. And stars, often being the motivating force behind the movie being made at all, are known to freely change their dialogue and "tinker" with everyone else's right on through the final day of shooting. Except in unusual circumstances, in the heart and mind of almost anyone connected to the film, the writer may as well have ceased to exist.

Sure you will want to be involved, your advice sought in picking the director, cast, locations; you'd like to be consulted on those critical choices to be made in the editing room. If there is any rewriting to be done, you would like to do it. And you may get that chance. If you learned to play with the big boys and appreciate the talent and clout they brought to your script, they may tend to keep you in the loop. Friends make movies, remember? But in truth, more often than not, your work is done; thanks and goodbye.

Will you at least be invited to the set? Probably, but that depends on the director. If you are, a chair will be provided for you, discreetly out of the way. Do not bring your camera or expect to get chummy with the actors. If one does stroll over to discuss his part, it's best to smile and nod your support, but mum is the word. Directors are known to get frosty fast and withdraw their invitation in the face of any possible second-guessing at this point. And if your services should be called upon for dialogue changes or last-minute edits, do not expect additional payment; the budget is set. The producer may furnish your accommodations and meals, and if generous, a modest per diem for the days you actually reworked the script, but no more.

In the evenings, you may be invited to dailies (when the day's work is shown for a select audience), but it's best not to comment unless your comment is solicited, and, even so, be very tactful. Anything you say can and will be held against you. During post-production, your thoughts should be sought, but it is again up to the whim of the director (for television, it's the producer) whether or not you will be invited to the editing room to help smooth out any story wrinkles. If you are a Guild member, there will usually be a screening set up for you, but whether your comments are taken to heart will depend upon the goodwill you have stored up. Do not expect to be asked for your marketing advice.

Finally, your bio will be included in press kit materials (and, budget permitting, you may get to tag along at press junkets) and you'll be invited to attend premieres (though rarely previews). Hopefully, your contribution will be mentioned in reviews of the film.

And that's all, folks—unless, of course, you've won a huge marketing gamble with your script and successfully attached yourself as a director, producer, or lead actor. Woody Allen and John Sayles see their vision realized all the way through to release on any film they write. Award-winning screenwriters Matt Damon and Ben Affleck could paint you a rosy picture of their experience as writer-actors on *Good Will Hunting;* so can writer-director-actors Billy Bob Thornton on *Sling Blade* or Roberto Benigni on *Life is Beautiful.* And certainly, Sylvester Stallone can serve as the poster child for launching a full spectrum mega-career by writing the one screenplay which, arguably more than any other in the history of Hollywood, has brought the most success to its author—*Rocky.*

Those success stories (and others) notwithstanding, most screenwriters can better relate to the lament of Academy Award winning screenwriter Peter Stone (who traded his screen career for the less lucrative but more professionally satisfying world of the stage): "Minutes after the script leaves my computer, it's best I be put to sleep."

Q. I've read a lot about battles between the screenwriter and director and/or producer (and sometimes actors) over changes in the script. Can you tell me how much control a writer can expect to have once a script has been [purchased]? And what about rewrites? Does a writer always have to go along with the changes requested? Can you ever say 'No?' If you disagree with the changes, do you have any recourse?

Melana, Montclair, NJ

A. The author owns and controls 100 percent of all rights that attach to his work until those rights are optioned, sold, or otherwise contractually bargained away. No rights are relinquished during the ordinary submission process unless you agree to somehow limit or bargain away certain rights as part of the submission (for example, by giving a company—not an agency—an exclusive window of opportunity to shop those rights in search of a deal). Conversely, once you option or sell the film, television, and allied rights to your work, you have surrendered control of the screenplay. As one writer put it, "You sell a screenplay like you sell a car. If somebody drives it off a cliff, that's it."

For this reason, if no other, the day you sell your screenplay is the day you must learn to let it go. Any purchaser of those rights, absent specified contractual or Writers Guild restrictions, can treat your screenplay as their property, to do with as they please, including hiring other writers to perform writing services on the script. If the author is a member of the Writers Guild, certain rights are "separated" out and transferred back to the author of an original work, including the right to perform the first rewrite.

After the first obligatory rewrite, further changes will most likely be out of your hands. Unless you have contractual guarantees to the contrary (which are rare) you will have no right to say "no" and no recourse with respect to changes with which you may disagree. If such changes are truly abhorrent to you—to the degree that you believe the final work no longer represents your authorship—you may sue to have your name removed from the credits as author of the work and a pseudonym used in its place.

from the trenches: MY FIRST TIME

I wasn't a total outsider when fate came knocking. In fact, I was still hot from having produced seven feature films in three years while under the age of 30. (I know, I'm supposed to say I had 20 bucks in the bank, slept in the bathtub, worked as a stock boy, and wrote scripts by candlelight—sorry, not my story.) But if it helps any, I was in a deep funk. I found myself entangled with a project that languished for two years in pre-production—the refurbishment of my home. During the off moments when I was not making my own bricks or threatening deportation, I was busily pursuing MGM to produce a comedy entitled "Chalk," about teachers in an inner-city high school. (They did produce the film, much later, with big stars and a different title and without me, but that's another horror story which, via the terms of our lawsuit settlement, I'm only at liberty to obliquely mention here.) My point is I was getting nowhere fast and ready to take a gig for hire.

I had only recently suffered through a long, fruitless experience with an independent distributor whose best intentions at funding my "three-picture deal" were ultimately undone by an appalling lack of funds. So when I received a call from a "major" about producing a movie they had in development, I was ecstatic at the shot to work my way back into the mainstream. My then agent, fearful I was "out of the loop" too long already, suggested none too subtly that I jump on it.

Collecting my coveted drive-on pass at the studio gate, visions of a "go" film danced in my head; the script, budget, and talent were surely set—awaiting only a strong hand to hammer the last nails into place (I was still in remodel mode). It was nothing of the sort. I expected to meet with the creative team. Wrong again. Just a single exec greeted me: "You're it," he said, when I asked about the team. Then he filled me in. The studio had recently acquired a film for U.S. distribution from a small, foreign distributor with designs on the production side of the business. As part of the deal, the studio had agreed to back that company's first film. The project they settled on was in the form of a 15-page rambling "story," based on an idea by the company's president, who would be making his producing debut on the film. The studio wanted me to find a writer,

continued

supervise a script, "handle" (handhold) the new producer, and pull the film up by its bootstraps.

It's not like I didn't know what I was getting into. The studio could have cared less about this project. They knew it was amateur time in Dixie. I was to be their silent accomplice, paid well to supervise a script that would never rise from development hell. I was insulted, but in no position to be choosy. I read the pages right there under the distracted gaze of the exec. By the time his secretary buzzed him with a call, I had tossed in the towel. The story was a disaster in all respects: plot, plausibility, character development, and structure. It was also embarrassingly dependent on countless recycled movie images. I didn't tell him this, of course. I thanked him, said I'd give it some thought and made a hasty retreat, citing "pressing obligations" (not unconcerned about burning one of the last bridges open to me).

By the time I reached my car, I had worked myself into a rage. I stopped at a diner for a quick bite and tried my agent to let off steam and get him to do the formal "pass," but he was out. Infuriated over the total inanity of the pages still fresh in my mind, I began doodling on my dinner napkin. The plot had the main character moving from continent to continent like a seasoned CIA operative, yet he was supposed to be a 16-year old country boy still wet behind the ears. In the race to save his father, he's supposed to co-op the assistance of and then double-cross and elude the best military and police in three countries. The only elements that intrigued me were his adolescent combo of bravado/vulnerability when faced with the potential loss of his estranged father and the implication that this kid could really handle himself on a motorbike. Also, I had always wanted to make a movie (or take a long vacation) in Africa, one of the settings imposed by the story. At the least, and I don't have a clue why this idea popped into my head just then, I knew it would be a great place to write a script.

There is precedent for what happened next. A top literary agent once refused to let me pitch a film premise to his superstar client on the basis that "if you give a writer an idea, no matter how half-backed and idiotic, he'll let it percolate in his brain for weeks and be good for nothing else." Only it didn't take me weeks. By the time I finished my burger, I had convinced myself that I was the right—no, the only—person to write this script.

I should point out that I had *read* a ton of screenplays; I had never attempted to write one. Aside from some published poems and a few short stories, my writing had been limited to a daily journal, a Law Review note, and a series of well-deserved A's on school term papers. Of course, in my heart I had always known I was a writer. And I had filled the margins of many a script with the scribbles, notes, and assorted drivel that producers believe entitles them to some sort of shared writing credit, so here was my chance to test my own conceits.

After a couple of long nights fooling around with the concept (when I get a story in my head, I can't let it go. It haunts me; I can't sleep—each time my head hits the pillow I think of a new angle, a better word, a phrase I must jot down or lose forever), I called the studio exec. I said that while I didn't think the original idea was one I could, in good conscience, recommend to any screenwriter with whom I had a relationship, I had some thoughts for making it work. He listened, grunted indifferently at the plot and character changes I was proposing, and sent me on to the "producer" whose idea I was mangling.

This guy was all European charm, down to the cuffs of his Italian suit, but within the small world of foreign distribution he was known as "The Wolf." He worked out of a chrome and glass office in Venice, furnished in black. Normally, I ate guys like that for breakfast, but my guard was down. My appointment had cut into an impromptu tryst with his adorable little daughter, whom he clearly doted on. As she bounded out, he beamed with paternal pride; now how can you dislike a man like that?

And things started out well. I told him my problems with the story and he surprised me by agreeing to toss it and start fresh. I then screened a reel of commercials I had produced a year or so earlier (when the cash flow from that home renovation was draining me dry) and suggested we use similar storytelling techniques. Getting him on board with the more character-driven angle in which I wanted to take the script took more persuasion, but by afternoon's end we were getting along famously. He even agreed to accompany me to the old Getty down the road in Malibu and to the Norton Simon in Pasadena to check out African artwork and nail down the visual landscape. (However the script turned out, I shamelessly wanted that African trip as a perk for taking this thankless job.)

The next day I had my first writing assignment. It was non-Guild through the small distributor's company, but subject by contract to all Guild minimums and protections (I had learned a few things as a producer). I soon signed a step deal for a treatment and two drafts of an original screenplay with me being paid through the first draft, though I could be terminated at any point after the delivery of the treatment. I remained attached as producer (he was amenable to receiving executive producer credit), but we both knew that without a viable script there would be nothing to produce. All that remained was for me to write it.

continued

And that's when it sunk in. Up until now, it had been about the deal. Deals were my forte. I could make deals in my sleep. But this time, I had tossed all the lifeboats overboard, pitched a whole new route through the icebergs, and sold myself as the captain *and crew* of the ship. And serious men had paid good money for the ride. Now was the time when everyone else sat back to tan on the sun deck and enjoy the shuffleboard and tennis while I delivered the goods. I was, after all, *the writer*. Hell, I didn't even own a typewriter.

I headed straight to an appliance wholesale store and purchased a used IBM Selectric II. I thought about phoning other screenwriters I had worked with for pointers, but concluded that would be cheating. So I went to a bookstore and purchased a copy of—are you ready—the only how-to scriptwriting book on the shelf—Syd Field's *Screenplay*. It confirmed what I had intuited from reading scripts—there is a structure to most movies more or less ingrained in the audience's viewing history which you violate at your own risk. It also helped me reduce the looming enormity of 120 pages into manageable ten page chunks.

Emboldened by Syd's cobbler-like approach to the craft, I stitched together a two-page outline with an elaborate teaser and a big-budget ending and submitted it for The Wolf's approval. At this early stage, he may still have been deferring to my "expertise"—he gave the green light and the studio gamely followed suit. From there, it was a mere matter of designing a relentless chase down an ever-narrowing tunnel and creating deep characters that would stay in the hearts and haunt the minds of moviegoers for generations to come.

Right. Over the next six months the two-page story outline ballooned to a 12 (then 22)-page treatment to a first draft submitted in 30 page spurts. It wasn't a seamless journey. Life (and my home remodel) went on. There were also many times when I put down my pen, sometimes right in the middle of a scene, doubting that I had the stuff of which writers are made. But the blank page endures. Matisse once wrote that the great thing about art is that no matter what happens to the painter, whatever the interruptions or vicissitudes of his life, the daffodil or the patch of sunlight waits, utterly unchanged, so that he can make it complete. Eventually, I picked up my pen. I finished the scene. I finished the script.

I endured all the notes and the knockdown, drag-out story fights, inevitable rewrites, light-bulb inspirations, and midnight sweats, but it got done. I had written it. And, miraculously, it got produced. (Not the way I intended, not by a long shot. Not by the studio I had originally assumed would release it, and not on the locations I scouted nor with the stars or the budget that were attached and committed when I was still the working producer of record. But it got made, even if that's the best you could say about it in the end.)

That first original script led to pitch meetings on other stories, which led to assignments. I soon found myself a member of the Writers Guild making a living in my softest flannel shirt and moccasins. I also learned a valuable lesson: compared to a home renovation, screenwriting is a walk in the park.

from the trenches: DODGING BULLETS ON A SCOUT IN MOROCCO

Writers are limited only by the boundaries of their imagination. If you can dream it, they can find a way to film it. And if you dream of foreign lands and exotic cultures, and would like to travel there first class, all expenses paid, screenwriting can offer a hidden delight, the perk of perks: the location scout.

This was impressed upon me early on, during pre-production of the first screenplay I had ever written, *Riding the Edge*. The storyline centered on an American youth who braves a hostile North African environment to rescue his father from terrorist abductors. The screenplay had a key climactic scene set around the blowing up of a dam and the resultant flood that engulfs the valley below. I was asked to accompany the director and producer on various location scouting trips over and through the southwestern deserts of Arizona and New Mexico and on to uncharted terrain and virgin vistas that lay somewhere from the sacred temples of Jerusalem across the vast, shifting Sahara to the winding souks and donkey markets of Marrakech. I had set the movie there, read travel books, and generally did my homework, but it was an area of the world I had visited only with my muse.

Your basic North-African atmosphere aside, like kasbahs and camels and mosques and medinas, what we really needed to find was a dam. Water effects are among the most difficult to achieve. Models, blue-screen, even the magical use of Intro-vision often fail to yield the scope and the volume necessary to validate and lend credibility to the effect. To actually flood the village below and its sleazy, high-profile occupants, we needed a real dam, a filmable dam, preferably one with dry, flat land below it in which we could construct a terrorist village. This could later be duplicated with a wood and Styrofoam model that could be rigged to explode. Large dump tanks filled with reclaimable water would provide the actual flood.

continued

And finding that dam became like the quest for the Holy Grail. We started in the good old U.S. of A. Very helpful film commissions all over the southwest had already arranged fly-bys over every available dam in and around seven states. The film's director, James Fargo (*The Enforcer, Every Which Way But Loose*), was happy to hold my legs while I leaned precariously out of helicopters dipping wildly between low mountain peaks (a location scout quickly identifies the most expendable member of your group) and lost my lunch on all-terrain vehicles with balloons for tires to get us over the desert sand. No luck.

So we repeated the exercise in sunny, mysterious Morocco. I couldn't pack my bags fast enough.

Of course, I knew that we would be *working*, that scouting wasn't all belly dancers, eight course dinners, and floating on salt in the Red Sea reading the newspaper. I expected my share of frustrations with language and customs. I knew that it wasn't going to be a bed of roses slaving away for a cheapskate producer and an affable but myopic director. (He nixed one location because the script called for "white houses dotting the hillside." The hillside we stared at, a match in every other way, had a few blue houses. I pulled the script from his hand and crossed out the word "white"—that satisfied him.)

I knew too that success on the location trail never came without jet lag and dysentery and eighteen hour days and sleepless nights and families growing up without you and endless compromises and broken promises and dashed ambitions. I had my sleeping pills and my salt pills and my nice, soft American toilet paper and my emergency stash of good old USA green. I was prepared.

But negotiating for my life with a contingent of Arab soldiers who had just sprayed my immediate area with gunfire from an Uzi was more than I had bargained for.

As my mom might have put it, "Is this any way for a grown man to make a living?"

It turns out that we had arrived in the middle of Ramadan, the ninth month of the Muslim year religious fast governed by the moon in May, or something like that. The point is no food nor drink, not even cigarettes or water, between sunrise and sundown. They're serious. And sunrise is something like 4 a.m. and it doesn't set till around midnight. So you're left with a bunch of very easily irritable people and not a healthy choice of food or drink. The good news is that if you can find a restaurant open, you won't need a reservation.

Our producer opted for the opulent swimming pool and buffet lunch back at the hotel. The director, location scout, and I piled into an old Mercedes, hand-pumped ourselves a tank full of gas and packed a lunch. Then we played chicken on one-lane roads with truck drivers, their eyes glazed over from hunger and thirst, who were in no mood to slow down or give up an inch of ground.

Finally, in Taourirt, the ruins of a Berber kasbah at the foot of the Atlas mountains, an old man who sold camel rides to tourists directed us to a nearly abandoned dam not far from the southern Moroccan town of Ouarzazate. We were encouraged to take his camel with us for the climb over the mountains.

This was just good business sense on the old Berber's part. Since camels are national treasures, able to cross unpatrollable and shifting desert borders, you can buy them, but you can't take them out of the country, so you must sell them back, usually to the person you bought them from, for a third of the price you paid. Nor are camels the cute, cuddly things you might think or the noble creatures you remember from *Lawrence of Arabia*. This Moroccan breed can hit a fly at a hundred yards with a spot of spit and have a decidedly New York cab driver temperament. We chose to go with the old Mercedes.

Unfortunately, the dam was located in a high-security area bordering Algeria and terrorist activity had been a real concern. With some "my father is from the same village as your father" diplomacy by our location scout, Sarim Fassi-Fihri, the local governor kindly granted us passes to visit the premises—on the strict condition that, for security reasons, absolutely no photography would be allowed. These were the king's rules, only the king could change them, and His Excellency wasn't available.

Of course, a key purpose to any location scout is to take lots of photographs so the executives back home can choose and approve the locations and the production designer can plan for their use, dressing, and/or duplication. If successful, we would *film* there after all, so how could a few photos harm? But at this point in our month-long trek, we held so little hope of actually finding a usable location that we readily agreed to terms just to move things along.

Our Mercedes was escorted by two jeeps full of soldiers armed with automatic weapons. As soon as our caravan rounded the final curve in the mountain, we knew we had found it—the perfect dam. A small lake of water behind it despite the long drought and a stony but dry picturesque valley below. Just the right size for construction of our terrorist village. The spot also had an available power supply, plenty of parking, was far from gawking crowds, and had no pesky merchants to pay off for "loss of business." Yet it was close to the market town of Ouarzazate, which boasted a luxury hotel and two gourmet restaurants sure to satisfy the demands of even a star-studded cast. It may have qualified for the dream location hall of fame.

continued

But the governor had said no pictures. We, on the other hand, had a sworn duty to our film. Fortunately, the soldiers escorting us looked bored and Sarim, whose purring voice was the verbal equivalent of a warm bath, agreed to distract them with a round of mint tea for everyone while Jim and I strolled the valley floor. I strung my camera under my leather jacket (it gets cold in the desert) and Jim, a true giant of a man, blocked me from the guards' view while I snapped away.

The shutter echoed in the canyon like a rifle shot. Still, the guards seemed oblivious. From then on, Jim coughed loudly and on cue to mask the noise. We shot enough film to change rolls under my coat when Jim suggested that we move up to the top of the dam to cover the angle from the lake as well.

There was about a five foot wall surrounding the dam, but things were going so smoothly that we figured either the guards knew nothing about the photo ban or could care less. Raising the camera over my head, I brazenly began to click away when the entire world seemed to explode around me—in a shed overlooking the dam, hidden below a ridge in the side of the mountain, a guard I hadn't seen was firing his weapon at us.

Fortunately, he was either a lousy shot or aiming high on purpose. Either way, our smiling and friendly contingent suddenly went ballistic. A soldier snatched the camera from my hand, the film was exposed and removed, and Sarim's butter voice had gone shrill, spouting Arabic in a desperate attempt to calm the guards, apologies spilling out as fast as Humphrey Bogart let Mary Astor know she was taking the big fall in *The Maltese Falcon*.

I managed to get the mouse out of my voice long enough to try to explain that these were "just harmless vacation shots," just photos of local folk, "pretty girls, that sort of thing." This seemed to soften them somewhat. Then, my immediate fear having subsided along with the threat of instant execution, my adrenaline kicked in and I decided to take the offensive with all the bravado of a lone cop at a Hell's Angels convention.

"Do you realize who this man is?" I said pointing wildly at Jim. "This is the director of Clint Eastwood movies! We are the invited guests of your king."

The American who has endeared himself to indigenous populations all over the world had reared his ugly head, for which I am today duly ashamed, but this was an emergency. In any event, it gave them pause. They gently steered us to the car for the escorted ride back to the governor's office to determine what should be done with us.

Sitting in the governor's anteroom, like school children summoned to the principal's office, Jim and I devised a strategy, patently absurd on its face, but with a twisted logic all its own. When we were brought before His Honor, I rationalized our side of the story while Jim's attention appeared to wander. Not a subtle actor, he soon began to check out angles in the office with his director's viewfinder.

Raising my finger to stall His Honor's lecture on breach of trust and possible detainment and other consequences, I said, "Excuse me a moment, please," and asked Jim, *sotto voce*, if he was thinking that this room could be the location that we had been seeking for that key scene with Clint, with emphasis on "Eastwood." And, I continued, didn't the scene require a local man to play the king's aide? Well, it wouldn't hurt to ask, would it? Straining to hug him across the desk with my question, I asked softly if it was possible... I mean, did His Honor think perhaps he could consider lending us—for a fair price, of course—this splendid office for our modest movie? And perhaps, if it was not too much to ask or too great an imposition on his busy schedule, could he also agree to appear in the scene alongside our stars? We promised not to inconvenience him by more than a couple of days.

At this, the governor beamed. It seems His Honor had actually considered a career in the movies before he came to public service and we were not to worry about this silly incident today. After all, his men had recovered the offending film and he could just dispose of it. At which point he tossed it in the waste can.

No one ever noticed or inquired about the full roll that I had shot and removed back at the dam and that now bulged out of my pocket. In the opinion of our production manager when we finally delivered it stateside, "No terrorist could have gotten a better set of photos of that dam."

Postscript: Due to "budget considerations," the film was ultimately shot in Los Angeles and Israel, the stars were virtual unknowns, and the big dam scene was faked, using a real dam in Pacoima, some 30 minutes from our L.A. production offices. But I still have the hand-stitched rubber camel, silver tea pot, and red Fez I haggled for in the souk in old town Casablanca, where I shared tea on the roof with the proprietor one sleepy, sun-drenched African afternoon.

Chapter 14

A Writer's Notebook

There is more to the business of screenwriting than writing. It's a war out there and writers go into the trenches daily with no better weapons than a sharpened pencil or a mouse. We need a survival manual—our own uniquely tailored *Art of War*—that has nothing to do with what to write or how to write or why we write or even what to do after we write. There are manuals enough to fill a lawyer's bookcase on all that. No, we need a political guide, something with the expediency, craftiness, and duplicity of Machiavelli's *The Prince*. So I've raided my store of "life's lessons" (and borrowed from my well-worn copy of *The Wisdom of Baltasar Gracian*) to share with you these "notes to myself" and six basic "laws" for surviving as a writer in Hollywood.

On the Writer's Life

- Write every day, if to be a writer is your aim. A salesman without inventory is a hollow boaster.
- Avoid those who do not understand the value of what you do (even if what you do all day is stare at a blank page).
- Find a mentor. Inspiration, technique, success, strategy, and contacts rub off.
- Consider a writing partner. Two people have ten times the strength of one. Partners give the illusion of a club; each conferring grace upon the other, they are harder to attack.
- When you're having a bad day, turn off the computer, reschedule the lunch, go work out or read a book; retreat and regroup. There is always tomorrow.

- Do something positive each day to advance your career goals, character, or knowledge. Boring person = boring writer.
- Set higher, more far-reaching goals—and then set deadlines to achieve them.
- Store goodwill like a squirrel stores chestnuts for the winter; people really do make movies with their friends.
- Enjoy the creative process. It's that long second act and not the big finish that makes a life.

On the Work

- Reason, ruminate, plot, and outline—but eventually, write; the world spins while you stand still in your bathrobe.
- Write for yourself—not for money; there are easier and faster ways to earn money. Not for fame; those who achieve fame are condemned to spend the rest of their life in fear of losing it.
- Expose your work to the marketplace; but submit your work carefully. A merchant must exhibit his wares to attract buyers, but never brings forth his best cloth first.
- Remember: only completed scripts sell. A 30-page screenplay is a dust collector.
- Never rush to market. Submit too soon after the first blush of completion and a script's imperfections will forever taint it. Even nature does not bring forth her children until they are ready to be seen.
- Hold your tongue. In a story conference, when receiving those script "notes," wait until you fully comprehend the problems in your script before offering solutions.
- Dwell on the work that has brought you pride, rather than on the crumbled pages. Writer's block and depression are the triumph of the few losses over the many victories.
- Creative work invites rejection, so be good to yourself. Find things that bring you joy and indulge in them from time to time; treat yourself generously if you expect others to.
- Write more. A famous race car driver once shrugged off his long record of victories with a simple explanation: "I win more because I race more."

On the Business

- Become an optimist. There is pleasure and pain to be had in almost any situation—it is all a matter of perspective.

- A thin line separates friendly rivals and bitter enemies. Be careful about sharing your best ideas or work-in-progress.

- Some people will forever misunderstand your clear meaning, twist the plot of your best writing, misinterpret every character's actions—just don't have this person for an agent.

- Never celebrate your "horror stories"—especially to a prospective buyer or employer. Nobody follows a man who can't swim into the water.

- Keep your weaknesses and your losses to yourself so they don't mark you as a loser even after you overcome them.

- Maintain the long vision; do not be easily discouraged by the script that hasn't sold.

- Be slow to believe (or to doubt) all those rumors of your talent. Persistence, opportunity, and hard work may have had something to do with it.

- Accept responsibility for your failures. Learn from them and move on. Don't make excuses or waste energy trying to explain them.

- Speak well of those who speak ill of you; it will make you appear invulnerable to their enmity. To put others down only reduces your own esteem.

- Accept that, in any profession there are monsters. Work with, around, through them, but never let them know they are the enemy; why let them plot even harder against you?

- Be careful in sharing your secret hate list. Your confessor today can be lunching with your enemy tomorrow.

- Avoid speaking of your successes (lest you diminish them) or your failures (lest you magnify them). If others praise you, it will be heard tenfold; if they scorn you, it will be discounted.

- Avoid placing your happiness on the outcome of events you cannot control. Don't allow the accidents of fortune to determine yours.

- If you play, play to win. Stop repeating losing patterns. Not every script will sell, but consistency in failure is no virtue.

- All fails the desperate and the unlucky; find or make little successes and hold on to them until you change an unlucky pattern (and never let them see you sweat).

- Good friends are your best asset. Work hard at keeping them or ten times harder making new ones.

- Your words are powerful; be careful. A letter sent can never be recalled; joy and anger fade, but the written word burns on the page.

- Follow the dictates of *your* vision, not those of a development executive. As Baltasar wrote three centuries ago: "talent outshines position."

- Run your own race. Stay focused on your goals, not the speed of others in the race. In Hollywood, as in life, there can be more than one winner.

- You can't please everyone or win every argument. Listen, take notes, but never argue with an arguer. A well-timed retreat can leave your nemesis flailing at the wind.

- A handshake is not a contract. (Not in this business.)

- Success is the best revenge. Enjoy your work, your spouse, your friends, and you make the whole world envious.

- Do not envy the success of others; it suffocates your own spirit, dwarfs you, and gains nothing.

- Never celebrate a victory or bemoan a defeat until after the battle is over. Take advantage of the ebbs in your work to gather strength and allies for the next surge.

- Never forget the value of good public relations—to have your achievements known is to achieve them twice.

Six Laws of the Screenwriter's Career

1. **The Law of Rejection—Don't let rejection dissolve your resolve.**

   Don't let the big desk intimidate you. Behind it sits some cherub-faced Senior Executive Vice President in Charge of Worldwide Production, 27, fresh from Harvard Business School and genuinely frightened for his job (his predecessor was traded for two development execs and a future draft choice). Fear rules here. Remember: it takes only one person to say "yes."

2. **The Law of Change—There is no job security in Hollywood.**

   Executives change jobs like a con changes aliases; every 18 months on average they show up somewhere else under a new title. So should your screenplay; then, it can be considered all over again. And, new doors open up every day so keep knocking on them.

3. **The Law of Changes—We all have to make them.**

   If your screenplay is rejected by many for the same reasons, consider rewriting it. Until a screenplay is produced, it is always a work-in-progress.

4. **The Law of Birth—Keep those babies coming.**

   As soon as you finish one screenplay, start another—you'll still be fresh and brimming with ideas and undeterred by rejection.

5. **The Law of Burying the Dead—Gulp and move on.**

   There comes a point when you've done all you can. It's only one screenplay. Sometimes you must learn to let it go. They can't all be winners.

6. **The Law of Survival—Don't quit your day job.**

   But never forget why you started writing—because you had to!

PART V

"FORGET IT JAKE, IT'S CHINATOWN"

Chapter 15

ROCKY—A Case Study

This is a true Tinseltown story. The kind where souls are lost and no names have been changed to protect the guilty. All the *de rigueur* party zingers are here, like how certain superstars were made "overnight" and how huge careers began with a whimper, not a bang. As befitting any good horror story, there's even a skeleton in the closet. I heard it moan again just last week, as grating as fingernails on a chalkboard. It was day two of my ten-week screenwriting seminar at UCLA Extension. From the rear of the room, a student murmured that a real writer should be able to "knock out two screenplays in a good week." I countered that even veteran hacks take an average of three months to deliver a well-structured, polished final draft. Then I saw him straighten up in his seat. Twenty-something, a belly full of fire, he was holding onto the fantasy for dear life: "*Sly did it!* He wrote *Rocky* in THREE DAYS and wouldn't sell it unless he could star in it."

The great *Rocky* myth. Once, it may have made good grist for the publicity mill, but not a word is true. Put a pot of java on the burner and come back thirty years with me. I'll give you the *real Rocky* story, the inside scoop on "business as usual" on *this* planet Hollywood. Not to "set the record straight." In an industry where reality is ethereal, the books are cooked anyway. And not to spoil Sylvester's anniversary party. Mine is not a suit for alienation of affections; I *love* the movie, and not a whit less because I once carried Sly's script to hell and back seeking someone, anyone, to trust my instincts, share my vision, give this film that I had nurtured through puberty a chance. But only because as a case study of the one script that did more for its author's career than any other in motion picture history, I know of no finer abject lesson, from script to screen, in the Business of Hollywood.

"Fasten your seat belt, it's going to be a bumpy night."

—Bette Davis

The setting is Century City, the former back lot of Twentieth Century Fox, sold at fire sale prices in the wake of the financial disaster of *Cleopatra*. A steel and glass high-rise oasis, a half-mile from the elm-shaded canyons and trendy boutiques of Beverly Hills. At 24, I practiced entertainment law there for the likes of Goldie Hawn, Jack Nicholson, Warren Beatty, Steve McQueen, and Paul Newman. But I wasn't having any fun. Sequestered in a ten by twelve foot cubicle, the phone umbilicaly tied to my ear, I felt as much a part of the movies as my 96-year-old grandmother. The client contact was minimal, the deals largely "done" (if Beatty got $4 million last time, he got $5 million now), and I was hardly breaking legal ground in scoring plane tickets for the nanny and the cook and matching stretch limos for the rock star's kids. I took to leaving the office earlier and arriving later. I soon made up my mind to do something else.

To keep my sanity, I performed *pro bono* legal work for a non-profit group called Advocates for the Arts. There I met two earnest young men from Carnegie Tech; Charles Haid, a blustering and talented actor with production credits on Broadway, and John Roach, the only director I had ever met who was so frugal with his words that a grunt counted as a conversation. They asked me to fly to Houston, all expenses paid, to meet John's father-in-law (everyone called him "CJ"), an oil magnate, to discuss funding a film production company. For a kid from South Philadelphia who had never been to Texas, there were worse ways to spend a weekend.

We met CJ for lunch, at the head of a table full of lawyers and bankers, all deferring to his power. Nobody continued to talk when he interrupted. Governor Connally was one of his attorneys. I was impressed. Our host was both charismatic and expansive in his love for movies. An associate called me in the next day and said that the "seed money" we sought was "liquor money" to CJ, but all would feel more comfortable if *I* was a part of the venture. So that I might juggle film theory with actually paying my rent, I presented an alternative: set up a slush fund to cover expenses in case we found any viable screen material and we could all keep our day jobs.

"Make movies with your friends."

—Robert Towne

I have to admit that we got lucky early. One of the first scripts presented to us was a heartwarming story of a clubfighter trying to fight his way out of post-war New York, *Hell's Kitchen* written by Sylvester Stallone. Charlie had it handed to him by Henry Winkler, a friend of Sly's since they acted together in the 1974 film *Lords of Flatbush*. Scenes and dialogue in the script sprang to life: vulnerable characters mired in a grim reality, with a visceral sense of who they were, of right and wrong. We loved it. We arranged to meet Sly for dinner at Joe Allen's restaurant, a hangout for theatre types in West Hollywood.

Sly's career after *Flatbush* had floundered (guest shots on a *Kojak* and *Police Story* and parts in films like *Capone* and *Death Race 2000* notwithstanding), so when he mentioned that he had written the starring role for himself, I winced. First-time producers touting a period piece for an ensemble cast with the writer holding out to star made for a tough sale. But he *did* fit the part. Granted he wasn't all that tall, but he had the bulk of a fighter and a fighter's hands. And he was, well, *sensitive*. At least the script would be producible for a price, which was what we were seeking for our first film.

Fred Spector, Sly's agent at William Morris (today a super-agent at CAA) closed the deal in April 1975. We paid Sly $2,000 for an option, i.e. the right to own his script for a year, and an additional $1,500 for a polish of his first draft. At year's end we would have to come up with another $21,500 to purchase it outright or give it back to him. Peanuts today, but back then $100,000 bought you a house in Beverly Hills. Moreover, *Hell's Kitchen* (formerly known as *The Italian Stallion*), was the first screenplay Sly had sold. Having earned less than $1,400 as an actor that year, the money was "like manna" to Sly. I believed so strongly in the project that I handed in my law resignation that same week.

A month later, we held a reading at Sly's cramped two-bedroom apartment, tucked into the winding hillside north of Hollywood Boulevard on Las Palmas. The white stucco, elaborately balustraded facade was typical of this part of Hollywood, all flash and no substance. It was a sweltering afternoon and the air conditioning was broken, but the atmosphere could have been designed by a set decorator; Sly's own abstract paintings of urban chaos competed for wall space with his collection of knives and guns and a rusting bear trap. A punching bag hung from a beam in the ceiling. And we were blessed with a dream team of Sly's actor-pals; Hollywood has a way of creating a gypsy family around a hot film script. Henry Winkler was the first to arrive and also, as the *Fonz*, the first to hang his leather jacket in twinkling stardom. He read the role of Lenny, the crippled war-hero brother. James Woods' rapid-fire banter inhabited the role of Cosmo, a live-by-his-wits troublemaker. Ray Sharkey and Charlie Haid divided up the rival gang parts.

Sly read the lead of the clubfighter, Victor. His tiny, bubbly blond wife Sasha and an actress friend traded off the female roles. At evening's end we knew we had a winner. Sly even got me to spring for tickets to the old Wiltern Theatre on Wilshire and Western for an evening of fights. I don't remember who fought, but we nearly sprinted home afterwards to work on the script until the sun came up. Our goal: to transform an ensemble actors showcase into a star vehicle for Sly.

Two days later, Charlie Haid was offered a co-starring role in a TV series with Judd Hirsh. It was too much for him to resist. Charlie went on to play the popular "Renko" in fellow Carnegie Tech alumnus Steven Bochco's *Hill Street Blues* and pursue a lifelong desire to direct. John and I named our new partnership Force Ten Productions, after a champion racehorse owned by our Texas partner. We quickly acquired other film projects, Century City offices, and a front-page "coming out" story in *Variety*.

> *"Nobody knows anything."*
>
> **—William Goldman**

The first copy of Sly's revised draft went to agent Rick Ray. Rick was one of the smartest men I had ever met and the driving force behind a "Rolls Royce" literary agency. He was also a friend. He told me that I could paper my wall with the script. "No one is interested in sports stories anymore, let alone a fight story."

By that evening, we had relegated Rick's feedback to the trash bin. Not *everyone* can share your passion—but we *were* kind of counting on Sly. When we answered the phone at John's house the first words out of Sly's mouth were "I need to get my script back." He had an offer to sell it. "Pardon me if I'm missing something here, Sly, but haven't you already sold it to us?" But this was different, he said, these guys were *really* producers. John got on the extension as Sly's story spilled out like bargain brand ketchup. He had signed with a new management team, FAME, and had "left a copy" of the script with a partner, Larry Kubik. Larry had slipped it to Gene Kirkwood, a young development exec with the producing team of Robert Chartoff and Irwin Winkler. With 25 pictures under their collective belt, including the Oscar-winning *They Shoot Horses, Don't They?*, I could see how their interest might turn a hungry actor's head. And Kirkwood had sworn to Sly that he could deliver a deal—"for big money," Sly said. He wasn't even going to be in it; they wanted "Paul Newman or someone like that." What about his determination to star in his own script, money be damned? He wavered, his muddy voice cracking, and said he had a baby on the way and "like 200 bucks in the bank."

Desperation is like strong perfume; you can smell it coming from the parking lot, and it lingers long after the party is over and the guests have gone. I tried hard to put myself in Sly's boots. Still, I had left a law practice to make his script, believed he *should* star in it, and had partners in Texas who had paid him good money when no one else was looking at him cross-eyed. I told him that we would talk with Chartoff/Winkler to see if there was a way for all of us to do the movie together.

Charlie, yet a partner in spirit, arranged a meeting with Kirkwood at his apartment on Sunset Plaza Drive, a stone's throw from the courtyard singles complex that would one day inspire *Melrose Place*. Surrounded by framed film posters, Gene came off as a sharp guy from New York—curt, bossy, and of the opinion we should leave the film business to him. He offered to pass the script around town for us if we would grant his company an option on it, for free of course. I asked to use the phone to call our lawyer, Gordon Stulberg, former President of Twentieth Century Fox, at his home. Gordon was leery about the prospect of us getting into bed with Chartoff/Winkler, with whom he had prior dealings at Fox, and was loath to give anything free. "You paid for an option and rewrite, let them at least split the costs," he said. Which I conveyed to Gene; he got upset, the meeting degenerated from there and we left.

The next day, Bob Chartoff phoned, inviting us to his offices on the MGM lot as "Gene Kirkwood does not represent the final answer at this company." I didn't know then that the script had already been seen and approved by United Artists. That very afternoon we agreed to pull it off the market. The lawyers were to draw up a co-production deal between Force Ten and Chartoff/Winkler. But Chartoff did not want Stallone in the lead. He wanted a real leading man, a star. We offered to screen *Flatbush* for him, compared Sly with Rocky Marciano, told him we were *committed* to Sly (we were, but not on paper—we had a standard "pay or play" deal; once paid, his services as an actor did not *have* to be utilized). Chartoff said he would consider Sly if we agreed to a rewrite to bring the story, for budget considerations, up to present day. We made plans to meet again on his return from a trip abroad.

The day of the meeting, John and I waited outside his office, and waited...and waited. Finally, we were called into Winkler's office and told simply "the rush is gone." There would be no deal, no producing partnership. They had changed their minds.

"If you're fucking over your partner for the good of the project, that's different from just plain fucking him over. In fact, if you're fucking him over just for the hell of it, but you can make it seem like it's for the good of the project, you're applauded for being 'professional'."

—Julia Phillips

There's a certain snob appeal to the big screen. Moving Sly's film script over to television felt like salivating for a smoked salmon and crème fraîche pizza at Spago's and ending up with a Big Mac at McDonald's. But it was our first picture and we were in no position to ignore a helping hand from Henry Winkler (no relation to Irwin). Together, we convinced Paramount and ABC (home of *Happy Days*) to develop a two hour movie of the week. The support we received from Henry almost assured the film a good chance of being made. But again no one was thrilled about "this Sly guy." He was not a professional fighter, nor to their mind had he ever demonstrated particular magnetism as an actor. Once more, we screened Sly's work, implored, and cajoled. The Suits delayed, asking us first to supervise a new script, one that included a beefy role for Henry Winkler. Rick Ray, the agent who had first tossed ice water on Sly's script, now enthusiastically endorsed a hot young writer, Robert Garland, to deliver a treatment for the TV version.

Three pivotal things happened while the treatment was in progress.

First, we acquired an agent, or rather an agency: five men who had just defected from the William Morris Agency and formed Creative Artists Agency. These were the kind of guys you wanted for your brothers, street-smart, aggressive, and supportive. Our primary agent was Bill Haber, a dapper, savvy, wheeler-dealer, with Mike Rosenfeld and Mike Ovitz chipping in advice as needed. We were building our team.

Second, I attended a party at producer Si Litvinoff's (*A Clockwork Orange*) home in Malibu. Speaking with his neighbor, Ryan O'Neal, himself a ring fighter and known fight fan, the storyline of our script came up. Ryan said he had *already read* the script ("I got it from Irwin Winkler; he said he had a green light from UA") and that a number of other stars, including Burt Reynolds, Gene Hackman, and James Caan, had seen it as well. "Shopping" a screenplay to which you do not own the rights is unethical and potentially legally actionable; sadly, it is also done all the time. Our lawyers promptly reminded Chartoff/Winkler and United Artists of our exclusive ownership of the rights.

Third, John Roach's sister-in-law had been dating Harvey Keitel in New York. During a dinner party, director John Avildson pitched Harvey a fight story he was involved in with "a guy named Sly Stallone," for none other than Chartoff/Winkler. Having struck out with "stars," Chartoff/Winkler apparently reconsidered the budget that weighed in so heavily at our first meeting and decided to knock the movie off for under $1 million ("B" movie range even at that time). The strategy was clear: go directly to Sly, get the rewrite, do not pass go, do not pay John and Ron. Two more producers suddenly became extra baggage. And at that price, they would go with Sly in the lead after all. We were only mildly surprised. By the amoral standards of Hollywood, it was nothing more than business as usual.

No one was home at Sly's apartment, so I sat on the steps and waited. He arrived with Sasha, who carried two bags of groceries. Sly, dressed in a muscle shirt and gym shorts like he had just returned from a workout, held only keys in his hand. My first words were, "Who's Rocky Balboa?" Sly actually blushed and said he had written a "new" script. Why follow a screenplay about a fighter with another about a fighter, both for him to star in? Sly said it was "a love story and not a fight story." "Let me see it," I prodded. Seems he didn't *have* a copy of his own script, but he had "written it in three days." Or had he *rewritten* it to mask similarities to the script he had already sold us? But what really had me hopping mad was what I had heard via the grapevine: Sly's script would be shot in South Philly, not only the neighborhood in which I had grown up and shared with Sly in stories told into the night, but in the very block where my grandmother still lived! I left shaking my head; how slight are the ties that bind in a town where friends share no more than the prospect of doing business together.

Appropriately for this scenario, next came a frantic call from Henry Winkler. Henry was a gentle soul, and his fame had risen considerably over the preceding months. He wanted *out* of the project, citing new commitments, etc., but implying that he risked serious physical damage if he stayed attached. John and I were forced to quietly let the project die at the network as a major lawsuit loomed. But the fat lady had yet to sing.

"Cannes, where everyone is on a hustle, starting with the increasingly impossible French, who are as bitter as their coffee, as dim as their lightbulbs and who make you feel as welcome as Hitler at a Bar Mitzvah."

—*celebrity columnist Ruth Batchler*

A few nights before I was to leave for the Cannes Film Festival, I had dinner with a fine actress named Nancy Wolfe, also headed to France for her role in the film *Helter Skelter*. She had heard about *Hell's Kitchen* and asked for a copy to read. Nancy lived with an actor-writer named Bill Tepper who had done a film with Jack Nicholson at Universal. When Bill read the project he phoned his old buddy, Edward Pressman, in New York and read him the script over the phone. Pressman had produced a number of films, including *Phantom of the Paradise* and the Jon Voight film *The Revolutionary*.

Ed phoned, asking me to stop in New York "on my way" to Nice and discuss the script. I warned him about the blooming lawsuit; that didn't faze him. He said we could beat Chartoff/Winkler to the starting gate. He had a deal at Fox and his family owned Pressman Toys, so he thought he could raise financing for the film. David Saunders, one of my lawyers (later President of Triumph Films for Sony), vouched for Ed, so I rescheduled my flight to pass through New York.

I arrived at dawn and took a taxi to Ed's brownstone. For a man awakened from a dead sleep, he couldn't have been more gracious. He offered me coffee and while waiting for him to don a three-piece suit, I perused a pile of comic books on his table. Later he told me of his hopes for a movie based on the action character *Conan the Barbarian*.

At breakfast, the diminutive Pressman spoke almost in a whisper so I had to lean down to hear him clearly. He hoped to deliver production financing in exchange for serving as executive producer. With his connections and experience, Ed looked like a viable partner. We ceremoniously signed a cocktail napkin to seal the prospective deal.

Almost as an afterthought, I mentioned a script that I was taking to Cannes in the hopes of attracting foreign pre-sale financing: *Mood Music*, a love story written by Alan Trustman (*Bullet* and *The Thomas Crown Affair*). I had interest from Jacqueline Bisset for the lead and from Canadian director Harvey Hart and had tried for weeks to get the script to Dustin Hoffman. Ed perked up immediately and said he and Dustin were old friends and were having lunch in two days. I arranged to overnight the script to him and an hour later I was on a plane to Nice.

A taxi took me to the Martinez, a few doors down from the famous Carlton and its famous terrace, where "Hollywood on the Riviera" held court every May. There was a hotel strike going on, dogs running loose in the lobby, and all eyes darted over shoulders to see who they were missing or being missed by. I lugged my own bags to a room that had clean sheets, if not room service, working telephones, or a staff.

Having retrieved my festival credentials and film passes from the chaos at the *Palais du Festival*, I headed to a lunch scheduled with Maggie Abbott of the Paul Kohner Agency, and her client, actress Charlotte Rampling. Charlotte was as hot as a bowl of Chasen's Chili that year, honored as one of the judges at the festival. She was also my choice to play the lead in a film I hoped to produce with my pal, Si Litvinoff—*Out of Africa*. Based on the stirring memoirs of Isak Dinessen and photographer Peter Beard's tome on animal conservation, *The End of The Game*, Si had interested Nicholas Roeg in directing.

My goal was to land Charlotte in the role of Dinessen. Outmatched by this high-powered agent and her high-profile client, I pointed out that Ed Pressman, my possible co-producer on another film, was lunching with Dustin Hoffman that very day in New York. Next morning, Maggie left a note in my box at the Martinez: "Spoke to Dusty this morning. He never heard of Pressman or *Mood Music*." A chink in my credibility that would no doubt cost me Ms. Rampling. Furious, I spent the day locked in my hotel room, waiting on French operators trying to get a call through to Ed. His response: "I don't *personally* know Hoffman, but my friend is his good friend" or something like that. Regarding *Hell's Kitchen*, he was "waiting for a read" from director/partner, Paul Williams. By now, I had lost faith in Ed and only a check in a production account could revive it.

> *"…I'll know I'm not just another bum from the neighborhood."*
>
> **—Rocky Balboa**

Back in Los Angeles, *Rocky* was on the fast track, a freight train that couldn't be stopped. I didn't see much hope in pushing further for financing on essentially the same movie Chartoff/Winkler was deep into production on, but I still agreed to meet with Pressman, if out of nothing more than a desire to make a circle of friends for future films. During our lunch, into our patio area strode a bodybuilder and actor who had acquitted himself well, I thought, in the one film (*Stay Hungry*) and one documentary (*Pumping Iron*) I had seen him in—Arnold Schwarzenegger.

Arnold was not yet a movie star, but those *arms* turned heads. I had spent some time with him through Jack East, the legendary publicist for *The Hollywood Reporter*, so I nodded a greeting. Remembering Ed's hopes to film *Conan the Barbarian*, I introduced them and commented, "Here's your Conan." Their handshake led to the film that would jumpstart Arnold's career as an action star and revitalize Ed's as a producer. Lunch over, Ed left, saying he would have his accountant confirm he was indeed out of the project. We agreed that he gave it a good try and maybe in the future we'd find something to do together.

A fateful day all around. An hour later I received word from our lawyer, Gordon Stulberg, that Chartoff/Winkler had begun principal photography on *Rocky*.

There was nothing to do but wait. Gordon finally arranged a rough-cut screening of *Rocky* at MGM's lot in Culver City. Scenes were missing, the print was not the best, and there was yet no music to punch up the drama, but we expected that. Worse, the film seemed to have no pacing, no drive. They seemed to have committed the cardinal sin of filmmaking: They had made it boring. Then came the moment that Sly ran up the Art Museum stairs and jumped up and down with his hands in the air in triumph. I guess sooner or later in this business you develop an instinct. I turned and whispered to John, "A hundred million dollars. This film is going to make a hundred million dollars."

Somewhere from the thumb-breaking thug Sly portrayed at the start to the poignant if trite love consummated with Talia Shire, the movie had developed real heart. But I knew that: *It was almost beat for beat the screenplay I held in my hand, the one sold to us almost a year ago by Sly himself!* John and I were hell bent on getting our pound of flesh.

But the sharks were already circling. First came a call from Stan Kamen at William Morris. In the face of a well-orchestrated media blitz positioning him as the new "great white hope," Stallone had signed with Stan, Morris' senior motion picture agent. Among his clientele was Goldie Hawn, my former law client, on whose behalf he and I had had a few meals together. I both respected and liked Stan. When he said he thought Sly, John, and I all had good careers in front of us if we could straighten out our differences before the lawsuit put a halt to everything, I listened.

A meeting took place at the Morris agency on El Camino in Beverly Hills. Sly was there sporting a beret and looking every bit the flavor of the month. And he was; a month before *Rocky* would even open, Sly had graced the cover of two national magazines, one captioned "Rocky: The Launching of a New Superstar." His entourage included his lawyer, Jake Bloom, and his personal managers, Jane Oliver and her husband. John and I were supported by our agent, Bill Haber, and our lawyer, Gordon Stulberg.

Stan started the meeting by conceding, on behalf of Sly, that *Rocky* had "mirrored" significant parts of *Hell's Kitchen*. He reasoned that, hey, Sly was a struggling actor faced with his big chance at stardom, could you blame him? Sly piped up that he didn't understand how it was possible to steal from himself; his lawyer wisely saved that legal lesson for later.

Stan continued, noting that John and I were free to sue the makers of *Rocky* for the purloin of our material, but surely not Sly if we were to *work together* on *Hell's Kitchen*. Apparently, Stan didn't think the damage was irreversible. After all, with a "few changes" to *Hell's Kitchen*, like the characters (Sly to play a creep instead of a fighter with a heart of gold), and the plot (club wrestling rather than a heavyweight title fight), it would be a whole new movie, wouldn't it? (*Yeah, Stan, the other one went on to make two hundred million dollars.*) Besides, Sly had repented, wanted to work with us again, and Stan was sure he could set a studio deal, based on the promise of a glossy rewrite, within 48 hours.

Don't lose this testament to Hollywood's herd mentality. Based on one heralded performance in a yet-to-be-released low-budget film, Stan was saying that a major film studio would agree to make essentially the *same movie* as *Rocky* from essentially the *same script*. And he was right! New acting blood is the oil that greases the Hollywood machine. Witness the millions that gushed from studio coffers in the mad scramble to sign Jim Carrey after *Ace Ventura*, Julia Roberts post *Pretty Woman*, and Alicia Silverstone, only seventeen when her payday leaped over $10 million following her smash hit *Clueless*.

As the afternoon groaned on, Chevy Chase popped his head in to say hello to Stan and immediately backed sheepishly out. Later he told me, "There was a cold draft coming from that room." I looked over at Sly, but his head was bowed, sucking his teeth. He was going to have his cake and eat it too—two movies from one script, two paychecks and no lawsuit! He finally sprang to life when our lawyer began absently referring to him as "Sy." Leaning over, he said in a menacing tone, "It's Sly, not Sy, okay?" For a long beat nobody spoke, at which point Stan quietly turned a page and, perhaps inspired by a scene from that year's other Best Picture front runner, *Network*, said, "Let's turn to net profits, shall we?"

"They have obviously opted to make movies, not lawsuits."

—gossip columnist Rona Barrett

Stan delivered on his promise. John and I soon found ourselves on Universal's lot in the producer's building. Sly was a floor below us, in a three-room suite sandwiched between Steven Spielberg and his *Jaws* editor and mentor, the late Verna Fields. As the first order of business, *Hell's Kitchen* was retitled *Paradise Alley*, after the lyric of an old New York street song:

"There's a little side street such as often you meet,

where the boys of a Sunday night rally.

Though it's not very wide, and it's dismal beside,

yet they call the place Paradise Alley.

Despite misgivings that the script changes we made to avoid looking like a *Rocky* clone were harming the commerciality of our film, we understood that for Sly to follow one role as a fighter with another would be a bad long-range career move. We also dutifully held off any lawsuit on *Rocky* until after the upcoming Academy Awards so as not to taint our star's chances at an Oscar. We had the future promotion of *Paradise Alley* to think about and we were rooting as hard as anyone for Sly to win.

Universal assigned a production executive, Peter Saphier, to the picture, his job presumably to please Stallone at all cost. Even when our reasoning prevailed behind closed-door meetings, many of which Sly spent distractedly signing pictures of himself, Sly could later bang his fists on Peter's desk and we would find our hard-won concessions reversed again. In any case, Sly set about polishing the script and he, John, and I set about interviewing production managers, production designers, editors, and DPs.

But not directors. Sly had lobbied us to let him direct. He was an amateur painter and we had toured museums together to find the right textures for the film, had strolled the back lot bouncing around casting suggestions and acting out the images of every scene. To pick someone else would have been like taking the canvas from an artist just as it went from sketch to the richness of oil. And he was, for all his lack of experience, a double Oscar nominee.

We delivered Sly's wishes as a demand to Ned Tanen, the president of Universal, half expecting to get tossed out on our ear. To our surprise Ned listened long and hard, saying only that, "Well, this has certainly been a no bullshit conversation," before giving the green light. Regret it as we would later, we now had a writer-director-star rolled into one.

Sly had the ego of a director, that was for sure. Often, on those strolls about the backlot, he became most animated whenever a Universal tour tram passed within viewing distance. He also raided Universal's prop storage house for memorabilia from horror films to decorate his office. This desecration of Universal founder Jules Stein's carefully orchestrated somber tones and fine antiques eventually landed him out of the producers' building.

It was Stan Kamen who suggested that Sly get some needed big picture experience before his directing debut. He lined Sly up to star in Norman Jewison's labor epic, *Fist*, penned by then unknown journalist Joe Eszterhas. We would have time to carefully prepare our first film, and establish some distance between the two "fight" films. Universal agreed to wait. It all made some kind of twisted sense.

> *"Enter Ophelia: the mad scene."*
>
> **—Woody Allen**

Then our erstwhile "partner" Ed Pressman crawled out of the woodwork. He had read about our cozy arrangement at Universal and wanted a piece of the action. The piece of paper we had drawn up months earlier at breakfast, though by its terms null and void, was enough to make a claim against the rights. Gordon said not to worry, "any idiot can sue; we'll crush him." One big problem: Universal. Stories were filtering back that Sly was having problems with everyone in Iowa. Also, our budget had climbed from a rose-colored $2.5 million to a more risky $6 million. Whether or not Universal was getting cold feet, one thing was certain: Clear up the cloud on the rights now or they might use it as a means of breaking their "go picture" commitment to us.

We tried to reason with Ed. John sent him a letter suggesting we chat. At the Bel Air Country Club, a deal was reached. Apparently John and I really did want to make pictures and not lawsuits, because we agreed to pay money to someone who had as much to do with getting our movie made as the man in the moon. Ed had never met Sly. It was pure blackmail in our eyes, but we just wanted the whole thing to go away.

The next morning, we got a call from our lawyer. Ed wanted more: points, an interest in any lawsuit settlement, and screen credit. Horror stories are a staple of Hollywood's fireside anecdotes. But I have never witnessed such a bold-faced turn around in character as Pressman displayed that day. I phoned him and he was a veritable madman, swearing and claiming that we tricked him and that he'd never agreed to anything. He even went so far as to claim that he and I had *never spoken*, let alone met for a drink at the Bel Air, the previous night. I was beginning to feel like a real person trapped in a cartoon world.

But this time we wouldn't cave in. A meeting was set by the lawyers for the next afternoon. Ed was smart; he stayed home and let his lawyers take the heat, and I was boiling. While both sides groaned on about percentages of this and that, I rose and fired my lawyers. I glanced at John, but he knew better than to pick this moment to speak. I must have had the look of the possessed in my eye because no one else spoke as I laid out *my* agenda. If unearned credit was Ed's style, he could have executive producer, even a small percentage of our profit share, but he would have no contact with the film or anyone connected to it. He was in fact to be barred from the lot during filming. And if he didn't agree by 5 pm that evening, all deals were off; we were going to court. By 5 pm, we had a binding deal. John and our lawyers congratulated me on "a brilliant move." I felt like I had been mugged in broad daylight.

We held back on our own lawsuit until the Academy Awards were over and *Rocky* was named Best Picture. Maybe a day or two. The press had a field day. Variety's headline screamed: "*U Continuing with "Kitchen" Despite Suit Filed By Its Producers Against UA, C-W.*" The Hollywood Reporter was more blunt; "*Force Ten files $30 mil suit against Rocky.*" We weren't suing *Sly*, of course, though by now we had exercised our option and owned his script, just producers Chartoff/Winkler and UA, the film's distributor.

We had in fact agreed to *indemnify* Sly so as not to rock our current working relationship. This proved costly. Even if we won, had Sly signed the standard "warranties and indemnities" contract with UA, they could in turn sue him. Sly could then look to *our* indemnity to pay UA. A complete circle and a lot of *Sturm und Drang* for nothing. Nonetheless, we made a good show of it. Our lawyers dumped a pile of interrogatories on Mike Medavoy, then the president of UA. Medavoy promptly phoned Gordon to assure him that, in a manner of speaking, John and I would never eat lunch in this town again. A game of telephone followed. Gordon informed John Roach of the "threat," who told his Houston attorney, Frank Smith, who related it on to CJ, our benefactor in Texas. CJ was a mover and shaker in higher Democratic Party circles which included his crony, Arthur Krim, the chairman of UA. Krim received a call from Gov. Connally, Smith's Texas law partner, to the effect of "Who the hell is this Medavoc or Medowlark that had the balls to threaten

CJ's son-in-law." It was shortly after that when we received our first serious settlement offer. If it sounded an alarm that UA knew they were in big trouble, we slept through it.

At one point during the negotiations, Chartoff gave us another signal that we missed. He offered us a share of the net profits of any *Rocky* sequels, but our lawyers advised against it. Nobody made sequels. Only *The Godfather* and this was not *The Godfather*. Of course, hindsight being 20-20, we should have pressed our suit all the way to the Supreme Court if need be—and taken profits over a cash settlement in a heartbeat. But who knew? Five "Rockys" later, Chartoff & Winkler are richer than God. Our settlement repaid our backers and covered our legal fees. And in an ironic twist, we even had to fork over a percentage of it to Pressman. I feared that I had "gone Hollywood" when I found myself actually admiring Ed's pure nerve in reinventing a career out of a signed table napkin!

> *"Agents, you can't live with them and you can't shoot them."*
> **—Jim Jarmusch**

I won't elaborate on the slings and arrows of making *Paradise Alley* except to say that pre-production went well until Sly's manager, Jane Oliver, died suddenly of cancer. Jane's sweet nature had been the glue that held us and Sly together through all the rancor. Sly worshipped her. Probably so as not to worry him, Jane had kept her illness a secret from him. Knowing the news must have devastated Sly, John and I planned to fly to Iowa to be with him, but Stan Kamen stopped us. In confidence he told us that he had reservations about the state of Sly's mental condition just then and that he thought it best to let things lie for a while. We did, but personal manager Jeff Wald, husband of singer Helen Reddy, did not. He flew to Dubuque, signed Sly, and in quick order announced that if we, the producers, wished any contact with our star-director-writer that we would have to go through him.

Ignoring this latest nonsense, we commandeered Universal's largest sound stage, hired crew and staff, and began set construction. We also planned 12 days shooting in New York, from a principal location on West 80th Street, on the outskirts of Hell's Kitchen, to the Hudson River docks and the Knickerbocker Icehouse in Brooklyn. The pros we had brought on to guide us through the rough spots soon melded into a well-oiled team and, for a time, we touched on the fun gig filmmaking promised to be. Steven Spielberg, on location for *Close Encounters of the Third Kind*, had left an enormous rubber chicken hanging over his desk and that pretty much set the mood of the office. We were kids making movies. But the calm only signaled a new storm on the horizon.

Weeks earlier, just before Sly departed for the Dubuque location of *Fist*, we met one morning to plan the "crewing up" of the production. Only this time, a new face, with a beard and an attitude, sat next to him. Sly introduced his "unassociated Associate Producer." Arthur was, we were informed, to be Sly's eyes and ears while he was on location. To us, he was a hanger-on sorely in need of a bath, and a distraction when we needed Sly's attention most. We were wrong, he was worse.

On our first location scout we included Arthur in the trip. On our second day in New York, my key crew complained to me that working with Sly's "disassociated AP" was proving impossible. At every turn he knew what Sly wanted, and with Sly still away in Iowa, *he* would decide locations on Sly's behalf. On our return, he announced that Sly wanted to begin casting the three female roles in the film. As Sly was due back any day, we opted to wait for him and left town on business. Upon our return we learned casting sessions, held without our approval, had netted a new girlfriend for Arthur and a string of complaints from actresses and agents about professionalism.

I phoned Sly and was told that he was not there. I marched to his trailer where a line of beauteous women led all the way to his door, which was locked. I knocked, but Sly buzzed his secretary to say that he couldn't see me. I sent the actors home, folded my arms and sat. His secretary called security and finally Sly emerged. In the course of asking him what he thought he was doing, I'm told I called him a "scumbag." (*Ten years later*, at a Grammy party at the Mondrian Hotel in West Hollywood, Sly motioned me into a cordoned-off circle of his own bodyguards, only to tell me the word still festered in him. I told him I had forgotten calling him any such thing, as I assumed he had, what with two divorces and his huge career and all, but "now that you've reminded me..." I probably should have tipped his bodyguards.)

At Universal, it was a Mexican standoff until we were advised by our agent, for the good of the picture, to reach out to Sly in a personal letter. Hat in hand, we laid out problems that threatened to undermine the production, along with potential solutions. We avoided the scud missiles of who was to blame. It was to be for Sly's eyes only. Next day everybody on the lot had a copy and there were no FAX machines back then. Hollywood respects the code of silence like the Cosa Nostra. If a complaint is put down on paper for a whole gossip-ridden business and public-company bureaucracy to *have to* respond to, the hatred of the messenger grows in proportion to the truth of the message. BOOM, we lay out this memo that says that the production is in trouble—and the reason is that we are at odds with our star. *Ipso facto*, that makes *us* the problem.

Universal tried essentially to replace the entire production team, invoking the "pay or play" clause along with the usual "creative differences." John and I were forced to produce the movie from across the street, getting production reports from spies and giving notes through intermediaries. Sly had finally acquired the *auteur* status he so coveted, surrounded by a coterie of fawning "yes" men.

"What so ever ye shall sow, so shall ye reap."

—The Old Testament

In September 1978, the film was offered to the public. It received a mixed reception from preview audiences. Theater owners and local publicists were at a loss as to how to market the "new" Stallone. A logline proclaiming "Three Brothers: One Had The Brains, One Had The Muscle and One Had The Suit" (even I couldn't figure that one out) and a running time listed as "tentative," seemed to beg advice.

Why had *Rocky* lifted them cheering from their seats, while *Paradise Alley*, using essentially the same theme, mood, characters, and structure of a club prize fighter who would build a reputation as such until a climactic fight which he would lose, written by the same writer and also starring Sylvester Stallone, was leaving them cold? The answer to me was simple. Movies are about dreams, about heroes, about trying to answer the eternal question of "Who am I?" Audiences may come to the theater to *see* Dustin Hoffman, but they want to *be* Sly Stallone, or more precisely, Rocky Balboa.

Paradise Alley was Victor's story, told from the fighter's point of view. Sly was *always* Victor. After *Rocky*, so Sly would not repeat himself, the role of Victor went to Lee Canalito. Sly inherited the part of Cosmo, whose acerbic wit was written as a *counterpoint* to the simple, sweet Victor. Fans were put off by Stallone as this wisecracking, not-so-funny n'er do well. The kiss of death came when Sly, their working-class hero, not only wrote, starred, and directed, but had the audacity to also *sing the title song*, in a voice one critic characterized as being like "a recalcitrant bathtub being drained."

I lobbied for Tom Waits or Joe Cocker to re-record the title song. Universal said no deal. We hired our own ad firm. Their copy was ignored. I asked to cut early expository scenes which were repetitive and in which Sly came off as a jerk, not funny or endearing as intended. They made the cuts—in the TV version. There was still time to restore footage that completed the storyline of the female leads, all of whom disappear after the second act. Universal kept mum on that request—perhaps deemed too hot to handle. During filming, Sly had become embroiled in a well-publicized affair with Joyce Ingalls, a former model who portrayed his girlfriend in the film. When Sasha took a contrite Sly back into their marriage, much of Joyce's part hit the editing room floor. If Universal held its hand from interference in order to curry favor with Sly and garner high-profile publicity for the film, they had miscalculated. Sly alone had the muscle to make things happen, but he had already moved on, transferring his affections to *Rocky II*, on which *Paradise Alley* had paved the way for him to direct.

Paradise Alley would do "boffo box office" in Italy, where perhaps Sly's "I'm nobody's fart catcher" lines mercifully lost something in the translation. But American audiences never warmed to its forties ambiance nor the Damon Runyon qualities that won the film and its director a rave review in the industry bible, *Daily Variety*. In fact, other critics were downright vituperative. One lashed out that Sly had "taken every bad habit since film began, since *Birth of a Nation*, and made it worse…We could only recommend that he cut his vocal cords and stand as far away as he can in a crowd scene." Maybe that's why, at its premiere in Westwood, Sly spent the final hour in the projection booth. My most memorable moment that evening was watching co-star Armand Assante repeatedly kick the back of Peter Saphier's chair.

The next morning, syndicated columnist Stephen Farber headlined his review: "…Never before has there been such a grossly appalling example of egomania run amuck as Sylvester Stallone's *Paradise Alley*."

"And so it goes."

—Linda Ellerbee

My Hollywood education had two more lessons to go. A month or so *before* the release of the film, when *Paradise Alley* was in final edit stages, I was awakened by a phone call from Sly's business manager, offering a million dollars (upped to "a possible two" before lunch) for our producers' profit share. Sly and his manager, Jeff Wald, had mutually determined this film would be bigger than *Rocky*. From their mouth to God's ear. In any case, they wanted to buy us out.

Our sage lawyer advised us to wait for "the big bucks that could really change your lives." Maybe he knew about the future California lottery. When I conveyed the offer to Pressman (who had a small share in *our* profits), he was ecstatic, saying, "I'm making more money with you guys than I am making films." (Maybe *that* was why we turned down the money.) Despite a revenue stream of over $30 million box office with a negative cost barely north of $6 million, according to Universal's unchallenged accounting, the film is hopelessly mired in red ink. We're told we'll never see a penny. Lesson number one: Never turn down a million dollars.

The next lesson followed two years later, when I got my hands on Oliver Stone's screenplay about his Vietnam experience, then entitled *The Platoon*. It was a compelling coming of age story that grabbed you by the throat and didn't let go for 136 pages. It was writing that was *about something*. I wanted it.

But Ed Pressman had a vise lock on it. By now, Ed had built a modest reputation for spotting and nurturing new talent (he "found" Arnold, remember?) and had offices on Warner's Burbank lot. Not so long ago I had been sued by, lied to, cursed at, and, to my mind, legally blackmailed by him. But Hollywood has a notoriously short memory and I was a quick learner. It wasn't personal, it was business. I would help raise financing and co-produce *Platoon* with Pressman. We may have even toasted to it.

We shopped that little gem of a script to every deep pocket east of Saudi Arabia and north of Australia. Call it a hard sell: A war film about an unpopular war. Call it bad timing. I had made enough films to know that sooner or later a great script has its day. *Platoon* would get made, even if it took six more years, which it did. But how did Ed and I—*Paradise Alley* still an open sore—come to break bread together in the first place? Through our then *mutual* attorney—Gordon Stulberg, who had once vowed to crush Ed on my behalf! In small town Hollywood, stranger bedfellows are made everyday. But that shouldn't surprise any reader of this book.

Nor should the Capra-esque ending to this story. *Rocky*, *Platoon*, and even *Out of Africa* all went on to become Academy Award winning Best Pictures. The real victory, as *Rocky* taught us, is to just hang in there. Success in Hollywood is about taking the long view. And if you want to be a producer, a "hot" screenplay is still the key that opens the door. I produced nine other films before having my fill of deals and dealmakers and turning my passion to screenwriting. John Roach packed his bags and moved his family to New York where he kept his soul, became a Broadway impresario, and remains my best friend to this day. Ed Pressman, who ultimately lost his option on *Platoon*, went on to produce films for Oliver Stone and others. And Sylvester, with multiple paydays of $20 million a picture now behind him, and despite suffering from a selective memory as to the roots of his success, has spent his life living up to his *Rocky* persona.

At age 60, he still hasn't hung up his gloves.

Rocky VI is on the drawing board.

...a final note

"Go to London," they said to me.
"In the great city you will make songs
from the sore hard light of your breast."
And I strove with myself for many years
    thinking of those streets,
    men with sharp power in their gaze,
    and illuminated glittering taxis
    lighting the windows of my mind.
But tonight sitting by the fire
and the hills between me and the sky
listening to the empty silence
and seeing the deer come to my call
    I am thinking of another man
    who spoke the words that are true:
    "Look directly down through wood and wood.
    Look in your own heart and write."

—Iain Crichton Smith

SUGGESTED READING

A select cross-section of books can sometimes provide as deep an education in a given subject as an exhaustive bibliography. These ten have made my short list:

Aristotle's Poetics. Translation and commentary by Stephen Halliwell. Chapel Hill: University of North Carolina Press, 1986.

Bach, Steven. *Final Cut.* New York: William Morrow and Company, 1985.

Booth, Wayne C. *The Rhetoric of Fiction.* Second Edition. Chicago: University of Chicago Press, 1983.

Campbell, Joseph. *The Hero with a Thousand Faces.* Second Edition. New Jersey: Princeton University Press, 1982.

Dunne, John Gregory. *Monster.* New York: Random House, 1997.

Egri, Lajos. *The Art of Dramatic Writing.* New Jersey: Simon & Schuster, 1972.

Eszterhas, Joe. *Hollywood Animal.* New York: Alfred A. Knopf, 2004.

Froug, William. *The New Screenwriter Looks at the New Screenwriter.* Hollywood: Silman-James Press, 1992.

Gardner, John. *The Art of Fiction.* New York: Knopf Publishing Group, 1991.

Goldman, William. *Adventures in the Screen Trade.* New York: Warner Books, 1983.

GLOSSARY

The following are some common screenwriting terms.

ad lib—extemporaneous dialogue created by actors appropriate to a given scenario. Often used in party or other group scenes.

aerial shot—a shot taken from the point of view of an airplane or hot air balloon.

backstory—an expository event that takes place before the story begins. Often given to the main character.

beat—can refer to a plot point, a scene, or even a single thought, emotion, subject or idea within the story. Also often used to indicate a brief pause in dialogue.

b.g. (background)—any action or prop secondary to the main action.

business—props written for actors' use, making dialogue-heavy scenes more active and physical.

blue screen—a visual effect whereby an actor is filmed in front of a colored screen, which is later digitally replaced by an image.

CGI (computer generated imaging)— a visual effect or image created by computer.

character arc—an imaginary line tracing a character's personal growth over the course of a story.

close-up (CU)—a camera shot which emphasizes some object or some physical part of an actor.

Cut to—a scene transition, falling out of favor but still used often for cutting back and forth between two locations in action sequences.

denouement—the final unraveling of the plot, usually coming after the climax and before the conclusion.

Deus ex Machina—an "act of God" ending which once worked in ancient Greek theater, but which modern audiences find too convenient for the author trying to write his way out of the plot and too unbelievable in the context of the story to accept.

Dissolve to—a scene transition in which the final shot of one scene fades or bleeds into the first shot of the next scene.

dolly—a camera cue used to indicate movement in, out, or with the actors during a scene.

Establishing shot(s)—a shot or series of shots of the house, building, neighborhood, or general environment within which the action will take place.

EXT. (Exterior)—mandatory abbreviation for a scene heading indicating that the scene will take place outside.

extreme close-up (ECU)—a camera shot that focuses particularly close on some detail.

extreme long shot—a camera shot from a considerable distance from the subject.

Fade in—used to open most screenplays.

Fade out—a scene ending used to denote the end of a feature film or the end of a television act.

f.g. (foreground)—action taking place or object closest to camera.

flashback—a scene showing an earlier event is inserted into the normal chronological order of events in the film.

freeze frame—a shot in which the film stops and becomes a still photograph. Most often used at the end of a screenplay.

high-concept—a story premise easily reduced to a single sentence or catchy one-liner.

inciting incident—(AKA a story hook or primary incident)—the necessary early story event which propels the main character into the action of the plot.

insert—a stand-alone shot of a specific object such as a watch, a diary, or a calendar.

INT. (Interior)—mandatory abbreviation for a scene heading indicating that the scene will take place indoors.

log line—a catchy one-line description of the movie, used in movie ads or in TV Guide.

long shot—a camera shot taken from a distance.

A MacGuffin—a term coined by Alfred Hitchcock, it's a red herring that triggers the plot but has no other inherent story value. Sometime an object of desire for the conflicting characters (for example, the statue of the Maltese Falcon from *The Maltese Falcon*).

Match cut—a scene transition in which the last shot of the scene matches the same or similar subject in the first frame of the next scene.

medium shot—a camera shot of a character from the waist up.

montage—a series of shots without dialogue, making a connected story point.

motif—an image or sound which recurs in the story, often related to theme.

on the nose—dialogue which too plainly reveals exactly what the character wants.

O.S. (off screen)—(used interchangeably with O.C.—off camera)—sound or dialogue heard out of camera frame, such as dialogue coming from another room in a house.

pan—a side to side camera move.

payoff—the necessary result of a complication for which the audience has been prepared.

P.O.V. (point of view)—a camera positioned from the viewpoint of a particular character.

premise—the basic story idea that usually states the character, situation, and conflict.

red herring—a story device that misleads the audience into expecting an event, result, or problem that never materializes or has an effect on the outcome of the story.

SFX (special effects)—everything from snow to heavy traffic to an atomic explosion that must be created by a film crew on set or on location.

story hook—see **inciting incident**.

subplot—a secondary plot line to the principal action that is driving the main character.

super (superimpose)—the photographic effect of one image over another.

synopsis—a summary of the story told in present tense.

treatment—a prose narrative of the film story, not a summary but the story itself.

tripling—creation of action which occurs in three distinct beats in the story.

V.O. (voiceover)—dialogue heard, but not spoken by a person also physically present in the scene, such as in narration, or dialogue coming from a television, radio, or over the telephone.

Zoom—a camera cue that indicates a manipulation of the lens to move the camera in and out on a subject.

INDEX

ACKNOWLEDGMENTS

The man behind the author in this case is Kevin Harreld, who approached me to write this book, kept at me when I wavered, and made the whole process so easy I could not turn him down, despite my prodigious duties as coach of my son's little league baseball team. Right behind Kevin was Jenny Davidson, who helped me to bring this book to completion and endured all those e-mails written at 3 A.M. importuning advice on every tiny concern my sleep-deprived mind could conjure. Thank you, Kevin, Jenny, and the Thomson team.

To Dr. Linda Venis, director of the Writers Program at UCLA Extension, and Erik Bauer, publisher of *Creative Screenwriting* magazine, you have, as ever, my heartfelt thanks and appreciation for your unfailing guidance, encouragement, and support through the years.

To Lew Hunter, writer, teacher, bon vivant, and legendary all around good guy, being your friend is an honor and being in your company, always a pleasure.

To every person who has attended my classes, lectures and workshops over the years, this book is as much yours as it is mine. If you learned half as much from me as I have from you, then we all profited greatly from our time together.

To my children, Nicolas and Gianna, whose sweetness, laughter, and boundless energy have enriched my life in ways I never could have imagined, thank you for playing outside when I got that look on my face.

And to my mother, Grace, who passed away this year, I bow down in thanks for the unconditional love which she made a constant in my otherwise unbalanced life and for the immense courage which she displayed throughout her long illness, but particularly in her final years, which shall always be a source of unending inspiration to all who knew her.

Finally, thank you to my readers. Having come this far together, I look forward to great things from each of you.

What Ron Suppa's Students Are Saying...

I was fortunate enough to attend the first course held by Ron Suppa in the UK. As a successful advertising copywriter, I must say it was undoubtedly the most interesting, informative and valuable course I have ever had the pleasure to attend. Consequently, I have no hesitation whatsoever in recommending Ron Suppa's course to anybody interested in developing a career in screenwriting.

The best way to describe the course is two days packed full of very positive personal experiences, frequently punctuated by priceless polished gems of advice and guidance. Even "produced" screenwriters would benefit enormously from Ron's knowledge. Aspiring screenwriters quite simply cannot afford to miss this opportunity.

—Doug Kissock

Your course was the best one I ever took at UCLA Extension. It was precise, insightful, and extremely useful in launching my career. My career in TV has taken off and I've just had my first screenplay optioned. Thanks for helping me. (Now can I have that "A"?)

—Ned West

The class in Chicago was great. In my case, you took a physician with absolutely no knowledge of screenwriting and transformed him into a physician who knows a lot about screenwriting, is motivated to learn more, and most importantly, is writing regularly. Just as you said, the rest is up to me. How you were able to do that for me, while doing the same for a group with such a wide range of background, experience, and talent, will have to remain your secret, because I have no idea.

So watch for me, Teach, I can't thank you enough for the introduction to a new mode of expression. I thank you, my wife thanks you, and my right brain thanks you.

—Roger Landry

Just a few lines to say what a gratifying experience your "Designing The Screenplay" weekend course was. At 35, I guess I'm a late starter in screenwriting, so I was particularly interested in new insights and angles on the profession and business. Well, I sure got it. Having completed a feature screenplay, I am revising aspects of it, based on what I learned, before submitting it to Hollywood. Can't thank you enough.

—David A. Russell

ABOUT THE AUTHOR

Ron Suppa is a member of the Writers Guild of America, west, Inc. and a former entertainment lawyer. He is also a published author, a produced screenwriter, an international script consultant, and the producer of ten feature motion pictures. Mr. Suppa is a regular contributor to *Creative Screenwriting* magazine and is also a Senior Instructor in the UCLA Extension Writers Program, where he received the Outstanding Teacher Award for his seminars in screenwriting. He lives in Westlake Village, California.